BURMA AND GENERAL NE WIN

General Ne Win

(*Courtesy*: *Myoma Studio*)

Burma
and
General Ne Win

Maung Maung

Asia Publishing House
Bombay · Calcutta · New Delhi · Madras
Lucknow · Bangalore · London · New York

Copyright © 1969 Maung Maung

Maung Maung (1925)

PRINTED IN INDIA

BY G. G. PATHARE AT THE POPULAR PRESS (BOM.)
PRIVATE LTD., BOMBAY 34 WB. AND PUBLISHED BY
P. S. JAYASINGHE, ASIA PUBLISHING HOUSE, BOMBAY-1

Acknowledgements

Many people have helped in many ways in the preparation of this book; many of them prefer to be unnamed. But I thank them all.

The following are among the most generous helpers, with advice and suggestions, information and valuable references: Colonel Ko Ko, Secretary to the Council of Ministers; U Ohn Khin of the Foreign Office; U Khin Zaw, the poet; U Thein Han, University Librarian, and U Than Htut, director, Institute of Culture; U Ba Kyaw, editor of *The Guardian;* U Htin Leong of the Central Press; and officers of the Ministry of Information and the Defence Services Historical Research Institute.

The following Japanese officers of the Minami Kikan and the Burma Independence Army contributed useful notes: Maj.-Gen. Suzuki (Bo Mogyoe), Maj.-Gen. R. Sawamoto, Mr. Mitsuru Sugii, Mr. H. Akai (Suzuki), Mr. Tatsuro Izumiya, Mr. Shigemoto Okuda, and last but not least, Mr. H. Takahashi (Capt. Kitajima). Mr. Takahashi spent several years at the DSHRI in Rangoon, translating into Burmese available Japanese-language material on the independence movement and the BIA. His translation of the diary which Mr. Sugii kept while on the march is a valuable source. Through the good offices of Mr. Takahashi and Colonel Hla Maw, then our military attache in Tokyo and now our ambassador to India, I also obtained a copy of a thesis on the Minami Kikan, presented by Mr. Hirano Jiro to the International Christian University in 1963. The thesis has proved to be another useful source.

It is also my pleasant duty to acknowledge my gratitude to the following authors and publishers for permission to reproduce extracts:

Maurice Collis, *Trials in Burma.* Faber and Faber Ltd., London;
Field-Marshal Sir William Slim, *Defeat into Victory,* copy-

v

right 1956 by Sir William Slim, by permission of Cassell & Co.
London, David KcKay Company Inc. and Harold Ober Associates Inc., New York;

Lord Louis Mountbatten of Burma, *Report to the Combined
Chiefs of Staff by the Supreme Commander, Southeast Asia,*
by permission of the Controller of Her Majesty's Stationery
Office, London;

Brigadier Bernard Fergusson, *Return to Burma,* William Collins Sons & Co. Ltd., London;

David Wise and Thomas B. Ross, *The Invisible Government,*
Random House, New York;

Mamoru Shigemitsu, *Japan and Her Destiny,* E. P. Dutton &
Co. Inc., New York;

Nevil Shute, *The Chequer Board,* William Morrow & Company,
New York.

And to son Aung Naing, tireless prodder, father U Sin, unfailing
inspirer, and wife Myint, constant critic, many thanks.

MAUNG MAUNG

Rangoon,
March 27, 1968.

Introduction

May Day, 1964, was celebrated in Burma in a memorable way. It was, in fact, more than a celebration; it was a milestone in the march forward of the nation, and a rendezvous with history.

The day was well chosen for the purpose. On that day, after many days of discussion and debate in committee and in plenary sessions, the working people adopted a charter of their fundamental rights and responsibilities. Delegates had come from all over the country and from all walks of life: workers from the factory, the wharf and the railway, the oilfield and the mine, the public services—clerks and officers, and policemen too—and teachers, professors, artistes and intellectual workers, all elected by assemblies of their fellow-workers. Truly a parliament of the workers, as one of the principal draftsmen of the charter said, and the purpose was to proclaim that the working men and women shall thenceforth be their own masters, to manage their affairs by their own elected councils, vested with full rights, and always fully aware of the duties that come with the rights.

The place was right for the rendezvous, for it was below Chauk, the oilfield town, and on the sandy shores of the Irrawaddy river. Chauk and Yenangyaung were developed by British oil interests, and their wells had brought wealth to generations of shareholders in Glasgow and Edinburgh, Manchester and London, cities whose chambers of commerce had persuaded the British government to annex all of Burma to the empire of Queen Victoria. The high steel towers of the oil extraction plants standing stark over the sandy wasteland of that dry zone became constant reminders of the sharp contrasts of the age: the poverty of the people who lived on the land, the wealth that lay beneath it, the poor returns for the workers who toiled long hours by shifts and kept the industry humming day and night, the luxury and comfort in which the British managers and even their favoured local assistants could live and the huge profits which the owners divided among themselves. Chauk and Yenangyaung therefore served, in course of

vii

time when the nationalist movement gathered momentum, as
living proof of the injustice of alien rule and capitalist exploitation. The twin towns saw the quickening of the labour movement
which later merged into the larger struggle for national freedom.

From Chauk, on December 1, 1938, oilfield workers went on
strike and marched to Rangoon, 405 miles south, to lay their
case before the country. That was a restless year, the "year of
revolution" the nationalists called it, with the workers marching
or striking, the students striking or staging demonstrations, the
clamour insistent for justice and fair shares and for freedom itself,
political parties leading the people or following them, with a shooting here and a charge by mounted police there, making martyrs of
Buddhist monks and students, boys and men. In that year, so
packed with incidents and events which historians who will one
day write on our times must notice, the march of the oilfield
workers from Chauk was certainly a highlight.

General Ne Win, chairman of the Revolutionary Council and
the Revolutionary Government, thus personally chose Chauk as
the meeting place for the "parliament of the working people" and
as the historic site where the charter of the working people should
be proclaimed.

On May Day he addressed the rally of people who had come
from all over the country by rail or bus or on foot, by boat up or
down the Irrawaddy, people who filled the river's bank and made
another surging river of beaming faces that flowed on and on as
far as the eyes could see in that early dawn.

On the stage sat the chairmen whom the workers had elected.
Also sharing the stage were a few of the colonels who had spent
several weeks on the site, supervising the building of the residential halls, the exhibition stalls and the huge assembly hall—named
the "Po Hla Gyi Hall" after the leader of the 1938 March—and
looking after the needs of the delegates and providing the facilities for their work. On the stage also, proud and happy,
were the honoured guests who had taken part in the march a
quarter of a century or so ago, or supported the marchers as
members of the Dobama Asi-ayone.

Master of ceremony was U Chin Sein, better known as Shwe
Nyar Maung, actor, singer, film director, a comrade in the Burma
Independence Army. Shwe Nyar Maung was suffering from a bad

cold, and the strong wind that came up the river gave him no comfort. But the occasion so moved him, his voice came strong and clear, and swallowing the pills which Gen. Ne Win passed up to him every few minutes, he went on with the programme.

Gen. Ne Win spoke from notes he had scribbled on pieces of paper the night before. He attempted no oratory, but engaged in a chat, and it was as if the two or three hundred thousand people were gathered, not in a huge rally, but just round him in a room, squatting on the floor together, sipping plain tea and having a friendly conversation. He spoke of the need to work harder and produce more so that the fair shares for all would be enough for a decent living and leave more for social services and the care of the very young and the very old. Workers have come into their own, and they must rise to their responsibilities. There is need for national unity and sustained endeavour to carry out the socialist plans. Thus he spoke for 45 minutes, rambling a little, filling in here and there with reminiscences and anecdotes, and returning to subjects which were uppermost in his mind.

The attitude of the Revolutionary Council, with its declared socialist goals, towards Buddhism and religion was being questioned at the time, and the Council had reiterated its policy of freedom of religious faith and conscience. "We are Buddhists too," Gen. Ne Win said, addressing himself beyond the May Day rally to Buddhists and Buddhist monks everywhere in the country, "and we hope Buddhism will continue to shine forth in its pristine purity." The Buddhist monks, he suggested, should lead in purifying the religion, and in upholding the dignity and discipline of the Order.

In the evening, after six sets of tennis in which he tired out some of his younger officers, Gen. Ne Win visited the honoured guests at their camp in the state high school. The reunion was happy. "Dobama!" they shouted in salute when he arrived, remembering those days in the Asi-ayone when they used this greeting with fellow-members, and called each other Thakin for men, and Thakin-ma for women. "Thakin Shu Maung, you look well," observed one of the elderly Thakins, and Gen. Ne Win, who was known as Shu Maung in his youth, and was a Thakin in the late 1930's, beamed to show that he was, and also felt, very well. The founders of the Dobama Asi-ayone were there, and the marchers of 1938—or those who had survived. They were younger in those days, now they were older, but their spirit was as strong as in those days when they had shouted "Light the torch, and let its flame light up the entire country!"

Gen. Ne Win knew all the hundred-odd old comrades by name, greeted each one of them, looked tenderly when Thakinma Daw Sai rolled up her *htamein* to show a large sore on her thigh. Some others were ill, with old age simply or undernourishment for they were poor, and he made arrangements for them to receive medical treatment or help or suitable jobs. But they were tough, the whole lot of them, the women tougher perhaps, and certainly sharper-tongued, than the men. There were many reminiscences, of the struggle in the oilfields, the clashes with the police, the long march to Rangoon which took some 40 days, the hunger on the road, the harassment by the British authorities, the mounting enthusiasm of the people.

Reminiscences there were, and recriminations too. He was a shirker, one Thakinma accused, and yet he was included in the honour roll of the guests. He dropped out half-way, one Thakin said, but another comrade who was active and loyal all the way had been left out from the list. "He knew I was alive," one said, "yet he reported I was dead, just to put me out too, and fortunately I heard and had the omission corrected, and so I am here!" The story of the resurrection was received with good-humoured laughter.

One irrepressible man at the meeting was Thakin Sein Kho who wore a beard, a string of beads round his neck, and the coarse dull-brown robe of a hermit. He rose several times, successfully resisting the efforts of those who sat next to him to pull him down, and asked many questions. Then he made a little speech, declaring that he had vowed to wear the robe till the day the aspirations of the marchers were fulfilled; now the day had arrived, and Gen. Ne Win, leading the Revolutionary Council, had done them honour by bringing them forth from history's forgotten pages; the people were going forward together under dedicated leadership. His vow was fulfilled, Thakin Sein Kho declared, and he might discard his robe, and there was laughter.

"Let us forget and forgive what was bitter in the past," Gen. Ne Win responded, after shyly smiling through the compliments that were showered on him, "let us remember what was sweet and happy. We did much together, you and I and the others, and these young men,"—pointing to the young commanders who were sitting around—"who took part in the movement as students and later served in the B.I.A. and the resistance. Let us work together, build national unity, and march together again to our goals." History, he said, must one day be written, and records must be compiled now, fully and objectively. Omissions in issuing the invitations, he explained, were not deliberate. The last decade and more had been so turbulent in the country, so full of change, people had scattered while some of the old comrades had hidden themselves away in frustration. "Let us remember what was sweet and happy in the past," he repeated, "and forget and forgive what was bitter. We cannot build on bitterness."

It is in this spirit that this book is written. Its object is to remember the past without bitterness. This book is not a history of contemporary Burma: that is for our historians to write, when the time is ripe for objective appraisal, with all the facts before them. Nor is this a biography of Gen. Ne Win. A biography needs a responsive subject, which he is not, and access to the archives and private papers which cannot be so open at present. Gen. Ne Win has repulsed many abler men than I who want to write his biography, saying that his story must be read in his deeds.

This, therefore, is neither the history of a nation nor the biography of a man. This is served simply as an aid to memory, to help us remember the past few decades of Burma's political life through some of the main events and some of the people who played their parts in those events. By remembering and reviewing that past we may perhaps get a firmer feeling of roots, a better sense of history and a clearer perspective of the present. We may even learn a little from the past, for though we may think that we are very wise, we have yet to find total wisdom or the whole truth or all the sure answers to all the sore problems which have confronted the society of man since its beginning. Learning from the past may give us humility, and help us grow big. So, we shall remember, as Gen. Ne Win said, without bitterness. And without intention to judge harshly for, as Churchill said on assuming wartime leadership in embattled Britain, "If the present tries to sit in judgement on the past, it will lose the future."

Gen. Ne Win appears often in the narrative: as a boy at school in the years of comparative calm, as a young Thakin when the fight for national freedom began to capture the imagination of young men and women throughout the country, later as one of the now famous "thirty comrades" who slipped out to Japan to seek military aid for the liberation of Burma. He returns as a commander of the Burma Independence Army, and serves on to lead the Resistance. In the post-war years and after Burma's Independence, he plays strategic roles in the fast-moving drama: as commander of the Burma Army which fights back the rebel hordes many times its numbers; as Deputy Prime Minister in a Cabinet so besieged that foreign observers call it the "Rangoon Government"; as builder of the modern Armed Forces which take on the well supplied Kuomintang divisions which have swarmed over the country's north-eastern borders; as leader of the "Caretaker Government" invested by Parliament when the ruling party splits and a constitutional crisis of perilous proportions poses a threat of civil war. Gen. Ne Win holds the country together, conducts general elections after 18 months, and hands over to the winner, U Nu. Within two years, however, things are back where they were, probably worse, and Gen. Ne Win returns to defend the integrity of the Union, unite the nation and lead in the march forward.

Thus, the story of Gen. Ne Win is an essential part of this narrative, and also a convenient focal point round which the narrative revolves.

This is not a history book but I hope that it will be of some assistance to the historians when they start to write. Our records are scanty, our library and archival resources are yet far from adequate, and research on Burma can be a task of more than the usual toil. The dates and some of the details given in this book may, therefore, lighten the labours of the historians somewhat by providing them with clues in their pursuit of facts, and in their excavation of the whole truth.

I have used Burmese sources as far as possible, and when they happen to be published material, I have listed them in the bibliography and the notes to chapters. More people are writing in Burma these days; memoirs, essays, biographical accounts are becoming increasingly available. Participants are, for example, compiling a record of the Dobama Asi-ayone. This great flowering has been a great help to me as it will be a delight and help to scholars who have an interest in Burma's political history.

It has also been my good fortune to be able to interview, with the help of willing friends, several people who have taken part in the events described in the book. Their oral history can fill volumes, and we are missing something valuable and vital in not getting those volumes done. Some of those whom we interviewed are quoted, some are not, but all of them have been a great help.

Contents

Contents

1

The Early Stirrings

1

BURMA FELL under British rule in three wars: in 1824, 1852 and 1885. After the second war the kingdom was shut in and weakened, its sea ports, the fertile valleys and the Delta occupied. Burmese missions went to Europe to search for allies and aid for building a strong modern nation. But it was too late. The British, having taken half the country, must take the whole, for the doctrine was that half-measures in colonial ventures were dangerous.

Also, the merchants in England had their eyes on fabled China, the land of rubies and emeralds. They demanded an early end to the farce of co-existence with King Thibaw. Annex upper Burma, they demanded, open up the road to China and her treasures.

There were incidents between Thibaw's kingdom and the British in lower Burma. In these days and in normal circumstances, similar incidents would call for perhaps a protest, mild or severe depending on the merits of the case, and in response perhaps an apology, cool and correct or warm and profuse according to those merits. The incidents in 1885, however, unleashed war. An impossible ultimatum was served on the King at Mandalay laying down brutal terms to be undertaken in the briefest time.

At the receiving end, Thibaw was ineffective; Supayalat, his queen, was proud and angry, but she had only enough ability to eliminate her rivals, not to lead a nation at war. The wise ministers were weak, the strong were not so wise.

The Burmese were willing to talk, but not capitulate; the British, bent on conquest, had no patience for talks. On November 11, Lord Randolph Churchill in London cabled Lord Dufferin, the Viceroy of India: "Please instruct General Prendergast to advance on Mandalay at once."

The General was ready; his troops were poised for action. The advance on Mandalay took less than three weeks. On December 3, King Thibaw, his family and a small entourage, all numbering 68, were taken aboard the British vessel *Thuriya* (The Sun), and taken down the Irrawaddy river to Rangoon. There, on December 15, they were transferred to *H. M. S. Canning* and taken away to India and exile.

Annexation was smooth and swift, but pacification, the British found, was slow and costly. Led by some princes and strong leaders the peasants engaged in long and resolute guerrilla action from bases in the jungle or the Shan hills. The Sawbwa of Wuntho and the Saopha of Kayah were among those leaders who stood against the British for many years after Mandalay had fallen. In the north the Chins in their hills resisted and the best British troops had to be thrown in under the ablest generals to reduce stockade after stubbornly held stockade. The British used force as well as gentle persuasion; defeated rebels were often treated with honour and generosity. In course of time peace was restored; the country was opened up; roads and railways were built; agriculture and some industries were developed. A new prosperity gave the people some small benefits. A stable government was gradually established, highly centralized, efficiently coordinated. Emphasis was on law and order without which business would wither.

Burma as a nation was broken up. No leader could unite the people and make them rise again. The society, in its very nature, had discouraged unity, encouraged individualism. Every village was a little republic; the kings and their courts who lived far away in the capital were counted among the five "evils", on the same standing as fire, floods, thieves and one's ill-wishers. Now one evil was gone and another come; the going and coming would continue, the peasants knew from their Buddhist philosophy, till the end of time. Members of the royal family who were left behind in Mandalay preserved their state as best as they could, some on meagre British pensions. A few old ministers lived on their memories, keeping up a dignity which they could ill-afford, ghosts of an era that was dead and gone. U Gaung, the *Kinwunmingyi,* whom Supayalat had taunted as a coward, became an adviser to the British government, received titles and a pension, and compiled treatises on Burmese customary law.

Defiance could be shown towards the British, and the ancient dignities of the Burmese court kept up with a vengeance, but armed rising on a national scale was out of the question. The superiority of British arms was manifest. Their cannons could blast the brick walls behind which the Burmese kings had lived their lives in an illusion of security and the hope that the walls would keep away the world outside.

It was not, therefore, any call to arms that set off the first stirrings. Religion and education were what set the minds moving.

Buddhism became a convenient rallying point of the nation. Under alien rule the people drew closer and more jealously to their religion. Buddhism teaches tolerance and peace, stresses the impermanence of things, points out the roots of suffering and exhorts man to cut them clean and set himself free. Such a religion may not help to fan the glowing embers of nationalism into leaping flames. But the religion provided a forum where people could meet and think together. A thought would set in motion a train.

Education was both a stimulant and a hope. It provided the means of obtaining jobs in the government service which in turn gave prestige and a shadow of power. It also opened up a vast and exciting panorama of knowledge and ideas. The British believed in and provided facilities for a liberal education. In this age of science and technology a liberal education alone is no longer enough. In the first decades of the twentieth century, however, the arts, philosophy, political science, history and pure mathematics for the exercise of the mind and such subjects helped give young Burmans ideas and dreams of a braver future for the country. Dreams launched them on the search for the realities.

2

The Young Men's Buddhist Association (YMBA) was started in Rangoon in 1906 on the model of the YMCA. The declared aims of the YMBA were to promote Buddhism, education and the national cultures. There had been earlier efforts in those directions: the Buddha Sasana Noggaha Association in Mandalay, started in 1897, which set up a high school which gave birth to several national leaders; the Asoka Society founded in 1902 in

Bassein by the Bikkhu Asoka, a European convert to Buddhism. The YMBA, however, took deeper roots and spread country-wide. U Ba Pe, U Maung Gyee, Dr. Ba Yin, U Sein Hla Aung and their contemporaries, then students of the Rangoon College, gave their spare time to organize the association. College students were gentlemen of leisure, with time for philosophical discussions, debates, writing articles for the small press or letters to the editors, or parading in the streets in the evenings respectably dressed as became collegians. Jobs in the government service were not too plentiful. The higher grades were filled with Englishmen and the lower clerical grades with Indians who could live on very little and save the remainder of their small salaries. Graduates were so few, however, that employment was assured as a township officer, an inspector of police or excise, a junior officer of similar rank in the various departments. For young officers there was prestige and if one had waited patiently enough, prospect of marrying money. For the clerks there were the tips, the "tea-money", the "outside" income—which compensated amply for their meagre salaries.

The YMBA, led by the collegians, drew its membership from young officers and clerks. It was not, therefore, an angry association at all. Its meetings were orderly, its activities were above reproach, and its resolutions were couched in the choicest prose. The *Burman Buddhist,* a monthly bulletin issued by the association, did not cause the government any anxiety. The importance of the YMBA in the growth of the nationalist movement was that it became a gathering ground of the young intellectuals; its branches, which spread to the district towns and villages provided a network of communication covering the entire country. From modest beginnings, with membership of less than 20, the YMBA grew fast in the number of its members and the branches. In 1911 the first national conference of the association was held in Rangoon at which a general council was elected with U Po Bye as president. The annual conferences rotated among the principal cities. At the Mandalay conference in 1915, Mr. J. S. Pillay was elected president. At the Henzada conference, in the year following, U May Oung, a young barrister, was installed in that office.

The conferences would begin with "God Save King George V and Queen Mary!" At the end the prayer "Long Live Their Majesties" was sung. Speakers would affirm in flowery language their unswerving loyalty to the British Crown. Thus U Pe, addressing a conference as President, dwelled lovingly on the merits of British rule, the bounties it bestowed, and declared that the delegates assembled were loyal subjects, with an English education, a deep fondness for the English way of life, and they were all, therefore, in the true sense of the word, "gentlemen". Suggestions submitted to the government were couched in the language of prayer. Yet, they ranged over a variety of educational and social questions: equal educational opportunities for Burman and European; more scholarships for study abroad; non-discrimination on passenger transport such as the railways; the need for legislation to protect the rights of Burmese Buddhist women who married non-Buddhist men; courtesy in court and the dropping of the demeaning prefix, *Nga,* in addressing or describing an accused person. The purification of Buddhism, the need to encourage young monks to acquire a modern education and qualify for teaching in the monastic schools, registration of the monks at each monastery by the presiding *Sayadaw* to uphold discipline in the Order and keep out false monks, the folly of showy alms-giving. These were some of the religious and social questions taken up at the YMBA conferences.

The *Thuriya* (The Sun) newspaper, was launched in 1911 by U Ba Pe as editor and U Hla Pe as manager. The paper gave full support to the YMBA movement. One issue which the newspaper took up was the "shoe question". Burmans take off their shoes or slippers when entering pagodas, monasteries or sacred grounds, or on approaching their elders. This etiquette became a pinprick to British envoys who sought audience with the Kings and their reports would often exaggerate it almost into a cause for war. Now the question took on a new complexion. Europeans claimed the privilege to enter pagodas with their shoes on, and Burmans resented it.

One cartoon in *The Sun* showing barefooted trustees of the Shwedagon pagoda carrying a European and his lady on their backs so that the privileged visitors might look around without the discomfort of walking barefoot, made the readers laugh and Mr. Shuttleworth, the Police Commissioner of Rangoon, fume. U Ba Pe and his manager were called in by the offended official and gravely warned. They made an appropriate retort, and later

convened a general meeting of the YMBA to consider the shoe
question.

The drift to such drastic action alarmed the older men in the
association such as U Ba Tu, U Po Tha and U Thin—the "Tu-Tha-
Thin" trio, as they were promptly dubbed. The younger men,
prominent among them being U Ba Pe, U Thein Maung, U Paw
Tun, U Ba Dun and Dr. Thein Maung, decided to fight on. U
Thein Maung took the chair at the meeting at which speeches were
delivered and resolutions passed which were strongly worded—
by YMBA standards.

World War I quickened the political tempo. Britain, having to
rely on manpower and material resources of the empire, felt compelled to promise an "increasing association of Indians in every
branch of the administration and the gradual development of self-
governing institutions, with a view to the progressive realization
of responsible self-government in India as an integral part of the
British Empire." Burma—an administrative unit of the Indian
empire since annexation, and a province under a Lieut.-Governor
since 1897—was vitally interested.

Also, the "fourteen points" proposed by President Woodrow
Wilson as the basis of a happier post-War world excited the imagination of all peoples who longed for independent nationhood. For
Burmans, Wilson's call for open covenants of peace openly arrived at was unimportant. Nor the freedom of navigation of the high
seas; nor the arrangements for the reorganization of Europe. What
was important and precious was the fourteenth point which envisaged "a general association of nations" with "mutual guarantees of political independence and territorial integrity to great and
small states alike."

Self-determination and "home rule" became goals as well as
slogans. When a mission led by Mr. E. S. Montagu, Secretary of
State for India, arrived in India in December, 1917, the YMBA
discovered that Burma was not on the tour programme of the mission. Delegates were therefore sent from Burma to meet the mission. U Pe, U Ba Pe, U May Oung and U Su went from the
YMBA. The Tu-Tha-Thin trio, determined not to be outshone,
went along too. U San Win and Mr. Pillay from Mandalay, and
Dr. San C. Po and Mr. Sydney Loo Nee representing the Karens,
also went to India. The meetings in Calcutta reassured the dele-

gates, but when the Government of India Act of 1919 was passed, introducing administrative reforms, Burma was left out because the mission had reported that "Burma was not India."

Sir Reginald Craddock, the Lieut.-Governor of Burma, had attributed Mr. Montagu's promise of "the progressive realization of responsible self-government in India" to "an extraordinary lapse of an otherwise brilliant brain." Sir Reginald put forward his own schemes for local government through municipal bodies. Neither the "Craddock Schemes" nor their author, however, proved popular. U Ottama, a young Buddhist monk who had worked and studied in India and Japan, toured the country, lecturing for the YMBA, spreading the cry, "Craddock, Go Home!" U Ottama was jailed for sedition several times, but he carried on. He was one of the first monks to enter the political arena. Many more were to follow. U Wisara, another famous monk, was to die fasting in jail and attain martyrdom.

The YMBA sent a delegation to London consisting of U Ba Pe, U Pu and U Tun Shein—the "Pe-Pu-Shein" mission—to try and gain the ear of Whitehall for Burma's cause. For seven months the delegates worked hard to establish contacts, to find listeners, open doors. But Englishmen, with their famous reserve, do not speak unless properly introduced, and the Burmese delegates could not get the proper introductions. Those they could meet felt more comfortable talking about the weather. Besides, Britain was still weary after the war; resettlement of the soldiers and economic problems engaged her main attention.

U Tun Shein died a few months after the return of the mission to Burma. He was then thirty and at the height of his popularity as a young patriotic leader. After taking his degree from the Rangoon College he had gone to Mandalay to teach at the B.T.N. High School. He was outspoken and energetic. As a student he took up boxing to use up some of his energy, and joined the Rangoon battalion of the Burma Auxiliary Force, giving his name as "T. O. Shane" as enlistment was only for those of European descent or pretensions. U Tun Shein was active in the YMBA which he served as a full-time worker towards the end. His death was nationally mourned.

Another YMBA delegation went to London in 1920 with U Thein Maung taking the place of U Tun Shein. Persistence paid off, and this time there were some interviews, some sympathetic editorials in the newspapers, some friendships made. Questions on Burma were even put down in the House of Commons. The Burmese delegates waited eagerly in the visitors' gallery, but there was no quorum that day, and therefore no answers. The cold streets of Westminster seemed colder to the Burmese delegates as they sadly left the House and came away. But they kept plodding on in the cold.

3

In 1920 the YMBA, meeting in annual conference at Prome, decided that time had come for a larger, wider organization to spearhead the nationalist movement. The General Council of Burmese Associations (GCBA) was thus launched with the 2,000 or more branches of the YMBA as its nucleus. The emphasis was now shifted from "Buddhist" to "Burmese"; the avowed aim was to promote the nationalist cause. The people responded with enthusiasm and emotion. There was no call to arms but *wunthanu* or nationalism had a powerful appeal. Even the call to the people to wear Burmese clothes, smoke Burmese cheroots and be Burmese touched tender chords.

GCBA meetings drew huge crowds. The annual conferences at Thayet, Paungde, Mandalay and other cities were attended by 100,000 people, or more, delegates, observers and supporters. The Buddhist monks, with their *Sangha Samaggi,* gave their hearts to the movement; only the eminent and elderly monks, withdrawn from mundane affairs, stayed aloof. The women formed their *Wunthanu* associations. Houses in town and village proclaimed in bold letters on their doors that their dwellers were Wunthanu. Teashops in the streets, hairdressers, general stores and the like, vied with one another in taking the Wunthanu name.

Still, the GCBA did nothing to displease the government. At meetings the customary praises for British rule would be said, the prayer "God Save the King" would also be sung. A later innovation was to invoke the Buddha, instead of God, to save the King, and history does not record that King George was displeased with this show of Burmese nationalism.

Leadership of the GCBA came from lawyers, businessmen,

land-owners, journalists. U Chit Hlaing, whose star rose high with the GCBA, was a wealthy young barrister. A man of integrity, he was sought out in his home-town of Moulmein and urged to accept the presidency of the organization. His associates looked upon his wealth as a great qualification. They expected him to pour it into the movement, which he generously did.

U Ba Pe, editor of *The Sun,* U Ba Hlaing who later became prominent in the labour movement, and U Maung Maung Ohn Ghine who served in the movement for national schools, were some of the leaders of the GCBA. But U Chit Hlaing was the prince among them all. When he came to conferences—often dressed in European clothes, complete with winged collar and waist coat—golden umbrellas were opened to protect him from the colonial sun. Women knelt along the way and spread their long hair on the ground to make him a carpet to tread on. The people called him, when he was the unchallenged leader of the GCBA at its peak, the *Thamada,* "the uncrowned king".

The GCBA did not remain united, nor did U Chit Hlaing's leadership remain unchallenged, for long. The more popular it grew, the stronger, the more bitter, became the internal struggle for the leadership.

4

In December, 1920, students of the Rangoon College staged a strike in protest against Sir Reginald Craddock's proposal to establish a residential university on the pattern of Oxford and Cambridge. Residential universities were fine but they would be open only to a privileged few, and closed to the many young people who hungered for a modern education. The strikers demanded that the new University should take as many non-residential students as possible, and camped out on the Shwedagon pagoda declaring that they would not return to classes until the demand was satisfied. A few of the strikers took a solemn vow to carry the fight to the very end. Po Kun (in later years better-known as Bo Po Kun), Ba Shin, Nyi Paik, Ba Khin and others were among those who took that vow.

On Sunday, December 5, when the strikers took up their residence in *zayats* on the Bahan foothill of the Shwedagon, Dr. Mat-

thew Hunter, principal of the College, and U Ba, lecturer in chemistry and chief warden of the hostels, went to the strikers' camp
to persuade the students to return. Teacher-pupil relationship in
those days was such that the strikers received their teachers with
the customary respect, addressing them as "Sir". "Do you mean
to say, Sir," asked Ba U of Dr. Hunter, "that the Government
will not move to settle the strike?" The Government would not
move, the Principal replied, but the students would not be penalized for what they had done. "We are sorry, Sir," Ba U retorted,
"but we can't come back on those terms. We want satisfaction for
our grievances. The stubborn attitude of the Government only
shows its true colours!" When Dr. Hunter and Saya Ba turned
away to leave, there were tears in their eyes. The strikers then
sat humbly down and clasping their hands, bowed low in respect.

The students' strike—the University Boycott as it came to be
called—was a huge success. The GCBA gave full support to it,
and also earned great credit for itself. The Rangoon University
which was inaugurated in 1922 was open to all; residence was
not a requirement. Encouraged by the victory, the nationalists
formed a Council of National Education to build a system of national schools with a national college in Rangoon. The schools,
however, did not long survive. Resources were lacking, and without government recognition the schools could not, in the long run,
attract students who after all needed jobs in the public services
after school. Among the few national schools which were able to
struggle on were the Myoma High School in Rangoon, and the
National High School in Mandalay.

The National College, housed in sheds and monasteries in
Bahan attracted a few young idealists to its teaching staff. One of
them was Maung Hmaing, writer, scholar, journalist, who as a
young boy had seen King Thibaw and Queen Supayalat carted
away by red-coated British soldiers through the streets of Mandalay. That was a painful experience for the boy who later grew
up to be the Grand Old Man of Burmese letters and politics, Thakin Kodaw Hmaing.

The ninth annual conference of the GCBA was held in October, 1921, at Mandalay. The conference unanimously resolved
that the day on which the Boycott began should be observed every
year as the National Day. More than a decade later, Dr. Ba Maw,

as education minister, had the National Day declared a public holiday.

The conference was not, however, all unanimity. The fight for the leadership was becoming bitter, and when U Ba Pe proposed that the presidency should rotate to replenish the leadership, U Chit Hlaing would not concede. There were allegations too that funds were being used by some members of the executive committee to run their private banks for their private profit. These allegations did not help to preserve harmony in the committee.

The coming of Dyarchy, the lure of office and power, the periodical elections and scrambles for office through new alignments, all these hastened the break-up of the GCBA. There was no cohesive force to keep the GCBA marching in unity through temptation or trouble. No haunting dream of national independence, or of a happier society for the people, drove them. A few social reforms, increased number of seats in the legislative council to provide a larger platform for the educated elite, political jobs and other good jobs for the elite, these were the aspirations. At the slightest hint that these aspirations would be fulfilled the scramble would begin.

5

Notification No. 225 published in the Gazette of India Extraordinary dated October 7, 1921, accepted the principle that Burma should also be included in the Montagu-Chelmsford reforms and made a Governor's province. The preparations to establish the province took some time. In November, 1922, the first elections were held to fill 79 out of the 103 seats in the Legislative Council. On January, 1923, by Notification No. 1192 published in the Gazette of India, the creation of Burma as a Governor's province in the Indian Empire was announced.

To participate in the dyarchical scheme or to boycott it became an issue that divided the GCBA. Dyarchy would hand over a few innocent subjects, such as education, public health and local government, to ministers accountable to the legislative council. Law and order, finance and revenue, were among the "reserved subjects" in the care of the Governor and his counsellors. Though some subjects were transferred to the ministers, the Governor could exercise the veto, and also held the purse. Yet, it was an experiment in representative government which helped to quicken political life.

U Chit Hlaing, with the Buddhist monks and the people massively behind him, decided to boycott, and his prestige as the uncrowned king rose to new heights. U Ba Pe and 20 others broke away from the GCBA to run for the council and office. They were quickly dubbed the "Twenty-Oners", and this name stuck until the twenty-one too broke and dispersed and were twenty-one no more. In 1923 the *Boo* associations sprang up, taking their name from the Nay (or boo) which they said to everything: co-operation with the government, participation in the reforms. But nay to everything, aye to nothing, was somewhat too negative for a political programme. The Boo and the booers quickly went out of fashion.

The monthly salary of a minister was Rs. 5,000, which was a small fortune. A peasant would have considered himself fortunate in those days if he averaged as much as Rs. 50 from his year's toils. A minister also had power and prestige—items which were easily convertible into gold. The politicians who scrambled for seats in the legislative council were many, but the ministries were yet too few; "more dogs than bones," Mister Maung Hmaing remarked in his pithy, stinging verse. The "Dymen" or Dyarchists, as they were scornfully called by some people, were unashamed. The legislature provided a forum where they could make speeches and gestures, indulge in intrigue, dream and hope. Rules of procedure, speech-making, splitting legal hairs, these were important in the new system, and lawyers, skilled in the art, shone like stars in the political sky. Lawyers who had been called to the bar by one of the Inns of Court in London were preferred for they had been anointed in the holy temple—and they spoke English with an accent.

If there was disarray due to the scramble for office in the dyarchical fold, things were no better outside. The Wunthanu GCBA began to disintegrate with jealousies among the leaders, accusations and allegations, conceit and complacency, and generally for lack of long-term goals to which the people could march together. U Chit Hlaing fell out with the Sangha Samaggi who switched their support to other men who were waiting in a queue to climb

on the throne of the uncrowned king. The split in the GCBA
reached deep down, dividing the women's associations, the Buddhist monks who were often more intense than the politicians,
the lay organizations which had once stood together under the
GCBA banner.

U Soe Thein was elected president of the GCBA at the conference in Shwebo in 1925 and this promptly led to the emergence
of the "Chit Hlaing GCBA" and the "Soe Thein GCBA". Educated at the St. Peter's missionary high school in Mandalay and
the Government High School in Prome, U Soe Thein had served
for a while in the Burma Oil Company, a breeding ground of
many future politicians. Later, he came under the influence of U
Ottama and went to Japan for study and travel. The journey led
him on to the United States where he studied mining and geology
at Stanford. U Soe Thein returned, full of ideas, ready with many
plans for political emancipation, economic progress and industrialization, impressed deeply with the speed and smoothness of
progress in Japan and America, impatient with the endless talk
and groping in Burma. Direct action was what was needed, U
Soe Thein often thought aloud; pay no taxes, have nothing to do
with the government. In his time U Soe Thein was a revolutionary
and people were yet a little shy and suspicious of men of his kind.
They wanted peace and were content with the small incomes which
were enough for their daily needs. Even the Buddhist monks
who at first supported him found U Soe Thein too hot to handle
and they transferred their support to U Su, a chemist of the British-owned Burma Oil Company, who had received his training
in Germany.

The GCBA lasted as a united organization only for a few years.
As the 1920's closed, there were three GCBA's, not one, three
kings—U Chit Hlaing, U Soe Thein, U Su—who would sit tight
on their thrones while their kingdoms were fast melting away. New
parties began to grow like mushrooms after the rains: the Home
Rulers, the Swarajists, the People's Party, the Progressives, the
Twenty-Oners, the splinters from the Twenty-Oners, the Twenty-
Oners of Mandalay. All hit the high road to the legislative council, political jobs and privilege. The techniques, the procedures,
the tactics, the lobbying, the intrigues, the bargainings, the whole
bag of tricks of the parliamentary game was acquired very quick-

ly by the politicians. But political activity swirled round the council, the secretariat, the Government House, the headquarters of
the party—if there was any—the homes of the politicians, the
hotels where the members of the legislative council were offered
their inducements to cast their votes at the proper moment in the
right way. A vote, just one tiny vote, how much for a vote?

The peasants continued to toil in the fields. Dyarchy gave them
nothing. They listened when the politicians came to talk; they
heard promises from the politicians at the time of elections; then
they were forgotten. Dyarchy therefore failed to win their support;
and the peasants, if only the politicians and the government could
count numbers, were the massive majority of the people. "Dyarchy has almost become a term of abuse," remarked Sir Harcourt
Butler, the first Governor under the scheme, "I have heard one
man say to another: 'You are a Dyarchy'." Those remarks were
made in 1926 and were in sharp contrast to the buoyant optimism
with which Sir Harcourt had launched the scheme three years previously. Then he had said: "We start with favouring breezes."

6

Roads and railways and communication systems were built or improved under British rule, but the principal aim was more profits
for British business, not the welfare of the peasants, law and order
rather than social justice. The export of rice and other agricultural
products, the volume of which was fastly expanded by better domestic production and the opening up of Suez, was largely in the
hands of British firms. Long leases to rich forest reserves were
held by British firms, such as the Bombay Burma Trading Company; the Burma Oil Company was British, so were the major
mining companies which extracted silver, tin and wolfram.

For the rest, however, the British practised laissez-faire. Peace-
keeping was the main concern of the centralized and efficient
bureaucracy. The headman kept the peace and collected revenue
in the village, the basic unit of the administration. The township
officer, the subdivisional officer, the deputy commissioner, the
commissioner supervised those main tasks in their respective
charges with responsibility in that ascending order to the Secretariat in Rangoon. The senior district officers were British. They

worked conscientiously, "fathers" of their charges. Many of them wrote reports, diaries, gazetteers, about the things they saw or learned wherever they went. Much of what they recorded remain both classic and current today. But they were British, not Burman. They might grow fond of the country, the people, the birds, the flowers, the elephants in the jungle. They might be impressed with the art, the cultures, the history, the customs of the ancient land. Their hearts, however, were in England; their ultimate loyalty was to Whitehall.

Laissez-faire left the Burmans vulnerable. Indian labourers were cheaper, and they were imported in large numbers, pushing the Burmans out of employment in the factory, on the dockyard or the railways. On the land the peasants were prey to the money-lending chettyars. The Burman likes his fun, the seasonal pagoda festival, the merry-making after the harvests. He also likes to give generously, because he is kind and hospitable by nature, and because Buddhism teaches him that giving is a meritorious deed, a good investment for his hereafter. To be able to give generously he borrows freely on lavish rates of interest. The law permitted him full freedom to borrow on mortgage of his land, and the chettyar full freedom to foreclose in default of repayment. After a few decades of this freedom, the Burman cultivators became labourers on their former lands, working for their new chettyar landlords.

Things thus became gradually bad for the peasants; poor crops and the general depression which hit the country in 1928-29 made them worse. They could not pay the taxes; U Soe Thein of the GCBA preached: "Don't pay!" Many were frightened by such a radical suggestion, but one man, Saya San, was impressed. Besides, he felt his call coming.

Since the fall of Thibaw, simple villagers had waited for the rise of another king. Astrologers would announce the arrival of the time and the man; there would be whispers in the villages and excitement; the pretender would appear and declare that it was he. For a brief spell he would reign over the believers. Then the law would arrive and it would be time for the embryo-king to say his hurried farewell to his people. Many pretenders had come and gone, but the villagers continued to wait. The depression and the insistent tax-collectors made them yearn with deeper longing.

Saya San had placed some hopes on the Soe Thein GCBA at first, but the endless talking and the vague resolutions made him impatient. He had headed a committee of the GCBA which investigated the plight of the peasants. He had seen and felt the appalling poverty and hopelessness of the villagers in the many lower Burma districts he visited. A man of many names and many parts—alchemist, teacher, preacher, politician, practitioner of indigenous medicine—Saya San had considerable influence and following in Tharrawaddy and the neighbouring districts. He had always felt that he was born to a greater destiny than curing coughs and colds, or listening to those wind-bags of politicians. Originally from Shwebo, the home of Alaungpaya—founder of the last Burmese dynasty—Saya San had both the right background and the following to lead a rebellion. He would be no idle pretender. The peasants were ready for the revolution, he calculated, and he was ready to lead them. On October 28, 1930, Saya San, attended by a small entourage of faithful followers, went in the night to Mya-Sein-Taung-Nyo pagoda in Insein district and got himself crowned King of Burma. Rangoon, the stronghold of British power which he was pledged to overthrow, lay wrapped in sleep only a half-hour's drive away.

The symbol of British power was, at that time, a Burman. Sir Charles Innes, the Governor, had left on August 12 on four months' home-leave, and Sir Joseph Augustus Maung Gyi, a Burman notwithstanding the 'Joseph Augustus', was acting Governor. It was the first time that a Burman was appointed Governor, even in an acting capacity, and fate had in store for the first Burman Governor the first rebellion of serious proportions.

Sir Joseph had seen the world but did not know his own country too well. He had been called to the bar by Gray's Inn in London; he had held senior appointments in Siam; he had been appointed minister under dyarchy; he had served as a justice of the High Court in Rangoon; he was Home member of the Governor's council before he was appointed acting Governor. Sir Joseph had thus occupied seats of high power continuously for more than a decade, without having to exert great effort or beg for votes, when Saya San appeared on the scene.

On December 21, Saya San gathered his men on Alantaung hill, a few miles from Tharrawaddy. He styled himself Thupannaka

Galon Raja and called his men the Galon Army. Galon is a mythical eagle, conqueror of the Naga dragon. It is "the symbol of victory over the Naga," a witness explained at one of the subsequent rebellion trials, "the Naga represents foreigners such as the English, the French, the Italians, and the Russians." (The existence of Americans was apparently unknown then.) Saya San ordered his troops to march and hurl the British into the sea whence they first came.

In Tharrawaddy the day before Saya San made his declaration of war on top of the hill, Sir Joseph Augustus Maung Gyi held a durbar where he distributed prizes and invested titles for loyal service. One question that was causing great anxiety to the peasants was whether the government would force the collection of capitation taxes in those times when they were impoverished. The villagers who attended the durbar hoped that Sir Joseph, a Burman Governor, would say kind words on that issue.

Sir Joseph, however, was acting Governor only for four months, and he was determined to put up a good showing; if he had a soft side to him, he was not going to show it in that short period. He was also an honest, forthright man. Once, as Home member, he was asked in the council about U Ottama who was then spending one of his frequent sojourns in jail. Sir Joseph had haughtily replied that the monk was just one of the thousands of convicts held in the many jails all over the country; he could not be bothered with the details about one convict out of so many thousands. At Tharrawaddy, he was similarly forthright on the capitation tax issue. He came out bluntly that he could provide no relief to the peasants, and that collection would be punctual and, if necessary, forceful. There were present at the durbar several Galon men. If they had chosen to pounce on the few guards and seize Sir Joseph, they might well have succeeded. That, however, did not happen. Perhaps the auspicious hour was not yet; perhaps the Galon were only after the Naga, and Sir Joseph was a Burman, not a Naga.

7

Tharrawaddy is just 75 miles north of Rangoon. It is a quiet town, a haven of pensioners who have consistently refused to have a cinema house in their midst lest the morals of their young should

2

be spoiled. Those who feel the need for some amusement must go to Rangoon or cross the bridge to Thonze. The town, which is marked as village tract number 37 on the administrative map, has been a district headquarters for many decades. The British liked the quietness of the town, its golf course, the wooded hills eastward which offer good hunting.

From those hills the Galon Army swooped down on December 22. The first encounters were off Phar-Shwe-Kyaw village where several hundred men of the Galon Army, dressed in their black jackets and baggy pants, armed with swords and spears, marched on the police. Several police officers fell; victory in the first rounds went to the Galon Army. On December 24 a party of Galons surrounded the dak bungalow at We village and overpowered the resistance. One Mr. Fields-Clarke of the forest service fell.

The rebellion, however, was an unequal affair from the start. The Galon Army was armed with primitive weapons, a supreme confidence in the cause, charms and amulets which were supposed to confer immunity from the bullet and the bayonet. Into battle the Galon soldiers would march, beating their gongs, waving their banners, chanting their songs, brandishing their swords. On the other side were the well-armed police, and the better-armed regular army troops which were poured into the field from the bottomless reservoir of British imperial resources. The rebellion was an act of deep faith and great courage, but it was doomed to defeat from the start.

Not without a great fight did the Galon Army go down, however. The rebellion spread from Tharrawaddy to Prome, Insein, Thayet and Yamethin, and across the Irrawaddy to Henzada, Pyapon, Dedaye and the Delta districts. Almost all of lower Burma was thus affected. Sir Charles Innes, on his return from home leave, found a full-scale war on his hands. A few thousand Galon troops, under the leadership of Saya San, U Aung Hla and others engaged the police, the military police, the regular troops such as the 2/15th Punjab Rifles. Reinforcements of some two divisions of troops—mainly of the Mahrathas and the Dogras—and aeroplanes were rushed over from India. The Galon side was led by Saya San, "a desperado and reputed alchemist" as the judges of the High Court scornfully described him in their judgment in

U Aung Hla's appeal case, and men like U Aung Hla himself, peasants and leaders in their villages. Opposed to them were Sir Charles Innes, with all the might of the British empire behind him, Maj.-Gen. Coningham commanding the Burma independent military district, Brigadier C. F. Watson commander of the Rangoon brigade area, and a host of civil and police officials who were trained to lead, to obey, and be loyal in the service of the British crown.

In that unequal tug of war the rebellion gradually gave way. The government used force on the one hand, driving the lesson home by frequently displaying heads of fallen rebels at police stations. This crude method raised loud protests from the press and the public which were heard in London. On the other hand, sweet persuasion was employed, district officers in grey flannel suits going round to convince the people that armed rising against such superior power was futile. Those of the Galon Army who wished to come in were offered amnesty. Go home, go back to your fields, the villagers were urged, what had happened would be forgotten and forgiven.

Only the leaders of the rebellion were relentlessly hunted down. A reward of Rs. 5,000 was offered for the capture, dead or alive, of Saya San. When things became hopeless in the plains, Saya San moved into the Shan hills, disguised as a monk. The Shan chieftains, alarmed lest their own tranquillity should be shattered, offered their own rewards for his capture. Saya San had fallen ill with malaria; a wound in his leg greatly reduced his mobility. He kept on stubbornly, however, hoping to cross the border into China in search of arms and aid. On August 2, 1931, Saya San was captured near Hokho village in Nawnkhio township. He was kept in stocks for one night at Hokho, then securely chained and taken to Hsipaw. Under heavy guards and in heavy chains, he was taken by railway from Hsipaw to Tharrawaddy. Shan peasants, numbering some 2,000, gathered at the police station to see Saya San taken away. The older peasants, who remembered the British annexation and the taking away of Thibaw, wept.

The rebellion was much bigger than anything that had happened since annexation. The politicians secretly admired Saya San for doing what they did not dare to do, but they had to be careful about what they said about the rebellion. Sympathy could be expressed, but in guarded language, with the utmost care given to the law; it must fall safely short of providing 'sinews of war" to those who were waging war against His Imperial Majesty. The newspapers reported the development of the rebellion, but the editorials were careful. Political parties were quick to declare that they had nothing to do with the rebellion. Only the Soe Thein GCBA, to which Saya San once belonged, was declared illegal.

In Rangoon members of the legislative council, in its 7th and 8th sessions of the year 1931, denounced atrocities committed by the government in suppressing the rebellion, moved that amnesty be granted generally and totally, asked many questions. They also stoutly opposed a bill to set up a special tribunal to try the captured rebel leaders. The existing machinery of criminal justice was adequate, it was argued; a special tribunal would be unnecessary, unfair, even illegal. The voting was 41 against 39 for the Burma Rebellion (Trials) Bill; but after more speeches, the usual give and take, after the members had placed themselves on the record that they were strongly against it, they voted for it, and the bill became law.

Justice J. Cunliffe of the High Court was appointed chairman of the Special Tribunal, and U Ba U, a Sessions Judge, and A. J. Dawood, a retired Sessions Judge, were named its members. The Tribunal tried U Aung Hla and other leaders in Pyapon first. Young lawyers with political ambitions sprang to the defence: Dr. Ba Maw, his brother Dr. Ba Han, U Pu, and several others. Mr. Arthur Eggar, the Government Advocate, prosecuted. Mathematician turned lawyer, Eggar was an energetic man with a touch of eccentricity, a love for rowing—he helped found the Rangoon University Boat Club—and for dogs. He slyly suggested to the defending lawyers that they might usefully consider whether they should not take the line that all that happened was a riot, not a rebellion. When the lawyers took that line—there was no other available—Eggar had the accused brought out daily to the courthouse under heavy guards. "It was a brilliant piece of stage management", Eggar said, pleased with his tactics, "for how could the Tribunal look upon such dangerous men who needed to be so heavily guarded as mere merry rioters?"

U Aung Hla, "an old man of over 60, mild in manner and respectful in behaviour" as U Ba U described him, was found guilty, but his life was spared by the Tribunal which gave him a life sentence. A bench of three judges of the High Court, presided over by Sir Arthur Page, the chief justice, dismissed the appeals of U Aung Hla and others with these imperious words: "Be it known throughout the length and breadth of Burma that the life of every person who wages war against the King-Emperor is forfeit to the State, and that upon conviction he is liable to receive the sentence of death. Let there be no illusion."[1] The Court, on its own motion, issued notices to the appellants to show cause why they should not be hanged. "On hearing this" wrote U Ba U, "the Governor, Sir Charles Innes, broke into a cold sweat. He knew that if Sir Arthur Page carried out his threat, the rebellion would break out afresh, and that if it did, it would not be confined to a few districts, but would spread all over Burma. He sent for Page and begged of him not to alter the sentences. Page agreed not to in all but the case of Aung Hla whom he insisted should be given the death sentence. The Tribunal's sentence of transportation for life was accordingly set aside and Aung Hla was sentenced to death."[2] Thus did Sir Arthur Page, who built himself a reputation for his learning, show that while British justice would hold an even balance between the chettyar and the peasant, between citizen and citizen, yet when British power was challenged the justice would no longer be tampered with mercy and the extreme penalty would be decided upon even before the appellant had spoken.

Dr. Ba Maw who defended U Aung Hla and argued his appeal in the High Court also saw him hang. U Aung Hla and his son were hanged the same morning, on opposite gallows. They faced death bravely. The son bowed to his father, paying his last respects and begged for forgiveness for any disrespect that he might have shown in the past. The father replied with perfect composure: "Let nothing distress you, my son. You and I die noble deaths. The merit of dying for nation and religion will certainly bring us rewards in rebirth after rebirth down *samsara*. Just remember that, my son."

The trial of Saya San by the Special Tribunal took place in Tharrawaddy in the new courthouse which was completed only in March, 1927. U Thu Nge, Thakin Mya, Thakin Seint, U Chit

---

[1] See *Aung Hla* vs. *King-Emperor*, I.L.R., 9 Rangoon, p. 404.
[2] Dr. Ba U, *My Burma*, p. 110.

Nyunt, U Ba Shein and several other lawyers defended him. Tharrawaddy U Pu and Dr. Ba Maw also put in their appearances for Saya San who himself, U Ba U recalled, "refused to say anything in his own defence. He treated the whole affair with an indifferent air." Judge Ba U saw Saya San as "a thin, small man of medium size. Nobody who did not know of him would have taken him for a leader; but what he lacked in size and height, he made up for in his face and eyes. He had a strong, determined face, and his eyes glowed."

Saya San was condemned to die and the High Court promptly confirmed the sentence. His followers urged him to appeal to the Privy Council, as a last chance and also to make Burma's case better known in London and to the world. "So many of my associates and followers have been killed or hanged," replied Saya San, "I should also go their way."

On Saturday, November 28, 1931, at dawn, Saya San was hanged in Tharrawaddy jail. He went up the gallows with head erect, and waved good-bye to those who had to be present at the execution. Outside the jail a few thousand people waited, hoping to get a last glimpse of their leader. After he was safely dead, they brought his body out and let the people have a brief look at his face. Then they buried his body in an unmarked grave.

8

It took some two years before the rebellion could be extinguished. Its leaders were executed and buried or put away in jails; its members were dispersed. The fighting ended in the field but the ideas which were let loose, the eyes which were opened, the nationalism which was set aflame by the rebellion, these were more difficult to quieten or kill.

A British historian attributed the cause of the rebellion to "superstition pure and simple...spread by an ex-monk who claimed magical powers."[3] Maurice Collis, who saw the rebellion as "an ordinary observer" just a few months before winding up his many years' tour of duty as a civilian in Burma, had, however, a deeper analysis to offer. "The peasants rose," he wrote, "because

[3] G. E. Harvey, *British Rule in Burma*, Faber & Faber, London, 1946, p. 73.

that was their way of expressing the national dislike of a foreign government. Every man and woman in Burma wanted to get rid of the English government, not because it was oppressive or lacking in good qualities, but because its policy was pro-English instead of being pro-Burman. The educated classes, realizing that they were living in the twentieth century, adopted the tactics which the times offer to unarmed and subject peoples; they presented their claim for a free government to Parliament. The peasantry, whose education was confined to reading, writing and arithmetic, had no notion what to live in the twentieth century might mean, and having no way, except the traditional way of insurrection, of showing their dissatisfaction, they broke out as best they could. Their best was the best of an age that was gone."[4]

The rebellion launched many young men on their political careers. Dr. Ba Maw was one of them; his star was to rise high. U Saw, a young lawyer of the third-grade, was another. Calling himself "Galon" Saw, he set out without delay to storm his way to political power. Such were the moods of the times, he too succeeded.

Saya San made yet another bequest to posterity. He gave a small sum of money to U Tun Pe, who was then reporter on *The Sun,* to start a library. "When the Tribunal started at Tharrawaddy," U Tun Pe wrote in *The Guardian,* dated March 5, 1965,—by which time he had become a member of the Public Service Commission—"I covered the trial with Ko Han Gyi as my photographer. Ko Than Aung of *The Truth* (now in Pyapon) also was with us. The two of us, Ko Than Aung and myself, contacted Saya San in the jail—of course with the permission of the authorities concerned. Saya San authorized us to take the sale proceeds of his book *Lakhanuzu Kyann* (Symptoms of Diseases) from the Sun Press at which U Ba Gale (ex-mayor of Rangoon) was the managing director. With this money (more than Rs. 100) I bought books from the Burma Book Club for Saya San's Library. Accidentally or otherwise, the books were all leftist literature. The book list was copied from Pandit Jawaharlal Nehru's book, 'My Impressions of Russia'."

Several young men who were later to become leaders in Burma's militant nationalism used the library and read up the leftist litera-

[4] Maurice Collis, *Trials in Burma,* Faber & Faber, London, 1937, p. 276.

ture. Unwittingly, thus, Saya San, the leader of the peasants' revolution, helped to pave the way for the socialist revolution that was to come.

9

On December 21, 1959, Gen. Ne Win addressed a conference of the Security Councils from all over the country. The Councils, coordinating all government agencies in the field, specially the security forces, had worked for more than a year to restore law and order in preparation for parliamentary elections. The Anti-Fascist People's Freedom League (AFPFL) had broken into two factions in May, 1958, after enjoying a monopoly of power for a decade and more. The split posed a serious threat to the constitutional process, to the integrity of the Union itself. Gen. Ne Win was invited, when the crisis became desperate, to take over and lead a "Caretaker Government" until elections could be held. U Nu himself, leader of the one AFPFL faction which survived in office on a thin majority of 8 votes in Parliament, moved in the Chamber that Gen. Ne Win be entrusted with the task. The motion was carried by acclaim.

Now this was to be the last conference of the Security Councils under the Caretaker Government. The task was, by and large, accomplished. Lawlessness had been put down, illegal arms had been gathered in, the private armies of the rival AFPFL groups had been disbanded. Conditions were favourable for free and fair elections. The Government would act as umpire in the game, and Gen. Ne Win laid great emphasis in his speech on the vital need for strict neutrality on the part of public servants and military personnel. Personal attachments must be put aside; the dominant loyalty must be to the people.

Gen. Ne Win gave a brief review of the country's political history in his speech. The GCBA and the nationalist movement which won the massive support of the people, the students' boycott of 1920 behind which the nation rose united as one man. Yet the unity never did last long. Factions would appear, with allegiance to personalities rather than principles. Dyarchy raised a crop of parties. "It was the country's bad fortune," Gen. Ne Win said, "that unity had been so transient. One consolation, however, was that the factional struggles did not end up in violence and bloodshed. The British Government could afford to stay neutral, the entire administration kept aloof. Hence the fight was contained in a narrow arena."

On the Saya San rebellion also Gen. Ne Win had his observations to make. In his address to a mammoth rally in Rangoon on Peasants' Day, March 2, 1965, Gen. Ne Win as chairman of the Revolutionary Council, pointed out that the rebellion was no mere incident, nor any small rising, but of revolutionary purpose and proportions. Some might call it a foolhardy affair, but his own analysis was different. The rebellion must be viewed against its own proper historical background. The peasants were in deep despair and dire circumstances. The economic depression had hit them rather hard. The capitation taxes introduced and exacted ruthlessly in such circumstances drove them to desperation. Exploitation by the money-lenders, the businessmen, and the hangers-on to the government, coupled with oppressive measures by the government, made the peasants feel that they had to fight back. They saw no alternative, no salvation. Death was preferable to the misery and humiliation they had to suffer. In rising they chose the path of courage and honour.

"It was a peasants' revolution in our way of thinking," Gen. Ne Win said, "and no foolhardy act done on impulse. That is why we honour the veterans of the Saya San Revolution who are here as our guests. We cannot trace all the survivors or bring them all here. The honoured guests here are a token of how we feel." The veterans, who shared the dais with Gen. Ne Win, beamed with pleasure at these words.

The weakness of the Saya San rebellion lay, Gen. Ne Win analysed, in reliance on charms and amulets which were supposed to confer invulnerability to bullets. With that misplaced faith the men rushed on guns and cannons with the result that their casualties were high. Strength, Gen. Ne Win said, could not come from superstition, only weakness.

"Another lesson we should draw from the rebellion," Gen. Ne Win said, "is that those who wield power must always be on guard against its corruptive influence. Leaders of the Saya San rebellion began well in all true sincerity. In later stages corruption set in among some leaders. They took to themselves many wives, or

queens as they called them, and exacted tolls and tributes from the
villagers. They rolled in wealth and luxury, turning their backs on
their cause. That is what power can do to men. We must watch
out always, and vigilantly, against the evil influence of power."

For Gen. Ne Win the YMBA, the GCBA, the Wunthanu movement, the Boycott, the Saya San rebellion, were partly things of
hearsay and partly things seen and felt by him as an observer,
aware but too young to be an active participant. He was born on
May 24, 1911, at Paungdale in Prome District. His father, U Po
Kha, proud of his first son, called him Shu Maung—the apple of
one's eye.

10

The stump of a *pe*-tree (fan palm) half-covered with cactus, a
fence, an ancient tamarind tree, these are what remain of the
first home in Aung-thwe-ma-shar to which U Po Kha brought his
bride, Daw Mi Lay, the home where Shu Maung arrived.

The family later moved to Paungdale. U Po Kha retired after
a time from government service as revenue surveyor and devoted
himself to managing the family estate and looking after the growing family. There were the lands to cultivate—paddy, groundnut,
corn, the varied and abundant crops to sow, nurse, harvest, sell.
There was enough work for all: U Po Kha with his friendliness,
Daw Mi Lay with her sound business instincts, relatives and
villagers who shared in the toils and their rewards, young Shu
Maung who enjoyed taking a turn at the plough or a place in the
spread-out formation of sowers, planters, reapers.

The father tended to spoil the child. Daw Mi Lay gave him all
her young mother's love and character and a good upbringing too.
She was thrifty, she taught the boy to be so. She worked hard, she
taught the boy to acquire a steady working habit. When the boy
was a little older, and a young sister was born, he washed the dishes
and the diapers. The mother taught the boy how to make a small
piece of soap go a long way, how to wipe the diaper clean first
with a thin piece of bamboo before dipping it into the bowl of
water. She showed him how to pound the paddy grains into rice
of the right quality. She taught him how to cook, keep books of
the household account. The boy also swept the house and looked

after the baby when his mother went out to the bazaar to shop. "What would you like me to bring for you from the bazaar," she would ask him on leaving. "Some *kaukswe* (fried noodles), Mother," he would reply, well-pleased.

Paungdale had a good middle school, but Shu Maung would soon outgrow it. The parents therefore sent him to Prome where he stayed with friends and attended the National High School. It was soon after the Boycott, when national schools were in full flood.

U Tun Maung of Prome was reading for his B.A. degree when the Boycott was declared. He left his studies and joined, as many of his classmates from the University College and the Judson (American Baptist) Mission College did. Many of them never returned to their studies. Some, like U Po Kyar, the Burmese scholar, and U Po Kun of Toungoo, served as inspectors of national schools. Some, like U Tun Maung, went back to their home-towns to start such schools so that the education of the boys in the districts—who had heartily joined the Boycott—might not be interrupted for too long.

In Prome, as elsewhere, the elders of the town gave full support to the movement. Students from the Government High School, who had been on strike, came over to join. The school thus started full-blown with attendance of some 600 in grades one to ten. U Tun Maung, the principal, drew a monthly salary of Rs. 80. The teachers received Rs. 60 or Rs. 70, depending on qualification and responsibility. Low salary was amply made up by high enthusiasm.

The school did not last very long, however. A promise by the Government to provide aid to national schools set off a controversy as to whether such aid should be accepted. There were those who thought acceptance would amount to surrender; there were those who thought refusal would be self-denial and suicide. Up and down the country the controversy raged, dividing the national school movement, splitting the Council of National Education. That was the beginning of the end of the movement. The School at Prome died after one general meeting of city elders, boycotters, the principal and teachers. Angry speeches were made, but no unanimity could be reached on the concrete issues. The School split.

Young Shu Maung stayed for a while—he was then in his fourth grade—with the part of the School which had resolved to carry on without aid. U Tun Maung, before leaving to find himself a career, called the boy in and advised him to transfer to the Government High School towards which there was a general exodus. The boy moved when he saw that his principal was going away too.

Shu Maung was steady in class, quiet and well-behaved. He had a curious, keen and questioning mind, the memory which he had perhaps inherited from his mother, willingness to learn, energy for study and sport and fun. He played football, hockey, tennis, with sportsmanship and studiously developed skill. He hated bullies in the classroom or the playing field. The weak found in him their champion, the bully their foe. He disliked the unjust, the snob, the pompous.

Those years at school were relatively tranquil. Economic depression was to hit the country only in the twilight of the 'twenties. Peasants were beginning to feel the pinch of the system of free competition. The chettyars had started to foreclose on the mortgages of their lands. But U Po Kha and Daw Mi Lay in Paungdale were holding their own quite well.

Shu Maung worked steadily at School without want or worry. A monthly allowance of Rs. 30 was ample; Rs. 15 for boarding fee, Rs. 5 for tuition and sundry expenses, leaving Rs. 10 for pocket-money which would buy the favourite dish of *kaukswe* and the cinema tickets for himself and friends. There was a spirit of sharing among the friends, and Shu Maung was among the most generous sharers. He was, at the same time, thorough and thrifty, as his mother taught him to be. He would wear and keep his clothes well. When packing to return home for the vacations he would remember the smallest item of his belongings. Back home, his mother would check, to find everything there, including the worn vest with gaping holes in it, and she would feel pleased.

Political consciousness was spreading in the country. The GCBA was attaining the peak of its popularity. U Po Kha, with his following and influence, was much sought after by the politicians. His blessing meant much. His friendly good nature also made him a good mediator between factions. The leading political leaders visited the home of U Po Kha and Daw Mi Lay, to seek support, or to stay a few days during their campaign tours. U Chit Hlaing, the uncrowned king, came and stayed. U Ba Pe, U Tun

Shein, U Thein Maung, Dr. Thein Maung, Dr. Ba Maw, all came except "Galon" U Saw whose ways went against the grain of U Po Kha.

In the early years, before the Dobama Asiayone was born, the comings and goings of the politicians at the home did not affect young Shu Maung too deeply. He did not dream great dreams of leading the country in revolutionary times. He did not hear whispers that he was born to greatness. He did not listen much to the politicians who spoke long about home rule, dyarchy, reforms and the rest. If political leadership required the ability to talk endlessly in a learned way on nothing in particular, he was not cut out for political leadership.

He wanted, in fact, to become a doctor. His record in school was good. Always with the top few in class, by steady work rather than strenuous striving, he was more than adequate for the medical school.

Parents in those days wanted their sons to attain the Indian Civil Service, later the Burma Civil Service, class One. If not class One, then class Two; if not class Two, at least the Subordinate Civil Service, whose pay might be small but whose prestige was high, higher than that of a senior master in a school. Shu Maung, however, aspired to be a doctor, not a Class One officer, not any officer at all; a medical doctor who could cure and heal, not a Ph.D. of a doctor who could show so much learning about so little. His parents did not care much for the civil service. They encouraged him to go to medical school and come back home a doctor. Ko Maung Nyi, uncle and counsellor, thought it was a fine idea. So did Ko Chit Khine and Ko Chit Hlaing, the maternal uncles.

So, to the University College in Rangoon went Shu Maung in June 1929. He enrolled in the intermediate of science course, with biology. If all went well, he would pass out into medical school after two years.

2
The Struggle Gathers Momentum

1

THE INCIDENTS of 1930 set many young minds moving.

There were racial riots in May. The economic depression made the unemployment problem acute. Immigrant Indian labourers, willing to work on cheap wages, made up most of Rangoon's labour force. There were, however, limits to how cheap the wages could go. Some Indian labourers went on strike when they felt that the limits had been exceeded; the employers quickly filled their jobs with Burmese workers. The result was the riots which spread through the city, claiming casualties at random from both the Indian and the Burmese communities.

Nerves were on edge. After the Indo-Burmese riots came the Sino-Burmese riots—a brief affair which flared up over a small incident. Restlessness and frustration were widespread.

The riots stirred nationalist feelings. Pamphlets appeared in the streets calling on Burmans to rise and defend national honour. "Burma is our country. Love her! Burmese is our language, cherish it!" The call—indeed the command—to love and cherish Burma and things Burmese struck deep responsive chords throughout the country. Looking back across the years which have been so full of war and revolution in which so many clarion calls have been sounded, the call to honour that was sounded in 1930 must seem feeble. In its time, however, it was a great thing. It awakened the nation to the need for greater endeavours, beyond speech-making and grabbing office, for larger sacrifices and bolder deeds. It also brought forth into the political arena several angry young men.

The beginnings of the *Dobama Asi-ayone* (Our Burma Association) took shape that year. Ba Thaung, the author of the pamphlets, wanted to be a writer; he would wield his pen to rouse and rally the people, recapturing for them the shining glories of Burmese days. Ohn Khin, a friend, was destined to be a successful publisher and journalist. There were also Ohn Pe, Hla Baw, and a few others, and together these friends formed an informal group to meet, talk, write, and go round lecturing wherever they could find people who would listen. At the University, Ba Sein, Lay Maung and others were willing to listen; later they too became so excited they listened no more but only lectured. Thus emerged the founders of the Dobama Asi-ayone whose members titled themselves "Thakin" or Master. The founders were emerging, but they did not yet know what they were destined to create. A few years were to go by while the growing group of young men groped for directions.

Unknown at first to the would-be Thakins, the whole village of Wekkathe, on the road from Prome to Taungdwingyi, had gone Thakin in 1927. An Englishman who was subdivisional officer for the area took to himself a Burmese wife. The relatives of the young lady felt so honoured by their new connection with the ruling gentry that they would talk about the "Thakin" (Master) on every occasion. The villagers were disgusted. U Wayama, the abbot of the village monastery at Wekkathe, an ardent GCBA man himself, decided that time was ripe to make a grand gesture of defiance. He had a meeting of the villagers convened, at which he pointed out that the real masters were the villagers who paid the revenues that paid for the government machinery. Hence the villagers were Thakin, and the officers, Englishman, Indian or Burman, were their servants. "Let us call ourselves Thakin henceforth, to remind ourselves of our true status, and the others of their's," resolved the villagers without a note of dissent. Thus, Ko Toke, the farmer, thenceforth became Thakin Toke; Chet-gyi, the blacksmith, became Thakin Chet-gyi, and so on. Name-boards were put up on doors to announce the rebirth of the villagers as the masters. U Ba Thaung, working as a translation tutor in the Burmese department of the University College, Rangoon, heard from friends about the assumption of the Thakin title by the villagers of Wekkathe, and thought it was a fine idea. How would "Thakin Ba Thaung" sound, he asked himself, and decided that it sounded very noble indeed.[1]

[1] Thakin Myat Saing, *The Source of the "Thakin" Designation,* article in the *Botataung* Burmese-language daily, Aug. 17, 1964.

The Saya San rebellion sparked off many things. It also happened at a time when, in London, the Statute of Westminster had been passed by Parliament in recognition of the Commonwealth idea. The mood and thinking of London increasingly favoured a family of nations free and equal, bound together by a common allegiance and common interests. That was the dream; the realities in Burma were the nightmare. The peasants were having to be mown down by machine-guns. British rule was unpopular, British intentions were suspect, British words were fast losing their weight.

The Simon Commission, which had studied the working of dyarchy in India and Burma, recommended reforms. It also re-emphasized that Burma was not India; separate constitutional reforms were therefore advised for the two countries. The Saya San rebellion helped to persuade the British Government that commissions and select committees were no longer adequate. More direct links were needed between the law-makers in London and the peoples in India and Burma for whom the laws were made. Conversations round the table between representatives might solve a number of problems. The answers that eluded a formal, fact-finding commission, might emerge easily in such friendly chats. That would also be the British way of getting things done by conversation and compromise.

To London, therefore, the politicians were invited. They were invited often during the few years that followed the Saya San rebellion. They went in bigger delegations. Even U Chit Hlaing, the great boycotter, at last became interested, and went to London with his friends.

2

The issue which dominated the domestic scene for the next few years was, in fact, no issue at all. The question was whether Burma should separate from India; the answer had always been "Yes". The commissions of inquiry had said "Yes". The British Government in Rangoon had said "Yes"; His Majesty's Government in London had agreed to draft a new constitution for Burma on that basis. Everything was practically settled, but the politicians in Burma needed an issue to fight over, a great big issue that would engage the attention of the people for the last remaining years of dyarchy.

To separate from, or stay with, India thus became the burning issue of the day. The Separationists came up, and the Anti-Separationists. The two schools divided into many sects. There were those who agreed in principle but differed on methods. There were those who differed to agree; those who agreed to differ. The "Hlaing-Myat-Paw" party, made up of U Chit Hlaing, U Myat Tha Dun, and U Paw Tun were against separation. Dr. Ba Maw, U Kyaw Myint, and "Ramree" (Yan-Bye in the Burmese pronunciation) U Maung Maung, making up the leadership of the "Maw-Myint-Bye" group, were also against. U Ba Pe, U Pu and U Thein Maung, leading the People's Party, a relic of the Twenty-Oners, were for separation. So was the Independent Party, nicknamed the 'Golden Valley Party' after the aristocratic suburbs in which its leaders, Sir J. A. Maung Gyi and others lived.

The Anti-Separationists were not without their reservations. "Separate! But do not let go of the association with India!" That was what Dr. Ba Maw urged, with his eloquence and enigma, when the tides seemed to turn against his group. It would be a blunder, it was suggested by the Anti-Separationists, to part with India at a time when constitutional reforms were being considered. Burma had been excluded from dyarchy before; part now, and she might again be left out in the rains. Non-separation did not have to mean eternal union, it was argued. At the proper time, Burma could ask for secession; another statute, an order in council, and the parting could be effected, with no ill-feelings on either side, no tears shed. Thus, the debate went on, up and down the country, dividing parties, the Buddhist monks, families, friends.

The elections of November 1932 were fought over the separation issue. It was an issue without any real validity, for London had already decided on separation. This was ruled by Lord Peel, chairman of the Round Table Conference in London, who drew the attention of the delegates to the Government's announcement made on August 20, 1931: "The primary task of the Burma Conference will be to discuss the lines of a constitution for separated Burma." The November elections, however, gave a resounding victory to the Anti-Separationists who won 42 seats in the Legislative Council and 415,000 votes, against the Separationists who won 29 seats and 250,000 votes.

Two rising political stars emerged from the elections. Dr. Ba

3

Maw, barrister, doctor of philosophy of the University of
Bordeaux, had made his name as defence counsel in the rebellion
trials. He was made for success. He was a handsome man who
looked good even in the eccentric dresses which he invented for
himself. He spoke Burmese with an English accent and a little
stutter which made his speeches sound musical. He had wit,
charm, intellect, ambition, cunning. His French experience made
him think and talk like a leftist. When he later started the Sinyetha
(Poor Man's) Party, he set a new fashion by issuing a manifesto.
In 1934, after ousting one of his own former associates, U Kyaw
Din, by a no-confidence motion, Dr. Ba Maw took office as minister for education. Thenceforth his rise was to be meteoric.

U Saw was the other star which appeared on the political firma-
ment. He did not have much formal education. He took out a
lower grade pleader's licence but did not have a practice. He
volunteered to defend Saya San, but Dr. Ba Maw and the other
barristers, who rushed to offer their services, outshone him. But
U Saw had guts, and a fierce ambition. He had the ability to recognize opportunity when he saw it, and seize and exploit it with
ruthlessness. Calling himself "Galon" U Saw, in revered memory
of Saya San, he began without delay to bulldoze his way to power.
He won a seat in the Legislative Council, quickly mastered its
procedures and tactics, and was soon making his presence in the
Council very much felt all round. Only those silken, smooth-
tongued barristers had attained ministerial office so far; there was
no precedent of a lower grade pleader reaching that high. U Saw
was determined to make a precedent with himself by becoming
prime minister, not a minister merely.

The Legislative Council debated long and loud about separation, anti-separation, or a federation of convenience, but the political centre of gravity had shifted to London where, in the palace
of St. James's, proposals for a new constitution were being considered. The Council was without serious purpose, but its members sharpened their skill in the mechanics of the parliamentary
game, intrigue and manoeuvre. Debates were heated. Objections
were raised, nice points of order taken. The Speaker had to use
his gavel frequently; members often ignored him and kept talking.
Vague resolutions worded to invite the best legal hair-splitting,
were moved. Marathon speeches were made, precisely timed to

kill unwanted motions by lapse of the session. U Ba Pe set a handsome record of 40 hours of speaking in a debate before the Council was prorogued on May 6, 1933.

London, puzzled and confused by the goings-on in Rangoon, invited a delegation to another round of talks. Off went Dr. Ba Maw, U Thein Maung, U Chit Hlaing, U Ba Pe, and others, including a lady, Dr. Daw Saw Sa. A joint parliamentary committee talked with the Burmese delegates. Major Clement R. Attlee, Labour M.P., who took active part in the discussions and the Burma Round Table conferences, probably had no inkling then that he would, one day, as prime minister of Britain, supervise the abdication of British power over Burma.

The joint committee found, after the delegates from Burma had fully expounded, explained and elucidated their case that "they have no real desire to see Burma included in an Indian Federation; and indeed they frankly admit that on their own terms they would unhesitatingly prefer separation." The issue was thus finally laid to rest. A new constitution for a separated Burma was drafted. The Government of Burma Act of 1935 passed the constitution into law. Time was needed to prepare the ground for the new system of government. General elections were scheduled for 1936; the Act was to be fully operative on April 1, 1937.

3

The Rangoon University to which Shu Maung came to work towards a medical degree was calm. Intellectual ferment went on below the surface; there were no violent eruptions. Students were young, but they were "collegians"; they bore themselves with dignity and distinction.

The buildings were still coming up. Sir Harcourt Butler who had inaugurated the University, after a delay caused by the strike, had been its great supporter and fund-raiser. Ava Hall, into which Shu Maung was admitted as a residential student, was fresh and new. Pinya and Sagaing were next door; residents of the "central halls" dined together in a common mess. Food was only good for grumbling about, but then the hostel fee was Rs. 24 per month which covered board and lodging. A student could get by comfortably on a remittance of Rs. 60 from home; many pulled along on much less.

Classes were scattered over the town; the buildings mushrooming on the campus were not yet enough. Science students had to travel back and forth by buses for their lectures and their practicals. Few students took science courses, though. The courses were considered to be tougher. They were certainly rougher too, for some of the professors, like D.H. Peacock of chemistry and F.J. Meggitt of biology could be holy terrors. There were dear eccentrics too in the science departments; one brilliant lecturer in physics went quite mad. The arts subjects were more popular with the students also because they held out better chances to candidates for the civil service. There was a sprinkling of Burmese staff in mathematics and oriental studies: Professor Pe Maung Tin, later to become the first Burmese principal of University College, U Ka, U Po Thon, U Hla Paw Oo and others. The rest were English or Indian. Mr. D. J. Sloss, an Englishman belonging to the Indian Education Service, was principal.

Shu Maung organized his life in college with his usual thoroughness. He attended classes regularly; the practice of his more Bohemian friends to miss classes was not for him. He played football, making the University Eleven, and won trophies in inter-hall hockey. An inquiring mind, supported by a capacity to learn, led him into the company of campus poets U Thein Han and U Wun, and Burmese scholars Saya Lin and Saya Pwa. Many verses learnt, indeed absorbed, in those days still remain fresh in his mind. He polished his English, made entries in his diary in that language, for its pure delight, and also to perfect it as an essential tool. He had an ear for music, a fondness for classical Burmese songs. He would also walk from the campus, alone or with friends, on the fullmoon night of Waso or Tazaungmon, to the Shwedagon pagoda to worship, to pray. He often undertook, with unrelenting strictness, the rigours of the sabbath.

So much time, Shu Maung would plan, for sports, so much for study, leaving so much for play. Rangoon was an exciting playground for the country-boy who went out studiously to try everything once. He would join friends out on a spree, for he was a good joiner, or he would slip out alone, for he could be a lone wolf too.

Political repercussions came only in mild ripples to the University as the 1930's began. The Saya San rebellion was followed with interest by the students; its wisdom was questioned, its courage was admired. But the call of Dobama, our Burma, our language, our culture, drew good response. There was a movement for a boycott of imported foreign goods; students, wearing coarse home-spun clothes, would go round asking their friends to wear likewise, and change from English cigarettes to Burmese cheroots. The young ladies of the College were asked to give up English voile—nylon was not in vogue yet—and wear *pinni* blouses instead.

A typical campus politician was Ba Sein who was active in the All-Burma Youth League. Ba Sein had a thin purse—he managed on a bare subsistence allowance of Rs. 40 a month—and a supreme self-confidence. With him, the coarse pinni jacket was both a matter of necessity and principle. He read widely; talked endlessly. Much as he liked talking, he disliked listening. He would go to the lectures at the College Union given by Dr. Ba Maw, U Ba Pe, U Tun Win of Moulmein, to heckle, not to listen. His smile of self-satisfaction grew wider as he opened up in fuller flower every day. He shaved off his head, to rid himself of the western style hair crop, and earned the nickname, "Gandhi Sein" after the great Mahatma.

Lay Maung, a founder of the Youth League, earned his degree in science in 1931 but left without taking it, too absorbed in political work. He went to India for a close look at the Indian National Congress. On his return he devoted himself to the building of the Dobama Asi-ayone.

Ko Nu, another leader of the Youth League, was the University orator. He could wax eloquent on any subject: a beautiful face, literature, Shakespeare, the National Day. Once, when the burning issue of separation or anti-separation was rousing high passions, he waxed eloquent at the College Union on anti-separation. That was a blunder which he soon found out, for after the loud boos came the brickbats. He kept doggedly on, unflinching in the din. Ko Nu was, however, more sensitive than Gandhi Sein. The reception apparently hurt him, for he retired to Pantanaw to teach at the National High School. There Ko Nu's wounded feelings were healed when he met and married Ma Mya Yi. Ko Thant, a fellow teacher, acted as negotiator, practising an art which he was to perfect in later years as

Secretary-General of the United Nations.

Shu Maung hardly ever went to the debates and lectures at the College Union. He would, instead, borrow a car from a visitor, and take a trip to town. He found the talks boring, and he considered the wearing of pinni and the smoking of cheroots by some students as little more than showmanship. Perhaps a little showmanship was essential to enliven things up; he himself believed only in organization, strong, solid organization, long sustained. Life was getting to be dull; the excitement of Rangoon was wearing off. Meggitt of biology was becoming unbearable. The professor had the annoying habit of pointing a formidable finger at random at some unfortunate student, shoot questions by rapid fire, then turn the still-stammering victim out of the class. "What a bully," Shu Maung would mutter to his friends at such frequent displays, "what injustice!" But to get to medical school one must score good marks in biology, and biology meant Meggitt.

In March, 1931, Shu Maung took his examinations in the senior intermediate of science. Meggitt and biology failed him. He did not go back to the University. Beyond the campus there was a world waiting, calling, and to that world he went.

4

The early 1930's saw the gradual emergence of the Dobama Asi-ayone as an organized party. First there were the few: Ba Thaung, author of the pamphlets, Lay Maung, Thein Maung, joined by Ba Sein and friends. The Dobama song, composed by "YMB" Saya Tin, a song full of memories of the nation's glorious past, was adopted as the anthem of the group. Young men in pinni jacket, longyi worn short, wooden slippers instead of leather shoes on their feet, went round lecturing, shouting slogans, singing the Dobama song. They called themselves Thakin or Thakin-ma (for women) and addressed each other by the title. They spoke in the language of command, preferring the master's "you" and "I" to the polite, customary "respected Sir" and "Your humble servant". The sound of their wooden slippers, and the direct, forceful, even rude, voices of the Thakin's and the Thakin-ma's announced the arrival of a new force on the political scene.

They were young men and women drawn together by national pride and a desire to do something to revive national pride, redeem lost national honour. They were without programme or philosophy at first. They groped, they searched, earnestly, urgently, reading copiously, discussing diligently, willing to borrow, copy, imitate. They drew their inspiration from a wide variety of sources. The Indian National Congress, with its saintly sage Gandhi, its young leaders Nehru and Bose, attracted Ba Sein, Lay Maung, U Ottama and several others. Japan, that Asian nation whose people western books of history and geography had always pictured as short and insignificant, had won a great victory over Russia in the very first decade of the 20th century, and to the young seekers Japan was the land of the rising sun. U Ottama taught Pali in the University of Tokyo and came home to tell many wonderful stories about the unity and industry of the Japanese people in building a modern nation. U Saw, who did not have a Cambridge, Oxford or an Inns of Court education, went to Japan in 1935 to complete his education, and wrote a book about his impressions. The young Thakins found Japan a source for inspiration, though not for philosophy.

The philosophy was supplied, to a large extent, by the books. "We read a lot in those days," recalls Thakin Kyaw Sein who did his share of writing and publishing for the Asi-ayone and is now, appropriately, directing the book trade for the Trade Council. "We read whatever books we could lay our hands on. We made notes, shared the books with our associates, discussed. We would walk long distances in town—we were generally poor and could not afford bus fares—to borrow a book or spend a few hours in a library. Ideas excited us. A catching phrase or a potent word in a book would keep us awake at nights."

The Burma Book Club, started by J. S. Furnivall who retired from the ICS to lecture, write and publish, provided a good meeting ground for the young intellectuals. The Club launched Thein Maung by sending him to London to learn bookstore management. There he was drawn into leftist circles, the League against Imperialism, the company of Hyde Park orators. His London experience equipped Thakin Thein Maung to lead actively in the Asi-ayone in its formative years. "We can accomplish a good deal without money," he would tell his comrades who showed

signs of weakening for want of material things, perhaps remembering Hyde Park where all that was necessary to give voice to an idea
was a soap-box, a firm faith, and strong lungs.

Thakin Ba Thoung found a haven in the Burma Book Club. So
did U Khant, a young writer. *The World of Books,* a bilingual
journal published by the Club provided an outlet for the young intellectuals; the *Burma Research Society Journal,* in the starting
of which also J. S. Furnivall took a hand along with U May Oung
and others, carried more scholarly studies on Burmese history and
culture.

The Bernard Free Library, set up in 1883 with the funds of an
Englishman, Sir Charles Bernard, was another place where the
young men received nourishment for their minds. Their appetite
was huge. Books on economics, history, literature, and, of course,
politics, were hungrily devoured, resulting in some intellectual in-
digestion, but leaving the appetite still unsatisfied. The library
established with funds left by Saya San was another attraction.
Thakin Than Tun, Thakin Soe, and several others who are now
leaders of the Communist parties—White Flag, Red Flag—drank
deep from the fountain of Marxist thought at the Saya San library.

Dr Thein Maung, an associate of Dr Ba Maw, brought back a
collection of books on Marxism from the London Round Table
Conference. These books too went round from hand to hand, to
be read and re-read. Japan defeated Russia in battle and set Asian
nationalism aflame. In Russia the people overthrew the Czar,
feudalism, the old oppressive order; this aroused enthusiasm for
a revolution to end exploitation, privilege, inequality, and to usher
in a new socialist society of justice. Nationalism must be guided
by the ultimate aim of building a new society of social justice. But
to cast the society in a new mould there must first be freedom
from foreign rule. The Thakins therefore took nationalism as their
ideological guide and programme, for it was the essential means
to freedom and the promised land.

The methods varied. Boycott of foreign goods and competition
with foreigners were mild ones for the start. Cheroots instead of
cigarettes, pinni instead of imported textiles. The boycott was
not a great success economically, but it had its emotional
appeal. In the field of competition the young intellectuals could
not take on the big businessmen, but they thought they could

beat the small retailers.

After leaving the University, Shu Maung, living with friends in 101st Street, Rangoon, decided to have a try. Charcoal, which Prome produced, could be procured at the kilns at so much a bag. Transportation to Rangoon would cost so much, so that at such a price they could under-sell the Indian charcoal merchants and still make a margin of profit. Thorough research convinced Shu Maung that it would be a sure thing, and it would soon drive the Indians off the market.

Ko Maung Nyi, in Prome, was game to join the venture. He sent buyers around, procured the charcoal and sent them down to Rangoon. Everywhere, all down the line, the venture ran into opposition. The producers, suddenly offered better prices by the Indians, were unwilling to sell. Transportation somehow did not run smoothly. In Rangoon the merchants teamed up and undersold their competitors at impossible prices. The venture failed, but a lesson was learnt that puny measures could not dislodge the massive interests which were so deeply entrenched.

Talking at street corners, standing on improvised platforms—not much more substantial than the Hyde Park soap-boxes—was another method. At first few listened, but slowly the crowds grew. The Dobama song was appealing, if not the rather rude language used by the young men. The tri-colour flag of the party evoked fond sentiments of the past, stirred hopes for the future. Green was the colour to denote the abundance of agricultural resources; yellow was the colour for the purity of the Buddhist faith; red was for valour. In the centre of the flag, framed in a circle, was the peacock in its pride, the peacock which had led the Burmese armies to victories in the glorious days. The flag, the song, the slogans, the speeches, the fiery young men with their intense dedication, these began to gradually win recruits and supporters.

No formal ceremony was needed to initiate a recruit into the Asi-ayone. In the first years, no applications for admission were demanded. It was by association, and by habit, that a man became a Thakin. Going along to lecture meetings with a Thakin, or joining in a discussion, reading a book lent, sharing the speaker's platform and being introduced to the audience as a comrade, these were the steps which led a man slowly but surely into the Asi-ayone.

Thakin Ba Sein left the University in 1934 with due fanfare and devoted himself entirely to the movement. Thakins Thein Maung, Ba Thaung and Tun Shwe made up the small group of the original founders. In 1933 the Asi-ayone was properly proclaimed, with the All Burma Youth League and the Youth Improvement Society forming its elements. In 1934, the four founders went to Shwebo, the famous starting point of the armed rising by which Alaungpaya built the last Burmese dynasty. A pagoda at the entrance of Shwebo has a plot of ground which, it is said, was the exact starting point of Alaungpaya's march. The ground is therefore symbolic of victory, and he who has trodden on it is assured of victory in any grand venture that he may set upon. That is what the people say, and the Thakins went to Shwebo to tread on victory soil, thus establish a direct link with Alaungpaya, and to contest a bye-election for the Legislative Council.

The four Thakins went from the victory soil practically straight into jail. The deputy commissioner of Shwebo was not too pleased with their visit, and served this order on each of the Thakins: "Whereas credible information has been received by me that your presence in the Shwebo district is likely to lead to a disturbance of the public tranquillity or a riot or an affray, I hereby direct you to abstain from residing in or entering into the Shwebo district for two months from the date of this order." The visitors refused to leave, and they were prosecuted and sentenced to jail terms. On appeal the High Court ruled that the deputy commissioner had no power to pass the order. The Thakins were set free, but not until they had had a taste of jail.[2]

Shwebo was not exactly an unalloyed victory, but it aroused people's interest in the movement. Thakin Ba Sein and his comrades received publicity, even made headlines. Victory in the High Court made languishing in jail worthwhile. There would be many more jails, many more victories, before the end of the road, to be attained only by those of stout heart.

Ko Maung Nyi in Prome was one with such a stout heart. A friend, Ko Sein Chaw, came to his wedding and talked about the Thakin movement, and its young idealistic founders. The bridegroom became keenly interested. Ko Sein Chaw stayed on, talked

[2] See *Thakin Ba Thaung & Others vs. King-Emperor*, I.L.R. 12 Rangoon, p. 283.

some more, courted a girl next door and married her. Ko Maung Nyi met Thakin Lay Maung and Thakin Ba Sein, and decided that a life's mission was opening itself to him. A bridegroom of not many months, he joined the same day with another man, Tun Oke. Thakin Nyi was to give all of himself and his wealth to the movement. By association with him, Shu Maung was to become a Thakin too.

5

At the University, in the academic year 1934-35, a clan of young politicians gathered. Ko Nu was back for a third time, this time to read law. Also on the scene were Aung San, the future founder of New Burma; Kyaw Nyein who was to play important roles in politics; Thein Pe who was to acquire both fame and notoriety as author, social reformer, champion of controversial causes.

Kyaw Nyein and Thein Pe had passed from the Intermediate College, Mandalay. With their contemporaries in the College, Khin Maung Gale, Tun Ohn, Hla Maung, and others, they had staged a brief strike in 1932 to protest against the Government's proposal to close down the College for economy reasons. The strike drew strong support from the city elders. The Government yielded, the College survived. Thus when these comrades came down to Rangoon to work for their degrees they had behind them a record of organization, agitation, victory.

The Rangoon University Students Union offered the clan a home. The Union, established with the blessing of the principal, had been a social club run by the sons of government officers. It gave no trouble to the authorities. It organized sports, literary and social activities; now and then political leaders would be invited to lecture or engage in debate. Thus Dr Ba Maw, a frequent guest, had spoken on education in France, of which he had first-hand knowledge, at the investiture of Mon Po Choe as president of the Union in 1929. U Ba Pe and Dr Ba Maw had debated on the separation issue at the Union. U Saw, dauntless, defiant, had stood up well in debate against Dr Ba Maw.

The comrades decided that the RUSU was too tame, and needed a good shake-up. The Union needed them, and they needed

the Union. The first attempts to get into the RUSU executive were,
however, strongly resisted by the traditional managers of the club.
But resistance to the new forces could not hold out long. Times
were changing, the tide was turning, a new spirit of challenge and
crusade was astir on the campus and beyond. In the elections of
August 1935 the comrades swept into victory *en bloc;* Ko Nu was
president, M.A. Raschid vice-president, Ko Thi Han secretary,
Ko Ohn treasurer, Aung San editor of the *Oway* journal, Ba Set,
Tha Hla, and Tun Tin members of the executive committee.

The new committee thought in big terms, planned big things.
The inter-hostel debates, the lectures, the activities, were to be
bigger, bolder. The National Day would be celebrated on a gran-
der scale, and Ko Nu would deliver an even more eloquent speech.
Aung San, in charge of publicity, solicited messages of felicitations
from Thakin Kodaw Hmaing and prominent personalities. Tha
Hla's grand assignment was "Inter-University Affairs". Writing
in 1958, Dr Tha Hla recalled that he had "no notion whatever of
the duties connected with that high office. As there was only one
college outside Rangoon, the Intermediate College of Mandalay,
he decided that he must try and establish a liaison with students'
unions in foreign universities. "Accordingly, with my entire budget
of ten rupees," he wrote, "I addressed complimentary letters to
the Unions of Oxford and London Universities and also to that of
the Imperial University at Tokyo. I requested them to send us a
copy of their constitutions. My efforts were totally ineffective. I
have received no reply from any of them to date".[3]

Liaison with Tokyo, London or Oxford might be difficult to
establish, but with the Dobama Asi-ayone and the politicians it
was close and easy indeed. Thakin Ba Sein kept up his contacts,
taking upon himself the role of philosopher and friend to the up
and coming young men. The politicians found the RUSU a valuable forum; invitations to speak or debate were always welcome.
Than Tun, studying at the Teachers' Training College, came often
to share meals and thoughts at the mess with Ko Nu, Ko Aung
San, and comrades. The young leaders of the RUSU were asked
to share the speakers' platform at lectures or rallies in town. *The
New Light of Burma,* the *Deedok* journal edited by U Ba Choe,

[3] Dr Tha Hla, *The 1936 Rangoon University Strike, New Burma Weekly,*
June 21 and 28, July 5, 19, and 26, and Aug. 2, 1958.

the *Dagon* magazine and the *New Burma* English-language tri-weekly journal, welcomed their contributions, supported their cause.

The University authorities did not view the RUSU activities with great favour. They decided that they had to nip things in the bud. One student who failed to say "Sir" in responding to a roll call was dismissed. There were several who were gravely warned for lesser crimes. Ko Nu, the president of the RUSU, in a speech delivered at the RUSU on January 31, 1936, took the principal to task for the high-handed behaviour of the authorities. The speech drew critical comments from the English-owned *Rangoon Gazette* English language newspaper. The final examinations were only a few weeks away then, and the authorities decided that they could expel Ko Nu without provoking the students who would be deep in their studies. Thus they served the expulsion order on Ko Nu, who quietly pocketed it.

The Oway came out soon after, the pride and joy of Ko Aung San and Ko Thein Tin, the co-opted assistant editor. Both had worked hard collecting articles, reading proofs, soliciting financial support. Now the first copies were off the press Thein Tin—who sported the pen-name of Nyo Mya—had spent many laborious hours with Roget's Thesaurus to compose a satirical piece aimed at a member of the University staff. "A Hell Hound at Large", he called his piece.

The editor was immediately called upon by Mr. Sloss to disclose who wrote the offensive article. Aung San, quite properly, refused, saying it was a matter of journalistic ethics. Sloss knew, for Nyo Mya was jubilantly going round boasting that it was he, but needed an official disclosure from the editor. The upshot was that Aung San was expelled, making one expulsion too many. The RUSU rose in anger. Executive committee meetings led to a mass meeting at which angry, emotional speeches were delivered. Raschid who took the chair announced that the committee members had decided to forgo the examinations in protest, but a general strike was not planned. But one by one, the speakers called upon the students to rise. National honour was invoked, supreme sacrifices demanded. "I cannot recollect my entire speech now," Dr Tha Hla wrote, "but I did make an effort to appeal to their sentiment. I painted a pathetic picture of myself as a very poor student,

relying entirely for my upkeep upon the collegiate scholarship and
a stipend. The future of my poverty-stricken parents hinged upon
my struggles and upon my passing the forthcoming examinations. . . . I had plunged into the decision (to strike) because
I could no longer put up with the high-handed attitude of Principal
D. J. Sloss. I think I concluded by saying that national self-respect
and personal prospects did not go together, or some such thing."

Shouting slogans, the students proceeded from the Union Hall
on that day, February 25, 1936, into waiting buses—which some
thoughtful members of the committee had assembled—and drove
round the campus, calling on residents of the hostels to come along.
In their hundreds they poured out. Young ladies from Inya—Ma
Ma Gyi from Ahmyint, Ma Ah Mar and Ma Ohn of Mandalay,
Ma Khin Mya and Ma Yee Yee of Pegu, among others—and
students from Judson College which, though not always regarded
as a source of high patriotic fervour, provided staunch strikers all
the same.

The strikers camped on the Shwedagon pagoda, living on food
parcels sent by the people and funds given generously. The people
were no mere supporters, they were participants, for their sons and
daughters were there. The press gave their full support. City
elders, such as "Deedok" U Ba Choe and U Kyaw Myint, the
barrister, set up watch and ward committees; some of them gave—
as perhaps they rightly should—more attention to the young ladies
at the Moulmein Zayat, the Inya Hall of the strikers' camp. The
politicians were fully behind the students, some shrewdly seeing
definite possibilities in the strike. U Saw came to the camp to give
promises and suggestions. The Dobama Asi-ayone helped.

The strike lasted many months. It spread far, it went deep. The
College at Mandalay joined the strike. So did the high schools all
over the country. Ko Nu, Ko Kyaw Nyein, Ko Hla Pe, Ko Thein
Pe, Ko Aung San, Ko Tun Ohn, Ko Ba Aye, Ko Nyo Tun, and
such leaders of the strike became national figures overnight. They
were in demand in the districts, and they went round to speak.
rouse support, raise funds. The response and the applause pleased
the young leaders. Ko Nu posed often for photographers, sometimes making gestures, sometimes sweetly smiling. Rumours started after some weeks that a split had occurred between Ko Nu and
Mr. Raschid, and that called for a photograph, for public con-

sumption, of the two eating happily together. Ko Khin Maung Gale had his picture of him taken, showing him reclining in an easy chair, intently reading a book about Mussolini.

The expulsions dwindled into insignificance with the strikers as time went by. The amendment of the University Act—Raschid had to do diligent research to first find out what was wrong with it—the reform of "slave education", and graver, greater national issues occupied the minds of the strike leaders. Dr Ba Maw, the Education Minister, was sympathetic. He made promises, offered to meet the students half-way: "If your minimum demand is 12 annas, ask for a rupee; I shall offer 8 annas, and we shall compromise at 12."

On May 10 the strike was called off. Many of the many demands were met by the Government and the University authorities, but the important thing was that once again a students' strike which grew into a national movement had succeeded by united effort.

The students went back to prepare for their postponed examinations. Many lost one full year because of the strike. "It took me four years," U Kyaw Nyein recalled in later years, "to complete the normal three-year English honours course. And I passed out third class. If I had stayed five years, I might have got a fourth class."

Ko Nu did not go back to the University. Nor did Ko Tun Ohn, Ko Hla Pe, and several others. Politics, the irresistible, demanding mistress, claimed them for their own. Ko Aung San went back for a year, to serve as president of the RUSU, and the All Burma Students' Union which was born of the strike. But his heart too was no longer in his studies; compared to politics, law classes were drab and dull.

For many of the young leaders, the strike was the starting point of their political or public careers. In the national movement it was an important milestone.

6

Meanwhile Ko Shu Maung, who had a job at the post office and shared an apartment on 35th Street, Rangoon, with friends, was being drawn deeper into politics. Thakin Nyi, the uncle, was by now spending all his time with the Dobama Asi-ayone, pouring his money into it. At first the nephew was somewhat skeptical. "They are only exploiting you," he warned, "they will have no more use for you after your money is gone." But the fervour of the movement, the ardour of its men, impressed him. Thakin Ba Sein, with his direct, brusque and blunt manners, always blurting out the brutal truth, or what he thought was the truth, also impressed Ko Shu Maung deeply. A quick reader who could retain everything he read, Thakin Ba Sein was a mine of knowledge; his nationalism and eloquence rarely failed to excite and inspire.

The Thakins were talking their way into jail in increasing numbers, with increasing frequency. Sedition, defined in section 124-A of the Penal Code, was their passport to jail. There was no shortage of volunteers who sought the honour. A Thakin who had been "in" was a veteran. Young Thakin recruits also got their jail sentences. As time went on, and the wrestling between the struggle and the suppression grew really rough, it became a popular saying that "Thakin tenderfoots get six months of jail."

Thakin Nyi, being a leader, got more than that, and more often. Once he was in for quite some time, and he went into a fast to protest against something or other. For 46 days he kept up the fast, growing feebler every day. He was a man of wealth, coming from a well-to-do family; he was not accustomed to hunger or hardship. But there he was, going hungry with unbending will, suffering. Ko Shu Maung watched his uncle's progress, or decline in strength, with sympathy and admiration. An amnesty proclaimed on the Coronation of King George VI set Thakin Nyi free, and Ko Shu Maung nursed and nourished him. Here was vivid proof of a burning faith, Ko Shu Maung thought, and a movement that kept the faith aflame.

"Light up the torch," was the cry that was growing louder, spreading wider, and before long Ko Shu Maung was taking up the cry himself. He spent more and more of his spare time at the Dobama Asi-ayone headquarters where he met the young leaders and listened. He did odd jobs to help, such as hunting for a suitable place, along with Thakinma Daw Khin Khin, the wife of Thakin Ba Sein, to house the headquarters—they found rooms on Phayre Street. He worked on the Thakin newspapers, editing, reading proofs, helping in the distribution. They were shortlived papers.

always short of funds, and publishing them involved long hours of labour contributed by a few volunteers. The printing was done where credit was available. Thakin Ba Sein printed his *Meedok* journal at Daw Khin Khin's press where he got both credit and, later, a loving loyal wife.

The Communist Manifesto was translated into Burmese by Thakin Ba Sein and prepared for publication in book form. Thakin Shu Maung—so the comrades called him now—helped with the proofs, and read the translation and the English copy many times. He did not fall in love with the words of the Manifesto, but its dream of a fair and just society began to haunt him.

7

The Dobama Asi-ayone held its first national conference at Yenangyaung from February 28, 1935, in the full flush of the victory at Shwebo. A resolution, passed unanimously, recorded the gratitude and admiration for Saya San and those who fell with him in the rebellion, "whether they were right or wrong." Thakin Ba Sein was elected president of the Asi-ayone for the next year; the central executive included Thakin Lay Maung, vice-president. Thakin Tun Oke and Thakin Nyi, joint secretaries.

The second conference met in Myingyan for three days from June 27, 1936. Several resolutions were passed on affairs relating to the peasants, the students, and the youth. In the unavaidable absence of Thakin Ba Sein, who was serving a jail term for sedition, Thakin Lay Maung was elected president. Thakin Nyi became vice-president and Thakin Tun Oke was elected secretary. One important decision made by the conference was to organize a parliamentary wing of the party, the *Komin-Kochin* Group and put selected candidates into the field in the impending elections. The new constitution was to come into force after the elections, and it was thought that a two-pronged attack against it, from outside as well as from within, would be more effective.

It was late when the Thakins started to campaign, but with youthful zeal they went to the villages, the wards in the towns, demanding of all patriots that they cast their votes for them. The elections were really a scramble for the seats in the new House of Representatives. Nobody was boycotting. U Chit Hlaing, leader

4

of the boycotting GCBA, had given up, gone into the Legislative
Council under dyarchy, and ascended the Speaker's chair after
repeated no-confidence motions had ousted the European Speaker,
Sir Oscar d'Glanville. He was honest about the whole thing, U
Chit Hlaing. He held out as a boycotter as long as he could, but
his wealth and his wife's patience gave way. She told him not to
return home unless he had found his way into some office; he told
his followers what his wife had told him, and joined the scramble.

The parties and alignments that fought on the issue of separation had become obsolete very quickly. The GCBA, the Anti-
Separationist League, the Golden Valley Party of Sir J. A. Maung
Gyi were gone but for a few lingering memories. U Ba Pe and the
survivors of the "Twenty-Oners" put together an alliance of the
Nga-Bwint-Saing (Five Flowers), but the flowers were faded.
Prince Htaik Tin Wa was made a leader of the Nga-Bwint-Saing
in the hope that his name would get the votes of those peasants
who still remembered King Thibaw. But there were no real issues
to campaign for. All contestants were willing to promise the voters
everything. All were driven by the same hunger for office.

Dr Ba Maw, finding himself without a party, started one, making
himself its leader. The Sinyetha Party, the party for the poor man,
he called it. He addressed his promises principally to the peasants.
He promised them lower taxes, higher loans, protection of land
tenancy, free education.

The Fabian Party founded by "Deedok" U Ba Choe, U Ba
Khine and Ko Nu of University Strike fame, issued a statement
making 31 points, one of which was an undertaking to stay per-
petually in opposition, resisting the lure of office.

Money was spent lavishly. Dr Thein Maung of the Nga-Bwint-
Saing flew to India to bring over U Ottama, who had been sojourn-
ing there in a state of retirement from Burmese politics. In his
time U Ottama had drawn huge crowds to his meetings. He had
roused the country, shaken up the Buddhist monks, captured the
Sangha Samaggi. His words had always been direct, pointed to the
hearts. But by 1936 U Ottama was a little tired and confused.
Shin Ariya, his brother, was another spell-binder, but the times
denied him the opportunities which U Ottama had.

The parties vied with each other in wooing U Ottama when he
came. Thakin Ba Sein, Thakin Aye and the Dobama Asi-ayone

gave him receptions at Jubilee Hall. The Nga-Bwint-Saing was, however, the lavish host, with the means to get together big crowds by holding out many attractions. Shin Ariya was with the Thakins, but U Ottama was a little too old to want to cast his lot with the young politicians—he had done that two decades ago, and once was enough for a lifetime. Seeing U Ottama on the side of the older politicians, Thakin Ba Sein plunged into attack. He called U Ottama names; he made many accusations. Diplomacy would have indicated a smooth swimming along with the currents, but Ba Sein was no diplomat, he was a fighter. His blunt attacks on U Ottama brought down the wrath of the press and the public on himself and the Asi-ayone; many thousands of votes were lost at the elections in which the Thakins were branded by the older politicians as ungrateful, impulsive, hot-headed young upstarts.

Yet, the Asi-ayone put up a good showing. Of the 132 seats in the popular lower house 92 were non-communal and open to the general elections. The remaining seats were reserved for the Karens, Indians, Anglo-Burmans, Europeans, Commerce and Industry, Rangoon University, Indian labour, and non-Indian labour. The allocation of seats was therefore such that no single party could expect to win an absolute, or a workable, majority. "Give me 67 members who will decline office," Dr Ba Maw promised, "and I shall stay out of office with them." That was when the electors demanded of him, in his campaign, that he should go to the House but decline office to concentrate mainly on wrecking the new constitution. It was a promise he could safely make.

"Burmans had the numerical majority," wrote Furnivall, commenting on the experiments in representative government, "but they had no place in industry and commerce, and capitalist interests, European, Indian and Chinese, dominated economic and social life. In the legislature it was an obvious move in political tactics for Europeans to support the numerically weakest section of the nationalists, with the paradoxical result, inherent in the system of communal representation, that politicians could obtain office only on terms that prevented them from exercising power. The Burmans had the men but Europeans had the money and the influence, and the leader of the British mercantile community was popularly regarded as the uncrowned king of Burma. Thus the constitutional reforms from 1923 onwards, though purporting to be an experiment in parliamentary democracy, were in practice an education in political corruption."[4]

Dr Ba Maw commanded 16 votes in the new House, and the Nga-Bwint-Saing 46. The Komin-Kochin group of the Dobama Asi-ayone, which had put only 28 candidates into the field, won 3 seats, polling 100,000 popular votes—a good showing, considering their late start, and the size of the electorate. The Fabian party squeezed in with one seat. More than a dozen were elected as 'independents'; some of these members showed their independence by independently selling their votes. Other members were little better. Party loyalty was loose; desertions were frequent and unashamed. Votes were for sale to the highest bidder. The House of Representatives was the political stock exchange at which fast and furious buying and selling was done. Thus, Dr Ba Maw, with his 16 votes, could form a Coalition Government by splitting the Nga-Bwint-Saing which went into angry opposition. "Politics is a tical of virtue and a viss of sin," complained U Thein Maung— who should know as he had been in politics since GCBA days —and he left to assume high appointive offices in the Judiciary where the nightmare of elections and no-confidence motions could not disturb him.

The new constitution turned over, in theory, 91 government departments to the Cabinet which was responsible to the House of Representatives. There were reserved subjects in the absolute care of the Governor, and there were subjects over which he exercised control in consultation with his ministers. The administration of the "Excluded Areas", such as the Shan States, the hill tracts of Arakan, Kachin and Chin, was a reserved subject.

The "91-Departments-Scheme", as the new constitution came to be called, fell far short of expectations. It provided jobs for the few, while the many remained unfulfilled. Burmanization of the services was pushed to some extent. The Indian Civil Service became the Burma Civil Service, but the in-take was small, while the new young graduates emerging from the University were many. Some got in by sheer merits, but patronage counted heavily. The peasants were poor and were becoming poorer; a few laws were made to protect their tenancy, to extend them relief from the money-lenders, but those were totally inadequate.

[4] J. S. Furnivall, introducing U Nu's *Burma under the Japanese*.

The House was preoccupied with the no-confidence motions which were brought up several times every session. With all his skill, Dr Ba Maw was kept busy most of the time just fighting for survival. They had their laughs in the House, pulling Dr Ba Maw's leg by reporting to the Speaker that he was not properly dressed, for he wore on his head a skull cap of his own design rather than the traditional *gaung-baung*. Some other day when the debates were dull some member would start to speak in Burmese, to court a reprimand from the Speaker who would point out that the official language was English. There were the three members of the Doba Asi-ayone—Thakin Mya (Tharrawaddy), Thakin Hla Tin (Henzada) and Thakin Ant Gyi (Pakokku)—with their tactics and their vows. When the Governor, Sir Archibald Douglas Cochrane, entered in ceremony to inaugurate the first session of the House, the Thakins sat tight while the other members rose. Of such gestures they had many. They also perfected the various weapons of protest such as the walk-out. U Saw was another member who was always bristling, booming, busy. All in all, the honourable members gave U Chit Hlaing, the Speaker, a hard time.

The new constitution, with its "cleverly written reforms", Dr Ba Maw wrote in retrospect, "produced governments which did not govern, having little time or power to do so, but mostly shared the spoils of government among a few; and while these administrators or a large number of them were occupied with their deals to keep on in office the administration as a whole drifted just as ever before with nothing changed, nothing really done. It became more and more a government by deals and drifting."[5]

8

The year 1938—1300 Burmese Era—was the "year of revolution". The pent-up feelings of the people began to go off in explosions, now here, now there.

Most active politically were the Thakins who began to effectively organize labour, the peasants and the students. To the masses we must go, decided the Thakins, with the masses we must march. Thus resolved, and suitably informed on methods by the latest

[5] Dr Ba Maw, *Burma at the Beginning of the Second World War,* in *The Guardian* magazine, October, 1959.

books, they went to work among the labourers on the dockyards, the bus-drivers who plied between Rangoon and Insein, the rickshaw-pullers of the city, the labourers in the factories. Kamayut, off the University campus, also attracted the eager organizers who could brush up on theory at the RUSU, and go out to practise in the umbrella factory, the hosiery works, or the plant where aluminium pots were made. A few strikes were staged, some as sit-downs, some with noisy demonstration; some were successful, some were not. The strike, however, was soon sharpened as a political weapon, even more than as a bargaining force.

The young intellectuals were reading more too. The *Nagani* (Red Dragon) Book Club, founded by Thakin Nu, U Ohn Khin, Saya Tun Shwe, and friends, began to bring out translations of leftist literature. Membership of the Club quickly expanded. The *Nagani* journal gained several hundred subscribers in a very short time. The selections were made from a wide range of sources. The Little Lenin Library, available in a few rare sets, was a rich source. Publications of the Fabian Society were also read and tapped. John Strachey's *Theory and Practice of Socialism,* the writings of M. N. Roy, the philosophy of Nietzche and Karl Marx, Palme Dutt's *World Politics,* books on the Sinn Fein movement for Irish freedom, these were widely read, reproduced and translated. Thakin Nu wrote and translated plays also, with ambition to become the "Bernard Shaw of Burma"; he also translated Dale Carnegie's *How to Win Friends and Influence People.*

Marxism certainly had a strong attraction for the young politicians, partly because the rise of Soviet Russia was regarded as proof of its power. Socialism, Communism, Marxism, all these were interchangeable terms in their minds, and all meant national independence as the essential foundation on which a society of affluence and social justice would be built. "I am a Socialist," proclaimed Thakin Nu in an article, explaining that he had seen a child die of hunger which could not have happened in a socialist society. "Long Live Stalin!" exulted Thakin Ba Swe, waxing eloquent on the love of the great leader for all mankind, and the power of Marxism to cure all human ills. A few of the comrades even started a Communist group. "One day, about that time," wrote Thakin Hla Pe (later to be Bo Let Ya) "we had a meeting at our apartment in Barr Street. Ko Thein Pe, Thakin Ba Hein, a friend from Calcutta, Aung San and myself were there. We decided to form the Burma Communist Party, of which Aung San was to be the general secretary. We were able to meet only occasionally as the Party, and our activities were limited to discussion. The Communist Party was not a legal association at the time, and we had to meet in stealth. The larger Dobama Asi-ayone claimed most of Aung San's time, however, and the C.P. slowly faded away."

The Dobama Asi-ayone had adopted the tricolour flag. It later added the hammer and sickle to the flag. It had also used the emblem of a peasant, or worker, marching towards the promised land of humming industries and abundant fields, while behind him was the desolation of the royal palace of the Burmese kings, its spires down, its big drum shattered. To that emblem too the hammer and sickle were added. The gestures, however, meant that the Asi-ayone was marching in revolutionary directions, rather than that Marxism as an ideology was embraced.

In July of the year of revolution, there were riots between the Burmese and the Indians. Nationalism, roused to high passion; feelings of political frustration; the sense of being economically exploited; these ingredients made up the explosive. An obscure writer called Maung Shwe Phi, who had published a pamphlet making some critical remarks on Buddhism, was the unwitting, unfortunate spark. The explosion was big, and affected many. The politicians tried to take advantage of it, and Premier Dr Ba Maw came under heavy fire in the House. U Saw, who had broken away from the Nga-Bwint-Saing and started his own Myochit (Patriot) Party, was the most vehement of all of Dr Ba Maw's opponents. *The Sun,* of which U Saw was by now a controlling director, was proscribed for a time.

The oilfield workers of Yenangyaung and Chauk made their demands from the Burma Oil Company. Thakin Lay Maung and Thakin Soe, of the Labour Organization set up by the Dobama Asi-ayone, went up to help. The workers went on strike and, under the leadership of Thakin Po Hla Gyi, styled Bo Ahlarwaka, they began their march to Rangoon on December 1. It was a long march, covering more than 400 miles in more than 40 days. The British authorities flung several obstacles across the path of the marchers, but they continued. Several arrests were made, men and women roughly handled or thrown into jail, but the remaining marchers continued. Dr Ba Maw sent one of his close associates in the Cabinet, Dr Thein Maung, to attempt a peaceful settlement, but the Company was adamant.

At Magwe the marchers were told by F.H.C. Mullerworth, the deputy commissioner, to go home, and submit memorials from there. But that was not the marchers' mood. Ko Ba Hein, president of the All Burma Students Union, and Ko Ba Swe, the secretary, went to Magwe to support the marchers. To the mounted police Ba Hein challenged: "One stamp of a hoof shall strike the spark that will set the whole country ablaze!" Ba Hein, Ba Swe and Thakin Soe were arrested, provoking a protest meeting of the RUSU in Rangoon on December 13. Ko Hla Shwe, the vice-president of the ABSU took the chair; Ko Aye Kyaw acted as master of ceremony. It was resolved that a big demonstration around the Secretariat was called for.

U Saw and the Myochit Party demonstrated on their own. Gathering at the U Ba Yi *zayat* on December 12, a crowd of impressive size heard U Saw make an impressive speech. The stage display was brilliantly done. A huge banner showed the Galon bird gripping the Naga dragon in its deadly claws. After the speeches were delivered, the crowd melted away, leaving U Saw and a few hundred men to march down to the Sule pagoda, carrying torches and banners. At the pagoda they dispersed, well pleased with their own show.

On December 20 the students, led by Ko Hla Shwe, newly designated the *Arnarshin* (Dictator) by his loyal comrades, marched round the Secretariat and posted their pickets. A tense atmosphere persisted the whole day, but there was no mishap. The students observed strict discipline; the mounted police and other police armed with batons kept their distance. At the end of the day, however, when the pickets were being withdrawn and students were getting ready to march back, the police charged. A hail of stones thrown at the police by someone outside who wished to provoke an incident, or the stampede of an excited horse, or a coldly calculated plan, what exactly it was nobody could tell, started the police attack. Several students, including several young ladies, were struck down. Some went down under the flying hoofs of the horses, some were felled by repeated baton blows. One young student, Aung Gyaw, aged 22, received several severe injuries on the head, and died in hospital on December 22. A hero's funeral and fiery orations marked his martyrdom.

The incident touched off strikes by students—called by Ko Hla Shwe, the *Arnarshin*—and demonstrations throughout the country. The crew cut that Aung Gyaw wore became a badge of patriotism; many young men gave up their hair voluntarily or under persuasion from monks. In Mandalay the Young Monks went about asking the young ladies to give up wearing voile and transparent blouses and take to pinni jackets instead.

On February 10 a giant rally was held in the Aindawya pagoda under the leadership of the Young Monks, students and other organizations. Demonstrations, without prior permission of the police, were illegal. The authorities warned that firm action would be taken to disperse such demonstrations, but the rally dared. Along 26-B Road, up to the Telegraph Office, making for the old royal palace, the demonstrators marched. There they ran into the police party headed by Mr. H. N. Lett, the deputy commissioner, and Mr. C. H. Raynes, the district superintendent of police. The warnings were repeated. The monks at the vanguard, bearing banners, refused to turn back. The police, backed by the military, fired into the crowd, killing 7 monks and 10 laymen, including one Maung Tin Aung, a student, 12 years old, of the National High School. Seventeen martyrs were thus made in as many minutes.

There were hero's funerals for the martyrs, mock funerals for Dr Ba Maw. In the House there were stormy scenes. The British members, representing commercial interests, decided it was time for a change—all the restlessness was doing grave harm to business. On February 12, U Saw moved a no-confidence motion against the Coalition Government. Public anger against the Government, whipped up by the students and the Thakins, and the prevalent feeling in the House among the groups representing special interests, combined at last to bring the Government down. The voting was 70 for the motion, and 37 against. A few minutes after the count, Dr Ba Maw drove to the Government House and tendered his resignation to the Governor. He had survived in office for nearly two years which was, in that mad-house of a Legislature, a feat approaching a miracle.

The students naively called upon U Thwin, member of the Senate, to form a Government, pledging himself to resign on their

instruction. But power politics was a sharp game, in which words
of honour meant nothing. U Pu formed a Government, discarded
a minister in a few months, and brought U Saw in as minister for
forests. The mock funerals conducted in the streets, the beating
of empty drums traditionally done to drive the evil spirits away,
and the calling of names were now directed against U Pu and U
Saw.

More and more, however, amidst that din, young minds were
turning to more serious purpose. They had broken Governments;
now they would go ahead and make the Revolution.

9

As the Thakin movement gained in strength, the rivalries between its leaders grew. It had started as a freak, which few took
notice of. When it became a force, many wanted to use it for their
own ends. The older politicians were skilled in the parliamentary
game and cunning in the play for power. But the Legislature, in
the context of fast-moving events at home and in the world outside, was becoming an empty form, a farce. The young Thakins
were going to the people in their wards in the towns, in their
villages, organizing, working together, inspiring, instigating, un-
locking long pent-up energies, releasing powers hitherto seething,
stored up, unused. In Kamayut, Kemmendine, Sanchaung, Pazun-
daung and Yegyaw, of Rangoon the young Thakins built their
strongholds. They spoke at street corners; they canvassed from
door to door; they sold their newspeapers—*Daung* (The Peacock),
the *Meedok* (Burning Torch), the Thakin Bulletin; they waged a
tireless campaign to win more recruits for their growing army.
They even started an undertaker service to serve the poor people
in the wards and to win more supporters. They ran a bus for the
service, and for a modest fee of Rs. 20, the poor could give their
dead a decent funeral, with coffin draped in the tricolour flag. Thus
the Thakins strived in their grass-roots organization.

The Dobama Asi-ayone, with its growing popularity, became a
desirable prize. The first crack showed at the Prome conference in
March, 1938. Thakin Lay Maung took the chair. The election of
president for the following year brought the factions into the
open. Thakin Ba Sein and his group had expected that Thakin

Nyi would be elected by acclaim, as he had served his terms as secretary and vice-president. They accused that Thakin Lay Maung, instead of observing the traditional neutrality of the chair, took active part in the election, casting his vote twice—as a participant, and, when there was a tie, as chairman of the convention. The opponents put up Thakin Thein Maung as a candidate, and had their own things to say about Thakin Ba Sein and his friends. After a great amount of heat, Thakin Thein Maung was elected president, and Thakin Nyi became secretary. The unity of the leadership, however, was irreparably broken.

Another issue that split the Asi-ayone at Prome was the question whether the Komin Kochin members of the House of Representatives should take their salary. The decision at Myingyan had been that they must not. The salary, Rs. 200 a month, was not princely, but in those days it was something. The Government was applying pressure on the three Thakin members with a law that allowed only three months for drawing the salary—after that the salary would be forfeit. The prospects of the Asi-ayone's winning more seats in bye-elections looked bright. Why, some delegates wanted to know, must the Thakins continue to struggle in poverty? Let them draw their salaries, contributing to party funds, eating decent meals. The preponderance of opinion, advanced by the Ba Sein faction, was that there must be no softening, no relaxation of a solemnly taken vow.

The advent of the young politicians from the University, flushed with the victory of the Strike, also contributed to the split. Ko Nu, Ko Aung San, Ko Than Tun and others had decided to dedicate themselves to politics, and they needed an organization. Time was pressing, they thought; they could not join the organization as ordinary members and work their way up. The Dobama Asi-ayone needed them, they decided, and they needed the Asi-ayone. As there was room at the top only for a few, and as they were the chosen few, the others must be pushed out or relegated to minor posts on the executive committee. They were quite sincere in their approach to the problem. Only, Thakin Ba Sein, Thakin Tun Oke, Thakin Nyi and others who had been there before them did not entirely see eye to eye with them.

The new Executive Committee took steps to expel Thakin Ba Sein on several charges on which he was not heard in his defence.

He was arrogant, it was charged, and indeed he was. He had spoken
out against U Ottama at the very critical time of the first elections
under the new constitution. He had roundly cursed Ko Nu. He had
gone to U Ba Choe, the Fabian leader, who was fond of music
and culture, and accused the older man of being false: "You play
the harp while all the time thinking of this, don't you?" he asked,
making with his fingers a sign both vivid and crude. Thakin Ba
Sein was a man of high passions and many weaknesses, but he had
his strengths too, and he was sincere.

Thakin Kodaw Hmaing tried to mediate. He heard complaints
from Thakin Thein Maung and his group, and from Thakin Ba
Sein and his. "I am like a High Court judge now," chuckled the
arbitrator, as he examined witnesses. His verdict in the end was
that both Thakin Thein Maung and Thakin Ba Sein should take
long leave from the Asi-ayone. The verdict had commonsense but
held out no appeal to either side. Thakin Ba Sein, energetic and
robust, exclaimed, "Politics is my life, how can I retire?"

Thus, the split in the Asi-ayone became final. "The Dobama
Asi-ayone was," Thakin Nu recalled, "at that time divided into
two factions one led by Thakin Kodaw Hmaing and the other by
Thakin Ba Sein. We deplored the division, particularly in those
crucial times when unity was so vitally necessary. The Asi-ayone
and the Thakin members were, after all, the best that we got in
politics, and we did not want to see the party disintegrate due to
lack of vision on the part of its leaders. We decided to go in and
give a hand to unite and rally the party. Ko Aung San, Thakin
Than Tun and myself joined the party on the same day."[6] That
was one version of the story.

Thakin Shu Maung stayed with Thakin Nyi and the faction
which came to be known as the "Ba Sein-Tun Oke" Dobama Asi-
ayone. Thakins Kyaw Yin, Aye, Kha, Ba Gwan, Thin (Sandoway), Thin (Bogale), Aung Than, and Khin Maung were among
the prominent members of the group. Thakin Ba Sein was a hero
to Thakin Shu Maung, Thakin Hla Tun (the younger brother of
Shu Maung), and other young Thakins. They believed in him and
were willing to blindly obey him, such was the spell he cast on
them.

Around Thakin Kodaw Hmaing grouped Thakins Aung San,

6 U Nu, in *Aung San of Burma*, p. 16.

Nu, Than Tun, Hla Pe, and the rest. Soon, the younger men took over, and Thakin Kodaw Hmaing and Thakin Thein Maung were eclipsed.

Both factions of the Dobama Asi-ayone, however, had one common goal—Burma's freedom. Both worked diligently and dangerously to that end. Both also arrived at the same conclusion, working independently, that only by armed rising could the goal be attained. They were ready—so were the people—to move from words to deeds.

3
The Land Of The Rising Sun

1

1939 WAS the year of contrasts. There was mounting enthusiasm for revolution on the one hand, and frustration on the other. Bright hopes alternated with dark despair. Frantic energy, used in organizing the masses and in searching for means of action, would be followed by aimless drifting. The people were ready, but they knew not for what. The leaders, especially the young ones, were sounding the clarion call to rally and march, but they knew not where.

Hopes turned in many directions. They soared on wings of song. The *Nagani* (Red Dragon) song, sung by Khin Maung Yin, the popular actor, singer, recalled the glories of the past, promised the people a brave new future. In riddles which were quite simple to read, the song spoke of the dynasty which Alaungpaya built, the fall of the dynasty to the British, and the day British power would be shattered by the Mogyoe thunderbolt. In another song, in a different vein, Khin Maung Yin anticipated the emergence of Bo Bo Aung, the legendary figure of great powers, who was believed to have attained immortality—his contemporary King Bodawpaya was long dead and gone—through alchemy and religious pursuits.

Some of the songs were banned and their recordings proscribed. So well did they sell, however, that British companies, such as Columbia Records, bought them. The mournful song about the martyr, Bo Aung Gyaw, written by Thahaya Saya Tin, was another best-seller.

The newspapers were staunchly behind the nationalist movement. *The New Light of Burma,* managed by U Tin, and edited by U Chit Maung, was a great supporter of the young Thakins. U Chit Maung later started the *Journal-gyaw* (Weekly Thunderer) to give mightier support. *The Deedok,* edited by U Ba Choe, *The Bandoola* journal edited by U Sein, *The Dagon* monthly magazine, and such journals were partisans in the nationalist movement, though with loyalties to their own groups. *The Nagani* was, of course, an important organ of the Dobama Asi-ayone. There were other Thakin newspapers and journals that appeared and disappeared, starved for funds, suppressed by press laws. *The New Burma,* tri-weekly journal in English, founded by Dr Thein Maung, provided a forum for the young politicians; Thakins Aung San and Kyaw Sein worked on it as sub-editors, filling its pages with the writings of M. N. Roy, the constitution of the Soviet Union with glowing commentaries by the Webbs and George Bernard Shaw, and such material. *The Sun* came under the control of U Saw, who had a translation done by Shwe U Daung of Hitler's *Mein Kampf* serialized in the paper. The two British-owned English newspapers, the *Rangoon Gazette,* and the *Rangoon Times,* reported the news fully, but were, of course, pro-Government.

Political parties raised private armies of their own in the fashion of those of Hitler and Mussolini. The Thakins had their *Letyon Tat* (Army of the People), the RUSU and the ABSU their *Thanmani* (Steel Corps) the Sinyetha Party of Dr Ba Maw its *Dama* (Woodchopper) *Tat,* and U Saw's Myochit Party its Galon Army. The armies drilled and paraded, with their wooden staves; their leaders in fancy uniforms—Dr Ba Maw sported baggy pants while U Saw preferred riding breeches and top boots—reviewed parades and took the salute in style. The Letyon Tat and the Thanmani were bent on more serious purpose. Selected volunteers began to learn the use of firearms from students who had turned instructors by reading up a few stolen training manuals of the British army. Did not Comrade Stalin say: "Arms decide everything?" There were no guns available—yet. But if the will to fight for freedom could be sharpened, the guns could be found.

The search for ways by which revolutionary zeal might be translated into revolutionary action led the parties along different paths. The Indian National Congress was a source of inspiration to the young Thakins. Its proclamations and methods were studied, indeed often copied. Thus at a conference of the Dobama Asi-ayone (Thakin Kodaw Hmaing group) held in Moulmein from

April 6-9, 1939, the current programme of the Congress was placed before the Conference by Thakins Aung San, Nu, and others, and adopted in toto. These, however, were programmes and words which failed to satisfy the hunger for action.

The outbreak of war in Europe called for reappraisal of policies. Concrete programmes also became urgent necessities. The war, all parties saw, opened opportunities to Burma to advance her cause. For the Thakins of both factions, time had come to strike. For the politicians in the House, the war was an opportunity to extract promises from the British Government of constitutional reforms to establish the country as a self-governing and equal member of the Commonwealth.

A Freedom Bloc was forged with different elements of the political parties in October of that year. Thakins Aung San, Mya, Nu, Than Tun of the one faction of the Dobama Asi-ayone; Dr Ba Maw, Dr Thein Maung, U Tun Aung; Saw Pe Tha; U Ba U and U Ba Shwe of Mandalay, were among the prominent members who proclaimed the birth of the Bloc. Dr Ba Maw was chosen as the leader, with title of Dictator, and Thakin Aung San the secretary. With a flourish and appropriate publicity Dr Ba Maw resigned his seat in the House of Representatives, declaring that the struggle for freedom must be waged outside, on the national scale.

The "Ba Sein-Tun Oke" Thakins, out-manoeuvred for a time after the split by the other group, met in conference on November 12 at Panzwe monastery in Thonze, Tharrawaddy district. The abbot U Vilasa was an active supporter, and harbouring the Thakins was with him a routine. The discussions revolved round the need for drastic action. The British, it was agreed, could not be pushed out with words. An armed revolution was called for, and for that, it was recognized, foreign aid was essential. There was a meeting of minds among the leaders on this, but the proclaimed resolutions did not say so in so many words.

Sometime later, the Executive Committee of the party met one night in a monastery in Chawdwingone of suburban Rangoon. Police surveillance was vigilant. The Committee had first assembled at a monastery in Thingangyun, but the abbot drove them out saying they would bring nothing but trouble. Thakins Ba Sein, Tun Oke, Nyi, Aye, Khin Maung, Chit Tin and others were at the meeting. They deliberated deep into the night. When the meeting broke, the Committee had decided, with one mind, that foreign contacts must be found in the search for foreign aid.

The other faction of Thakins met in May 1940 in Tharrawaddy where the Saya San rebellion had started. They proclaimed that they would struggle towards the goal of Burma's independence. As the Sinn Fein had seen opportunity for the Irish cause in Britain's troubles during World War I, so now the Thakins declared that Britain's difficulty was Burma's opportunity. The leaders then dispersed to take the resolution to the people and mobilize them for the struggle.

2

The Government adopted the traditional tactic of putting away the young revolutionary politicians in jail, while appeasing the older politicians with promise of more privileges for them and constitutional reforms for the country. The tactic did not succeed against the rising tides. There seemed to be no end of young Thakins to jail; when one was locked up, two appeared to take his place. "Our mothers brought us forth, the jails bring us up, the living is indeed easy," they cheered as they went on their way to enjoy the hospitality of the Government.

The older politicians in the House and the Cabinet joined heartily in the suppression of the Thakin movement. The "young upstarts" made them feel uncomfortable. U Saw even saw it fit to employ his Galon Army to break up meetings of the Dobama Asi-ayone by force. But the older politicians too had to justify their existence. In the House, therefore, they moved their resolutions calling for definite word from His Majesty's Government that Burma would be established in dominion status after the war. Such word was not forthcoming, and even the old politicians began to grumble.

Thakins Aung San, Than Tun and a few others made a tour of India in March, 1940, meeting leaders of the Indian National Congress. Before leaving on the trip Aung San worked through the night drafting a statement to explain the origin and purpose of the Dobama Asi-ayone. This statement, copies of which were distributed along the way, was later adopted by the Working Committee of Dobama Asi-ayone of which he was general secretary, and published as its manifesto.

"We stand," the manifesto explained, "for complete independence of Burma (including the areas excluded under the Government of Burma Act, 1935) from the present imperialist domination and exploitation and for the introduction of a free, independent people's democratic Republic . . . ." One of the basic principles of the Republic would be "democratic dictatorship of the proletariat and peasantry." Emancipation of the workers; "radical agrarian programmes providing for abolition of landlordism, free distribution of lands to middle and poor peasants with a view to ultimate nationalization and mechanization of all lands;" nationalization of all lands, forest, waterways, railways, mines, heavy industries, banks, etc., were to be definite goals in the economic field in the new Republic. Socially, there would be equal rights and opportunities for women, freedom of conscience and religious worship for all citizens, free universal education with special care for the moral, cultural and social elevation of the youth; cultural autonomy for all minorities; equality of all before law, irrespective of race, religion or sex.

The Asi-ayone also felt the need to define its foreign policy as "Burma and the world form one organic link." Surveying the European scene, the manifesto noted that "the Soviet Union alone is the constant and consistent supporter of human freedom." It then went on to proclaim: "We shall have no truck with any ideology that actually crushes other people's freedom and interest. We cannot contemplate even for one moment the question of participation in the present imperialist war for the freedom of another country so long as we are not allowed freedom of action in such matter. We stand for friendly and businesslike relations with any foreign nation, especially with those in our neighbourhood and the Far East in all possible matters." Finally, imperialism was denounced "for it fostered war which meant death and distress to countless millions. It entails the enslavement, poverty and death of several millions; we shall therefore strive for the speedy end of the war and shall strive to liberate the whole humanity from every form of oppression and exploitation."

"We reject the present constitution," the manifesto declared, and "demand that a Constituent Assembly be convened by the people of Burma to frame up their own constitution by their own delegates." The Constituent Assembly, it was pointed out, would spring "not from the stars above but from the people below. The people will create it out of the furnace of their own revolutionary experiences. We make no mistake about ourselves and our demands. We shall forge mass sanction to secure our ends. This is the main kernel of our strategy."

One hundred thousand members would be enrolled, the manifesto proclaimed, "in order to strengthen our Asi-ayone as an impregnable democratic bulwark of the workers, peasants and the rest of the toiling population." Enlistment of more volunteers for the Bama Lētyone ('Arm of Burma' or the 'Army of the People'), and intensive training and selection of cadres for the coming struggle were to be some of the immediate tasks. "We invite through this manifesto the co-operation and sacrifice of our enterprising youth."

"Within our organization all are welcome—Socialists, Communists, nationalists, if they accept and work our policy of anti-imperialist struggle for freedom. Our Asi-ayone is a potential democratic front of all the people in Burma." It was explained that the Asi-ayone was not a Communist organization. Not one of those who levelled the charge that it was could say, the manifesto countered, what Communism meant. "It is the 'Red Menace' all over again. Ours is not a Communist, but a freedom fighting body in the present phase of our country's history. However, unlike the reactionaries and vested interests, we are not alarmed by the 'Spectre of Communism'."[1]

That was a powerful manifesto, rather wordy, but strong in ideal and enthusiasm. It was a far cry from the prayerful resolutions of the GCBA, the carefully couched resolutions debated in the Legislature to be adopted finally in diluted forms. The difference in tone and temper between those prayers and resolutions and the manifesto and the demands of the Dobama Asi-ayone indicated not merely that the younger men were more hot-blooded or impulsive. It showed that the people themselves impatiently demanded clear, ringing words, with decisive action to follow. The young Thakins, with all their revolutionary fire, occasionally

[1] The manifesto is reprinted in full in *The Guardian* magazine, Jan., 1959.

got a rap or two from an impatient public. "The Dobama Asi-ayone should do something more than make speeches and hold demonstrations," reminded the *New Light of Burma,* in its issue of May 31, 1940.

Thakin Aung San addressed a political meeting at Zalun in Henzada district on June 1. Mr. D. W. Xavier, the district superintendent of police, after reading the stenographic notes of the speech, decided that action for sedition would be justified. A warrant of arrest was issued. A reward of Rs. 5 was offered to anyone who could provide information leading to the arrest of the wanted man. The small reward was insult added to injury, Ko Hla Maung, president of the RUSU thought, and he wrote to the editor of the *Rangoon Gazette,* expressing his indignation. The *Gazette* published the letter.

Dr Ba Maw, the Dictator of the Freedom Bloc, lost his freedom on July 26, when he was arrested on charges of sedition. He was tried in Mandalay. He sat through the trial, grandly displaying disinterest, walking out occasionally to address the crowd that had gathered outside the courtroom. The sentence was a year in jail.

U Saw, minister for forests in the Cabinet led by U Pu, decided that his time to take over the supreme leadership had arrived. He resigned from office, crossed the floor and tabled a no-confidence motion against his Chief of 30 minutes ago. The motion was carried. U Pu's government fell. U Saw became premier. The Cabinet was reshuffled. A few ministers, like Sir Paw Tun who was almost a fixture in every Cabinet formed under the new con-stitution, remained. But U Saw was the boss.

U Saw sent several older politicians to jail: U Ba Pe, his men-tor, U Ba U of Mandalay and U Ba Thi. The joke in town was that U Saw was not fond of people who had "Ba" in their names.

The Thakins went to jail in their scores and hundreds. Thakins Nu, Soe, Than Tun, Wa Tin and others from the one faction, and Thakins Nyi, Khin Maung, and several others from the "Ba Sein-Tun Oke" group. The Defence of Burma Act and Rules gave the Executive large powers of preventive detention. The formality of judicial trial could be dispensed with. All that was needed was to find the "subversives" and put them away.

The situation drove the young Thakins to search harder for

foreign contacts. They must evade arrest and go underground to organize, or get out of the country while they could. Or else, like stags at bay, they would be picked off one by one, until the whole movement was broken up and confined in so many jails scattered far and wide over the country.

3

Thakin Shu Maung kept working at his post office job for as long as he could. The position held out certain advantages. He could discreetly check the mail and the telegrams to discover what the police were up to and then warn his comrades. His intelligence sense was keen. The job also provided a good listening post. What he saw and heard were sometimes of great value to the "Ba Sein-Tun Oke" faction of the Dobama Asi-ayone which started out early to establish foreign contacts.

Not at his job alone, but at his usual haunts also, Thakin Shu Maung picked up useful information. The Turf Club was the gathering ground of so many people, and there his ears were pricked not for racing tips only. He would also go round and ask his friends, who were working in different government offices, for the latest news.

Thakins Chit Tin and Shu Maung would sometimes post themselves unobtrusively on Prome Road and take notes of the government cars that passed. By sight, or by the number that it bore, they could soon tell the ownership of a motor-car and even, to some extent, its mission of the moment. They did better with some cars. They made friends of the drivers, such as Ko Ba Chit who drove police commissioner Prescott's car, and found out where their masters spent the night before—usually at the Clubs, sometimes at emergency meetings.

Then there were the hiding places to organize, for the police hunt was getting hotter daily, and many of the comrades had to be lying low. The stables of horse-owner U Po We, father of Ko San Maung, a friend; a rented room on the 4th floor of a 29th Street building; the homes of trusted friends, such as Thein Aung of Bengalizu, or Ko Aye Maung with whom he had shared an apartment for many months; such were the places which Thakin Shu Maung kept in use, always a jump ahead of the police. His friends suspected that Shu Maung was up to something, but they did not ask. If they did, he would not have told, for he was quiet, tight-lipped, well capable of holding secrets. He was not the kind of young politician who had to go round the town, carrying a Shan bag stuffed with papers, telling friends he was engaged in highly secret political work.

Keeping Thakin Ba Sein in hiding involved a lot of hard work. He had to be kept fully supplied with his physical needs—which were many. Sometimes Thakin Shu Maung would take the food to him, and a concealed bottle of brandy—"Bisquit" brandy being Ba Sein's favourite. Sometimes, Thakin Chit Tin would go, or Thakin Khin Maung, for the same man going too often would attract notice. Thakinma Daw Khin Khin could slip in now and then, but not too often, for her going there might give her husband's presence away. Being away from her too long made Thakin Ba Sein lonesome, and that too had to be taken care of.

The "Ba Sein-Tun Oke" faction of the Dobama Asi-ayone set out early to look for foreign contacts, and the strongest possibility they found was Japan. They thought of Siam (Thailand), but there was only a mild interest at that end, and that only among adventurers. China was in the throes of civil war. After a flirtation with Marxism, Thakin Ba Sein had become more intensely nationalistic, more impressed with the power of the dictatorships of Hitler and Mussolini. A total war waged with the wielding of total power, that he thought was the sure cure for Burma's ills. The other Thakin group was talking a lot about Marxism and Socialism; so, to be different, Thakin Ba Sein talked more about nationalism and power. Forge a free nation first from the fire of war, then there would be time enough to construct the new society for the people. To this goal Japan seemed to offer the shortest road. Besides, it was easier to get Japanese contacts. A small Japanese community lived in Rangoon; its members were dentists, doctors, photographers, traders, all very polite, always smiling, good-mannered, bowing greetings and gratitude, ready to listen.

Thakin Ba Sein always preferred the direct approach, the frontal attack. He started talking to the dentists, first about teeth, then about politics. Some of the dentists grinned blankly, some showed a glimmer of interest. Dr Kokubu, who had a clinic on Barr Street, reacted positively to approaches. Thakin Aung Than, a fast fellow who had friends everywhere, served as a link between the dentist and the inner circle of the "Ba Sein-Tun Oke" group; Thakin Chit Tin was later assigned to go along with Thakin Aung Than to make things doubly sure. Kokubu, it turned out was a retired officer of the Japanese navy on the reserve list, or on active special duty nobody could be sure. The Navy was interested in getting to know nationalist groups in Southeast Asia who needed foreign aid in their struggle for freedom. Japan was planning to build the Greater East Asia Co-prosperity Sphere, with the catching slogan "Asia for the Asians!" Aiding the nationalist groups with arms—supplied stealthily by sea—could be a good investment. When these groups came to power in their new nations, they would be more favourably inclined to join the Co-prosperity Sphere as willing partners. The first thoughts of Kokubu, the department of the Japanese Navy which worked on those special operations, and those in the seats of power in Tokyo who had given their nod to the operations, were probably on those lines only. An all-out war waged by Japanese arms to the furthest frontiers, with a long drawn-out and expensive occupation to follow, was not, it may be conjectured, in the minds of the Japanese planners. So indeed thought Thakin Ba Sein and his comrades who negotiated with the agents in Rangoon.

Kokubu introduced another dentist friend, Mr. Hatanaga, to Thakin Ba Sein. One night in June, 1940, around 10 p.m., a meeting of the conspirators was held in an upstairs room of Jubilee Hall. This Hall, a heap of monstrous red-brick masonry, had been raised to commemorate the Golden Jubilee of Queen Victoria's reign. Weddings were celebrated there; public meetings were held there. The GCBA had convened a meeting there to protest on the "shoe question". Receptions for U Ottama had been held there by the political parties which contested the elections of 1936. The Jubilee Hall, therefore had its history, and its many varied uses. But never before, as far as it could be known, had it served as a meeting place for conspirators who were bent on the overthrow of British power with the aid of foreign arms. The choice of the Hall as rendezvous was not made for symbolic reasons. It only happened that the caretaker of the Hall happened to be Thakin Aung Than's father, and it was considered safe to use its facilities.

Thakins Ba Sein, Tun Oke, Chit Tin, Aung Than and Khin Maung were among those present. Kokubu and Hatanaga were there. The Burmese expressed their expectations, and the Japanese made their suggestions. Rangoon, it was suggested, was a rather unhealthy place for this kind of work; the British were on sharp watchout and did not view the activities with any great favour. Let a few leaders of the Ba Sein group slip across into Siam; there, friends would welcome them.

The meeting gave heart to the group. Now they were getting somewhere. Thakin Khin Maung had a nephew named Hla Maung who had established residence in Siam. It was a relatively simple matter to change the photographs in the passport to enable Thakin Ba Sein to travel as Hla Maung. Arrangements for the trip had to be carefully made. Thakin Ba Sein was a wanted man. His face and figure were difficult to disguise. The journey was therefore planned in stages, to be made by car, and by boat, until the border was reached. After several weeks of preparation, Thakin Chit Tin and Thakin Ba Sein started out by road early October, leaving families and friends behind, venturing into the unknown.

Slowly the two made their way, stopping with trusted friends, taking secluded paths through the jungle, travelling by canoe at night. Near the border, Thakin Chit Tin left his friend and turned back. Thakin Ba Sein was on his own, but nothing should go wrong now, for the worst part of the journey was over.

But at the border Thakin Ba Sein was arrested. Someone, the group in Rangoon concluded when they heard of the arrest, must have betrayed him. Thakin Ba Sein had the presence of mind to get rid of a letter of introduction given him by the Japanese agents in Rangoon, before the police unerringly searched his wallet in which he had hidden the letter. After a quick trial he was sentenced to a year's imprisonment for attempting to use a forged passport.

A round-up of the "Ba Sein-Tun Oke" group followed. Thakin Chit Tin was put away in jail at Moulmein, later to be moved to Insein. Thakin Tun Oke went into hiding, as did Thakin Khin Maung and those who could disappear fast enough. The rest landed in jail. Thakin Shu Maung, whose job at the post office provided a convenient cover, at last felt advised to resign and return home for a time. He had not been home for some time. News of him, of his leaving college, his living an apparently aimless life, had first angered, then saddened Daw Mi Lay, the mother. His father, U Po Kha, and his uncle, U Chit Khine, had occasionally gone to Rangoon to reason with him, but only once or twice were they able to run him down to one of his many hideouts. U Po Kha, more an elder brother than a father to his boys, so friendly was he, broke into tears when they met.

Daw Mi Lay, it was said, broke her heart over what she looked upon as the loss of her Shu Maung. She never quite recovered. When he went back to Paungdale, she had been dead a year or two. Only memories of her, indelible memories, remained.

4

Keji Suzuki, a colonel of the Japanese imperial army, arrived in Rangoon in May, 1940, in the guise of a correspondent for the *Yomiuri* newspaper. Two Japanese came with him: Mitzuru Sugii, businessman and part-time member of the *Koain* (a Japanese agency engaged in research on Asian affairs), and Inao Misutani, who was with the Manchu Railway Company. These two, and Takeshi Higuchi were recruited to the Minami Kikan by Suzuki in Shanghai.

Suzuki also took on the honorary duties of general secretary of the Japan-Burma Friendship Association. His task was to study the lay of the political land and establish useful contacts. The task was given him by the planners in Tokyo. It was also, in part, self-imposed, for Suzuki, a veteran of the China campaigns, a specialist on Southeast Asian problems, had dreams of his own for the expansion of Japanese power into the region. It was not, however, conquest that he dreamed of. His dreams were more noble— they were for the liberation of the subject Asian people, and their willing entry into the Co-prosperity Sphere of which the Emperor of Japan was the benevolent father.

Suzuki moved fast, skillfully avoiding the British secret service, yet meeting people who mattered for his work. U Saw sent for him and asked if Japan would give material assistance in Burma's fight for freedom. "He mentioned the type of aid he envisaged," Suzuki recalled, "arms, aeroplanes, money, and I made a quick calculation in my mind, and found the figures fantastic. I told U Saw that I was only a newspaper reporter, and he should discuss the matter at higher levels, perhaps with the Japanese Consul."

The Japan-Burma Friendship Association was a good place for meeting people, and there Suzuki met and made friends with Dr Thein Maung, an associate of Dr Ba Maw. The Japanese residents also gave "useful information" to Suzuki. "There was U Nagai, the Japanese Buddhist monk," he said, "whose monastery in Kamayut was a good meeting place. Mr. Oba, the chief of the Japanese trade bureau, and Mr. Kokubu. Nagai was arrested by the police later on, and the Japanese Consul ordered me to leave as things were getting too hot, but I remained for some months."

Suzuki did not meet the Thakin leaders of either faction. Many of them were already in jail, or in hiding. But he decided, on information he could gather, that they could be his most promising clients. The Thakins, specially those of the Aung San group, were widely regarded as Communists, and this put Suzuki off a little. One school of thought among the Burmese nationalists, noted Suzuki, looked to China or Russia for aid; the other placed its hopes in Japan, but that other school was a minority. "I wanted Japan to help," he said, "and we could do that by sending arms. But the Burmese had no military experience, and we would have to train some of their young leaders, and as that could not be done in Burma the thing to do was to smuggle the young men to Japan."[2]

Where to look for aid was, for Thakins Soe, Than Tun, Ba Hein, Saya Chit, Saya Tun Shwe, and their comrades, a question not merely of practical importance, but of deep ideological meaning also. The question called for much soul-searching, and provoked heated debates in jails, outside jails. Some wanted to fight Japan—whose entry into the war and advent to Burma were expected—even if it meant fighting alongside, instead of against, the British. The settlement of accounts with the British could be done after the war. There were other young nationalists who considered fighting alongside the British a betrayal of the cause. They would fight the Japanese invader—for they were staunchly anti-Fascist —but would also take on the British colonialists too. With what? That, they could not say. The others were eager to receive

[2] Keji Suzuki (Bo Mogyoe) in *Aung San of Burma*, p. 54.

Japanese aid—for aid from other sources was nowhere in prospect. If the Japanese stayed out of the country, well and good. If they chose to come in, they could be humoured with some concessions —a small price to pay for the vital aid they extended at the crucial moment.

The debate went on right up to the time the Japanese armies marched in. Then the situation took on a new complexion, and other practical and philosophical problems arose. Till the occupation became a reality, however, the debate engaged the attention of the nationalist groups almost as much as the organization of revolutionary activities. Thakin Ba Hein, the student leader who had attained prominence in the march of the oilfield workers, spent the evenings sub-editing the *New Light of Burma,* and the nights with the "Burma Revolutionary Party" (BRP), plotting and preparing for the coming showdown. A literary man, with artistic taste and curly hair, Ba Hein was a confirmed Marxist. He led the group which wanted to take on both the Japanese and the British. Thakin Mya, a Socialist, with seat in the House of Representatives, was the elder statesman of the BRP. A mild-mannered man, Thakin Mya could also be tough. He and Hla Maung once tried to cross the border over jungle paths into Siam, but without success. Saya Chit ran a co-operative store in Yegyaw and a network of activities which ranged from publishing a paper, *Burma's Revolution,* to conducting classes in ideology and courses in small arms training, and preparing suitable young men for special missions in the country or outside. Ba Swe of Tavoy, assigned to organize the students of Rangoon University, Kyaw Nyein who worked during the day as appraiser in the Customs department and Saya Tun Shwe, were among the top leaders of the BRP. Young members, wearing assumed names, went about their assigned tasks with great seriousness.

Thakin Nu, who wanted to write plays and poetry, took a detached view of the plans for violence. He spoke for the cause, earned a jail sentence, and went in to muse. Thakin Soe taught Marxism-Leninism to the young Thakins in jail; Thakin Nu taught English and lectured on Shakespeare and sex. Thakin Soe translated Marxist books, wrote *Burma's Revolution,* and theses on the coming struggle. Thakin Nu finished a few plays in jail. Thakin Ba Sein, when he joined the Thakins of the rival camp in the same jail ward, amused himself by baiting Thakin Soe on his Communism. "It's easy to become a Communist, my friend," he told a young disciple of Thakin Soe, "all you have to do is denounce Buddhism and call the monks bad names." The taunt, meant for Soe, effectively stung him. In a rage Soe went to have it out with Ba Sein, whose coolness angered him even more. Frustrated in his attempts to beat up his tormentor, Thakin Soe kept raving and roaring for some time.[3]

Thakin Aung San, with Mr. Xavier's warrant of arrest after him, had no intention of languishing in jail in that decisive period. He had proposed to his comrades that time had come to step up mass activities, culminating in guerrilla war. "In this plan I did foresee the possibility of an invasion of Burma by Japan," he later wrote, "but I thought we could forestall the Japanese, set up our independent state and negotiate with the Japanese before they entered. If we could not stop them coming in, we would launch a resistance movement." The plan, however, did not appeal very much "to many of my comrades because our middle class origins made us hesitant to make bold decisions and follow up boldly. We might talk big, and we might feel impatient with the masses. But most of us did not really believe in the effectiveness of mass action. Thus, I was asked by my colleagues how we could wage guerrilla war without arms, and my answer was that we should be able to find arms if even the dacoits in Burma could. I was not able to convince my friends, though. So we decided to send someone out of Burma to seek assistance, and as I was the leading exponent of the plan, that someone had to be me."

Dr Ba Maw sent word about the offer of aid from Japanese sources at this time. "After some hesitation, we accepted," recalled Aung San, "but the Japanese, on their part, did not seem too keen to go ahead. Later, we heard that they were rather suspicious of us, thinking we were Communists. We could not wait till the Japanese made their decision. I slipped out to China with the assignment from my friends to do what I thought was best for Burma."[4]

To Amoy by Chinese cargo boat *Hai Lee* his friends arranged for Aung San and another comrade to go, after attempts to get

[3] Thakin Tin Mya, *In the Socialist Life,* (in Burmese), Vol. I, p. 299.
[4] Aung San in *Aung San of Burma,* p. 32.

other transportation to mainland China had failed. From Amoy, it was hoped, the two comrades might make their way inland and perhaps get in touch with the Communist Eighth Route Army, whose exploits were heard of in Rangoon, or even the Chinese Nationalist Forces, whose leader Chiang Kaishek had spoken often in support of nationalist movements in Asia.

On August 8, 1940, *Hai Lee* sailed away from Rangoon for Amoy, carrying on board two young men who gave their names as Tan Luan Shaung and Tan Su Taung. They were Aung San and Hla Myaing of Syriam, set on a bold adventure, driven by no less an ambition than to win Burma's freedom. They had no friends in Amoy. Hla Myaing had never been out of Burma before, while the farthest from home that Aung San had been to was Calcutta and Bombay. All they had was their determination, and 200 rupees between the two which was all that their comrades could raise.

5

Thakin Shu Maung was in from the start on the activities of his group and the Japanese agents. Not all the members of the Asiayone, nor even all those who were in Rangoon, were party, for police surveillance was increasing. The arrest of Thakin Ba Sein at the Siamese border was also a clear signal to the few who worked together that disloyalty could breed even within the smallest, closest circle.

The plan, as it later developed, was to send young men to Japan for military training, so that when time came they could return to Burma with arms and skill to lead the rising. The road to Japan was to be across Siam, through Bangkok where agents would wait. Young men of education and ability, seriousness of purpose and willingness to sacrifice, were marked out and kept ready. All that was needed was a surer entry into Siam and more reliable transit arrangements there.

Two young men, Thakins Kyaw Sein and Thit, had been sent once into Siam. Their instructions were to pick up a quarrel with the Siamese police and land themselves in the police lock-up. There, in privacy, they must give the code words, "S.K., S.K., Itoda," and things would begin to move, all would be well. The

men went, managed to slip across, provoked a fight with the
police, arrived at the police station, uttered the code words, and
drew a blank. It was the wrong place. The men had to use all their
cunning to get back across the border and to Rangoon.

Thakin Aung Than slipped across, shortly after Thakin Ba Sein
was arrested. He got through, but for some time there was no
word from him or about him. For many weeks there was nothing
to do for Thakin Nyi, still at large at the time, Thakins Khin
Maung, Shu Maung, and comrades, but anxiously wait, and play
the hide and seek game with the police.

Thakin Shu Maung was one of those who had been chosen to
go to Japan. He wanted to go. Here was the adventure he had
been waiting for. Friends and he had planned during college days
to go to Bangkok in search of adventure; Thakin Nyi had then
thwarted them. Now the adventure would be bigger, the goals
larger. Thakin Nyi himself urged his nephew to go. They discussed
the prospects calmly, leaving out the sentiments and the heroics.
The mission was not a sure thing, anything could happen, even
death. But man dies, and if Shu Maung must die, it would be because his time was up, and what better way could be found than
dying in a brave cause? On the other hand chances of success were
not too bad. "Say, they are better than a sporting chance, a gambling chance," the uncle said to the nephew, "and if you win, you
will be a leader of the national army of independent Burma. We
shall need a strong army; you can have a hand in building it." The
younger man did not need persuasion; he had already decided.
He did not dream up a great role for himself as liberator of the
country, or leader of a revolutionary army. Here, he decided, was
a job to do, and he wanted to do it.

Ko Kyi, a horse-trainer, brought a message one day to Daw
Khin Khin. A Burmese fugitive in Mesauk, he said, had delivered
a letter for her. The man who received the letter, finding the situation on the Burmese side of the border rather unsafe, had left the
letter hidden away and passed on the word as to where to find it.
Daw Khin Khin took the word to Thakin Khin Maung who, after
carefully checking the story, sent Thakin Kyaw Sein to collect the
letter. Within a few days it arrived, blank, and suspecting that there
was more in it than the eye could see, Thakin Khin Maung took it
in the night to the home of the Japanese Consul-General in Halpin

Road. Mr. Homa, the Consul, held up the letter against the flame of a candle, and read the meassage which was in Japanese. It urged the Burmese comrades to send the young men, and the Japanese agents to help them get away.

Once more the Burmese got busy. The Japanese too were more decisive this time, and promised to arrange sea passages for the young patriots. Thakins Khin Maung, San Thein, Thet She, Hla Maung, Daw Khin Khin and the leaders of the group who talked with the Japanese sought assurances that they were sincere in their intentions to help Burma win her independence. Homa and Yusono of the Japanese Consulate-General's office nodded their heads violently in emphatic assurance. They suggested that perhaps somebody of Thakin Khin Maung's standing, or Thakin Tun Oke's, should go along to Tokyo, move about in government circles to negotiate, while the young men trained for war. The Burmese thought that was an excellent idea, and Thakin Tun Oke, who was anxious to stay out of jail, was considered an excellent choice. Thakin Tun Oke was then in hiding in a village; Daw Khin Khin went out to inform him and bring him back to Kamayut.

Thakin Shu Maung, his friends noticed, became more secretive. To those who were close he spoke of a noble future for the country. Time had come, he also said, to do or die. One day, Thakin Shu Maung went and bought a suit of European clothes, which surprised his friends for he had always dressed in Burmese. "I'm going upcountry to smuggle opium," he explained. Puzzled, half-believing, his friends saw him a few days later, dressed in those clothes in which he looked different, hail a rickshaw and ride away.

A Japanese cargo vessel, the *Kouryu Maru* lay in anchor in the Rangoon harbour that month of July, 1941. Japanese ships which called at Rangoon were getting fewer. The situation in the region was becoming more tense. Japan was angry about the Burma-China Road. The British were suspicious of Japanese designs. Several members of the Japanese community in Rangoon, dentists —including Mr. Kokubu—traders, photographers, and U Nagai— the *bonze* who used to walk the streets beating a small drum— had been deported. *Kouryu Maru* was one of the last of the Japanese ships to call, and the agents had instructed Thakin Tun Oke and his comrades to board it.

Thakins Tun Khin and Kyaw Sein, boarding first, disguised according to instructions, were mistaken for thieves by the ship's guards. An alarm was sent up, and the two comrades had to run for it. They arrived back in Kamayut, panting, with their pants on, but minus their wristwatches which they had dropped on the ship in the flight.

Thakin Tun Oke, instructed to take a sampan into the river, and climb up the ship by a rope ladder, came back to report that he could not find the ship.

Reports and complaints made to Mr. Homa resulted in better boarding arrangements. All that the comrades had to do now was dress up as sailors and go up the gangway, each carrying a bunch of bananas in one hand and an umbrella in the other. Each comrade was also given a number which he must shout out on going up. Thakin Shu Maung's was number. 7.

To make sure that Thakin Tun Oke found the ship all right this time, Thakin Khin Maung sent him off in style in the car used by Mr. Prescott, the police commissioner. The driver, Ko Ba Chit, whose friendship had been cultivated over the years, was told that a Chinese opium smuggler had to make a getaway from the country. Thakin Tun Oke, on his part, was told to keep his lips sealed on the drive to the harbour.

One by one, the comrades boarded the ship. The arrangements were improved when one of the ship's Japanese officers had the brainwave to show some nice pictures of naked girls to the police and the customs staff who were checking arrivals at the top of the gangway. The photographs were more exciting than the arrivals, and when Thakin Shu Maung went up, he did not even have to call out his number, he was passed in.

Below the deck, by many flights of stairs, the comrades were taken down quickly, deep into the bowels of the ship, to a hot steaming room close to the engine. It was a small room, so small, so low, they could neither stand up nor lie down together. A small bucket in a corner of the room was for the toilet. The ventilation was so poor, it was hard to breathe after a while. As the hours passed, many of the men grew faint or ill.

Six members of the "Ba Sein-Tun Oke" Dobama Asi-ayone boarded the ship: Thakins Tun Oke, Shu Maung, Kyaw Sein, Ngwe, Thit and Tun Khin. In the room, down below, they met five other Burmese who, they found out on inquiry, were members of the other faction of the Asi-ayone. The five were Thakins San Hlaing, Tun Lwin, Than Nyun, Maung Maung, and Hla. It was a matter of surprise to the members of either group that the other was also in on the mission. But they were glad to be together on the lonely voyage. They came from two factions of the Asi-ayone; they had been practically rivals. Now they were on the same ship, bound for the same destination, striving towards the same goal of Burma's freedom. When they came aboard they were six, and they were five. Now they were eleven and united as one.

6

Thakins Aung San and Hla Myaing were in Amoy for nearly three months. The police occasionally questioned them, and once they had to bribe their way out of threatened imprisonment. They took up lodgings in a small hotel, paying Rs. 4 per day for the room. They could not travel into mainland China. Amoy bristled with smugglers and spies, but they could not establish contacts which might be useful for their purpose. Their money quickly ran out and Aung San wrote to friends in Burma for more. The friends were scared, for Aung San's handwriting could be recognized by the police. Tun Ohn, Ba Gyan, T. K. Boon, and others, who had started a successful 'Varsity Co-operative Stores, raised the money and remitted it by telegraphic money order.

The BRP—or rather those few of the group who managed to remain at large—spoke to Dr Thein Maung about the two comrades in Amoy. Dr Thein Maung, in turn, spoke to Suzuki. "In September," the latter recalled, "Dr Thein Maung came to see me. He showed me pictures of Aung San and Hla Myaing, said they had slipped out and reached Amoy, and Dr Thein Maung and his friends wanted me to arrange for them to get to Tokyo. I left Rangoon on the 3rd October, and stopped in Bangkok for a few days to make arrangements with the Japanese military attache for young Burmese who might slip across the borders on their way to Japan. Then I flew to Taipeh, and visited the Japanese Army headquarters where I asked a friend, Colonel Tanaka, to send one of his reliable officers to Amoy to contact Aung San. Tanaka co-operated, and thus Aung San turned up in Tokyo."[5]

[5] Keji Suzuki, in *Aung San of Burma*, p. 56.

6

On November 12, 1940, a blowy day which indicated that an early winter was on the way, Aung San and Hla Myaing landed at the Haneda airport, dressed in their summer clothes. Suzuki met them, and took good care of them. "Two or three days later," Aung San wrote in an autobiography which he did not live to finish, "he took us to a country hotel, where he asked us if we would like to take a woman. We were abashed at that—I was up to that time a hundred per cent bachelor—and we replied, No. Suzuki said: 'You needn't be shy. It is nothing, no more than taking a bath. There's a woman's quarter here.' We thanked him but declined to enjoy ourselves in this manner, and I asked myself, 'Is it their intention to demoralise us first?' "

Doubts remained on both sides throughout the following weeks. Suzuki and his associates wanted to test the sincerity of Aung San and his friends in Burma; Aung San on his part wanted to know how sincere the Japanese were. "They wanted to know why I went out to China," Aung San recalled, "whether I was a Communist, and what attitude we had towards their China policy. I replied that I went to China seeking help; that I did not believe in imposing any foreign system on a country, and we wanted to study all systems and adapt them to our needs; we had serious objections to Communism, though we were impressed with its planned economy. Regarding their China policy, my reply was that we were more concerned with our struggle, and looked upon those who opposed our foes as our friends. I did not think the Japanese were satisfied with my answers, and they continued to watch and study me with some suspicion."[6]

Colonel Suzuki and associates were at first free-lance adventurers who had the unofficial blessing of the Army or the Navy in which they held their commissions. They drew from different sources for funds. When they ran short, they dug deep into their own pockets, or sold their things. They also enlisted the support of big business. The Daitoa Shipping Company, whose directors were one evening invited to dine with Suzuki and the Minami Kikan, pledged their full support in getting the young Burmese over to Japan. Several businessmen placed their country houses at the disposal of the group for use as transit camps. The Navy was to provide training facilities. The Minami Kikan received more open

[6] *Aung San of Burma*, p. 34.

support from the High Command of the imperial forces later on, and Suzuki was appointed its chief.

Mr. Sugii and Thakin Aung San were sent back to Rangoon in March, 1941, by a cargo ship which called at Bassein. They went disguised as pursers; Aung San wore false teeth which, he hoped, would put the police off. From Bassein Aung San made his way to Rangoon where, after some searching, he found the comrades of the BRP. Thakin Chit found a hideout in Thingangyun for a secret gathering of the clan. "One Japanese officer who called himself Mr. Minami Waka, was with Aung San," wrote Bo Let Ya, "we were eager for news and Aung San did not disappoint us. He said that understandings had been reached with the Japanese who would support our rising with arms and money, but would not, themselves invade Burma. To get us ready for the rising, the Japanese would train our young leaders in military camps abroad, and we must select and send them by land and by sea. We accepted the plans; we had no choice, and we were all agreed that British power could only be ousted by force. It was a long night for us, and when we had finished talking, we fell into the deep sleep of the fulfilled."[7]

Thakins Hla Pe, Ba Gyan and Aye Maung, and Ko Tun Shein of the RUSU accompanied Aung San and Sugii when they sailed back on March 10. In the next few weeks Thakins Shwe, Tun Shwe, Tin Aye, Than Tin, Saw Lwin and Soe, and Ko Aung Thein, a member of the students' Steel Corps, got away in one batch. In the next went Ko Hla Maung of the RUSU, Thakins San Mya and Khin Maung U. Thakins Aung Than and Than Tin of the "Ba Sein-Tun Oke" faction were able to cross into Siam and find their way to Tokyo. Ko Saung, resident in Tokyo, was adopted as one of the members of the now legendary "Thirty Comrades". The eleven who left by the *Kouryu Maru* were the last batch.

The Minami Kikan wanted more young Burmese to come out to the training camps. Thakin Khin Maung and friends selected 30 young men, or more. The arrangements were to take them out, in one group if possible, in a big Burmese sailing boat from Pyapon. On the high seas, just beyond the territorial limits of

---

[7] Bo Let Ya, in *Aung San of Burma*, p. 44.

British power, a Japanese ship was to wait for them. But the monsoon came; the seas became rough. Thus the plan was struck down by the storms.

7

Several steaming, uncomfortable, anxious hours passed in the engine room of the *Kouryu Maru* before the ship eventually set sail. Thakin Shu Maung, tall and lean, took off his shirt as he profusely sweated. The ship's doctor came down often to do what he could for the comrades. Food was brought down in trays: fried bacon and eggs, steak done Japanese style with plenty of sugar; but few could eat. Mr. Mitzutani of the Minami Kikan, a veteran of the China wars whose body was scarred all over, was in charge of the operation and he treated the men as precious cargo. There was no lack of attention, but not a sound, it was warned, must be made in the engine room, until the checking on the decks was done. "Let's sail as quickly as possible," Thakin Shu Maung urged an officer of the ship who came to visit, "if we must die we would rather die outside Burma's waters."

At last, on July 8 the ship could leave. Once Burma's waters were left behind, the comrades could come out on deck and breathe the fresh, free air. There was great rejoicing. The treatment given by the ship's officers to the comrades was royal. They were wined and dined and treated as heroes. Sea-sickness prevented all but Thakins Tun Khin and Ngwe from doing full justice to the feasts. Off Singapore, a British pilot vessel came alongside, and the comrades had to go into hiding for nearly two hours. It was not so bad this time, however, for they were put away in cabins below the deck and told to keep quiet. Then on, the ship sailed, reaching on July 22 a Japanese naval base off Shanghai, where Commander Hidaka welcomed the comrades with great warmth. From Shanghai, in the disguise of motor car drivers of the Japanese navy they were flown to Yokosuka naval base for a stop-over of five days, spent in sight-seeing, feasting, fishing—Thakin Tun Oke caught a small octopus and was thrilled. Then to Fukuoka, and to Hakone by bus, passing by the snow-capped Fujiyama. Sight-seeing in Tokyo, riding on the underground railway or resting in Japanese inns, pretty girls everywhere always sweetly smiling and eager to please. At Hakone the comrades were put up for a few days at the summer resort of one Mr. Iwasaki. The housekeepers, husband and wife, and Eiko San, the sister of Mrs Iwasaki, looked after them very well. The younger men in the group were somewhat apt to forget their purpose and succumb to the temptations of the moment. Thakin Shu Maung was one of the older members who kept the team moving along in harmony and discipline.

The training camp was on Hainan island. The team was the last to arrive, and it brought the number of the comrades up to thirty. A dark, stern man, wearing luxuriant whiskers walked about the camp with serious strides, and the arriving team took him at first to be an Indian Sikh, on a mission such as their own. The man turned out to be Thakin Hla Myaing who had gone out to Amoy with Aung San.

8

The going was rough at the camp. Time was short, Captain Kawashima, the commandant, reminded the comrades. Their task was huge. They must, therefore, work hard on training programmes in which years were packed into months. From early dawn every day to late at night it was drill, training, exercises, lectures, demonstrations. The comrades were not only taught, but toughened, for if Hainan was rough for them, their return to Burma would surely be rougher.

Life at camp was spartan. Food, brought over at meal times by naval boat from a base some distance off, was of the simplest fare. Boiled rice, sugary soup, some fish, some pickles, an occasional chicken or meat. After meals there was the washing up to do and the general cleaning up of camp, at which everyone must take his turn. For clothes the comrades were issued short-sleeve shirts and shorts, canvas shoes and boots. In the rough and tumble of training, in the bush, in the jungle, up the hill, or across stony stretches doing the crocodile crawl, the shirt and shorts were grossly inadequate. But scratched, bruised, bleeding, the comrades carried on. Emphasis made by exhortation and example by the instructors was on the fighting spirit, the will to win. Man himself is the mightiest weapon of war. Give him the skills, cast his spirit in a mould of steel, and he will ram through all opposition to victory. That was the constant theme on Hainan island. To drive this theme home, the instructors would drive the comrades hard, praise them, blame them, coax, console, encourage, deride or shame them by turns. This training, this treatment, compounded with the patriotism that brought them there made men out of the youthful comrades and gave them the necessary courage and confidence to lead.

The Japanese instructors were thorough. They prepared training schedules carefully. They marked the progress of each of the comrades. They graded and classed them on the basis of I.Q., ability, leadership, and perseverance. After basic training, each class had to specialize. Dai-ippan, the number one section, trained the would-be battalion commanders. It took somewhat younger men and put them through the usual course for troop officers. The Dai-ippan did a good deal of drilling and digging; its members grinned and called themselves the coolies, condemned to hard labour. The Dai-nihan trained a few comrades for fifth column activities and guerrilla war. The members were nicknamed the thieves, for theirs were tasks to be accomplished while the enemy slept. The San-pan, took a few who were marked out for high command. Thakins Aung San, Shu Maung, Hla Pe and Aung Than were in the group. Thakin Tun Oke, the oldest of the thirty, regarded himself as the political leader who must be preserved for no less a position than head of state or prime minister of independent Burma. He made himself available to the Japanese general staff for high policy discussions, and took only a polite interest in the military training. He was, though few realized it, under a serious handicap for field activities. Like a true Burmese he had had himself tattooed from waist to knees when he was a younger man. Wearing shorts would show the tattooes, which he was shy to do. Thus, Thakin Tun Oke in Dai San-pan preferred to wear trousers and work on jobs—such as writing the constitution of New Burma—which exercised the brain more than the brawn. The members of the San-pan were known, among the comrades, as the "Sampan-wallahs", the ferrymen who plied their sampans across rivers back home.

Aung San was a small man, but he was driven by a strong will power. He would fall down from sheer exhaustion in those field exercises which were specially strenuous. But he would get up and go on. The same spirit burned in all the comrades. Shu Maung was tall and lean. "We called him 'Takasugi' which in Japanese means a tall and straight cider tree. Takasugi is also the name of a Japanese hero of the Meiji revolution," wrote Mr. Sugii. Shu Maung asked questions in field and in class. Into whatever he did he put his whole heart. When he had a rare moment of leisure in the Dai San-pan, he would go along with the other groups to learn more. Once, in a battalion attack on a hill, he had to carry a machine-gun. The exercise covered several miles of hard terrain, and when they moved up the hill the comrades were near the limits of their endurance. Shu Maung fell several times under the heavy burden. But he rose after each fall and tottered forward. When he could not totter, he crawled.

The Japanese were deeply impressed with the performance of comrade Shu Maung. He was, they decided, fit for the highest commands. Aung San, who had at first looked upon the comrades of the rival "Ba Sein-Tun Oke" group with some caution, was unreserved in his agreement. "Shu Maung will be my right hand in the independence movement," he told Sugii. Thakin Aung Than, claiming seniority in his membership of the "Ba Sein-Tun Oke" group, felt displeased with all the glowing reports on Shu Maung. He complained to Thakin Tun Oke that his own grading should be much higher. "But, Aung Than," Tun Oke replied, "you and I are politicians. We can't possibly survive long in the army. We are not made for this sort of life. Besides, Shu Maung is doing very well. I think he has found himself."

The camp was in an isolated part of Hainan, itself an out of the way island. The sign at the gate of the camp read, "Sanya Farmers' Training Depot". The disguise was well kept. The Japanese made occasional security checks in the area to keep strangers away. There were a few small villages of the islanders not far from the camp, and the Burmese comrades would go there on their rare holidays to visit. The villagers lived a bare, primitive life. Coconut trees grew everywhere, providing the comrades with fresh, nourishing drinks of coconut juice in intervals between training. Lone Chinese guerrillas prowled the jungles preying upon lone Japanese soldiers. These guerrillas had crossed over from the mainland and lived in the jungle on fruits, figs, fish and frogs. When they were captured, they received cruel and summary treat-

ment from the Japanese, but they met their ends defiant. The
Burmese comrades saw how the Japanese dealt with some of those
guerrillas, and wondered whether, if the world situation made the
Burmese presence an embarrassment, the Japanese would not deal
with them also in the same manner.

As time passed, the comrades began to repeat their training.
The Dai San-pan did the same battles over and over again in its
map-fighting on the sand. Life became a little boring and anxious.
Tension grew at camp. There were suspicions and anxieties among
the Burmese whose one great desire was to get home and into
action. They felt restive, cooped up on the island, caged. The
Japanese themselves were not free from their own anxieties. The
rivalry between the Navy and the Army did not end with the
official birth of the Minami Kikan. Kokubu, the "dentist" from
Rangoon, turned up as a naval captain assigned to the Kikan.
Captain Kawashima, the commandant of the camp, was navy. In
fact the whole training programme had to depend largely on naval
resources. Colonel Kojima, Lt-Col. Hidaka and Maj. Nagayama
were other naval officers attached to the Kikan. But people came
and went, army officers, navy officers, civilians; ambitious, individualistic men who clashed and quarrelled often. Col. Suzuki himself was an arrogant man who was quick to assume to himself more
authority than the General Headquarters were willing to grant
him. From his Japanese associates he demanded absolute obedience. He never quite forgave Kokubu for dealing with Thakin
Aung Than of the "Ba Sein-Tun Oke" group without telling him.
When Aung Than managed to slip across to Bangkok, both
Kokubu and Suzuki happened to be in town. Kokubu kept Aung
Than from Suzuki for some time, until Suzuki found out for himself and accused Kokubu of trying to steal the Burma show for the
Navy. If there was any stealing of the show to be done Suzuki
would do it himself; the mission had become personal to him. "The
idea of Col. Suzuki" Sugii had noted in his diary, "was that instead of presenting a special kind of fruit to the Emperor, he would
present a country." Later, after long association with the Burmese
comrades, Suzuki became excited with their enthusiasm for
Burma's independence.

The General Headquarters in Tokyo could never quite make up
their minds about what to do with the Minami Kikan. Suzuki's

vanity and freelancing habits were trying; the world situation was fluid. The domestic situation too was sometimes hard to assess; many groups contended for power. If there was jealousy between the Navy and the Army on Hainan island, there was even sharper jealousy and endless intrigue between the two arms in Tokyo. The German invasion of Russia made the world situation perplexing to the policy-makers in Tokyo; it cast a cloud of despair over the Japanese staff and the Burmese comrades in Hainan. Now Japan would not go to war against Britain, the Burmese thought, and all the promises of aid in the fight for Burma's freedom would be forgotten. More, they themselves, incriminating evidence of Japan's designs, might be destroyed. The comrades lived in a state of nervous vigilance. Aung San, Shu Maung, and the leaders among them tried to keep the comrades calm. One night, Hla Myaing, more deeply disturbed than the rest, rose and shouted an alarm, "Comrades, the time has come!" There was a dash for the armoury to grab weapons, but fortunately peace was quickly restored and the whole affair was made out as an exercise. The Japanese, however, could read the signs. They smiled more, treated the comrades better, relaxed their training schedules, encouraged them to go fishing or shooting on Sundays and promised that the return to Burma would soon be arranged.

Thus the months passed, and October, 1941, arrived.

9

In Burma there was little to do but wait.

Those Thakins and politicians who opposed the Government had been jailed; those who were fast enough had gone underground. The BRP conducted its war by pamphlet and bulletin, and kept the people ready. The German invasion of Russia started a hot debate among the BRP and Thakin theoreticians, and called for an urgent reappraisal of policy. Thakin Soe in jail sent desperate messages to the comrades outside that the line of action must now clearly be to associate with the British in the fight against fascism; there was neither need nor time to bargain for Burma's freedom, for Britain's war had become the peoples' war. Those messages, those debates, however, were to be little consequence in the larger realities of the war in South-east Asia.

U Saw reigned supreme. He got on well with the British in the ICS. He became good friends with Sir Reginald Dorman-Smith, the new Governor. Satisfactory relations of give-and-take developed between the two of them. When general elections fell due in 1941, the Governor obligingly offered to postpone them by decree. U Saw, pleased and grateful, promised continuing co-operation. As leader of the *Myochit* (Patriot) party in a situation which was highly charged with nationalist feelings, he had to do something, show some results to the people. Sir Reginald, after some thinking and some cabling back and forth with London, decided that U Saw should go there and talk things over himself. U Saw was again pleased and grateful. He left early in October, 1941—just about the time the thirty comrades were preparing to leave Hainan on their way home.

It was a grand, well-publicized exit, for U Saw had that flair. He flew up, with his wife, in a private aeroplane he had bought from U Ohn Khin, and circling round the Shwedagon pagoda, paid his respects from the air. People thought that was an unwise thing to do. One adopts the most humble posture, on hands and knees, to pay one's respects to the Buddha's image. U Saw did the reverse; he took to the air and worshipped from above. It was a bad omen for him. Besides, the world was up in flames with war. It was doubted that U Saw would return from his mission.

In London, U Saw, assisted by U Tin Tut, a Burman ICS officer, made his rounds. He saw Mr. L. S. Amery, the Secretary of State for Burma, several times. He met the press and wrote letters to the *Times*. He addressed meetings. The climax of his visit was his encounter with Winston Churchill at Chequers. He gave Churchill a box of Burmese cigars and asked for a promise that Burma would be given dominion status at war's end. Churchill took the cigars but did not give the promise. U Saw was disappointed, and he said so to the British press. He flew off to America to return across the Pacific. The American reception was coldly correct. He reached Honolulu, the day after the Pearl Harbour incident. The wrecks of American ships, half-sunk, half-protruding out of the sea, announced in silence that war had come to the Pacific area. U Saw flew back, touching at Lisbon where he called at the Japanese Consulate-General. The British intelligence, intercepting Japanese messages sent out of Lisbon, found that U Saw had

U Saw reigned supreme. He got on well with the British in the ICS. He became good friends with Sir Reginald Dorman-Smith, the new Governor. Satisfactory relations of give-and-take developed between the two of them. When general elections fell due in 1941, the Governor obligingly offered to postpone them by decree. U Saw, pleased and grateful, promised continuing co-operation. As leader of the *Myochit* (Patriot) party in a situation which was highly charged with nationalist feelings, he had to do something, show some results to the people. Sir Reginald, after some thinking and some cabling back and forth with London, decided that U Saw should go there and talk things over himself. U Saw was again pleased and grateful. He left early in October, 1941—just about the time the thirty comrades were preparing to leave Hainan on their way home.

It was a grand, well-publicized exit, for U Saw had that flair. He flew up, with his wife, in a private aeroplane he had bought from U Ohn Khin, and circling round the Shwedagon pagoda, paid his respects from the air. People thought that was an unwise thing to do. One adopts the most humble posture, on hands and knees, to pay one's respects to the Buddha's image. U Saw did the reverse; he took to the air and worshipped from above. It was a bad omen for him. Besides, the world was up in flames with war. It was doubted that U Saw would return from his mission.

In London, U Saw, assisted by U Tin Tut, a Burman ICS officer, made his rounds. He saw Mr. L. S. Amery, the Secretary of State for Burma, several times. He met the press and wrote letters to the *Times*. He addressed meetings. The climax of his visit was his encounter with Winston Churchill at Chequers. He gave Churchill a box of Burmese cigars and asked for a promise that Burma would be given dominion status at war's end. Churchill took the cigars but did not give the promise. U Saw was disappointed, and he said so to the British press. He flew off to America to return across the Pacific. The American reception was coldly correct. He reached Honolulu, the day after the Pearl Harbour incident. The wrecks of American ships, half-sunk, half-protruding out of the sea, announced in silence that war had come to the Pacific area. U Saw flew back, touching at Lisbon where he called at the Japanese Consulate-General. The British intelligence, intercepting Japanese messages sent out of Lisbon, found that U Saw had vanity and freelancing habits were trying; the world situation was fluid. The domestic situation too was sometimes hard to assess; many groups contended for power. If there was jealousy between the Navy and the Army on Hainan island, there was even sharper jealousy and endless intrigue between the two arms in Tokyo. The German invasion of Russia made the world situation perplexing to the policy-makers in Tokyo; it cast a cloud of despair over the Japanese staff and the Burmese comrades in Hainan. Now Japan would not go to war against Britain, the Burmese thought, and all the promises of aid in the fight for Burma's freedom would be forgotten. More, they themselves, incriminating evidence of Japan's designs, might be destroyed. The comrades lived in a state of nervous vigilance. Aung San, Shu Maung, and the leaders among them tried to keep the comrades calm. One night, Hla Myaing, more deeply disturbed than the rest, rose and shouted an alarm, "Comrades, the time has come!" There was a dash for the armoury to grab weapons, but fortunately peace was quickly restored and the whole affair was made out as an exercise. The Japanese, however, could read the signs. They smiled more, treated the comrades better, relaxed their training schedules, encouraged them to go fishing or shooting on Sundays and promised that the return to Burma would soon be arranged.

Thus the months passed, and October, 1941, arrived.

9

In Burma there was little to do but wait.

Those Thakins and politicians who opposed the Government had been jailed; those who were fast enough had gone underground. The BRP conducted its war by pamphlet and bulletin, and kept the people ready. The German invasion of Russia started a hot debate among the BRP and Thakin theoreticians, and called for an urgent reappraisal of policy. Thakin Soe in jail sent desperate messages to the comrades outside that the line of action must now clearly be to associate with the British in the fight against fascism; there was neither need nor time to bargain for Burma's freedom, for Britain's war had become the peoples' war. Those messages, those debates, however, were to be little consequence in the larger realities of the war in South-east Asia.

4

The Burma Independence Army

1

THE THIRTY comrades, Suzuki and his staff moved from Hainan to Formosa in October, 1941. Like hounds on the leash, all were straining hard, ears pricked for the word, "Go!" Elements of the Kikan in Bangkok prepared to receive the force, recruit men and launch the invading columns into Burma. Several comrades were to be sent in first as "internal disturbance groups". These comrades, including Thakin Shu Maung who was selected to lead one group, were given training with special weapons and explosives.

The General Headquarters in Tokyo still refrained from flashing the green light. Japan was preparing for war while her diplomats were sweetly negotiating for peaceful agreements; appearances must, therefore, be kept up. Orders for caution and secrecy irked the Japanese and the Burmese alike. "Now the thirty comrades have completed their training," Sugii noted on October 25, "and would be bitterly disappointed if they were sent back to Japan instead of Burma. The Minami Kikan could not understand the attitude of the GHQ and decided to carry on as planned."

On October 30, the GHQ cabled orders to stop all movements as the situation was sensitive. Suzuki cabled in reply that "all the Burmese comrades had run away, only four had been caught, but the search was still going on." To give some truth to the message, the force had to scatter. The comrades and the Japanese staff, divided into small teams, started out for Bangkok, the rendezvous, by sea, by air, by road, by direct route, or through Hanoi or Saigon.

Bangkok was not yet ready to welcome the great adventure. For several weeks, the operations had to be done under cover. Some of the Burmese comrades, and the Japanese staff who arrived first in the city had to go about as "geologists" in Japanese

mining concerns; some posed as businessmen and even opened a
few shops. Surveillance was not strict; the Thai police were obliging; it was easy to move about. Home was near; time for action
was nigh; morale was high.

In Burma the people waited. There was nothing to do but wait,
for war that they knew must come, for changes they knew must
happen. In the war many people would die or get hurt, many lose
their homes, but they were so weary of this awful, endless waiting,
they would prefer to go through it all, and get it over with. The
young politicians, the BRP, the Thakins, waited in the jails, or out,
hoping, talking, debating, organizing, dreaming; there was little
else that they could do till help came. The older politicians kept
talking, but in subdued tones. Sir Paw Tun was acting prime minister, in the absence of U Saw, and there was little for the Cabinet
to do. The Governor and his staff had started work on civil defence; building air raid shelters in the streets of Rangoon was a
campaign. A small Burma Royal Naval Volunteer Reserve, with a
handful of young Burmese officers, and a small Burma Royal Air
Force, with another handful of young Burmese officers, were in
training. The Militia in Maymyo was turning out some young
Burmans to officer army troops which were not yet there.

In Japan, the weeks of waiting were imposing a heavy strain on
the nerves of the citizens. Governments were changing. Now it was
the Navy on top, now the Army, in the power struggle; now it
was to be peace, now war. On October 18 General Tojo, War
Minister, became leader of the War Cabinet, with a free hand.
Yet, the talks in Washington went on, a smoke-screen to cover
the preparations for war.

Then came the attack on Pearl Harbour. "In the early dawn
of December, 8," wrote Mamoru Shigemitsu who was Japan's
Foreign Minister in the last two years of war, "telephones in Tokyo
were busy. The great success of the attack on Pearl Harbour was
already known to those in the inner circles and communicated to
their friends. The radio announced the outbreak of war and read
the Imperial Decree. The citizens listened respectfully. They rejoiced at the good news and breathed a sigh of relief. It was not
entirely due to the good news. They had been held in a state of
suspense so long and now that waiting was over they sighed with
relief, as a Japanese might well do, and as Japanese they resolved

to go through with it to the end and smash the enemy. Nobody had time to reflect what it all meant."[1]

2

For the thirty comrades the start of war meant that they could come out into the open and get ready for the march homeward. For Thakin Tun Oke it meant that he could now deliver over the radio the speeches that he had kept locked up in his breast. He spoke many times. He invoked the glories of Burmese history, and called on the people of Burma to rise and restore them. Their hour, his hour, had come.

The Burma Independence Army was inaugurated on December 26, 1941. Volunteers from the Burmese communities in Bangkok and Chiangmai flocked under its banner. "That night," wrote Bo Let Ya, "we had a meeting of all those who had returned from the training camps in Japan, and Aung San suggested that we should each pick an auspicious name, a name that would give pride and sense of mission, a name to carry on our march. It was Aung San's idea, not one that we conceived by collective or prolonged thinking. We liked the idea, we made our selections, tried them out, liked them, and felt a few inches taller wearing the new names."[2]

Thus, Thakin Hla Pe became Let Ya, the Right Hand; Aung San was Teza, the Powerful; Shu Maung became Ne Win, Brilliant as the Sun. All the comrades took on new names, names that sounded brave and noble, some of which had belonged to the heroes of Burma's history. Thakin Tun Oke, whose ambition was for political leadership, did not choose a new name for himself. A ritual of the ancient warriors was also performed at the meeting. Each of the comrades cut open a bit of the arm to give blood into a silver bowl; then all drank the oath of loyalty in blood. It was, perhaps, a primitive ceremony, but then the comrades were setting out on the primitive—apparently eternal—mission of war, in which men settle their scores in fire and blood.

Each new name was prefixed with the title "Bo"—meaning

[1] Mamoru Shigemitsu, *Japan and Her Destiny,* E. P. Dutton & Co., Inc., New York, 1958, p. 267.

[2] *Aung San of Burma,* p. 47.

officer, commander, or leader of fighting men. Designating by rank
or function, in later years, the title "Bohmu" for officers of field
rank, major and above, and "Bogyoke" for general, commander-
in-chief, or supremo, came into use. But "Bo" was applicable to
all the officer brethren, from the young cadet officer to the commanding general, and this was the title that the thirty comrades
adopted with their new names. Bo Teza, Bo Ne Win, Bo Let Ya,
and so on, they became as they raised the BIA and prepared to
march. The names have stuck, except for Bo Aung San who used
the new name only for a while on the march.

Colonel Suzuki also received a new name chosen for him by
the Burmese comrades. Remembering the songs about the Mogyoe
thunderbolt which would one day strike and shatter the umbrella's rod—interpreted by the astrologers as British power—the
young comrades decided to call him Bo Mogyoe. The new name
pleased Suzuki immensely. It made him feel that he was sent by
some divine power to perform a historic role for Burma. He would
march at the head of BIA, drive the British out, and proclaim
Burma's independence. It was all very simple. "We shall occupy
Government House in Rangoon—the seat of British power—and
proclaim independence there," he kept saying to the comrades.
The Japanese GHQ asked Suzuki how many divisions should be
launched into Burma; Bo Mogyoe curtly replied, "None, we shall
do it ourselves, just give us the arms!" The GHQ, which found
the war going much better than they expected, had their own
thoughts, but they decided to humour Suzuki for some time. Meanwhile the GHQ contented itself with cutting down on indents for
arms for the BIA.

Bangkok was a busy city. The Hayashi Army soon arrived. The
Minami Kikan had its many offices, many camps. Jealousies between the Navy and the Army in the Kikan became acute again.
Bo Mogyoe's swagger and claim of priority for the BIA annoyed
the other Japanese units. He assumed the local rank of general,
and called himself General Minami or Bo Mogyoe. He was irrepressible. His arrogance, his demand for absolute priority for the
mission, his claim of star role for him and the thirty comrades in
the Burma campaign, these saved the BIA from being relegated
to a subordinate role. The generals in Tokyo and the Hayashi
Army went into fits when they heard about, or from, Bo Mogyoe.

The clashes between Army and Navy within the Minami Kikan, and the rivalry between Suzuki and Kokubu took on serious proportions in Bangkok. "Discussing these matters is not advisable," noted Sugii in his diary, "but in the Kikan the opinion was divided." That was a mild way of describing the situation, for the Navy tried to launch out into Burma on its own. The Burmese comrades, however, were uninterested in the quarrels of the Japanese. They were united under the leadership of Aung San. Bo Ne Win, a senior by virtue of age and standing in the "Ba Sein-Tun Oke" Thakin group which came out, helped to persuade the comrades to forget factional feelings and work together in the common cause. "The Naval side," Sugii therefore found, "could not obtain any members from the Thakin Party except Bo Setkya (Aung Than). The Army, however, through Mr. Sugii and Lt. Kitajima managed to secure many members so that the Navy naturally had to look to the Army for the lead."

Work saved the situation from getting out of hand. The BIA needed men; recruiting teams therefore went to the villages to enlist volunteers. Aung San's firm instructions to the recruiting officers were to take volunteers only, strictly avoiding anything that looked like compulsion, making it amply clear to them that it would be rough-going, no picnic, and it was a fight for freedom, not a raid for loot or plunder. Shans, Burmans, Thai, they came forward in their hundreds, pledging victory or death. Thai railways helped to transport the recruits to Bangkok; at railway stations women wept and wailed while their men sat impassive, impatient for the train to move off. Most of the recruits wanted adventure and an opportunity to strike a blow for Burma's freedom. Some wanted to pray at the Shwedagon pagoda in Rangoon.

At camps in Bangkok the recruits were given their basic training. One thousand pieces of arms—rifles, machine-guns, mortars—were obtained by Suzuki from Japanese troops stationed in South China. The shipment of arms arrived at Mitsuei wharf in Bangkok on January 1, 1942, just in time to arm the recruits who had started pouring in. Three thousand more pieces were supplied, and these were transported to Rahaeng, Mekan and Kanburi for distribution to the BIA troops. When the march into Burma began in columns, there were more men than arms.

Bo Ne Win, Bo Tayar, Bo Linyon and Bo Monyoe were among

7

a small group who were trained intensively for parachute-jumping.
The plan was to drop the group and arms behind British lines, so
that the revolutionary forces in Burma might rise. The "operation
airdrop", however, ran into red tape and inter-service rivalry at
the Area HQ. Week after week the operation was put off. There
was a shortage of aircraft against heavy demands for their services. The *Mayu Maru,* bringing a supply of arms and explosives,
was sunk, and with the ship went all hopes of operation airdrop.
Those members of the BRP who waited in Rangoon, looking up
eagerly skyward for help, had to wait in vain.

Bo Ne Win and comrades decided they would go in anyhow,
overland, through the jungles. Time was of the essence. Bo Aung
San was also anxious to have friends in Burma know the situation
and prepare. The struggle was not going to end with the collapse
of British power over Burma. That would only be the beginning;
a long, hard road lay ahead. Aung San wanted to get that message
across as quickly as possible, and well before the Japanese arrived. Bo Mogyoe on his part also wanted Bo Ne Win and party to
move on well ahead. He wanted a BIA victory, to get to Rangoon first.

Thus, the race began in earnest. Sugii's records of January 12
showed that on that day Bo Mogyoe, Mr. Uchida, Adjutant Kimura
and Staff Ijima left Phitsanulok for Rahaeng. So did "Bo Aung
San and the group for inside disturbance works, Bo Ne Win and
5 members together with 3 guides carrying disturbance arms."
On January 13 Sugii noted: "Bo Ne Win and 8 followers were
to leave Rahaeng on the 14th to create strife and disorder in
Burma. Major Taira and Kisako were to help him. Within Siam
the clothing of the group would be Siamese style. At the border
they were to change into Burmese clothes. They were to carry
arms—small size pistols, explosives, rifles, bayonets, etc. They
would also carry cash Rs. 3,000."

3

Rangoon received the first air raid on December 23, 1941, the
day before Christmas Eve. The bombers, some seventy of them,
escorted by about thirty fighters, flew in around 10 a.m.; the warning sounded, but curious people went out into the streets, instead

of the shelters. The Japanese raiders came in like a swarm of bees, dully droning; only, they were deadlier. They bombed the airfield in Mingladon, the dockyard and several other places in the city. A few archaic anti-aircraft guns barked at them. The lone Royal Air Force squadron sent up those of its Buffaloes which escaped the bombing at Mingladon. The American Volunteer Group sent up its squadron of Tomahawks. The ensuing dog-fights in the air were wonderful to watch, and people crowded together in the streets and the open spaces to enjoy the aerial circus. On them the raiders dropped anti-personnel bombs. It was Rangoon's first taste of war; a bitter taste it was.

There was utter confusion in the city, and thorough unpreparedness in the high places of power. Commands and commanders changed in rapid succession. Burma was under the "ABCD" (Allied S. W. Pacific Command) with General Wavell as supreme commander based in Java; when the ABCD command was broken up, Burma was placed under C-in-C, Singapore. The fall of Singapore returned the command to India. Commanders came and went. Wavell himself came from the deserts of the Middle East where he had fought Rommel. On his transfer to the Eastern theatre he handed over to General Auchinleck. General Slim, sent in at the eleventh hour to lead the Burma Corps, also came from the deserts of Iraq. General Alexander, who had fought on the beaches of Dunkirk, was given overall charge of the Burma campaign. Stilwell, the American General, arrived in yet later stages, with a vague command over a confusion of Chinese troops. The best of commanders thus plunged into the worst of situations, mingling with commanders of the old school who would only dig deep trenches and stay in. Promised reinforcements did not arrive. An Australian division which was on the way was recalled home by the Australian government; Churchill's urgent requests to send the division to Burma could not persuade the government who had to think first of home defence in that fast crumbling scene.

The *Prince of Wales* and the *Repulse,* battle cruisers of the British Navy, were attacked and sunk in Asian waters by a squadron of Japanese bombers. Reporting to the House of Commons in secret session on April 23, 1942, Winston Churchill recounted the many disasters which had befallen British arms in the course of a few, brief, anxious weeks. The two ships had arrived at Singapore on December 2. "It was hoped," he said, "that their presence there might be deterrent upon the war party in Japan, and it was intended that they should vanish, as soon as possible, into the blue. I have already explained to the House how they became involved in a local operation against Japanese transports in the Gulf of Siam which led to their destruction. On the night of December 9, in view of the news we had received about the heavy losses of the American fleet at Pearl Harbour, I proposed to the Chiefs of Staff that the *Prince of Wales* and *Repulse* should join the undamaged portion of the American fleet in order to sustain the position in the Pacific. The matter was to be further considered next day, but in the morning arrived the news of the loss of both these great ships. We had now no modern or modernized capital ships in the Indian Ocean."

The early fall of Singapore, with the surrender of 100,000 British, Australian, Indian and other troops to 30,000 Japanese who first landed on the island on February 8, was another disaster and humiliation the British had to take in the Asian theatre of war. "This episode," Churchill observed in his report to the House, "and all that led up to it seems to be out of harmony with anything that we have experienced or performed in the present war." Demands were made for the appointment of a royal commission of inquiry, but Churchill could not comply. "General Wavell, who was in charge of the whole ABCD area from January 15 onwards," he explained, "is far too busy grappling with new perils. We too have enough trouble on our hands to cope with the present and the future, and I could not in any circumstances consent to adding such a burden, for a burden it would be, to those which we have to bear."[3]

Rangoon, in those weeks, was a city wrapped in gloom. Rumours of impending disasters ran wild, driving the people to evacuate in desperate hurry. The railway stations were jammed. The roads were choked with the exodus. People moved out and on, carrying their belongings; where they were going mattered little, the thing was to keep moving. Some refugees who moved out of Rangoon, pushed on by the fast sweep of the invasion, ended up in Myitkyina or Bhamo in the far north.

[3] Winston S. Churchill's *Secret Session Speeches*, Cassell & Co. Ltd., London, 1946, p. 49 and pp. 54-55.

Events moved so fast that the Government had to change its mind often. Now it was going to hold Rangoon; next it was leaving. Now Sir Reginald Dorman-Smith was promising that the lines would be held firm, every inch of ground to be defended to the last man; next the order was to withdraw. Now the citizens of Rangoon were called upon to stay at their jobs; next they were told to evacuate. Sir Paw Tun, the prime minister, members of the Cabinet, and senior officials, packed their bags and kept moving; wherever they stopped, Prome or Mandalay, Maymyo or Sagaing, they drew their salaries on time.

In Rangoon, a few weeks before the general evacuation began, arrived Bo Ne Win after hard march and travel from Rahaeng.

4

The march across hill and jungle had been long for Bo Ne Win, Bo Tayar, Bo Monyoe, Bo Linyon, the two Japanese officers whose task was to get the comrades to the Burmese border, and the Thai and Karen guides whose duty was to lead the group through footpaths to the river Thaungyin which separates Siam from Burma.

Each of the comrades carried sword, bayonet, binoculars, rifle, grenades, pistols, and equipment all weighing about 60 pounds, which was a sizeable load for the jungle journey. A fast pace was kept up, for the urgent purpose was to get home, organize the friends, warn them, build postures of strength from which to bargain with the Japanese. The task forbade deeds of heroism on the way, Bo Ne Win warned his comrades whenever they wanted to engage in skirmishes. Strict discipline was also observed during the brief stops in villages. Some were Thai and some Karen, but the villagers were generally friendly though a little suspicious at first contact. In one village, after the usual exploratory greetings, the village elders became very friendly and made the visitors welcome. The girls, in their colourful sarongs then came and whispered to the elders, giggling and smiling shyly as they spoke. The elders conveyed the message to Bo Ne Win and his comrades that the girls would be glad to receive them in the late evening, the customary courting time. The invitation had to be politely declined. Taira and Kisako, who were told about it only the next morning, when the village had fallen far behind, were bitterly disappointed.

Ko Maung Gale, a Karen forest ranger, guided the party over a difficult stretch of jungle. The man moved like a leopard, fast, smooth, silent, through the jungle that was his home.

Thaungyin river was wide and wild. A raft was made to cross it. When the party climbed aboard, it barely floated. The swift current carried the raft downstream, against rocks, into sandbanks. It took some time to touch the Burma bank. Then, Taira and Kisako jumped off first, saying to Bo Ne Win, "Wait, let us put you down in proper style on your native land." They joined hands, making a chair for him to sit on, lifted him from the raft and put him down tenderly on the bank. It was a touching gesture, a moving moment for all. The Burmese comrades said farewell to Taira and Kisako who went back the way they came to report to Bo Mogyoe and Bo Aung San that Bo Ne Win's mission into Burma was well launched.

At Shwegun village, headman U Ba Han and his group of village defence men were suspicious. Bo Ne Win's explanation that he was a forest officer searching for a lost elephant failed to satisfy. The headman wanted to disarm and search the party, and Bo Ne Win felt compelled to take the headman aside and reveal the true mission of the party. The headman responded with great warmth. "All is well, go home," he told the villagers who gathered round, "these are our friends."

By boat down the Salween river the party went to Wetkyi village. There the monastery of U Zawtika, a monk who had given his heart to the Thakin movement, gave refuge for one night. Bo Ne Win whispered his identity to the monk in the gathering dusk of the evening, and the monk stood up and burst into a lusty cry of "Dobama!" Thakin Saw Maung, in the village, was hastily summoned so that he might also hear the good news that the BIA was coming.

At Theinzeik, the presiding monk at a monastery was less hospitable. He drove the party away, refusing shelter even for one night. In the streets, the party ran into a police patrol, and had to make a quick withdrawal into another monastery where, fortunately, the monk was kinder. The monk gave rice and dried fish to the comrades, and words of encouragement. "National freedom will give glory to our religion and enhance the standing of the *Sangha*," the monk murmured with delight when he was told about the mission, "it is therefore my duty to help you." A police search party arrived, however, and the comrades had to take to the fields where they took their rice and fish. Time had come, Bo Ne Win told his associates, to separate, and make their way as best as they could to their assigned areas. Bo Tayar was to operate in Pyinmana; Bo Monyoe in Pegu; Bo Linyon in Prome. Bo Ne Win himself and a Thai guide were bound for Rangoon, the headquarters of the BRP, the nerve-centre of the revolution, the fortress which the British still held stubbornly at that time.

Bo Ne Win and his comrade took the train at Hninpale station and arrived in Rangoon on February 2. Wearing old clothes and with a towel wrapped round his head, Bo Ne Win ran into Ko Aye Maung, with whom he had shared an apartment on 35th Street. It was not safe to exchange more than a few words in public; Ko Aye Maung therefore handed his long lost friend the key to his house in Shwegondaing. When they met in privacy there were many questions to ask of each other, much news to exchange. "How's Mya Than?" was one of the first questions Bo Ne Win asked, remembering their other room-mate of the 35th Street days. "He is dead," was the sad reply.

Thakin Nyi and several other associates were in jail. Those who had not been jailed were lying low, and it was difficult to run them down to their lairs. Bo Ne Win went to Kamayut looking for Thakin Khin Maung. A suspicious, frightened elderly woman drove him off saying, "Go away, no Thakin Khin Maung lives here." The next man whom Bo Ne Win sought was Ko Kyaw Nyein, an organizer of the BRP, who worked as an appraiser at the Customs House. Ko Than Maung of the Home Department went to see Ko Kyaw Nyein and fixed a meeting on the Shwedagon invoking the name of Ko Thein Pe, a mutual friend. The meeting led Bo Ne Win to the dens of the BRP. There, among the regulars were Thakins Mya, Kyaw Nyein, Ba Swe, Ba Hein, Tin, Chit, and Pu; Saya Hla Maung, once of the *Yetat,* Ko Hla Maung of the RUSU; Aung Gyi, who worked in the Defence Department as a clerk; Maung Maung, a medical student, who read up the stolen training manuals and served as an instructor in the use of small arms and the art of guerrilla war; Ba Swe (Rangoon), a sullen, scowling young man, intense yet Bohemian. Thakin Chit managed a Co-operative Store in Yegyaw quarter on 49th Street; the shop was also a convenient transit camp for young Thakins such as Tin Mya who took assigned tasks, under assumed names, observing iron discipline. The Varsity Co-operative Store in Scott Market was another BRP nest. There, men like Ko Kyaw Nyein, Ko Aye Kyaw, Ko Tun Ohn, T. K. Boon, and Ko Ba Gyan raised money—honest or otherwise—to supply the BRP with the sinews of war—hid comrades, took messages, ran errands.

Bo Ne Win and Toke Shwe, a young comrade assigned to serve as his aide, made one bold attempt to rescue Thakin prisoners who were being moved from Tharrawaddy jail to Mandalay. Information was received by Thakin Chit at the underground headquarters that the prisoners were to be brought down by train and transferred to the Mandalay Mail at the Rangoon central station. Thakins Nu, Soe, Than Tun and several others were reported to be in the party. Bo Ne Win and his aide found the station heavily guarded. Two carriages were reserved for the prisoners and a cordon of guards was thrown round the carriages. The rescue party of two walked in, mingled with the crowds, and quietly led away ten prisoners who were at the tail-end of the line just as they were being transferred from one platform to the other. Thakin Htain Win, U Tun Maung (New Burma) and a Thakin Buddhist monk were among the ten who were rescued. The rest were packed away to Mandalay where they languished in jail until Japanese bombs broke down the walls and delivered them.

The arrival of Bo Ne Win and a few of the thirty comrades, with some .22 pistols and cash, inspired the BRP to set out on a grand venture. Ko Kyaw Nyein, with his winning smile, was given the task of wooing Burmese soldiers of the few rifles battalions to come over. When the men came in with their arms, a force could be organized to fall upon the British troops then dispersed over a sector between Rangoon and Tharrawaddy, to Daik-U and Pegu. Decisive victory might not be obtained, the BRP modestly agreed, but blows could be struck, which would make definite contributions to victory.

Ko Kyaw Nyein went out merrily on his mission of seduction, riding bicycles which he had begged, borrowed or stolen from people. He was fairly successful. Once, without prior notice to his associates, he brought a man in uniform to a BRP hideout. The associates thought that it was a police raid, and that Kyaw Nyein had been caught. Someone sounded the alarm; all ran; one jumped out of the window and landed on his knee. Kyaw Nyein wanted to create an impression with his comrades; he succeeded.

A section of men from the Burma Rifles and a Havildar (officer holding the Governor's commission) agreed to come over. The next move was to pick them up at a rendezvous in Mingladon, off their barracks, and transport them to Tharrawaddy, the grouping area from which the BRP planned to strike. Trucks were needed for the move, and Ko Kyaw Nyein, dressed as a police officer, accompanied by Thakins Pu and Mya Thein, and Yebaw Toke Shwe went about to steal some. The party, by using straight-faced bluff, acquired one from the Road Transport Department. Encouraged and emboldened by the success, the party went to the Boat Club on the Royal Lakes to pick up some army trucks which were parked outside. Here, however, the guards were more sharp and fired a few shots at the prowlers who had to beat a hasty retreat. Bo Ne Win went ahead to Letpadan to organize.

Things went well until, in Tharrawaddy, a British army officer seized the truck. Fortunately, the Burma Rifles men had been safely dispersed by then, and Bo Ne Win, Ko Kyaw Nyein and party decided to walk back the 75 miles to Rangoon to recruit more men. It was a long walk; they started out under cover of dusk, at about 7 p.m., and reached Okkan around 2 a.m. The police at an outpost on the approaches of the town were suspicious, but the comrades told a convincing story that they were staff of a government department who had gone out in advance to make preparations for the evacuation of their office from Rangoon. The police gave the news that gangs of bandits were at large on the road ahead, and suggested that the comrades should rest at the outpost till daybreak. The suggestion was gratefully taken, for the comrades needed to stretch their tired limbs. In the morning they marched on, to hear, at Taikkyi that martial law had been declared and groups of people might be fired upon at sight. The party decided to break up, and make for Rangoon separately.

Bo Ne Win and Yebaw Toke Shwe followed the railway track, which was rather lonely, for few trains passed. Toke Shwe limped along, his feet badly swollen. Bo Ne Win did the scouting and the fetching of food and water from the villages. At Hmawbi the aide wanted to rest, but Bo Ne Win urged him on. They snatched a few hours of sleep under the shrubs, then pushed on. In the morning they reached Hlawga, just as a train pulled in, headed for Rangoon. It was a crowded train, with people sitting on the roof and clinging to windows. Bo Ne Win made a dash for the train, but Toke Shwe could only wobble along behind; so he stayed too, and the two of them slowly walked on. Tired and hungry, the two entered Kamayut at last, and begged for food and water from an old lady in a hut. The University campus was occupied by the Indian troops, and some sentries had to be passed in cutting their way to Bauktaw, but the two made it without any mishap. Back in Bauktaw, reunited with their associates, Bo Ne Win and Yebaw Toke Shwe ate large meals and fell asleep.

Thakin Chit soon left for Pegu to direct operations in that area. Bo Ne Win took charge of the BRP headquarters in Rangoon. U Shain and U Zaw Weik, pioneer physical culturists, brought food to the camp. British troops blew up some parts of Rangoon and left the city to the looters. Fires broke out here and there. Bo Ne Win and party organized to take over the administration of the city, restore law and order, and make ready for the arrival of the BIA. Buildings lay empty; there was no shortage of accommodation. The Methodist high school on Signal Pagoda Road, the Park Hotel, the Devon Court, and the row of buildings on both sides of the road were prepared to accommodate the BIA. Shops were open; people took what they wanted, and threw away in the streets things they did not want. Do not steal, do not rob, Bo Ne Win warned his men. Do not forget our mission, he always reminded them. Respect the lives and properties of the citizens, he told them. He gave his men sufficient pocket-money, and expected them to pay for what they wanted, in that city of free-for-all. Once a Thakin member of the headquarters brought back a case of whisky, pleased and proud with his rare acquisition, prepared for a few days of intoxicated bliss. Bo Ne Win kicked away the bottles, and sternly scolded the man for his indulgence. There was a war to be fought, and it would not be won with whisky.

On March 7, 1942, the first Japanese troops appeared in Taukkyant and Mingladon. Okuda, a young Japanese officer, and some

40 BIA men were in the spearhead of that thrust to Rangoon. On receiving news that the forward elements of the BIA had arrived, Bo Ne Win and Toke Shwe took a bus and drove out to Mingladon to fetch them. The meeting, which took place beyond Mingladon, was happy. The BIA soldiers, after their march, were tired and covered with dust. They were glad to have a bus ride home.

5

The main BIA columns came into Rangoon soon afterwards. "We marched in three columns," wrote Bo Mogyoe, "I commanded the main column, with Aung San as my chief of staff, and we had 2,300 men and 300 tons of equipment with us, and we marched across rough terrain. We made good speed. Aung San and I wanted to enter Rangoon first, ahead of the Japanese army, and we drove through British lines, fought a few actions, reached Pegu on the 1st March, and Rangoon on the 10th."[4]

From Victoria Point, low down south of Burma, through Mergui and Tavoy, one column ascended. Another marched through Myawaddy, and yet another through Papun and Pa-an. All the columns converged on Rangoon where, Bo Mogyoe had promised, the tri-colour flag of the Dobama Asi-ayone—minus, of course, the hammer and sickle—now adopted as the banner of the BIA would be unfurled on the flagmast of the Government House, and Burma's independence proclaimed. The columns sent out scouting patrols, or made brief diversions, but the destination was Rangoon. The ranks of the army became swollen with recruits from the villages and the towns through which it passed. Men, young and old, found the call irresistible. For more than a century—since, in fact, the days of Maha Bandoola who resisted the British in the war of 1824—the glory of Burmese arms had dimmed. There had been no victories, only defeats. Worse than mere defeat, there had been this long, dark mood of defeatism. Now the BIA was redeeming it all, in the buoyant spirit of victory. So thought the thousands who joined the columns that marched over hill and through jungle, that waded or swam the rivers and the creeks, and ultimately, in open country, through the paddy fields, leaving behind them clouds of dust. Often, the BIA troops would march

[4] *Aung San of Burma*, p. 58.

through the fields in several directions, raising great volumes of dust—the "smoke-screen" the Japanese called them—and then retire and do it all over again in another place. This gave the impression to British units, whose morale was sinking fast, that hordes of Japanese troops were upon them. Rumour was another weapon which the BIA skilfully employed. People in Pegu and Shwegyin heard with awe that a great Mongolian army led by one Bo Mogyoe, a Burmese prince, a direct descendant of Prince Myingun, was marching in with the Japanese. The great army might turn out to be no more than a platoon of BIA soldiers, dressed in shorts, breeches or longyi, wearing the tricolour arm-band, bearing assorted arms—from rifles and machine-guns left behind by the British troops, and arms of Japanese issue, to sword and spear which had been forged by the Burmese black-smiths. It was a motley army, moving on its feet, riding on bul-lock-carts, elephants and horses. All types of men joined it. Men who were afire with patriotism, driven by ideal. Men with loot and plunder in mind, or who had old scores to settle; men who were running away from the law, or from nagging wives.

There were skirmishes here and there between the BIA and the British troops which were on the retreat. There was an en-counter near the Sittang river where the British held the bridge, then blew it up, leaving some of their troops on the other side. In Shwegyin which Bo Saw Aung and a company of BIA occu-pied, Indian troops returned to encircle the BIA and a battle broke out in which Bo Saw Aung fell. These and a few other brief en-counters, were all that stood in the way of the BIA in its race to Rangoon.

More serious encounters took place between the BIA and troops of the Japanese 15th Army which took command of the Burma campaign. The Army itself came under Field-Marshal Juichi Terauchi who had his headquarters in Saigon. Two divisions, the 33rd which had been fighting in China, and the 55th made up the Army whose first task was to group and stabilize in Siam. Policy at the Imperial Headquarters at first seemed to have been un-certain as to whether the 15th should enter Burma. When the war went so well for the Japanese forces in the region, it became too tempting for the makers of high command policy to stay away from Burma. Thus, Lt-General Shojiro Iida, commanding the 15th

Army, went in. Once Burma became an operation, the role of the Minami Kikan and the BIA lost its importance to the regular soldiers who tended to look upon Bo Mogyoe himself, with his self-bestowed jump promotion from colonel to general, as an adventurer who had only some nuisance value. Bo Mogyoe was undeterred. He quarrelled with the staff officers at the Army HQ, and often argued with Iida himself that the whole operation should be called off because it was unnecessary, wasteful, and against the pledges that he, Bo Mogyoe, had made to the Burmese. But it was a futile thing to stop the Army which had started moving in according to plan.

The BIA entered Tavoy and set up a "peace preservation committee" to undertake the administration of the town. The 15th Army did not like that very much. The 55th Division, under Lt-General Takeuchi, entered Moulmein about the same time as a BIA unit led by Captain Kawashima and Bo Bala. The BIA prepared to establish a committee, but the Hiraoka organization of the 15th Army appeared on the scene to organize military administration. Kawashima did not possess sufficient weight to prevail against the Hiraoka people. In the eyes of the Japanese fighting troops, the Hiraoka organ had more regular status than the motley BIA and its Japanese irregulars. Terakura, the general staff officer of the division at Moulmein, suggested that Bo Mogyoe should settle the issue with Takeuchi, but Bo Mogyoe had pushed on. Thus, Moulmein came under military administration. To the BIA this was evidence of Japanese duplicity.

"Our first regret came," Bo Ne Win recalled in a famous broadcast made on May 7, 1945, when, after leading the resistance forces in the Delta area, he arrived in Rangoon to organize, "with the fall of Moulmein. Doubts began to awaken in Burmese minds when the Japanese for the first time broke their promise for declaring Burma's independence and handing over the administration of the town to the Burmese themselves. Since that time began discussions among the Burmese regarding the questionable character of Japanese promises."[5]

If Moulmein was bad, Rangoon was worse. The BIA did get

[5] This broadcast was first printed in *The New Burma in the New World*, Rangoon, 1946, and is often reprinted in the English newspapers on Resistance Day special issues.

into the city before the 15th Army arrived; but the race, it turned
out, was not for the quick, it went to the strong. The Japanese
Army was bigger, stronger, better-organized, and backed with
more power all the way from Rangoon to Tokyo. It was the 15th
Army, therefore, which occupied the Government House where
a department of military administration, headed by Colonel Yoshio
Nasu, started business from March 15. The BIA, quartered along
Signal Pagoda Road where Bo Ne Win had thoughtfully taken
a whole row of buildings, was a force under the 15th Army's
command.

The unfurling of the BIA flag at the Government House was,
therefore, out. So too the proclamation of Burma's independence.
Bo Mogyoe, who had enjoyed his role of deliverer, was furious.
He told Bo Aung San and the Burmese comrades that they should
go ahead and declare Burma was free; if the Japanese Army made
trouble, fight them, he said. "At one point," Bo Mogyoe remembered in later years, "I felt so desperate that I called in my Japanese officers and asked them if they would follow me if I fought
the Japanese. I also met Aung San and his colleagues and asked
them to rise against the Japanese, and Aung San said they would
not dream of doing that as long as I was there." Bo Mogyoe's
unrestrained utterances were heard in Tokyo. "Lt-Gen. Muto of
the General Staff came to visit Burma," Bo Mogyoe recalled, "and
he asked me if it was true I wanted to proclaim Burmese independence. I said it was, and he said that would be premature.
Muto was hanged after the war as a war criminal."[6]

The BIA did hold a parade in Rangoon in the Burma Athletic
Association football grounds and 10,000 troops marched past
the saluting base on which Bo Mogyoe and Bo Aung San stood.
Bo Ne Win, who had spent much time organizing with the BRP,
was without proper uniform or sword. A young Japanese officer offered to lend him his sword, for a senior officer of Bo Ne
Win's standing would not be properly dressed without one. Several of the thirty comrades were now most impressively dressed in
high boots that shone, in riding breeches; they carried sword, binoculars, revolver, whistle and whatnot. Those who were most fan-
cifully dressed were often those who had done the minimum of
work or fighting. Aung San looked grim and shabby: he had prob-

6 *Aung San of Burma*, p. 58.

ably been wearing the same shirt and breeches for the last few weeks. There was hard work ahead, and this parade was no victory parade; this was not the end of the journey but only the beginning. There was need for courage, perseverance, endurance; not much need for sword and fancy uniform in this parade. Bo Ne Win declined the loan of sword with a smile, and took part in the parade, erect and austere.

6

Marching orders came soon after the parade. Bo Mogyoe relinquished command of the BIA—though not without some persuasion from Aung San and the comrades. There was a dramatic scene at Bo Mogyoe's residence to which the comrades were summoned one morning. Bo Mogyoe came down the stairs, dressed in a silk kimono. Bo Aung San, Bo Ne Win and the comrades stood up and bowed. "Sit down," Bo Mogyoe grunted, and then threw down on the table a letter which the comrades had written him. He then drew his sword and with its tip pushed the letter towards the comrades. It was a tense moment, and Bo Aung San gripped his sword. Bo Ne Win cautioned him; there were Japanese sentries all round the place. Then Bo Mogyoe said: "You are all like my sons. You must not write to me like this. Come and talk to me, letters are not good. But whatever you say in the letter is correct!"

On the following day, Bo Mogyoe issued an order appointing Bo Aung San commander of the BIA, which was organized into two divisions. The 1st Division, which the Japanese called the Kaga Corps, was placed under Bo Zeya (whose Japanese name was Kaga). The 2nd Division, or the Takasugi Corps, was given to Bo Ne Win (Takasugi, the Tall Pine Tree). Japanese commanders handed over to the Burmese, and took on new roles as "advisers". Bo Mogyoe was content to remain the "father of the BIA", the military statesman who worried about making governments, high policy, and independence. Captain Kawashima served as adviser to Aung San. Captain Noda was adviser to Bo Zeya; Captain Kitajima went with Bo Ne Win.

The two divisions were ordered by the 15th Army to march up north, along either side of the Irrawaddy river. The 33rd was

the Japanese division to which the BIA was responsible. The
Japanese Army saw to it that the BIA did not win too much glory
in battle. It was, for the most part, slow plodding up the poor
roads for the BIA, or slow sailing in the big boats up the river.
It was, however, good training for the BIA, a good test of the
strength of its soldiers and commanders. Aung San and his associates had decided that they had to build a strong army which
would become not merely the right arm of the nation, but its hope
and a living symbol of defiance. The BIA could rouse the people,
forge national unity, and fight through to final victory. This resolve kept the young commanders going. This was the message
they took to the people.

Dropping in at Henzada, a Delta town, Bo Ne Win met town
elders, including Karen leaders, and U Mya and U Aung Tha
who were both of U Saw's Myochit party at that time, and spoke
earnestly on the need for unity. The only thing that the Japanese
respected was strength, Bo Ne Win told the elders, drawing from
his own personal experience and knowledge. Unity between the
Karens and the Burmese who were so mixed and mingled in the
Delta, between young people and the elders, between civil servants and the various classes of citizens, between the BIA and
the people, that unity was the only source of the needed strength.
The elders agreed that they must all work together.[7]

Off Shwedaung, on the road to Prome, BIA troops collided
head-on with the rear-guard of a retreating British column. The
BIA launched waves of frontal attack, to be mown down by machine-guns. The British had a few tanks left, and these were skilfully employed to beat off the attackers. The action was heated;
casualties were heavy on both sides. One Japanese officer, Lt.
Hirayama, whom the BIA soldiers called Bo Mokeseik for his
luxuriant growth of whiskers, fell. Another Japanese casualty was
Hiranobu who had been with the thirty comrades since Hainan.
Among the Burmese who went down at Shwedaung were students, teachers, boys from the farms, men who had come from
as far as Tavoy, Chiangmai or Bangkok. The battle of Shwedaung
and Bo Yan Naing became a subject for songs.

Most of the march was plain plodding. There were logistical

---

[7] Gen. Ne Win's *Statements of Policy on the National Races,* (in Burmese), Rangoon, 1964, p. 64.

problems to take care of, though not too many, for the troops lived off the land. Movement was slow, and most of the units were within hailing distance, so that communications did not pose difficulties. Bo Aung San would meet his field commanders, Bo Ne Win and Bo Zeya, and give a few simple orders. That was enough communication for a few days, for the orders would take that much time to execute. He would also go round and visit the camps, talk with the men and their officers, and with a quiet chuckle boost their morale.

Aung San had said on Hainan island that Bo Ne Win would be his right hand in the fight for freedom. The march from Rangoon to Myitkyina and Bhamo in the far north, lasting nearly two months, showed up nothing to shake Aung San's faith. The two men were, in fact, alike in many ways. They had the same strength of character, the same unbending will. Both were puritan and perfectionist, practical and realistic at the same time. They cared little for the welcoming parties, the eulogistic speeches. On a few occasions each on his own gave startled elders of welcoming towns a good tongue-lashing for giving him a great feast while leaving the soldiers hungry. The men came first with Bo Aung San and Bo Ne Win; the army came first, for it was their politics, their mission. The two commanders had neither time nor patience for the privilege-seekers—of whom there were many in every village or town. They invited members of the Dobama Asi-ayone to join the BIA, rather than chase the illusion of power in the peace committees which would be short-lived anyhow. Toughen yourselves, learn to fight, they told the Thakin comrades. The response, however, was not always good. Many of the members wanted power, or even the pretence of it, if only briefly to hold. Some Thakin members who were put on the committees immediately started to swagger. Some walked the streets with two pistols in the belt—status symbols to show that now they belonged to the ruling elite. Some went round with followers holding the golden umbrella over their heads. "We belong to royalty now," one Thakin, appointed headman of a village, was heard to observe to his daughter, "you should stop mixing with the common crowd."

The great response to the BIA came from the young students —sons of peasants, government officers or clerks—farmers and

8

village people, workers in the towns, school teachers. Patriotism, it was seen, was not the monopoly of the slogan-shouting politicians.

The two commanders also showed one quality: integrity. There were many temptations—power, riches, women, all there for the taking. But neither of them yielded, nor even showed a flicker of interest in the distractions. Lesser men, including a few of the thirty comrades, succumbed. Some grabbed gold. Some abused power to serve the interests of the flatterers. Some strutted in fancy uniform, complete with gold braid and plumage, and went courting.

Such practices were not for Bo Aung San or Bo Ne Win. Bo Aung San moved about without pomp or ceremony, accompanied by a staff officer. In the middle of the march, Aung San became bored with the clumsy uniform and paraphernalia; so he wore his khaki shirt and Burmese longyi, packing the uniform away in a bundle. That was the dress in which the commander-in-chief made his triumphal progress.

Bo Ne Win, taut, trim, and tall, dressed simply, worked hard, punctual, thorough, untiring. He was level-headed; no flatterers could sway him. He was correct with money. Funds supplied to his division were carefully accounted for. Funds collected were turned over without delay to GHQ. His soldiers must not steal, rob, or extract "gifts" from grudging donors, but they were well-fed and well looked after. To a large extent the division had to rely on food parcels given by the villages, or supplies that were locally bought. There was no shortage of people who wanted to wine and dine the commanders, but Bo Ne Win preferred to live and eat with his men.

Bo Mogyoe visited the troops now and then, taking time off from high politics. His influence on affairs was on the wane; Hiraoka and the 15th Army were on top of him. But Bo Mogyoe did not give up. He appointed Thakin Tun Oke as the chief administrator, and kept on issuing many directives addressed to the people. There were too many directives coming from too many sources; few people read them. With the help of Nagai, the Japanese *bonze,* Bo Mogyoe also tried to win over the Buddhist monks with whom he conferred in a Rangoon meeting. This, and other such moves, did not please the Japanese Army HQ. Once on a visit to the troops which were around Prome, Bo Mogyoe accompanied Bo Ne Win to Paungdale and Paukkaung. The villages warmly welcomed them. Conversations with U Po Kha and the elders of Bo Ne Win's family impressed Bo Mogyoe deeply. "Now I know why the BIA is so successful," he told Kitajima back at camp, "its leaders come from such good families with such broad support. Ne Win's father can get 1000 men for us if we need them; he is so influential in his area. Don't let Ne Win run too many risks: Burma needs him."

Kitajima was an able officer and a veteran of the China wars. He knew Siam well and was specially assigned to the Minami Kikan. Because of his intelligence and sharpness, he was specially chosen to be Bo Ne Win's adviser, for Bo Ne Win was held in high esteem by the Japanese Army HQ and regarded as one who should be helped as well as watched. "Bo Ne Win's division marched side by side with the Japanese forces aiming at Gangaw," Kitajima wrote, remembering the long march. "When we were marching along the Irrawaddy river above Prome, many BIA soldiers died of cholera. Bo Ne Win took the trouble of treating the dying soldiers, using his own medical knowledge and personally organized the burning of the dead—while I myself was very much afraid of contracting the deadly disease and kept myself away. I first had doubts about his ability to command a division in the battlefield because I knew he had received training only for a short period, but I admired him when I found he could lead the soldiers without trouble. He was a great disciplinarian and very diligent. Amidst all odds he would get the troops ready to move or do things an hour ahead of schedule."

7

The gathering of the political clans took place in Mandalay in March. The BRP was there, represented by Ko Kyaw Nyein, Ko Thein Pe, and Ko Khin Maung Gale who was a teacher in the National High School addicted strongly to leading students' strikes. In jail were Thakins Nu, Soe, Ba Hein, Kyaw Sein, Mya Thwin and others, and leaders of Dr Ba Maw's Sinyetha party and other parties. The politicians in the jail felt deeply frustrated, feeding all the time on rumours, while the war came up. Thakin

Soe, with his high passions, fumed and fretted because he was there, caged, while he should be out in the field rousing the people and fighting the Japanese Fascists. Behind the bars he could make war only in his dreams—or nightmares.

General Wang, a Chinese emissary, visited the Thakin group in jail. He had known Thakin Nu in Rangoon and in Chungking which the latter had visited on a goodwill mission. Deedok U Ba Choe, who also had Chinese contacts, had asked Wang to look up the young Thakin leaders, cheer them up, and take them out to China if possible. Wang was more than willing. Thakin Nu had his reservations. He explained to Wang that the Governor must get a promise from London that Burma would be given her independence as soon as the war was over; if the promise was forthcoming the Thakins would fight with the British and the Chinese against the Japanese with clear conscience, for their war would be a patriotic war. Thakin Soe was willing to fight the Japanese on any terms, for the German invasion of Russia had given him the clear ideological answer.

While Thakin Nu was talking with General Wang about resolutions, pledges, declarations, the BIA was marching up along the Irrawaddy, and the Japanese forces were pushing north through the Shan mountain ranges. By the time Thakin Nu and party decided to get out to Chungking the Japanese had blocked the roads. "So our trip to Chungking petered out at the foot of Maymyo hill," Thakin Nu wrote, "and we were back at the cholera-stricken central jail in Mandalay." It took the party a few more weeks and some patient negotiations with the jailer before they were able to get out into the deserted city.[8]

Across the river, at Sagaing, General Slim was trying to hold the remnants of the Burma Corps together in an orderly fighting withdrawal. A party of Burmese officials "dressed in morning coats, pin-stripe trousers and gray topis" called on the general and presented "a neatly typed resolution duly proposed, seconded and passed unanimously at a largely attended public meeting." They asked for an assurance that no military operations would be carried out in the hills, held in veneration by the Buddhists, and at that time a haven for the war refugees.

"I was terribly sorry for these people," General Slim wrote.

8 U Nu, *Burma under the Japanese*, p. 13.

"They were all high officials of the Burma government, commissioners, secretaries, judges, and the like; their world had tumbled about their ears, but they still clung to the democratic procedure of resolutions, votes, and the rest that we had taught them. They brought me their pathetic little bit of paper as if it were a talisman." Slim could only say that he himself had no wish for military operations in the hills, but the Japanese general might not be so obliging as to agree; the Burmese party went away polite but puzzled. "The impressiveness of the proceedings was somewhat marred," the general recalled, "by one gentleman who came back and asked could he not be issued with a six months' advance of pay?"[9]

Dr Ba Maw broke out of Mogok jail about this time. It took him some planning, some help from friends outside and from his wife who had been staying in town for the rescue. Then on the appointed day Dr Ba Maw slipped out to be picked up on the road by his wife who was waiting for him in a car. They drove out to a Shan village and waited for the proper time for the leader to step out onto the stage. Dr Ba Maw had a keen sense of the right and dramatic timing; he knew his time would come. Ko Kyaw Nyein searched him out and urged him to go back to Mandalay and join hands with the BRP group. Dr Ba Maw declined with smiles. With the group he would be one among many. Alone in the solitary mountains he would be more vividly seen as the one without whom the many would be lost. Besides, he could not go to the Japanese; they must come to him.[10]

And Dr Ba Maw was right. The search for him became a special task with the Japanese Army. General Tojo in Tokyo wanted him for he was the one political leader of sufficient stature to be appointed leader of the government in Burma.

General Iida wanted him, for some kind of government must be set up and a front-man was needed. Bo Mogyoe, Thakin Tun Oke, the peace committees, all these were becoming a little too much for Iida; he wanted something simple which he could understand.

---

[9] Field-Marshal Slim, *Defeat into Victory,* David McKay Co. Inc., New York, 1961, p. 70.

[10] Dr Ba Maw, *It Happened during Thingyan,* in *The Nation,* April 13, 1964.

Bo Aung San, Bo Let Ya, Bo Ne Win and the leaders among
the thirty comrades had agreed even in Hainan that Dr Ba Maw
should be given leadership of the wartime government. He was,
after all, the leader of the Freedom Bloc. The Japanese themselves, in sounding out the comrades, had hinted their preference
for him. If they must have him, they must. There was no need
for making an issue of what was, in calm analysis, a matter of
no great importance. The vital thing was to forge national unity.

The debate assumed urgency in Rangoon where the appearance of the military administration organs made for more confusion. In Mandalay, when the commanders of the BIA, the
Thakin leaders of different political thoughts, the BRP and other
groups met for the first time after a long separation, the debate
assumed larger proportions, covering wider range of problems,
generating greater heat. Some Thakin leaders urged Bo Aung
San to take the leadership of the nation as a Generalissimo, but
he was uninterested. It was not Aung San's ambition to lead a
puppet government. "You may have your head in the clouds," he
used to advise his associates, "but at least have your feet on the
ground." Aung San saw that whoever took on the leadership of
the country under the Japanese occupation would only have to
grapple with petty problems, wielding some pretence of power,
while the Japanese Army would make the big decisions reserving
to themselves the real power. The leader of the government would
therefore come out of the war exhausted, tainted as collaborator,
politically finished. Bo Aung San therefore decided to stay with
the army, build it, and prepare himself, for the right time and the
decisive struggle. "I am not ready, the job is too big," Aung San
told those who wanted him to become Generalissimo.

Thakin Ba Sein saw the severe limitations under which a war-
time regime must operate, and the perils. He realized that the
fortunes of war must change, the Japanese must fade away. But
a politician must stay in politics, move and manoeuvre in changing circumstances. He would, therefore, join a government, not
as an end in itself, but as a means to something better in the
future. He could not, however, accept Dr Ba Maw as the leader.
"How much had that man sacrificed in the national cause?" he
asked.

On May 13, 1942, the Japanese Kempetai made contact with

Dr Ba Maw. The "rescue" was suitably played up for publicity purposes. Colonel Furuki of the 15th Army and Colonel Hiraoka urged General Iida to appoint Ba Maw, without any delay, as head of a provisional administration which the Army was preparing to establish.

At Kyunhla in Shwebo district, Bo Aung San and Bo Ne Win decided to fall back to Mandalay to participate in political discussions. The future government of the country, the choice of leader, the future of the BIA, these were the big and urgent issues. Bo Zeya was left in charge of the march to Myitkyina and Bhamo, fixed as the grouping point of the troops. At Yinmabin in Monywa district, they met Thakin Than Tun who had just come out of jail, but there was only enough time to give him some news and drop a few hints on the situation. They ran into Thakin Thein Pe in Shwebo. Thein Pe, after circulating anti-Japanese pamphlets, was bound for Calcutta, which was some way away, and the Japanese were already hunting for him. Bo Ne Win, who was neither aware nor informed of the situation, was asked to take Thein Pe in his car to Amarapura where the BIA was assembling. He complied, and the drive was, fortunately, without mishap. The Ava bridge had been blown down, and the Irrawaddy had to be crossed by ferry. Bo Ne Win gave the code word to the Japanese guards and the ferry took them across. It was only much later, when Bo Ba Thein of Henzada who conducted Thein Pe part of the way to Calcutta returned and reported to him, that Bo Ne Win discovered that the ride to Amarapura had been a really perilous one.

Iida met the political leaders in Maymyo. Thakins Mya, Nu, Than Tun, Kodaw Hmaing, Ba Sein and Tun Oke were there. Bo Aung San, Bo Ne Win and Bo Let Ya represented the BIA at the meeting. Iida asked for the views of the leaders on the appointment of Dr Ba Maw as chief administrator. Thakin Ba Sein and Thakin Tun Oke spoke strongly in dissent. The BIA commanders said that as Iida seemed to have made the choice, they would raise no objection. Thakin Kodaw Hmaing, who had expressed himself in forceful words in private councils against Ba Maw, kept his silence at the meeting. Iida, and in fact Tojo in Tokyo, had already made the choice, and the meeting was mere formality.

Dr Ba Maw complained to Bo Mogyoe that some BIA soldiers were treating members of his Sinyetha party rather roughly. Bo Mogyoe promised instant action. It was true that the BIA had been high-handed in places, but Ba Maw's complaints were in token of his authority, to show who was the boss. Bo Mogyoe's respectful response also acknowledged not the bigness of issue, but the fact that Ba Maw was the chosen one. Both men were good actors, at home only in grand roles. That of Ba Maw was now beginning; Bo Mogyoe's was just about played out.

With the Japanese Army, however, Dr Ba Maw stood firm on the need for a strong national army. The BIA might have its faults, but it could be reorganized. There were, inevitably, bad elements in it; they could be weeded out. Bo Aung San and his commanders should be given an opportunity to build the army, using the good elements in the BIA as the nucleus. There were hard times ahead, Ba Maw knew, and without a strong national army the nation would be weak, helpless, vulnerable.

Iida's own respect for Aung San, and the strong support given by Ba Maw, helped to save at least the hard core of the BIA. Troops which had reached Bhamo were ordered to regroup in Mandalay. The campaign was over: it had been brief, all too brief. The British had withdrawn; the Japanese Army was in occupation of the land.

8

When the BIA ended its long march, it had rallied to its banner some 23,000 men. That was an unwieldy number for a force raised so quickly in the dust and din of battle. The army attracted the good and the bad elements, the best as well as the worst. More, it also provided an outlet for pent-up passions and deep-rooted prejudices. Troops committed excesses here and there because they were intoxicated with power or from sheer over-zealousness or short-sight. Mistakes were made which amounted at times to expensive blunders. Summary "justice" was done in the field which sometimes amounted to cold-blooded cruelty. Yet, all in all, discipline was maintained by the commanders of the BIA, and the troops gave valuable service to the people by protecting their homes and keeping law and order in the troubled transition. By its very nature and mission the BIA made the people feel good and hold their heads high with pride.

One ugly incident happened in the Delta. There, in some parts, Karens live with Burmese in villages, or Karen villages flourish as good neighbours of Burmese. The British had taken Karens into racial battalions long before they started to admit Burmese recruits. When the British forces withdrew, Karen soldiers returned to their villages with their arms. These soldiers, taking propaganda for pledge, believed that the retreat was only a tactical withdrawal. They therefore considered it to be their duty to resist the Japanese and the BIA. Besides the soldiers, many of the Karens themselves, classified by the British as "loyal", felt they had to live up to that reputation. Some elders, and some of those who had been associated with the rulers and the missionaries, felt that way and they wielded great influence on the villagers.

The BIA marched in, spoiling for a fight, searching for glory. Some Karen villages in the Delta, veritable fortresses, appeared to the BIA as a challenge. Clashes occurred near Bassein and Myaungmya between the BIA and the Karens, which soon assumed the proportions of a small war. Whole families, whole villages, were destroyed in the slaughter in which both sides took part, driven by the fiercest passions that the war had unleashed. In Rangoon, the BIA, a few thousand strong, was left under the command of Bo Setkya. The commander, however, spent most of his time at play, with little time to spare for troops, while Bo Kyaw Zaw, a younger man, supervised their training. Bo Aung San, Bo Ne Win, Bo Let Ya, Bo Zeya, and the senior staff were up in the north, plodding on with the army.

Bo Mogyoe organized a punitive force which he planned to lead to Myaungmya. A conference in Maymyo called him away for a few days, and on his return he heard that parts of the Delta were already in flames. His favourite aide, Kimata, was killed on operations in the area, and this made Bo Mogyoe hopping mad. He was a frustrated man. He had missed his role of deliverer of Burma. He was Mogyoe only in name—and perhaps in legend, which would soon fade—but the "thunderbolt" had struck nothing, made no visible impact. Now he would show the Karens what the Mogyoe could do. Besides, there was Kimata to avenge.

When Bo Mogyoe reached Wakema by river-boat, the devasta-

tion in the area was clearly visible: dead bodies of Karens and
Burmese floated down the river. That was not enough, Bo Mogyoe
decided. The rebellion must be crushed completely. After planning a campaign all night, Bo Mogyoe ordered Bo Kyaw Zaw and
a regiment of the BIA into battle at dawn. Karen villages near
Wakema were the target. Bo Kyaw Zaw, trained and indoctrinated
in Hainan to execute orders without question, waged the battle
with thoroughness. Only much later did Bo Mogyoe discover that
it was not at Wakema but at Begayet near Bassein that Kimata
was killed. Such mistakes, he said with a shrug of the shoulders,
were bound to happen in war.

"The Delta incident was an expensive mistake, a great blunder,"
General Ne Win told Karen leaders several years later, "it opened
gaping wounds in Karen-Burmese relations which were hard to
heal. We tried our best, as you know, to heal the wounds during
the war. Even when they did, the scars remained."

There was another incident in the Shan State which was less
destructive, but perhaps nearly as damaging to the popularity of
the BIA. One young officer, leading a force of one hundred men,
went on a spree through the State. The forces looted and plundered. In Hsipaw, they broke into the palace of the chief helping
themselves freely to what valuable things they could find. The
officer then mounted the throne and cursed the "feudal lord" of
the palace in pithy language. The force went round wounding feelings left and right. In Lashio they shot cows in the market-place
for meat. When Bo Aung San and Bo Ne Win heard of the misdeeds of the force, they sent out a party in hot pursuit. It was,
however, too late. The mischief had been done, and when the party
caught up it found that the young officer had fled into the hills.
Later reports said that he renounced lay life and became a Buddhist monk.[11]

There were many wounds to heal, many scars to erase, many
incidents to live down. The wonder was not that there were so
many, but that there were not many more.

9

The BIA was reorganized without delay. Only 3,000 men were
to be retained out of the 23,000. The rest were to go home. The

[11] Gen. Ne Win's *Statements of Policy on the National Races,* p. 63.

selections were therefore strict; the partings were sad. The older
men were asked to go back to their professions and their families. Thus U Ba Than, an old lawyer from Thaton, "as wily an
old rogue as a small town lawyer could be," as a comrade affectionately described him, was going home after receiving a promotion in the field. So was Yodaya U Ba Thein, so called because
he joined the BIA in Siam (Yodaya-pyi). So were some 150 Siamese nationals who had joined up in Bangkok, Chiangmai, or
Kanburi; they had come a long way from home, and some did
not even know how to return.

Not the elderly only, but the young too must go, for only three
battalions were to be kept. The divisions, the regiments, all were
disbanding. Day after day, the men were lined up for the selections which Bo Ne Win supervised with swift eye, sure judgement,
and fine memory for faces and names. Many young boys wanted
to stay, and to them he was kind. While selecting the men, cadets
for the first officer training course to be organized at an academy
in Mingaladon were picked out. A young boy, so lean he was
willowy, stepped forward at one selection parade and asked to
be sent to the academy. His company commander, Bo Than Daing,
decided he was too young and much too small. "Step back", he
told the boy kindly, "step back and go home". The boy persisted,
and Bo Than Daing decided to stop the boy the only way he knew
how: he hit him hard across the cheek, the way the Japanese liked
to do. The boy reeled but did not fall. "Hey, stop it," shouted
Bo Ne Win, "let the young fellow go to the academy if he is so
keen." Thus, the young soldier, Mya Thaung, went to Mingaladon,
then on to Japan for higher military studies, and service with the
army through its many campaigns.

One by one, the many melted away, taking their little bundles
of clothes, storing away their precious memories of the great
march. But all was not lost. Those who went home had been
trained to fight. They had tasted victory; they were confident, un-
afraid. When time came for them to rise again they would be
ready.

The few remained, the hard core of the national army that must
be built, future commanders of the army and leaders of the nation. Aung San received a colonel's commission from the Emperor, ceremonially handed to him by General Iida, and was ap-

pointed commander-in-chief of the Burma Defence Army. Bo Ne
Win was made a major and given the 1st battalion, which marked
him out as number two in the chain of field command. The battalions were scattered. The 1st was sent out to Arakan to defend
the border alongside the Japanese troops, and to help in the construction of roads. Captain Kitajima went along as Bo Ne Win's
adviser.

The Minami Kikan was officially dissolved on July 10, 1942.
Some civilian members of the Kikan, such as Sugii, Mizutani and
Higuchi, had considered that its mission ended as soon as the
15th Army gained a firm foothold and established military ad-
ministration, and that Suzuki had been talking too much and too
loud without authority. Those soldiers in the Kikan who chose
to stay on—they were the majority—were absorbed into the 15th
Army HQ and assigned to the advisory group attached to the
BDA. Control over the BDA itself was retained by the Army
HQ.

Col. Suzuki was promoted to be a major-general and sent back
to Japan to command the Home Guard in the Honshu area. A
remarkable man, he had given a fine performance in a unique role
cast by history. Now the role was played; the curtain must fall,
for the stage must be cleared for other players, other parts.

On July 27 the BIA was officially wound up and the BDA inaugurated. The BIA was seven months old when it was disbanded.
It had been seventy days on road and river, from Rangoon to
Bhamo, in that brief career. The thirty comrades were no longer
thirty when the BDA was organized with base at Pyinmana. Bo
Moe had fallen in a skirmish at Htugyi; Bo Nyarna had been killed in action between Bilin and Papun; Bo Saw Aung had been
felled by a sniper in the battle of Shwegyin. Bo Mya Din died
of illness at a hospital in Chiangmai where he had to be left against
his loud protests just before the BIA began its march. Thakin
Than Tin never even got back to Bangkok, never set foot on Burmese soil again, for he died of illness in a hospital on Formosa
island. Bo Saung alias Bo Htain Win never seriously joined the
thirty; in Rangoon he went over to the Hiraoka Organ. Thakin
Tun Oke had neither heart nor stomach for the army; he went
only after political office. Thus the thirty had dwindled, and there
were those among the survivors who tended to stray, and those

who would rest on their laurels. But nourished by rich new blood, the BDA began to gain strength rapidly.

On August 1, the Executive Administration was installed with Dr Ba Maw as chief. There were nine other members of the Administration of which five were his former political associates: Dr Thein Maung, U Tun Aung, Bandoola U Sein, U Ba Win and U Hla Pe. The four remaining members were Thakins Tun Oke, Ba Sein, Mya, and Than Tun. Thakin Tun Oke was appointed Executive for Forests, while Thakin Ba Sein became Executive for Communications and Labour.

Schoolmates had joined the BIA in their scores partly out of friendship for Bo Aung San, Bo Ne Win, Bo Zeya and others. Ko Thi Han, a pious man who had regularly walked to the Shwedagon pagoda from the University hostel; Ko Tin Maung who liked to sing and dance in college, and later acquired fame as an actor and director in the A-1 Films; Ko Chin Sein, also of A-1, who became better known as Shwe Nyar Maung; several actors, such as Tin Ngwe, Chit Swe and Tha Gaung; Ko San Maung, the son of U Po We who kept racing stables; these and many more had marched with the BIA. When they were demobilised, some had jobs to go back to, some needed help in placement.

Bo Ne Win took Ko San Maung to Thakin Ba Sein's house and told the former political mentor to look after him. When Thakin Ba Sein became Executive for Communications, he sent Ko San Maung out to look for books, the bigger the better, dealing directly or remotely with the subject of communications. Books were scattered all over the town, for offices and libraries had been raided, stripped and sacked. San Maung, however, turned up with a postal manual and a telephone directory. Pleased, and satisfied that he was suitably equipped to run his department, Thakin Ba Sein went to work. He appointed Ko San Maung superintendent of posts with office in Mandalay. Neither he nor Ko San Maung knew what the duties of superintendent entailed. Undeterred, Ko San Maung hunted round for a few more books, then hurriedly left to assume charge before someone else could make a grab for the job.

5

The Resistance

1

Building an administration from scratch was an exciting job and Dr Ba Maw loved it. He had a notice published calling the civil servants back to duty. They were to report at the Secretariat at the latest by September's end. Just as in February and March all roads seemed to have led out of Rangoon, now they led back to the city. By boat, bus, or railway, the refugees returned, among them the thousands of civil servants eager to get back to work. Thousands of young graduates or college students also sought employment, for the colleges were closed and they could not remain idle.

The Secretariat was the employment exchange. Every morning the seekers would come, bringing their applications and the letters of recommendation from their Thakin friends or their local Sinyetha party. Some wore the "pinni" home-spun jacket in the hope that that might please the Thakin members of the administration. Some did better: they wore the baggy pants and the skull-cap which Dr Ba Maw preferred. No more, however, the European suit, for this was the Burmese Era and one must move with the times.

When Dr Ba Maw arrived, accompanied by his Japanese "advisers" and bodyguards, the applicants would move forward, hoping to catch his eye. A few who were more bold would follow him and say a few words in respectful greeting. The Leader would smile, wave to the crowd, then pass on.

For the plums of jobs the Thakins and the Sinyetha party fought at various levels including the "inner circle" which Dr Ba Maw informally gathered round him. The fight remained a principal occupation of the leaders for some time. The Thakins enjoyed the advantage of having U Kyaw Nyein as secretary to Dr Ba Maw. U Kyaw Nyein would arrange appointment orders for the signature of the Chief, placing those for nominees of the Sinyetha party on top. Dr Ba Maw would sign away, pleased with the "fair" distribution of jobs. After a few orders were signed, he would stop checking the papers carefully and thereby miss the fact that the remaining appointments went mainly to Thakins.

The spirit of the Administration was good. It was a big challenge to build a brand-new State out of the ashes. The Japanese simultaneously helped and hindered, willing to participate in the building, yet anxious that they might no longer be wanted after independence was proclaimed. Swarms of their advisers descended on the Secretariat. They followed Dr Ba Maw like his shadow. They followed the other members of the Administration as well. U Thein Maung, who became Minister for Justice later, adopted an effective method of keeping his adviser away. "Study all these statutes," he asked the faithful shadow, "and advise me on which of them should be abolished, which amended." The man took the volumes of the Burma Code away, never to return.

Despite the Japanese, despite the odds and the hardships, the Administration was put into shape in a few short months, and its writ began to run throughout the war-torn land. Men went to their posts without grumbling. They did their best in the performance of their duties. The Administration was without large resources; the staff sharpened their own resourcefulness to compensate. Supplies were poor; few things came in while the Japanese took out much of what they found. The people, and the public servants, learned to manage with what they had. Senior officials rode bicycles to office. Wearing "pinni" became common, not because that was what the Thakins used to wear, but because that was all that the people could get. When the bombs began to fall—over the cities they rained—government staff moved their offices to the monasteries or the rest-houses on the pagodas, and carried on. The salaries were poor. The Executives (later Ministers) received Rs. 1,200 a month; Supreme Court judges Rs. 1,000; Secretaries Rs. 800; Deputy Commissioners Rs. 600. The Japanese Army printed paper currency—in dollars and cents—and circulated them in large volumes. Labourers would get their paper money crisp and sweet-smelling, moist with fresh ink. Inflation was rapid. The price of a cup of tea climbed from $ 1 to $ 10 in no time. A bag of rice cost a few hundred. Medicine went off the market. Quinine for malaria, and sulphur ointments to relieve the skin diseases caused by undernourishment, were in great demand. But the people, and the public servants carried on without losing their sense of humour. Government staff managed by selling off silk and fine clothes of their pre-war wardrobes. Their wives sold their gold. Some people in high places and some staff in the districts were rumoured to have made some fortunes during the war, but they were few. The majority worked with inspiration, and the will to prove to the Japanese—and to themselves—that Burmans could run their own country.

"One Voice, One Blood, One Command!" That was the slogan which Dr Ba Maw coined. "Let us be strong, for strength is the only medicine," he said. He called for a New Order built on a new plan "radically different from the old democratic plan which was based on vote-value instead of labour value. A real plan, that is a revolutionary plan, must be built on labour-value whether it gets the votes or not. The votes must wait till the work is done and the peril is averted, when people may go back to their old political play-acting if they should still want to be amused that way."[1]

2

For many of the BIA commanders and leaders of the BRP and political groups the end of hostilities marked the beginning of the mating season. Physically exhausted after the endeavours, mentally elated that the danger of death had receded at least for the time being, they began to marry to get nursed, or go into the military hospital to ultimately marry the nurses.

Bo Aung San followed the latter course. In hospital he met Daw Khin Kyi, a comely nurse, whom he married after a whirlwind courtship. He who used to growl at the weddings of his officers or comrades that they were going soft now discovered that domestic life had its delights. Young officers, eager to get on with the revolution, wondered for many months whether their Supremo would emerge in time from his prolonged honeymoon.

[1] Dr Ba Maw's *New Order Plan in Burma,* 1944.

Mandalay was where the BIA stopped for several weeks which gave time enough to the officers to get married. Bo Zeya got married to a Mandalay girl. So did Bo Bala. Bo Let Ya married a girl from Pegu whose older sister was a fellow striker in 1936. U Kyaw Nyein was united with the girl whom he had loyally wooed in college. U Hla Maung was similarly successful.

In Rangoon the comrades, now established in office and power, lived in the Golden Valley which was once the home of Sir J. A. Maung Gyi, ministers and high officials in the colonial government. In British days a man's Golden Valley address indicated to the nationalists that he was on "the other side". During the war, however, such an address showed that a man was in the "inner circle" or at least on the outer fringes of that inner circle. If a sentry stood with a rifle at the gate, then the man was in the inner circle. If not one sentry but two or three stood at the gate, then the man was a real big man and, as the popular saying went those days, "only an elephant would be bigger than he".

Thakin Kodaw Hmaing lived in the Golden Valley. He held court regularly for the young Thakins and cursed the Japanese and Dr Ba Maw in rhyme for their benefit.

The Japanese soldiers were becoming much hated, with their arrogance and their greed. The British had liked being called "thakin"; the Japanese liked to be called "master"; they came as masters all, only the Japanese were more rude. Daw Thi, the Burmese wife of a Japanese dentist, had broadcast from Radio Tokyo that the Japanese were coming to Burma as liberators. She spoke often about the cherry blossoms in Japan and the snow on Mount Fuji. Now those beautiful dreams were shattered. The Japanese soldier slapped people in the street, grabbed things, pursued women. The Burmese had not hoped for this kind of liberator. "What sort of a god have you invited into our country," Thakin Kodaw Hmaing asked Aung San, "can't you send him back?" That was good for a joke but unfair. "The Japanese would have come anyway," Aung San retorted. Thakin Kodaw Hmaing, however, only asked questions; he did not want the answers.

There was talk in the political and army circles of resistance, but it was just talk. No bridegroom of a few months wanted to become a guerrilla fighter. Besides, the Japanese were there solid and secure. There were some clashes, but they were minor quar-

9

rels. Some Burmese soldiers kept beating up the Japanese soldiers, and vice versa, but that was not the resistance. Things had moved too fast, and the people needed time to sort out a clear picture of the true situation, time to prepare for whatever they must do.

Bo Ne Win went to Arakan with his battalion. There in the mud and rain he lived with his men. Most of them were veterans of the long march, but they needed to be trained properly. So at Pyinmana, and in Lamu camp 100 miles north of Sandoway, the battalion was put through tight schedules of training, from the commander down. The day's programme would be first worked out by Bo Ne Win, Kitajima and the company commanders. The officers would then teach the non-commissioned officers, who would in turn teach and train the men. Through the day, day in and day out, this was done, and Bo Ne Win would join in till the end of the day's schedules. Kitajima would also translate Japanese military manuals and textbooks into English; Bo Ne Win would read up and translate into Burmese those which the officers and men should also study.

There was plenty of work to do: roads to make and keep in repair, from Padaung to Taungup pass and up; supply lines to keep open; sentry duties and security. Arakan was a frontline of the war, a spring-board for the projected Japanese offensive against India, a vital objective for the early British assaults. British aircraft would come over often and strafe and bomb. Units of the 1st Battalion, would shoot at the low-flying planes with their rifles and machine-guns, scoring fatal hits a few times, and attracting reprisal raids.

The rice, which was supplied by the Japanese depot, was often stale, and fresh meat and vegetable were rare. The men were thus undernourished, and prone to malaria and various skin diseases. Bo Ne Win would go to the cookhouse often to check the food, and he liked eating with the men in their mess. Kitajima would go to the supply depot occasionally to complain, and the supplies would improve, but only for a while. Bo Ne Win would also send Bo Aung Gyi, a supply officer of the battalion, to Ramree to buy fresh supplies for the men. Feed them well, work them hard, care for them with kindness when they were ill; Bo Ne Win drove himself hard to achieve those aims. The men loved and respected him. The discipline and the spirit of the battalion were good.

Among the officers were Bo Ye Tut, one of the youngest of the thirty comrades, who had the machine-gun company. Bo Saw Naung and Bo La Yaung, also of the thirty. Bo Tin Pe, who commanded the 4th company; Bo Kyaw Myint, the medical officer; Bo Than Maung who, as a clerk in the Home Department, had supplied information to Thakin Shu Maung.

It was lonely in Arakan, on the Yomas. But man often needs loneliness to build strength for his inner self.

3

Thakin Thein Pe trekked out to India through Arakan and Chittagong. The BIA sent Thakin Tin Mya and a few men to take him to the border. Thakin Soe went along, resolved to fight Fascism from India; his comrades, however, ultimately convinced him that he was needed in Burma where the resistance must be rallied.

Thakin Thein Pe was arrested at the first police outpost in India which he reached. They took his money and things and locked him up. The British intelligence interrogated him thoroughly before they decided that he was genuine and not a Japanese spy. Once he was cleared he was treated well. He was attached to the ministry of information, and later to Force 136, a secret service organization whose mission was to nourish the forces of resistance in Burma. His book, *What Happened in Burma,* created quite a stir. Edgar Snow, author of *Red Star over China* which had inspired many young Burmese nationalists, wrote a foreword to the book and recommended that it was essential reading for "every intelligent Englishman who wants to win the war."

The attention which Thakin Soe received in Burma was not so pleasing. The Japanese hunted him, and he had to go underground in the Delta region. He lived dangerously, prowling like a beast of the jungle, preaching to his disciples like a prophet who had risen out of the pages of a religious textbook. The villagers found him irresistible, especially the young girls. He was free from inhibitions. In those days of many privations and restrictions he was a welcome change, a breath of fresh air—or a gust of strong wind. He attacked everyone. Bo Aung San, whom he called a Japanese puppet, a military martinet. Thakin Than Tun had betrayed the cause, he said, and was enjoying his make-belief role of minister too well. Dr Ba Maw was beneath contempt. Puppets all, caricatures, traitors to the cause; only he, Thakin Soe, the great teacher, the prophet, was the saviour. Thakin Soe spoke, wrote his manifestoes, published his pamphlets, and kept on running. His untimely utterances and writings made much trouble for his comrades aboveground. They also helped to keep them awake.

Thakin Kyaw Sein, Thakin Pe Htay, Thakin Mya Than, Comrade Rajan and others formed a group to start the resistance. They tried to establish contacts with Thakin Soe but the prophet kept moving. They distributed anti-Japanese propaganda, but that was ineffective and premature. The Japanese Kempetai rounded the group up and gave them the treatment. When they were released they were broken men; their will to fight was gone.

A few young officers in the BDA kept plotting for the resistance. They too wrote their pamphlets and drafted noble manifestoes. They translated treatises on guerrilla warfare; they planned their grand strategy. But the young men were scattered, from Taungup in Arakan to Pyinmana, from Mandalay to Indaw up north. They had the will to fight, but neither the men nor the arms to do the fighting with. To his bookish aide, Bo Maung Maung, who was one of those young officers, Bo Aung San once put the question: "Can you find me someone who will do an assassination job and keep absolutely silent if he was caught?" The young aide had to admit that it would be difficult to find such a man, for most men might kill but would squeal under pressure. It was a question of will, Bo Aung San explained, a man of steel will could bear any amount of pressure. The Japanese will was forged in steel by hard training and indoctrination. "We must forge the resistance forces likewise," Aung San said, "before we fight the Japanese."[2]

Aung San was the living symbol of the army. The soldiers sang songs about him and the nurse whom he loved. Stories about the austere Bogyoke, the dedicated leader, became legend. But Bo Aung San could not visit the troops as often as he wanted; the Japanese Army must approve his tour programmes. His Japanese advisers always surrounded him. Closer to the men in the

[2] Brig. Maung Maung in *Aung San of Burma*, p. 67.

field, therefore, was Bo Ne Win who lived in the camps, worked and played with the men, sharing their hardships and hazards. The young officers found him a sympathetic listener; he might not always agree with them, but he understood. Bo Ne Win used the strong, salty language of the soldier—his schoolmates say that he had the language even before his army days—and the young men felt good with him even if he cursed them sometimes in his pithiest prose. To him they unburdened their thoughts and brought their literature. Bo Ne Win was young enough to be excited by the plans that were unfolded to him, but also old enough to know better. He too realized that the Japanese could not be pushed out of the country with pamphlets. He too stressed the need for patience, for thorough organization and preparation. The young officers would then retort that he was no more than an echo of Aung San.

Bo Ne Win was absolutely loyal to Bo Aung San who was a younger man, and junior in many ways. In politics Bo Ne Win had started out earlier. In wordly wisdom he could claim more breadth and depth, for he had learnt much at the hard school of life. In regard to some raw realities of life Aung San was an innocent. But Aung San had his great qualities. His integrity was unimpeachable; his patriotism was absolute. Aung San was selfless because he never learned to be otherwise, because there was no self but only country. In matters of principle Aung San never gave a thought to considerations of personality or faction. Since Hainan where members of the two factions of the Dobama Asiayone shed off their factional differences Aung San thought only of the one goal of national independence to which the people must strive as one force. Bo Ne Win thought and felt the same way. His loyalty to Aung San was therefore a natural consequence, not pretence, nor mere propriety in military behaviour towards an officer of higher rank. It was subordination of self not to a man but to a mission.

Some of the former associates of the "Ba Sein-Tun Oke" faction of the Asi-ayone were sometimes impatient with Bo Ne Win's absolute loyalty to Aung San. Why must he be so correct, they grumbled among themselves, why could he not side with his former associates in the tug-of-war for the leadership. If he would join them, or say a few right words in the right places, Thakin Ba

Sein and Thakin Tun Oke could win. Bo Ne Win, however, was uninterested in the power struggle. Bigger things were at stake than the appointment of the chief Japanese puppet.

4

In January, 1943, General Tojo announced during the 80th session of the Imperial Diet that Burma would be recognized as an independent state within the year. In March, a delegation led by Dr Ba Maw flew to Tokyo for talks. Aung San, promoted Major-General, Thakin Mya and Dr Thein Maung were on the delegation. "Let the political organization of New Burma be simple and effective," Tojo urged, "as for economic affairs Burma should promote her economic development by just and unhampered activities under her own authority as a unit in the general economic construction of Greater East Asia."

The Emperor received the delegates in audience and invested them with the Order of the Rising Sun. "I am profoundly touched and overawed," Tojo reported to the Diet in its 81st session, "by the boundless magnitude of His Imperial Graciousness." A scroll given by Tojo to the delegation containing the solemn pledge of independence was, however, less graciously received. Dr Ba Maw left it behind at a Manila hotel on the return journey, and remembered only in Saigon that he had forgotten to bring the precious document along. Major-General Isomura, shepherd of the delegation, went into a fit. It was, for him, a serious crisis, involving honour. The Burmese took the whole thing as a good joke. Isomura, however, suffered for several hours and seriously considered committing *harakiri* (suicide) in order to save his face.

In Rangoon an independence preparatory commission was appointed and given the task of writing a constitution without delay. It was a small but representative commission which included Aung San, Thakin Nu, Thakin Mya and Thakin Kodaw Hmaing; politicians of the GCBA vintage, such as U Chit Hlaing and U Thein Maung; Dr San C. Po, a Karen leader; Sir Mya Bu, the Chief Justice of the Supreme Court; U Khin Maung Dwe of Mandalay; U Kyaw, U Mya, U Aye Maung, U Tun Pe, and U Thwin. Isomura sat in during the deliberations of the commission. Hurry, hurry, he said, for General Tojo wanted to proclaim Burma's independence soon. The war was not going too well for Japan. The tide of victory was fast receding. Japan must march on India; a well-timed proclamation of Burma's independence might persuade the Indian nationalists to rise up in arms against the British and clear the way for a Japanese victory. Besides, the people of Burma were getting restive; independence might make them happy.

The jurists in the commission talked endlessly on abstract constitutional principles which they had studied long ago for their bar examinations. Was the constitution going to be flexible or rigid, was the state to be federal or unitary? They asked questions, they expounded, referring to rulings, quoting from books. Isomura's temper would rise in direct ratio with the length of the proceedings. A few weeks to the deadline, and the first draft of the constitution was not yet done; the old men were still discussing abstract principles and looking for further references. "Get on with the job," Isomura urged. "But we need to build safeguards into the constitution. No constitution is complete without them," the jurists argued. And Isomura fumed, "You don't need any. You have God!" "Which God?" the old men wanted to know. "The Nippon Imperial Army," was the imperious answer. The commander-in-chief of the Japanese Army had to invite the commission in for a strong lecture on how desirable it was for the constitution to be simple but effective and how time was of the essence, before the old men decided they had had enough fun and must now deliver the document on time.

On August 1, 1943, greatly to the relief of the commander-in-chief, the independence of Burma was proclaimed with proper pomp and ceremony. The military administration was withdrawn in the early morning. Dr Ba Maw was installed as the Adipadi, the Head of State. Thakin Kodaw Hmaing, who had consistently voiced his objection to Ba Maw, now crowned him and administered the oath which the kings took on ascent to the throne. The constitution vested supreme power in the Adipadi who was also the commander-in-chief of the national armed forces. Dr Ba Maw, suitably garbed in the uniform of commander-in-chief, read out over the radio a declaration of war against the Anglo-American Allies.

A new government was formed to assist the Adipadi who was also Prime Minister. Most of the members of the Executive Administration were retained. Thakin Tun Oke and Thakin Ba Sein were, however, dropped. They were sent with their families into exile, the former to Singapore, the latter to Java.

The Sinyetha party of Dr Ba Maw and the Dobama Asi-ayone were merged into the Dobama Sinyetha Asi-ayone to forge a united political front. Thakin Nu, who was appointed Foreign Minister, was a principal organizer of the new party. With him were Thakin Nyi, Thakin Tin and several of the old comrades of the early Thakin days.

Major-General Aung San was appointed War Minister in the new government. Colonel Ne Win took over as commander-in-chief of the army, now re-named the Burma National Army. "Our task is not merely defensive," Bo Ne Win told reporters at a press conference which he gave soon after taking up his new duties, "we shall wage war against all enemies."

The Army was quickly expanded; the training was improved and intensified. The BDA had started out with three battalions, which later grew into six. Now logistic support was added. Armour and artillery units were also got together. A Karen battalion was raised, partly with the political objective of restoring Karen-Burmese amity. Saw Kyar Doe and Saw San Po Thin, officers of the British army who stayed behind, were won over by Aung San to make a common cause.

Thus the army grew stronger and became more ready for the resistance.

5

Not the Army only but the people were ready to rise. The "independence made in Japan" whetted their appetite for the genuine, durable kind of independence. The fact that even in those impossible conditions Burmans could make a going concern of an administration and build a national army gave the people pride and confidence. The war also taught them that if they wanted something better than what they had they had to fight for it. They were ready to fight, therefore, for real freedom from foreign domination, from want and hunger, from privations and restriction, from humiliation. In their readiness they looked to the Army to lead.

The Army was of the people. The soldiers were boys barely out of their teens. Aung San, the Bogyoke, was not yet 30. They all came, these *yebaws* (comrades), from different parts of the country, from families of peasants, of workers, or working intelligentsia. Men from the different national races served together: Arakanese, Burmese, Chins, Kachins, Karens, Mons, Shans. They spoke with accents; they had different customs and cultures; the majority were Buddhists but some were Christians, some animists; but one common aspiration, which transcended all the differences, kept them marching together—the aspiration for the freedom of the one country in which they and their families made their homes.

Wherever the yebaws went they were received by the people as their sons. The boys were poorly paid, poorly clothed, but their complete dedication to the service of the country was patent on their faces, their behaviour and demeanour. They came like torch-bearers, bringing the flame of faith and courage, and lighting up other torches they passed on. Soon, the torches were burning everywhere.

The East Asiatic Youth League with branches in even the most remote parts of the country became an army in reserve. Young men and women who could not join the Army served in the League instead. They helped in the recruiting campaigns, in the supply of troops on the march, in building closer relations between the Army and the people. When preparations were made for the resistance, members of the League organized the partisans, laid the supply dumps, got the camps and hide-outs ready, and alerted the people. On the central executive of the League were U Ba Gyan, T. K. Boon and other associates of Aung San and the BRP; lady executives included Daw Thin Kyi, Daw Yee Kyain, Daw Ohn of Mandalay, and Daw Than Sein. From the central executive to members in the villages, the League was an auxiliary force of the Burma National Army.

The people were behind the Army, and the Army had its hero and leader in Aung San. It was one of those unique periods in a country's history when a man, his mission, and the people who were looking for the man came together and became one. Dr Ba Maw had called for one blood, one voice and one command. The people responded, but his was not the one voice nor his the one command which they were willing to accept. It was Aung San whom they wanted and needed. Dr Ba Maw was able, courageous, good in showmanship, clever with words, a man of good political style. He stood up against the Japanese as few men dared to do; in British days as a minister, he had stood up against the European businessmen and British I.C.S. officers. He was suave and silken. He knew that in time of war the uniform had its glamour; he wore his Field-Marshal's uniform on ceremonial occasions and cut a brave figure in it. He did what he could to inspire the people and win their trust. A free thinker, he went up the Shwedagon pagoda and prayed often—with due publicity. He invoked the aid of the *nats* (spirits) in holding the country together. He had a bucketful of victory soil brought from Shwebo to Rangoon for good luck. He tried hard to keep the politicians in his administration and the party working in harmony. He ran many personal risks. A clique of Japanese adventurers attempted to assassinate him. With all these, however, as the months went by, it was to Aung San that the people increasingly turned as the one leader who could pull them through.

Aung San was short and shabby. He could not look like a conquering general even if he tried, and he did not. He was curt in speech, blunt of manners. He had two suits of uniform, worn threadbare. When he took off the jacket on hot days, his vest grimaced with its many holes. He loved his family well, but his country better, and the people knew it. They knew he was honest, therefore poor. Their love for him and trust in him constituted his sole riches, but which patriot could ask for more?

Among Gen. Aung San's chief lieutenants Col. Let Ya was an efficient administrator, but a little too polished and sophisticated to be the soldiers' man. Bo Let Ya was fond of art, music, fine clothes, class distinctions. Col. Zeya was also a bit of a dandy. It was thus that the young officers gathered round Col. Ne Win to plan and prepare for the resistance. In his office the young men printed their papers and pamphlets, collected money and arms. His command network provided their distribution channels. The sinews of war were thus developed in the bamboo and thatch headquarters of the commander-in-chief at the War Office on U Wisara Road, Rangoon.

Goodwill missions to the Karen villages in the Delta led by

Thakin Nu and Bo Let Ya were successful. Even more so was the Army band conducted by Capt. San Po Thin, for the Karens are fond of music and love community singing. At the War Office secret discussions held between Bo Aung San, Bo Ne Win, Thakin Than Tun and other Burmese leaders and Saw Kyar Doe, Saw Henry, Johnson Kan Gyi and other Karen leaders laid firm groundwork for Karen-Burmese unity in the resistance.

Col. Setkya, sharp, shrewd and self-centred, learned that San Po Thin was in contact with Major Seagrim of the British army who had stayed behind in the hills of the Salween district to organize Karen guerrillas. "Arrange for me to get away to India," Setkya urged San Po Thin, who passed on the message—and the information that the BNA was preparing to rise—to Major Seagrim. Somehow the Kempetai came to know about this and promptly placed San Po Thin under arrest. Setkya was sent away to Tokyo as military attache in the Burmese Embassy where, the Japanese thought, he would be beyond mischief-making.[3]

Premature freelance activities by individuals or small groups could not mount the resistance. In fact they did more harm than good, frittered away valuable resources, exposed the people to Kempetai vengeance. Towards the latter part of 1944, therefore, efforts were made by Aung San and his comrades to forge all the forces into a common front. The first person to bring into the front obviously was Thakin Soe, the authentic rebel, the prophet, who had consistently followed one line of action. A party led by Bo Ne Win therefore went out to the Delta to pick him up at a rendezvous. In Rangoon, Thakin Soe, dressed up as an army captain, went into conference with the planners of the resistance without delay. Bo Aung San and Thakin Soe had long conferences on August 4 and 5 at the Burma Army's Sanpya (Model) School in Pegu—which conveniently kept the young firebrands in one place, within easy reach of the War Office. The conferences resulted in a meeting of minds on joint efforts for the Resistance, and the first statement of aims and purpose which Bo Aung San himself drafted.

Another important conference was held on March 3 and 4,

---

[3] Ian Morrison, *Grandfather Longlegs,* Faber & Faber, London, 1947, p. 199.

1945, at the residence of Aung San on Park Road (now Natmauk Road) by the lakes. Behind doubled security guards the objectives of the resistance, as well as the plans, the philosophy, the strategy and the tactics were discussed. The Burma Army was strongly represented by about thirty senior officers including Bo Aung San, Bo Ne Win, Bo Let Ya, Bo Zeya, Bo Kyaw Zaw, Bo Aung, Bo Yan Aung, Bo Aung Gyi, Bo Khin Maung Gale, Bo Maung Maung, Saw Kyar Doe, Bo Po Kun, Bo Win and Bo Ba Htu. Thakin Than Tun and Thakin Soe spoke for the Communist groups. U Kyaw Nyein, U Ba Swe, U Hla Maung and Thakin Chit participated as leaders of the BRP. Bo Ba Htu left for Mandalay soon after the conference.

Thakin Soe did not deviate from his original line of all-out cooperation with the Anglo-American Allies in the "patriotic war". There was, for him, no question of continuing the fight after the Allies had "liberated" the country. To do so would be to hamper the Allies in their war efforts. Aung San and his comrades were shy of "liberators". The resistance must, they decided, be aimed at higher objectives than supporting the Allies. If the war was prolonged, opportunities might even be better to consolidate the nation and bargain with the British for Burma's independence. The war in Burma should be short and swift, for the people and their homes must be spared as much as possible. But the aim of the resistance must be Burma's full and complete freedom. Thakin Soe thought that was all very lofty and unrealistic. "Blind, stupid young patriots," he said to his disciples about the army officers, "the war will wipe them out, leaving the field open to the Communist party."

The discussions finally produced a manifesto calling on the people to "Drive out the Fascist Japanese Marauders." Do you want to be free, asked the manifesto of the people, do you want peace and security? "Then drive away the Fascist Japanese barbarians. Set up a People's Government. Co-operate with the Democratic Allies." The manifesto was issued in the name of the "Anti-Fascist People's Freedom League (Burma Patriotic Front)". The "Victory Flag" of the AFPFL was to be a red flag with a white star in the left top corner. "Red symbolises bravery, the masses and unification of all the peoples of the world" the manifesto explained. "Red also draws attention easily. The star symbolizes the guiding star for the people to attain freedom and progress."[4]

The AFPFL was thus forged. The Army was ready, so were the people. The manifesto went out to the villages through secret channels to alert the people that the time to strike was approaching. The Flag had been designed; all that was needed was to unfurl it and follow it into the field of battle.

6

In June, 1944, Bo Ne Win organized a tour of BNA units for Gen. Aung San and Gen. Sawamoto, the principal Japanese adviser. Kitajima, who had been with Bo Ne Win since BIA days, also went along. It was a long trip taking the party to Mandalay and Maymyo, Shwebo, Namkham, and Indaw, Yenangyaung, Allanmyo, Prome and Paungde. Travelling was difficult, for air raids were heavy and frequent. Bo Ne Win, however, took good care of the party all along the way, and Gen. Sawamoto was well-pleased. For the Burmese commanders it was the last opportunity to meet the troops in the north and alert their officers. Wherever they went, they also met the elders and the local leaders, and urged them to work together.

In Mandalay, Bo Aung San asked U San Maung, the postal superintendent, to convene a dinner meeting of Burmese officials, city elders and young leaders. "Make sure no Japanese come to the dinner," Aung San instructed, "and let there be plenty to drink." The instructions were carried out faithfully. A jovial mood obtained at the meeting. The drinks dissolved the inhibitions. "Time has come again," Aung San said in a short speech, "to join hands in a common struggle. Let us sink personal jealousies and political differences in the larger cause of national freedom."

On August 1, 1944, the first anniversary of independence was celebrated. In Rangoon a public meeting was held at the Jubilee Hall at which Dr Ba Maw, the Adipadi, spoke. When his turn came, Gen. Aung San spoke briefly and bluntly. The independence that was being celebrated was not yet real, he said, and it was only enjoyed by the few such as himself and the ministers. The people were suffering. The struggle for the freedom of all the

[4] The manifesto is reproduced in *The New Burma in the New World*.

people of the land must yet be waged. The Japanese were not pleased with the speech, but the people hugged it to their hearts and understood its message.

Then came the secret meetings at which the AFPFL was organized and the manifesto drafted. The troops stationed in the north, with Bo Ba Htu in command at Mandalay, waited impatiently for the signal to strike. The Japanese march on Manipur, with the support of the Indian National Army which Subhas Chandra Bose had raised, was a disaster. On the plains of Kohima the Japanese divisions were beaten and broken. The time to strike was now. Later, the initiative would have been lost.

But the Allied Southeast Asia Command in Kandy, under supreme commander Lord Mountbatten, cautioned restraint. A premature rising would bring down harsh reprisals on the civilian population, it warned the BNA. Also, the SEAC received conflicting advice from its military commanders and the civilian administrators who were attached to it. The ICS officers, commissioned as colonels, and their chief, Major-General C. F. B. Pearce, had advised that issue of arms in large quantities to the BNA would "imperil the present and future security of Burma." The commander of Force 136, on the other hand, made out his case that "a strengthened guerrilla movement in Burma would greatly assist his own operations behind the enemy lines."[5] Mr. Pearce had his prejudices, and he owed a divided allegiance to his civilian chief, Sir Reginald Dorman-Smith who had been a governor without a country to govern since May, 1942. The Civilians did not want to go back to Burma to find the AFPFL established as a national government. If they did, all the fine plans of reconstruction that they had drawn up at Simla would be wasted. Besides, Sir Reginald and his staff had their honour to redeem.

Lord Mountbatten, however, did not personally have a wounded pride to heal, nor any strong prejudices against the nationalist forces in Burma. He was a man of stature and standing—which helped when he had to talk with the War Cabinet in London—and he had a broad mind which helped when he had to consider larger problems calmly. He had a war to win. If he did not re-

---

[5] Adm. Lord Louis Mountbatten, *Report to the Combined Chiefs of Staff by the Supreme Allied Commander, Southeast Asia*, 1943-45, London, HMSO, 1951.

cognize and support the Resistance, he might have to suppress it, and that would involve using troops which should be fighting the Japanese. "Moreover, I considered that armed intervention on our part, to prevent the Burmese from fighting the common enemy and helping to liberate their own country," he wrote in his Report to the Combined Chiefs of Staff, submitted after the war, "could not fail to have unfavourable repercussions in the United Kingdom, in the United States, and in other parts of the world." Though the Resistance was "not part of my plans, it would undoubtedly provide an acceptable bonus; and since the areas affected would be in the south, it might help to hasten the capture of Rangoon."

The War Cabinet approved, though not without reservations. SEAC must not discuss political issues with Major-General Aung San or other leaders of the movement, the War Cabinet directed. Also, Mountbatten wrote, the War Cabinet "instructed me to publicise by means of my Psychological Warfare Division, the fact that we considered the British and Indian forces, assisted by the Americans and the Chinese, to be the true liberators of Burma."

Who gets the credit for victory depends, of course, on who is looking for it. Orde Wingate, who led the Chindit long range penetration forces behind the Japanese lines, thought he would win it. Colonel Merrill, commander of the American Marauders, would consider that he had earned a large share of the credit. So did Gen. Joe Stilwell of the U.S. Army who fought with the Chinese. The Indian forces would say they bore the main brunt of the Burma campaign. So would the Chinese. And the regular forces would belittle the contributions of special forces, the Wingates, the Merrills, the Resistance.

But Hollywood had the last word on who won the war in Burma. It was Errol Flynn who, in *Jungle Victory,* won it single-handed.

7

The Allied Forces opened their offensive in a race with the monsoon. In December, 1944, the XIVth Army led by Gen. Slim, crossed the Chindwin. In a few weeks the 33 Corps broke into the Shwebo plain. Gen. Slim, pressing the advantage, decided to push further south and, crossing the Irrawaddy, draw the Japanese into a major battle in the plains between Mandalay and Meiktila. Major engagements were fought in February and March.

In these developments, Bo Ba Htu, the BNA commander at Mandalay, decided to strike. He gathered his forces, made his declaration of war against the Japanese on March 8, 1945, and began fighting. In the streets of Mandalay he and his men fought. He had a few hundred men, but a brigade of troops could not have raised more havoc and done more damage to Japanese morale. When Maj.-Gen. T. W. Rees arrived on the outskirts of Mandalay with his 19 Indian Division the Japanese were in flight. Only a handful of them remained, making noises in the palace which the British troops bombarded and destroyed.

Bo Ba Htu made a fighting withdrawal into the Shan hills. Knowing that the BNA was not yet deployed in southern Burma, and his action could seriously prejudice the plans for the resistance, Bo Ba Htu thoughtfully put out a terse statement that he and his forces had to rise because Dr Ba Maw and Gen. Aung San were puppets in the hands of the Japanese, and unable or unwilling to protect the people from the oppressors. The statement helped to allay suspicions of the Japanese high command in Rangoon. Maj.-General Sakurai, the principal adviser to the BNA and successor to Sawamoto who had gone to the 33rd Army as chief of staff, held a meeting with Kitajima and other advisers to discuss the Ba Htu rising. Japanese Army HQ wanted to know whether the remaining BNA troops could be trusted, or whether the troops should be disarmed. The advisers decided that there was no need to disarm the BNA. Bo Ba Htu, they thought, had acted on his own. He was an impulsive and excitable man, they agreed,—and a man from Tavoy where men were simple but stubborn. Bo Arlawaka, who commanded the anti-aircraft battery at Mandalay, was another inflammable man. When the two men combined in the critical situation around Mandalay, the result was the rising. The advisers also decided that the wise policy would be to issue more arms to the BNA, rather than disarm the troops, to show more trust and give opportunities to the troops to show their mettle and prove their worth.

Gen. Aung San had been suggesting just that for quite some time. Give us arms, he had been asking, and let us fight. The boys were spoiling for a fight, he told the Japanese, disperse them in the Delta and along the Irrawaddy, and let them have a go. The Japanese high command, under pressure of the Allied onslaught, bewildered by the political situation, finally agreed.

The BNA had these forces to employ in the resistance. Eight infantry battalions: the 1st commanded by Bo Tin Pe at Twante; the 2nd by Bo San Yu at Pyalo and Allanmyo; the 3rd by Bo Hla Pe at Pegu; the 4th by Bo Thein Maung at Mingaladon; the 5th by Bo Thaung Kyi at Toungoo; the 6th by Bo Sein Win at Pyalo and Allanmyo; the 7th by Bo Maung Gale at Mingaladon; the Karen battalion commanded by Bo Tun Sein at Rangoon. The 1st Engineering Battalion, led by Bo Aye Maung, was already in action in Mandalay; the 2nd of which Bo Monyoe was commander, was in Allanmyo where a regional command headquarters had been set up under Bo Aung. Units of the Light Anti-Aircraft Machine-Gun Battalion, commanded by Bo Myint Aung, were stationed in Sagaing, Mandalay, Maymyo and in the Sittang area. Bo Thein Oo, commanding the unit at Sagaing, fell in the fighting there. Bo Khin Nyo was commander of the Heavy Anti-Aircraft Battalion which had a unit in Mandalay under Bo Arlawaka.

There was also the Military Academy at Mingaladon. It had turned out four batches of cadet officers. Of the first batch of 300, thirty of the best had been sent to Tokyo for higher studies. The second sent about 40. By that time the cadets knew that if they went they would be missing the resistance, and those who went were reluctant; many feigned sickness so that they might be left behind. The third and fourth batches were close and sent none to Tokyo. The four batches produced an adequate corps of young officers in time for the resistance. The fifth was still at school with the youth corps—bright and hardy boys who were being carefully trained for future high commands. There were also the instructors and staff of the school.

There was then the War Office, with more officers than soldiers, more brain—it was hoped—than brawn. Some of the college mates of Bo Aung San, Bo Ne Win and Bo Let Ya had been brought in and commissioned. U Tun Ohn and U Thi Han, of the 1936 students' strike, were officers in the general administration and the directorate of supply respectively. There was even an art section at the War Office—with artists U Ngwe Gaing, U

10

Myat Kyaw and M. Tin Aye—which had been reconstructing in vivid colour the march of the BIA, the battle of Shwedaung and other such battles.

A Women's Corps was in the bud. Daw Saw Mya, Daw Khin Kyi Kyi and a few pioneers were already seriously at work when time arrived to take to the hills. They did their share in the resistance.

The infantry battalions, the engineers, the armour and the artillery, the War Office and its branches and the logistical units were armed and supplied and assigned their areas of operation. The Academy had to keep going, to put up appearances. When the resistance began the cadets and the youth corps, led by the instructors and staff, fought their way out to join the others.

March 27, 1945, was the Resistance Day. There had been several postponements of the date for several reasons. Now the day could no longer be put off. Time had come to do or die.

On March 17, a parade was held in the football ground (now the Resistance Park) on U Wisara Road, near the western foothills of the Shwedagon. Troops of the BNA who were going out to war were given their blessings by Dr Ba Maw and Gen. Sakurai. Gen. Aung San was, as usual, brief. He called on the army to go out and fight the enemy. He would, he promised, himself lead the army in the field. Who the enemy was, he did not say, but most of the men did not need to be told.

The citizens of Rangoon gathered around the parade ground to watch and weep. They lined the streets and gave sprigs of *eugenia* leaves to the departing soldiers for good luck. The city would be lonely and empty without the boys, and so open to the Japanese who were becoming so desperate.

A few Japanese aeroplanes, remnants of a decimated air force, flew above and flapped their wings in salute.

Then, the BNA melted away. There was no time to tarry, no time for tender farewells. The urgent need was to get to the assigned posts without delay. Most of the troops got there in time. Those who did not, and stragglers who wandered lost and unaware of what was happening, fell into Japanese hands and were cruelly butchered. From March 27 it was a fight to the death, with no holds barred, no quarters asked or given. The Resistance was an elemental struggle.

8

Gen. Aung San drove out from his house on the morning of March 23. On the outskirts of Rangoon an escort truck of BNA soldiers, and a small saloon car containing a few young officers, were waiting. Together, the small convoy sped fast on the road to Prome.

Maj.-Gen. Sakurai, calling at Aung San's residence later that day, found the house deserted. Alarmed, he drove out to Mingaladon in hot pursuit. Road blocks turned him back, and he went to the Military Academy, there to find the majority of staff and cadets gone. Collecting a *posse* of advisers and guards Sakurai went north again to investigate. The *posse* was received calmly at BNA camps along the way, which reassured the general. He returned to Rangoon to report to the Japanese Army HQ that there was nothing to fear from the BNA. Two days after he had reported, the resistance began.

Kitajima was the only Japanese adviser who had early hints of what was coming. He had been with Bo Ne Win all along, since the BIA, and friendship for him and the Burmese associates gradually ripened into a deep loyalty. When time to start the resistance approached Aung San dined with Kitajima a few times and sounded him out. "I am with you all the way," Kitajima responded, "I go wherever the BNA goes." Thus, Kitajima joined the resistance against the Japanese.

From Shwedaung Aung San sent a hurried note to Dr Ba Maw. "We shall have to be prepared to struggle alone for sometime," he wrote. "But I have every confidence that our cause will win ultimately. The struggle for our national independence must go on till it ends in victory."[6] The note was never delivered.

Thayetchaung village, west of Thayet, and hugging the foot of the Yomas, was where Gen. Aung San's headquarters was set up. The site was well-chosen. It was sheltered, yet close enough to the frontline of the war. An early meeting between Gen. Aung San and the commander of the Allied army could, therefore, be anticipated. The headquarters was also linked with the scattered resistance forces by reasonable communication systems. A few wireless sets, dropped by the SEAC, were available, but they did

[6] A photostat of the letter is in *Aung San of Burma.*

not always work. Road and river transport was available, though slow and unsafe. Relays of couriers and scouts kept Gen. Aung San in touch with the commanders in the different zones of the resistance.

Zone 7, under Bo Aung, had an operational sector covering Thayet-Allanmyo-Minbu. Bo Maung Gale, Bo Monyoe, Bo San Yu, Bo Sein Win, Bo Sein Hman and the troop commanders were with this zone. Gen. Aung San's command headquarters was in this zone, so that occasionally Aung San could personally take a hand in directing local operations. The departmental heads of the War Office were with the HQ which was therefore a War Office in miniature. Bo Zeya, Bo Yan Aung, Bo Min Gaung, Bo Win and Bo Khin Maung Gale of the supply directorate, Bo Shain of signals, Bo Tin of ordnance, Bo Maung Maung of the medical corps, Bo Hla Aung of the map and survey section, were among those at Thayetchaung.

The operational results of Zone 7 were good. There were skirmishes, night attacks, the hit-and-run, the ambush. Thayet, however, was off the war path, and no pitched battles were fought in the area. Discipline at command HQ tended to become slack as too many senior officers wandered around with too little to do. Gen. Aung San saw discipline and unity going downhill, but abided his time before he spoke out. He read, brooded, sent out couriers to troops which were scattered far and wide, read and re-read reports which came in. He worried about the fate of the cadets at the Military Academy, and sent out a courier to find out. The cadets and their instructors had, it turned out, broken through the Japanese cordons and taken up positions in Tantabin. This report kept Aung San happy for days. News came one day that Saw Kyar Doe had been arrested by the Japanese in the Delta. This worried Aung San a great deal. He sent a young officer out to see if Saw Kyar Doe could not be rescued.

Finally Gen. Aung San decided to talk to the officers and men at the headquarters. They were told to fall in. When all were lined up, some 300 of them, colonels to privates, Aung San gave them a piece of his mind. He was aware, he said, that discipline was bad, specially among the senior officers. There was a lot of rank-consciousness among those officers. Petty jealousy was rife. He knew that some of the senior officers slipped out of camp to return to their families for days on end. Some spent their time hunting in the jungles. This was no picnic, no sefari. "Don't think," Aung San warned, "that you are going to have a good time when the British arrived. Don't think you will get your promotions and live swanky and happy ever after. Get rid of your conceit and complacency. Hard struggle still lies ahead.".

9

Zone 2 had the whole Delta to take care of. Its area stretched from Hanthawaddy to Maubin, Myaungmya to Bassein and Henzada. The commander was Bo Ne Win. Among his lieutenants were Bo Aung Gyi, Bo Tin Pe, and Bo Kyi Win. Saw Kyar Doe, San Po Thin and Saw Tun Sein were given an area in Bassein-Myaungmya to lead the Karens in the rising. The arrest of Saw Kyar Doe, however, nipped the resistance in the Karen areas in the bud. In Henzada, Bo Aung Min, a few young officers and men moved about in the hills and the Karen villages, sometimes fighting the Japanese in the open paddy fields.

The Delta, in fact, was wide open country. Bo Ne Win's troops had to fight in the swamps and the sodden paddy fields without the benefit of cover. Night raids were possible, but costly. Ambushes were out. All war, at the start, was frontal war, with few opportunities for hit-and-run. The hardest fighting was done by the resistance forces in Dedaye and Pyapon where Bo Ne Win personally took command. The Japanese held the Delta in strength. Their commander, Lt-Gen. Hanaya was a ferocious old man whose boast was that he had never suffered a defeat in his long career of war. The Japanese set out to round up the resistance men, taking the offensive into the villages.

Political advisers were attached to zone commands. Several months before the resistance began Thakin Soe and associates were given full liberty to give classes in army camps. In secret sessions in Rangoon and Pegu Thakin Soe himself gave lectures to small groups of eager officers. Well-read in Marxist literature, he spoke with deep passion. His students would listen, rapt. A few lectures would convert most of them into faithful disciples. The classes, however, threatened to break up the unity of the army. Those graduates of the Marxist courses of lectures, began

to feel they were superior men; the other soldiers were blind patriots, devoid of philosophy—robots without the ability to think.
"The resistance and the call to arms came in time," Gen. Ne Win
once said, remembering those days, "to save the army from being split."

In the resistance also the Communists and the Marxist-indoc-
trinated partisans tended to look upon the soldiers as mere ins-
truments of war, to use, then to discard or destroy—if the war
did not destroy them. The soldiers, on their part, tended to look
down upon the politicians as mere talkers and a bit of a nuisance.
There was, therefore, no easy partnership between the politicians
and the soldiers during the resistance. There were, of course, rare
exceptions here and there. And there were partisans who came
in to help and fight; they were different; with them the soldiers
did not have any problems.

Thakin Soe looked upon the resistance as an operation in support of the patriotic war being fought by the Allied forces. This,
of course, differed basically from the viewpoint of Bo Aung San
and Bo Ne Win. The difference led to several heated arguments
between Thakin Soe and Bo Ne Win in the Delta. Once at Kun-
plai village in Dedaye area Bo Ne Win had to give Thakin Soe a
good tongue-lashing. Wireless communications with Allied forces
in India made a few air-drops of arms and supplies possible in
the later stages of the resistance. Thakin Soe, in requisitioning supplies, gave priority to nylon, lipstick and cosmetics, and fancy
pistols for the girls who were among the partisans. When Bo Ne
Win came to know about this he lost his temper. "This is the resistance," he shouted at Thakin Soe, "we are not playing spies or a
fifth column group. What will they think when they get your request? We must ask for arms to carry on with the fighting."

There was much fighting in the Delta. The Japanese at last
gave up the hunting and became the hunted instead. Hanaya's
division began the retreat. Night after night, its convoys passed
over the roads. The ambush became profitable for the resistance
forces then.

Nevil Shute, the novelist, wove a romance round the stories
of the resistance in the Delta which he was able to collect. In
The Chequer Board a British pilot called Morgan was brought
down by Nevil Shute in the Delta and into the hands of a resist-

ance unit led by one Utt Nee. The resistance men wanted arms and one Major Williams who had parachuted into the area had the wireless to call for air-drops. "I send him a present for a present," said Utt Nee to Morgan. "I give you to him as token of our good faith. As token of his good faith he must give us grenades and guns."

Utt Nee sent his pretty sister along with the party, telling Morgan: "My sister will go with Thet Shay to interpret with the Englishman. If he says he will give us arms, then I will come to see him with Colonel Ne Win, and we will arrange the details."

"If he says he won't give any arms," asked Morgan, "do you take me back and hand me over to the Japanese?"

Utt Nee laughed. "I do not think we should do that. We are not on speaking terms with the Japanese at the moment."

Morgan and the pretty sister of Utt Nee fell in love—of course—and married after the war and lived happily thereafter in a Delta town.[7]

Many men of the resistance were less fortunate than Morgan. They married death instead.

10

Zone 1, under Major Maung Maung, extended in area from Prome to Insein. Bo Myint Aung, Bo Thi Han, Bo Thein Maung, Bo Thein Dok, Bo Shwe, Bo Aung Min and Bo Min Thein were among his officers. In the first few weeks of the resistance the force confined its activities to blowing up railway bridges and locomotives, cutting down telegraph wires and felling telegraph poles. Japanese troops, massed in Prome and Paungde, were thus isolated. They did not venture forth to give battle. The guerrillas also ambushed convoys on the road. Villagers gave hearty support and took on small Japanese patrols. Thakin Nyi, who knew the area around Prome well, went as the political adviser at Zone HQ. When the Japanese troops withdrew, Zone 1 moved to Penwegon on the Rangoon-Toungoo Road. There, dispersed in villages along the Sittang, the guerrillas lay in wait for the Japanese troops which crossed the Pegu Yomas and tried to break across the

[7] Nevil Shute, *The Chequer Board,* William Morrow & Co., New York, 1947, p. 161.

paddy fields and the river. The most bitter battles were fought there in the mud, under the monsoon rains. The Japanese were broken up, hungry, and sick; but desperation gave the last ounces of strength to their customary defiance. The Zone HQ, established in a monastery near the road occasionally attracted Japanese visitors. They would stumble in at night, hoping to find a safe spot for rest. When they discovered their error they would try to throw a few grenades and run. There would then be shootings in the dark which were not good for one's nerves. Scores of prisoners were taken by the guerrillas in the fighting along the Sittang. The Japanese did not submit easily to capture; few of the Allied troops had therefore seen live Japanese soldiers at close quarters. When the resistance forces in Zone 1 handed over the prisoners, the Indian Brigade carried them away lovingly as prized souvenirs.

Zone 6, under Bo Yet Htut, in the Meiktila-Toungoo and Southern-Shan-State sector, joined up with the advancing Allied army after engaging in some heavy action. Bo Tauk Htain, Bo Tayar, Bo Thaung Kyi, Bo We Lin, Bo Nyun, Bo Bala, Bo Tun Lin, Bo Ba Yi and Bo Lwin the medical officer, were among the senior officers who alternated between running the Zone HQ and leading the guerrillas into action. Ko Mya led the partisans. The Zone command was also able to link up with Bo Ba Htu who had withdrawn into the Shan State. Thakin Tin Tun and Thakin Ba Hein were the political organizers. U Kyaw Nyein who was also assigned to the Zone did not make his appearance: he stayed behind in Rangoon with U Ba Swe whom the Kempetai arrested and later set free.

The Pegu-Shwegyin-Thaton area was allotted to Zone 4 under Bo Kyaw Zaw who had Bo Aung Shwe, Bo Lun Tin, Bo Lwin, Bo Ba Tin, Bo Aye Maung, Bo Thein Dan, Bo Hla Thamein, the medical officer, among his senior officers. The Model School at Pegu had provided cover for activities in preparation of the resistance, and for classes in Marxism. Organization was good in the area; publicity and public relations were excellent. The Zone HQ published a weekly bulletin of its own which carried reports on guerrilla successes and the progress of the war in the north.

The Japanese army planned to withdraw to Moulmein-Tavoy-Mergui—where it first entered Burma with the BIA—and then perhaps make their final stand. That area, marked for the regrouping of the scattered Japanese forces, was given to Zone 5 of the resistance. Bo Tin Tun was commander; Bo Kyaw Tun Tin, Bo Than Daing, Bo Pe Thet and Bo Hla Pe Gyi were among his lieutenants. The resistance could not accomplish much in the area because the Japanese soon began to arrive in overwhelming numbers. A few of the resistance leaders and partisans who fell into Japanese hands were cruelly tortured to death. The guerrillas, however, saved the villages from being put to the torch by the Japanese. In Thaton area they could group and fight. Some BNA units also attached themselves to Dr Ba Maw, his ministers and their families, whom the Japanese took along as hostages to Moulmein and Mudon.

The evacuation from Rangoon started on April 23. The Japanese high command had been divided on whether to make a stand in the city, or to leave. U Thein Maung, U Tun Aung and representatives of the Cabinet persuaded the commander to spare the city and, more particularly, leave the Shwedagon pagoda unharmed. Dr Ba Maw, U Tun Aung and a small delegation went to Tokyo in November, 1944, at the invitation of the Japanese government which wanted the leader of embattled Burma to give pep-talks to help the recruiting of *Kamikaze* suicide pilots. The visit provided an opportunity to the Burmese leaders to bargain with the Imperial Headquarters about Rangoon. It was then generally agreed that Rangoon would be saved, provided Ba Maw and his Cabinet accompanied the Japanese army on its withdrawal.

The departure from Rangoon, left till almost too late, was disorderly. Dr Ba Maw, Dr Ba Han, Thakin Mya, Thakin Nu, "Bandoola" U Sein, U Tun Aung, some staff, and their families were packed into trucks and driven off. The cars broke down often, or the convoys ran into ambush laid by the resistance, or they were strafed from the air by Allied aircraft which now had an open sky. In Moulmein the Burmese government continued to function, its main activity being the despatch of protests, through the Japanese Ambassador, Mr. Ishi, to the Japanese commander. There were many things to protest against: atrocities, arrests at random, failure to keep the Burmese government supplied with food and funds. Ishi promised, in proper diplomatic language, to speak to the army commander, and to send the notes to Tokyo itself. There were, however, no replies. This went on till August, when Japan, hit by atom bombs, decided to surrender. Dr Ba Maw then left alone, ending up finally in the Sugamo jail in Japan.

11

The monsoon was about to break. The British forces, eager to take Rangoon, yet cautious, prepared to bombard the city from the sea and the air. Messages had to be sent by the Resistance that the city was in its hands, but they were still somewhat dubious.

For the Resistance leaders who were already in Rangoon there was much work to do. There was urgent need to keep law and order in the city. Several hundred of BNA soldiers had been rounded up by the Japanese and thrown into Insein jail. They had to be organized and looked after. There were units of the Indian National Army who had to be persuaded to lay down their arms and cooperate with the BNA.

City elders, high officials, and political leaders had to be searched out and persuaded to stand together and talk with one voice for the national interest when the British arrived. Some agreed to come in. Many were uninterested. They did not know how the BNA itself would be treated by the British; it might prejudice their careers if they were seen in the company of the revolutionary elements. Anxious thoughts among Burmese officials tended to dwell mainly on back pay, seniority in service—which they hoped the war had not affected—and whether they might be penalized for having served under the occupation government. Some took out their morning coats from the dusty boxes, cleaned them and prepared to meet the returning British bosses in proper style. They also started to practise the handshake, the smile, the words of welcome, the excuses to offer for working in the occupation government.

On May 1, the Burma Revolutionary Party issued a proclamation that "the Burma Revolutionary Army has occupied Rangoon since 6 a.m. Burma Standard Time on the 5th Waning of Kason, 1307 Burmese Era. The BRP takes the fullest responsibility for the maintenance of law and order in the city and for the safety of the citizens' lives and homes. As the BRP is the People's Army and is fighting for the people at the war front, the people should give all help and cooperation. As a true representative of the people, the fighting forces of the BRP will serve for the cause of freedom of the country and the people, regardless of danger to their own lives."

Bo Ne Win returned to Rangoon on May 6, leaving the Delta area command with Bo Tin Pe. If things did not go well guerrilla war might have to be resumed.

On May 7, Bo Ne Win's report to the people on the aims and achievements of the resistance was broadcast. The report ended with a call to "comrades and countrymen to give us yet more of your willing cooperation and help, for before you all, ever loyal and true, we stand in readiness to fight for our cherished freedom, our one objective, our very life." The broadcast was picked up by the All India Radio and re-broadcast in gist three times—which was an unexpected bonus. The report, now famous, was an important one, made at the right time. Bo Ne Win drafted the report, assisted by U Chit Maung (*Journal-gyaw*) and Bo Aung Gyi. U Khin Maung Latt, the first editor of the *Working People's Daily,* helped with the translation. U Pe Shin, who had worked in the propaganda department of Dr Ba Maw's Government and whose hobby was wireless transmission, assembled a transmitter. When time came to broadcast, Bo Ne Win was away at the Government House in conference with Col. Holden, and Bo Aung Gyi arranged to have the report read out, in English as well as in Burmese, by U Tun Sein and U Htin Fatt, of the disintegrating Ministry of Press and Publicity, who had thoughtfully set up the "Rangoon Experimental Radio Station" with the transmitter.

In a letter dated May 19, despatched by courier from Rangoon, Bo Ne Win reported to Bo Aung San on the general situation. "I tried to reach you by wireless," he wrote, reviewing the past, "but the wireless was not working. Only on April 10, about 20 days before the Japanese started to leave Rangoon, could we pick up messages and transmit again. Thakin Chit has now returned to Rangoon from Pegu, Thakin Than Tun from Toungoo. So, I have a fair picture of the situation there. Ye Htut is engaged in the Toungoo-Pyinmana sector. The mechanized units of the XIVth Army would not assault Toungoo; our men went in instead. Thus

Toungoo was redeemed without any British effort. (The fall of Toungoo was announced on Radio Delhi, and due credit was given to the resistance on the radio and in the SEAC newspaper.) There have been successes in Pegu as well. The retreating Japanese are bombed by the Allies during the day and hunted by our guerrillas in the night. At least 10 per cent casualties are being inflicted."

"British liaison officers have come down by parachute in Pegu, and as in Pyapon and Toungoo airdrops of arms have been arranged. Japanese strategy seems to be to fall back east of the Sittang and make their stand there. British forces like to bomb everything out before advancing. That is costing heavily in the lives of the village people. We have offered to go in and clear the way, if they would only give us the arms."

"Three Japanese divisions, the British estimate, have crossed the Pegu Yoma between Tharrawaddy and Prome, and they are trying to break through in small groups of 50 or 100. Our forces are engaged in mopping them up."

"Rangoon was occupied on April 30 with a force of about 600 BNA and partisans. Bo Khin Nyo, Bo Thein Han, Bo Sein Tin, Bo Ba Ni and others commanded the force. Several of these officers and the 600 men were released by the Japanese when they left—which was on April 28. Ko Ba Swe, Ko Kyaw Nyein and Ko Kyaw Nyein (R.E.T.) helped to organize the occupation of Rangoon before the British arrived. We proclaimed the occupation immediately, and formed a Peace Preservation Committee with those Cabinet ministers who were around, and Justice Ba U. We broadcast the proclamation repeatedly from an experimental broadcasting station. Yet, the British apparently received information that the Japanese were massed for the battle of Rangoon. We got a message that the Indian Navy and the 15th Army Corps were going to bombard the city on the very day that we reclaimed it. We had to send Bo Aung Gyi urgently to Elephant Point to inform the British forces that the city was safely in our hands. The 15th Army Corps then took the credit for the capture of Rangoon."

"I came down to Rangoon," Bo Ne Win reported, "on May 6 to take stock of the situation. Col. Holden of the 15th Army Corps, the 26th Indian Division and V Force, came to see me.

He explained the need to collect the arms from our men while they are in Rangoon. He emphasized that our forces were not being disarmed. Indian troops of their forces have never seen the Japanese, and our men might be mistaken for Japanese, he told me, and Indian soldiers might therefore fire upon them, thereby damaging relations beyond repair. Holden told me they would supply us with uniforms and funds. I asked for Rs. 2 million; he said he only had Rs. 2,000, which he gave me. He asked for situation reports on the Delta and other parts of the country; I supplied it. We have good working relations with him, but no access to Gen. Chambers, the commander, who is reported to be assisted by ex-police officers, Loader, Orr and Hoope."

The political situation was fluid, which worried Bo Ne Win. "I thought Thakin Than Tun had settled the political problem with the British authorities," he wrote, "but apparently he hasn't. We presumed that the Burma Army would be recognized as a standing army, but it appears that that has not been agreed upon. We seem to be entirely on our own."

The British were saying that they could not discuss the future constitution of the country, nor even the future of the resistance forces. Gen. Chambers announced that he had assumed duty as "military governor" of Rangoon to Justices Mya Bu and Ba U, U Soe Nyunt, U Aung Chein and P. K. Chow. "The BNA was not invited to the meeting," Bo Ne Win reported, "which was an indication that they wanted to ignore our existence."

"We have been issuing press statements to clarify the aims and achievements of the resistance. On May 10 I met correspondents from the Associated Press, Reuters, United Press, the B.B.C., the London *Times,* All India Radio and others, and explained that we fought the British in 1942 because Burma was left out of the Atlantic Charter, while we were promised independence by the Japanese agents. When the Japanese broke their pledge and we saw the face of Fascism clearly revealed, we rose against them. All along, our one aim has been to win national independence, for which we are prepared to keep up the struggle. These statements are necessary, I think, because Mr. Amery has said that the Burmese would welcome the British back with open arms, and he might cite the action of our forces as example of such a welcome."

The White Paper issued by the British government, in which
the Governor's personal rule was envisaged for Burma for three
years at the end of which elections would be held, also disturbed
Bo Ne Win. "That would mean," he wrote, "that the British capitalist interests would return and resume their grip on Burma's
economy. After that, they would grant us self-government. Col.
Donnison (lately of the ICS) told Thakin Than Tun: 'I don't
know what to do with you and your organization!' So much is
now in the balance, the future of the country, the future of our
Army. These are crucial times. I think you should return to Rangoon without delay."[8]

12

Gen. Aung San left his command headquarters for Thayet on
May 6. From there he was to fly to a rendezvous with Gen. Slim
of the XIVth Army.

On May 7, at camp in Ponna village, word was brought that a
sizeable Japanese force was approaching. Northwards, along the
Irrawaddy river, battles were being fought between the Japanese
and the Allied forces. For several days, therefore, Aung San and
party were caught in the whirlpool of battle. A Japanese force entered the village, slipping through the guerrilla guards. Bo Aung
San, who had moved on to another village a few miles away, had
some things to say about the conduct of Bo Zeya and his men
who had charge of the area. On May 12, Gen. Aung San crossed
the river to Allanmyo. Gen. Slim sent an aircraft to take Gen.
Aung San to Meiktila where the two commanders met for the
first time on May 16.

"The arrival of Aung San," remembered Slim, "dressed in the
near Japanese uniform of a Major-General, complete with sword,
startled one or two of my staff who had not been warned of his
coming. However, he behaved with the utmost courtesy, and so,
I hope, did we." "I was impressed with Aung San," wrote Field-
Marshal Slim. "He was not the ambitious, unscrupulous guerrilla
leader I had expected. He was certainly ambitious and meant to

---

[8] The letter, in Burmese, is reproduced in *Armed Forces Day*, a collection of articles and material on the Resistance, published in 1960 by the
Institute of Military Science.

secure for himself a dominant position in post-war Burma, but I judged him to be a genuine patriot and a well-balanced realist—characters which are not always combined. His experience with the Japanese had put his views on the British into a truer perspective. He was ready himself to cooperate with us in the liberation and restoration of Burma and, I thought, probably to go on cooperating after that had been accomplished. The greatest impression he made on me was one of honesty. He was not free with glib assurances and he hesitated to commit himself, but I had the idea that if he agreed to do something he would keep his word. I could do business with Aung San."[9]

The meeting ended on a cordial note. The resistance forces were placed at the disposal of the Allied commander who in turn undertook to arm, equip and supply them. Lord Mountbatten, supreme commander SEAC, wrote in his Report to the Combined Chiefs of Staff: "On the 30th May, 1945, I held a meeting in my Rear Headquarters with Sir Reginald Dorman-Smith, which was attended by Lt.-Generals, Leese, Slim and Stopford, and by the new Chief, Civil Affairs Organization (Burma), Maj.-General H. E. (later Sir Hubert) Rance (who had succeeded Maj.-General Pearce on the 10th May). At this meeting it was agreed that there would be no political censorship on the activities of the Burma National Army; but that guidance should be given to our own military observers and to the Psychological Warfare Department, to confine themselves to stories of a factual nature. It was also agreed that the forces under the command of Maj.-General Aung San were to be re-named as the Patriot Burmese Forces. . . ."

For a few more months the PBF were kept busy along the Sittang River between Toungoo and Pegu. Perilous tasks did not end in that area with the Japanese surrender. PBF teams had to go deep into the jungles to contact the scattered Japanese groups and the stragglers. When contact was established, a Japanese officer, specially flown in from Bangkok or Saigon, and attached to the PBF team would go out to tell the lost soldiers that the war was over. There would then be weeping, some attempts at *hara-kiri,* followed eventually by a draining away of the emotions, until the Japanese soldiers, sick and covered with sores, simply sat or stretched on the ground, staring blankly, past care, past exhaus-

[9] *Aung San of Burma,* p. 83.

tion. The dangerous moment for the PBF team was when the Japanese were approached; their instinctive response was to open fire. Several PBF men, and some Japanese officers who had come from afar, were killed in carrying the message of peace to the Japanese soldiers who were lost in the jungle.

In the Delta, the PBF troops were disarmed. Their readiness, indeed eagerness, to carry on fighting until freedom was won became known to the British. Thakin Soe and Thakin Than Tun prevailed upon Gen. Aung San to order the disarming and demobilization of the Delta troops. The order was obeyed with extreme reluctance. There too the men wept when they had to lay down their arms.

On August 12, the commanders of the resistance, meeting in Pegu, issued a statement to the people calling for unity and unrelenting effort in the continuing struggle for national freedom. It was not for the benefit of a privileged few, nor for the personal glory of the commanders that the resistance had been waged and the heavy sacrifices made. It was for the freedom of all the people, regardless of their race or religion. "We call upon all our countrymen, and all the leaders, to rise above any differences they may have and forge the AFPFL as a national front. Let us apply ourselves, in full unity and without delay, to the continuing struggle for independence and the reconstruction of the country."[10]

The statement was signed by Gen. Aung San, Colonels Ne Win, Let Ya and Zeya, Majors Maung Maung, Aung Gyi, Kyaw Zaw, Ye Htut, and Aung. Captain Arlarwaka signed the statement as commander of the Upper Burma Zone, for Bo Ba Htu had died of malaria at Aung Ban in the Shan State on the hard campaign.

[10] The statement is reproduced in U Ba Than's *The Roots of the Revolution*, Rangoon, 1962.

6

The Union of Burma

1

THIS BOOK is not a catalogue of the names of people who bore their shares of the burden, ran their risks, and made their contributions in the struggle for Burma's freedom. Such a catalogue would fill not one volume but many. Nor can it be ever complete, for there are the unnamed people, the unknown soldiers, who gave their lives in the struggle. A victory of a resistance force might get recorded, or even be mentioned in despatches. But the villagers who supported the resistance, whose villages were put to the torch by the avenging Japanese troops, whose sons and husbands were mown down by angry Japanese machine-guns—they often got no more than a passing sigh.

But sacrifices there had to be. The resistance claimed the heaviest sacrifices from people—mainly the peasants, for war is mainly waged in the fields—and also drew the best that was in them. In giving, the people found their souls. No unity can ever be stronger than that which is forged in the red-heat of war between people who all become comrades-in-arms fighting for one victory under one leader. This unity, fortunately for Burma's cause, was kept up after the resistance. The call by the commanders for further endeavour in unity and under the AFPFL banner was heeded.

At the meeting in Pegu, the commanders decided that Gen. Aung San's time to assume national leadership had come. The Army must no longer claim him for its own; he must go out to lead the whole nation to independence. On August 19, 1945, at a mass meeting of the people held in the Naythuyain theatre hall in Rangoon Aung San (now affectionately called by the people "Bogyoke", the General, the Supremo) emphasized that the AFPFL belonged to the people. "Some people think it is an organization of Thakins," he said. "That is not so. The AFPFL is

161

11

not the Dobama Asi-ayone resurrected under a different name. I was a member of the Asi-ayone at one time, but I am not any longer. The AFPFL is separate and distinct from the Asi-ayone. Nor is the AFPFL the Communist party. There are some Communists in the leadership of the AFPFL but it does not belong to them. It belongs to the people; it represents the people."

"For me," Bogyoke Aung San continued, "politics has meant poverty, ceaseless striving, sacrifice, and running risks including that of death. I am in politics because I covet a crown, not to wear on my head, but the crown of freedom for Burma, for the people. That is the crown our boys in the guerrilla forces covet too, for when they die of wounds in the field, they say, 'Weep not for me, I have done my duty; carry on and do yours.' "[1]

On September 4 a delegation led by Aung San left Rangoon by air for Kandy to negotiate with Lord Mountbatten for the future of the BNA and the guerrilla forces. On the delegation were Thakin Than Tun, U Ba Pe, Saw Ba U Gyi and U Nyo Tun, providing the political talent. Bo Ne Win, Bo Let Ya, Bo Zeya, Bo Kyaw Zaw, Bo Maung Maung and Bo Zaw Min (Kyaw Winn) were also there to speak for the armed forces.

A settlement was reached in Kandy that the Patriot Burmese Forces would be absorbed into the reformed Burma Army. Some 5,000 soldiers with 300 reserves and 200 officers with 200 reserves would be taken from the PBF. That would exclude thousands of the BNA men and guerrillas, but the Burma Army could later be expanded to take them in. The agreement did not permit amalgamation of the PBF battalions and their officers, intact, as they stood, in the new Army; yet, it was better than nothing, better than total disbandment. It was going to be the BIA and the BDA all over again, but the men had been through it once, and they would survive this change as well.

Lord Mountbatten offered Bo Aung San a brigadier's commission and the post of deputy inspector-general in the Burma Army. "You must decide," he told Aung San at their friendly parting, "to be either a Churchill or a Wellington; you cannot be a soldier and a political leader at the same time."[2]

"The mission was a success," U Ba Pe told the reporters when

1 *Aung San of Burma*, p. 99.
2 *Aung San of Burma*, p. 89.

the delegation arrived back in Rangoon. "We were treated very cordially. We ate several times with Mountbatten, Bogyoke Aung San seated on his right, and I on his left."[3] U Ba Pe, however, did not disclose what Saw Ba U Gyi had said to him in private conversations in Kandy. That was not entirely relevant, nor too happy for the future. Discussing the wishes of the Karens, U Ba Pe had asked his colleague whether a Karen State within the Union would be adequate fulfilment. Saw Ba U Gyi had smiled and replied, "No, U Ba Pe, we want much more than that, much more than that."[4]

"We were getting on very well with Saw Ba U Gyi," recalled Gen. Ne Win in later years about the Kandy mission, "we had arrived at good understandings. Then, at the conference table, some British ICS men spoke up about the loyalty of Burma's highland people to the British, and the British obligation to protect them. This sort of talk swayed Saw Ba U Gyi and drove a wedge between us."[5]

2

Aung San and his comrades applied themselves to two main tasks on their return to Kandy: the building of the AFPFL into a national front with claim to form a national government and convene a constituent assembly for the drafting of the constitution for independent statehood; and the reorganization of the Burma Army. Aung San who had decided to lead the AFPFL wrote to Mountbatten declining the offer of a brigadier's commission in the Army. "Personally, I would have prefered a military career, above all others, for a permanent calling," he wrote, but bowing to the decision of colleagues in the AFPFL and the PBF, "I must now take leave of you before I go out from the Army to face the portentous perspective of a political career which, I hope, may not turn out to be as portentous as it looks."[6]

Bo Ne Win, to whom once again Bo Aung San gave the com-

[3] Report of a press conference given by the delegation on return to Rangoon, *The Sun*, September 11, 1945.

[4] Evidence of U San Maung, a prosecution witness, in *U Win Sein vs. U Ba Pe and Others*, Criminal Trial No. 1 of 1954 in the Court of the District Magistrate (Special Judge 1), Rangoon.

[5] Gen. Ne Win's *Statements of Policy on the National Races*, p. 66.
[6] *Aung San of Burma*, p. 90.

mand of all troops in the field, established his headquarters in
Pegu with the British IV Corps, and supervised the winding up
of operations, the demobilization of the men, and the selection
of those who chose to remain in the reformed Army. It was a sad
job, sending the young men home. Those who were selected to
serve could not stay together. Available commissions were not
enough for the young officers of the PBF, many of whom had
been in the field, leading men, since the BIA days. A few hundred
of the PBF officers had to start in the Burma Army as privates.
The changes were sad and souring, but the men bore them well.
Bo Ne Win, who made a point of visiting all the holding and
enquiry centres, did his best to give heart to the men.

Young officers who had graduated in the military schools in
Japan arrived back soon after the war, feeling sad that they had
missed the resistance. Rangoon made them sadder, for they were,
for some time, lost and forgotten. The few months in Japan before the war's end had been hard. They had been cold and hungry,
and, after the resistance had started in Burma, in constant danger
of Japanese reprisal. Bo Setkya the military attache, had collected the young officers, and civilian students together, and soon
after the Japanese surrender, had persuaded the Americans to
provide priority passages for the young men. Back in Rangoon,
they wandered about in their bright and shiny khaki gaberdine
uniforms supplied by the American armed forces. They had nowhere to stay, no money for their board. Some camped out at
the Youth League headquarters; some shared an old empty building which lacked sanitary facilities. Bo Ne Win provided for the
boys as best as he could and tried to get them on the PBF roll
so that they might draw their salaries and rations. The army
bureaucracy, however, stood squarely in the way. Bo Let Ya,
stiff, starched and formal, was no great help. After some futile
attempts to get some funds from Army HQ, Bo Ne Win blew up
with his choicest curses, "borrowed" from the AFPFL and gave
out fares and pocket-money to the boys to enable them to visit
their families whom they had not seen for more than three years,
before joining up. Most of the thirty who went to Japan in the
first batch received commissions. Almost all of the forty who were
in the second batch had to join as privates, and many of them
went to the 4th Burma Rifles which was given to Bo Ne Win.

Those were busy months for Bo Ne Win, but not without their frustrations. Seeing the PBF melt away was in itself a frustrating experience. In the streets he would run into young men adrift. He would recognize a face from afar, stop his car—or trishaw which was a favourite transportation of his in the lean period— and talk with the young man or take him home for a meal. His home was a transit camp for his associates and the young men, but then he himself was in transit. His old political associates urged him to revive the Dobama Asi-ayone. The Communist Party, which had started organizing early, with headquarters on Bagaya Road, was flourishing. PBF veterans and partisans, who were looking for a home, a cause, were flocking to the Party HQ. Thakin Than Tun and Thakin Soe were reaping a rich harvest of recruits; their classes were attracting even some of the young officers who had received commissions in the new Burma Army.

Friends therefore urged Bo Ne Win to leave the Army and lead the Dobama Asi-ayone. He was not uninterested. The prospect of starting all over again with a battalion and a Major's commission, was not attractive. The real challenge would be in the political arena, he thought. The Asi-ayone, which had done so much to unite the young nationalists, had ended a bright chapter of its career with the departure for Japan of the thirty comrades. During the war it had led a pale existence, merged with the Sinyetha Party, mingled with the Maha-Bama (Greater Burma), both led by Dr Ba Maw. Several Thakins looked for a leader. Bo Ne Win with his war record could make a successful one. A revitalized Asi-ayone could become an important force in the AFPFL and Bo Ne Win could take his place beside Bo Aung San in the political struggle. Bo Aung San, however, heard of the discussions among the Thakins, and advised Bo Ne Win to stay with the Army. "It needs you," he said, "and the country needs the Army." Thus, it was the 4th Burma Rifles, not the Dobama Asi-ayone, which got him.

The "4 Burifs" camped and trained at Legyun-Simee near Prome. Bo Ne Win, soon promoted Lt.-Colonel, shared the command of the battalion for the first few months with British officers of equal rank. Lt.-Colonels Vallance, Mitchell and Scott, were some of those officers who came and went. All down the command hierarchy, Burmese officers worked with British coun-

terparts. A strong team of young officers who were later to rise
high in the Army and share in its shaping were with Bo Ne Win.
Bo Tin Pe, Bo Aung Gyi and Bo Maung Maung who had all been
zone commanders in the resistance; Bo Ba Sein, Bo Kyaw Soe, Bo
Soe Naing, Bo Mya Thaung, and Bo Aye Maung; Bo Than Sein,
Maung Bo, Bo Ba Than. Several young PBF officers, and several
of those who had returned from Japan also chose to serve in the
battalion as privates: Gwan Shein, Hla Moe, Lu Maw, Ye Gaung,
and others. The *esprit de corps* was good. Officers and men worked and lived as comrades. Training schedules were meticulously
carried out. To encourage his young officers and the men to do
it all over again, Bo Ne Win himself would rise at crack of dawn
and go into the field to participate in the drill and the training.
He would often be the first in the field. No course was skipped
as elementary, no drill was avoided as dull.

There were lighter moments at camp. Saturdays and Sundays
were given to relaxation. At the mess there would be plenty of
beer to drink, and talk would wander freely, spiced with soldiers'
jokes. All week long the snobbery of some British officers, the
emotional problems of adjustment of some of the men, the rigours
of training, the restraints and discipline of barrack life, the uncertainty of the political future, all these had been borne with a
grin. Now over the week-end all could relax a little, laugh, dissolve the woes and the worries in rum and beer, and face the
new week with stout hearts. They would laugh in the mess at the
troubles of Bo Tin Pe, the Administration Company commander,
for the men's wants were never satisfied and supplies were never
enough. Once, in despair over a supply problem Bo Tin Pe had
ordered his assistants to stop issue of an item and not to relent
"even if *Thagyamin* (King of the Devas) came down from the
heavens to plead." The instruction was misunderstood. The assistants thought they had to stop the issue of sugar (*thagya*), and
promptly acted. The companies complained, first in whispers,
then aloud. For a few days the battalion drank sugarless tea. The
desperate situation led to an investigation which traced the source
of the error. The battalion laughed; tea was sweet again.

Bo Ne Win was a socialist by conviction, though his undivided
loyalty was to army and country. People he had closely worked
with in the political days and the resistance were Socialists: Ba

Swe, Kyaw Nyein, and others. By friendly association and philosophical affinity Bo Aung Gyi, Bo Maung Maung, Bo Tin Pe and other senior officers of the battalion were also closer to the Socialists than to the Communists. There was keen competition between the Socialists—who were slow to start their party—and the Communist party, which was early and fast, for support from the army. The politicians found willing recruits among some officers and men who, on their part, found it useful to have political associations. Some officers and men did not even bother to hide political ties.

Bo Ne Win, however, had seen what divided loyalties could do to the army and he fixed clear boundaries of loyalty for himself, his officers and the men. The building of the army came first. The aim and purpose of the army was to serve in the winning of national freedom, and in its protection afterwards. Mercenary motives must be kept out; the inspiration must be kept alive. Yet, discipline must be maintained, and the transcending loyalty must be to the nation, not to any party. It was a national army, a people's army, they were building, not a pocket army for any party, Socialist or Communist. Personal friendships must not interfere with the performance of duty; the soldiers could vote as they pleased at elections, but as men-at-arms they must obey orders and march as one. This was a code both of ethics and of conduct, which Bo Ne Win taught the 4 Burifs to obey. He himself obeyed the code strictly. On his visits to Rangoon he would call on Bo Aung San at his Tower Lane residence. Aung San was national leader, above party, above faction, and to him Bo Ne Win acknowledged his absolute loyalty, as he always had. Then Bo Ne Win would visit the Socialists and discuss the political situation. He would urge his friends to organize the Socialist party, recruit strong cadres and go to the country. Rousing and rallying the people for the march to freedom was the immediate task, but if a prolonged armed struggle was needed demonstrations and slogans would not be enough; grass-roots organization was called for which demanded sustained work. Beyond listening, beyond stressing the need for thorough organization, Bo Ne Win would not, however, go. He would not allow any party to use him or his men in its cause. There the boundary was clearly drawn, under no circumstances to be crossed.

3

The military administration, headed by Maj.-General Sir Hubert
E. Rance, was wound up on October 16, 1945, and Sir Reginald
Dorman-Smith, who arrived in Rangoon with his staff by the
H. M. S. Cleopatra on that day, took over. It was, Sir Reginald
hoped, a happy return. "Burma's fight for freedom is over," he
declared with a winning smile, pointing out that the statement
of policy towards Burma made by His Majesty's Government
contained all the solutions to all the problems. "Let us get on
with the job," he called out, asking the people to rally behind
him while he ran the country in a period of personal rule. He
would appoint a small Executive Council to give Burmans a
share in the administration, and a small Legislative Council in
which Burmans could speak. The tasks ahead were huge, the
aspirations of the people were high, but the Councils would be
small, their real powers tiny; all that Sir Reginald could offer
was big smiles for which the people had little use.

The people were undernourished, shabby, and without proper
shelter in the bombed-out city of Rangoon. In the country too,
the peasants had lost their plough cattle and were in dire want
for essential consumer goods. The roads needed repairs; the
bridges were down. The railways had been torn up; those locomotives that were still serviceable puffed and panted with little
strength to pull. Reconstruction and rehabilitation were undoubtedly the crying needs. The plans which were made in Simla by
the experts and the evacuee civil servants were, Sir Reginald
thought, what Burma needed most. The various "projects" and
"boards"—in which British business firms would play major
parts—would import needed capital and skills into the country
and get the economy going again.

Where Sir Reginald and His Majesty's Government went wrong
was in leaving out the wishes and aspirations of the people of
Burma, their unity and their spirit. They might be shabby, but
their spirit was all right. They needed consumer goods, but wanted
freedom from foreign rule first. They had come through hard
times, but were ready to face a harder future in the struggle. They
had found in Bogyoke Aung San their national leader, and with
him they would march to the final goal. The Japanese occupation

had taught them self-reliance and given them self-confidence. "We would have risen against the Japanese on our own," Gen. Aung San had said, "for the resistance was an essential part of our larger struggle for national freedom."[7] This, Lord Mountbatten had acknowledged in his directive to his military administration staff. "As regards the BNA and the AFO," he pointed out in his directive on "policy towards Burmans" of June 2, 1945, "they have risen before it was clear to them that British Forces would, or could, come to their rescue. And it can be said that they are rising for their own ends, and not for love of us. I think it would be unrealistic on our part to suppose that the people of any nation engage in war except in their own interests, however praiseworthy they may be."[8]

The end which the people kept in constant view was independence. Sir Reginald, who had to work within the narrow framework laid down by the White Paper, could only promise that he would rule gently for three years, then hold elections. "Let us get on with the job," he invited the people, but his goals and theirs, his priorities and theirs, were different. The White Paper prescribed the steps and phases by which "full self-government within the British Commonwealth" would finally be established in "Burma proper". The AFPFL asked for free elections without delay for a Constituent Assembly. As for the status of New Burma, the people must be free to choose, whether they liked to set up a republic. "Dominion status within the British Commonwealth," Aung San explained to a foreign correspondent, "is associated in our minds with inferiority and alien things. We must be free to make our own decision about our future."[9]

The White Paper also made the 'Scheduled Areas'—inhabited by the indigenous races of the highlands—subject to "a special regime under the Governor until such time as their inhabitants signify their desire for some suitable form of amalgamation of their territories with Burma proper."[10] This too was looked upon by the AFPFL and the people as another trick to "divide and

[7] Report on a press conference in *The New Burma in the New World*.
[8] *Report*, p. 230.
[9] Report on a press conference in *The New Burma in the New World*.
[10] The White Paper is reproduced in *Burma in the Family of Nations*, by Maung Maung.

rule". In a response to the Governor's policy speech, the Supreme Council of the AFPFL pointed out on October 17, that "the peoples of Burma have jointly and unitedly fought the Fascist aggressor and we can claim today that the peoples are more united than ever. The AFPFL is fully determined to ensure and safeguard the legitimate aspirations of the national minorities."[11]

Apart from the limitations imposed by the White Paper, Sir Reginald also felt himself to be under obligations to Sir Paw Tun and Sir Htoon Aung Gyaw, the ministers who had evacuated with him to Simla. Having spent three years in the cool safety of Simla, those elder politicians were out of touch with the moods and tempers of the Burma to which they returned. To them Aung San and the AFPFL leaders were mere boys. Give them office and appease them, or if they failed to respond to that classic treatment, put them all in jail. Sir Paw Tun had never seen the first method fail. He himself had always responded well to it; he had never refused a good offer of high office. If the first method did not succeed, the second could not fail. Lock up the loud young firebrands, and the crowds behind them would melt away. Sir Reginald was not so sure that Sir Paw Tun's methods would work. In fact he was not sure that Sir Paw Tun had a firm grasp of the situation. Yet, he could not dump the good old sport who had loyally followed him into the lonely exile of Simla.

Sir Reginald invited the AFPFL to participate in the Executive Council, duly recognizing the fact—though pretending hard that he did not—that the AFPFL represented the massive majority of the people. Bogyoke Aung San and the AFPFL decided that co-operation with the Governor on certain terms, would be expedient. Eleven nominations were made to the Governor for his Executive Council: Bogyoke Aung San; U Ba Pe, the veteran politician; U Aye and U Ba Ohn of the Myochit party, members of the Supreme Council of the AFPFL; U Razak, a Burmese Muslim, headmaster of the National School in Mandalay; U Mya (Pyawbwe) of the Sinyetha party, a Supreme Councillor of the League; Thakin Mya, Socialist leader, Supreme Councillor of the League; Thakin Thein Pe, the AFPFL's representative in India during the war, Supreme Councillor, general secretary of the

[11] Statements in *The New Burma in the New World.*

Burma Communist party; U Nyo Tun, leader of the resistance movement in Arakan; Mahn Ba Khin and Saw Ba U Gyi (Supreme Councillor of the AFPFL) leaders of the Karens. The Governor had proposed to appoint fifteen Executive Councillors; the League suggested that the Governor should accept and choose the remaining four Councillors himself. Participation by the AFPFL, it was also made clear, was only "a start and not an end in itself"; while co-operation would be extended in the reconstruction of the country, efforts would be made to conduct "a free general election based on universal adult suffrage for a constituent assembly for the purpose of drawing up a new democratic constitution for the country." The Supreme Council of the League also framed an instrument of instructions for its nominees. They must work the Executive Council as a popular government, mobilizing mass sanction to its support, stand up for civil liberties, report back to the Supreme Council, "function as a united team under a leader and a ship of their own," resign if directed by the Supreme Council.

The Governor could not accept the eleven nominees of the AFPFL. He decided that he would only have an Executive Council of eleven, in which he would offer seven seats to the AFPFL. Also, he found Thakin Thein Pe unacceptable. Thus the rift between the Governor and the AFPFL widened. Instead of co-operation there were charges and counter-charges. The Governor accused the AFPFL of adopting "fascist methods"; the League likewise called Sir Reginald a Fascist. "We want a National Provisional Government," Bogyoke Aung San declared at a mass meeting held soon after the deadlock had arisen. "We are not satisfied with the Governor's Executive Council. What he said fell short of our national aspirations, but we are prepared to co-operate if the Governor would form his Council consisting of national leaders who can truly be said to represent the people. The Governor says that we are Fascist. We say emphatically: 'No'; our methods are democratic. Our nominees are representatives and we only issue an instrument of instructions as any democratic party of any democratic country would do. We want to shoulder collective responsibility. If anybody is Fascist, it is the Governor, not we. The Governor says, 'There is no legal obligation on my part to form even an Executive Council. No one has

a right of representation on the Council.' These words show that
the Governor is showing fascist tendencies."[12]

Thus from the start of his personal rule the Governor ran into
the opposition offered by the AFPFL. The fight was not over, as
he had said and hoped, it was just beginning. The main issue
was not the allocation of seats in the Executive Council; it went
much deeper than that. The issue was who should govern: the
Governor representing the British Crown, or the AFPFL representing the people. If the Governor won, he could stay and rule;
if he lost he must turn over the country to the people and go. The
deadlock between Sir Reginald and Bogyoke Aung San brought
that main issue into the open. For Burma it was just as well. Had
there been no deadlock, had Sir Reginald smilingly welcomed
Aung San and the AFPFL into the Executive Council from the
start, the heat and urgency of the fight for freedom would have
been off, the main issue might have been lost in the endless
routine of government, and Aung San, the leader of the people,
would have been swamped and smothered by governmental
routine. Now Aung San was free to lead the people in the field.
In their eyes he remained their very own; he was not in the pay
of the Governor; all his dedication and allegiance was to the cause
of Burma's freedom.

4

The Governor made Sir Paw Tun and Sir Htoon Aung Gyaw
senior members of the Executive Council. Two British Civilians,
Sir John Wise and Sir Raibeart McDougall were also given their
seats. U Ba Ohn and U Aye of the Myochit party, who were included in the AFPFL nominations, left the League to receive
their appointments. U Lun, another Myochit, was also made a
Councillor. U Pu, whom U Saw ousted as prime minister, resigned
from the Supreme Council of the AFPFL to obtain an appointment. Politicians of standing were hard to get, and the Governor
had difficulty in filling all the seats in the Council. He managed to
tempt Mahn Ba Khin, also an AFPFL nominee; and U Yan Aung
who had once worn the Thakin name. U Tharrawaddy Maung
Maung of the Sinyetha party also received an appointment and

[12] Statement in *The New Burma in the New World.*

thus the Executive Council of eleven was complete. It was a mixed lot of Councillors who had some past but no future, who called themselves leaders but had no following, who were willing to talk but impotent to act. The Executive Council soon proved to be a millstone round Sir Reginald's neck.

A small Legislative Council was also got together by the Governor with some old Thakins, some members of the Myochit and the Sinyetha parties, some journalists, educationists, traders and professional people. The Legislative Council debated. Some members delivered strong speeches. Some good questions were asked; some ringing resolutions were passed. U Chit Hlaing, president of the Council, moved a resolution demanding general elections by November, 1947, on universal adult suffrage. Thakin Kyaw Sein demanded that reserved subjects be handed over to Burmans as independence was on the way. But the speeches and the resolutions did not stir the British Government in London into action, nor did they interest or inspire the people. Both looked upon the Council as a bit of a joke. U E Maung, the Advocate-General, had occasion once to explain to the Council that it was outside its competence to make laws. "Say no more," Thakin Lu Tun, a member, cried, "shame us no more! We are already ashamed because the people and the press are saying that we have no power and we are useless!"[13]

Sir Reginald too might well have echoed in his private thoughts the anguished cry of Thakin Lu Tun. His power had fast run away; only its shadow remained on paper. His writ ceased to run in the country. Nothing he did seemed to go well; nothing the AFPFL did seemed to go wrong. The AFPFL, in its efforts to assume the status of a united front, had taken on its Supreme Council leaders of the Myochit, the Sinyetha, the Dobama Asiayone, and other parties, and individuals like U Thein Maung who had long lost touch with party politics. The departure of some of the Supreme Councillors to accept office from the Governor strengthened the League and made for a stronger, closer leadership. The mass support for the AFPFL became stronger; AFPFL rallies and demonstrations became mammoth affairs. Sir Reginald had legal but no real power; he reigned but could not

[13] Burma Legislative Council, *Proceedings*, vol. I, No. 17, p. 606.

rule. The AFPFL had no legal power, but it ruled by mass support.

The AFPFL, in those exciting months, became the people. And Aung San was the AFPFL. The Communists, seeing the rapid rise of the League, tried to seize its leadership. They could not, however, do without Aung San. In January, 1946, the first national conference of the League was convened on the western slopes of the Shwedagon. Delegates, numbering 1,300, came from all over the country, and in the plenary public sessions more than 100,000 people attended. Behind the scenes, in the inner councils, there were trials of strength. The Communists wanted to have their men in the key posts of the League executive. Thakin Thein Pe, with his many gifts and the glamour of the Resistance agent who had fought his wars in foreign lands, was a contender against Aung San for the presidency of the League. So was Thakin Than Tun who had served as general secretary of the AFPFL and had signed the Kandy Agreement with Aung San for the delegation from Burma. The argument therefore was that though Gen. Aung San was the military leader of the Resistance, Thakins Thein Pe and Than Tun were at least his political equals. The Communist Party, however, was already showing divisions in its Central Committee. Thakin Soe was growling angrily about the treachery of the comrades and the AFPFL. Differences between Thein Pe and Than Tun were beginning to show. Splits in the leadership were forming beneath the surface.

The older politicians in the AFPFL also considered nominating U Ba Pe for the presidency. Aung San, some wanted to say, was too young. The veteran politicians knew the political tricks; the younger men were only good for fighting. So, the older men should lead, the younger should follow. This argument too could not prevail. The older men had little to show but their age. More than half of them had gone over to take office under the Governor. The remainder had wise counsels to offer, but no real following. They were clever with words, well-versed in rules of procedure, but the urgent need was for leadership in the field where the people were massed for the final march to freedom. For that leadership they looked to Aung San.

Thus Aung San emerged not merely the president of the League, but the national leader. First, he needed the AFPFL to establish his position; soon the AFPFL needed him to establish its own standing. The people, looking for a leader in the crucial phase of the country's history, had found him, and he had found his role. The Communists, the Socialists and the Elders in the AFPFL soon began to vie with one another to get closer to him; jostled in public to stand nearer to him, chat intimately with him, to be seen by the people as the Bogyoke's dear friends. Kyaw Nyein, the Socialist, served as general secretary and Thein Pe, the Communist, after losing to Kyaw Nyein in the election for the post, served as joint general secretary. Aung San was pleased with the arrangement, for his one great hope was that the leftist forces would unite and build a socialist New Burma.

Bogyoke Aung San spoke for several hours at the opening session of the AFPFL national convention. He had written his speech in flowery English, and the script ran into 75 type-written pages. The Burmese translation was much longer. In the middle of his reading, he lost his breath for a while, and an associate had to continue the reading for him. The people kept coming and going. Some, having brought their meals, ate under the shades. Some had come from villages far afield, by bus, by bullockcart, on foot. They wanted to see the Bogyoke; they wanted to hear his voice. Now they saw him, heard him, and they were pleased, no matter what he said. Whatever he said must be right; there was no need to hear it all, for they trusted him completely. The British director of information, the Reverend George Appleton, mingled with the audience—as did several foreign correspondents. "It looked as if the stage was set for a carefully planned and timed entry of the leader, on the totalitarian model," he wrote later about the opening session of the conference, "but when the time came, Aung San passed almost unobserved through the people to the platform and quietly began his speech. No ostentation, no rehearsed ovation. His speech lasted three and half hours; most of it he read quickly in an even tone. There were surveys of history, patriotic passages, vitriolic outbursts, Socialist and Marxist doctrine, for the manuscript was a composite one. Occasionally, Aung San put his manuscript aside, and then he spoke with fire and humour."[14]

A young lieutenant of the PBF, Tun Aung Gyaw, arrived back

14 *Aung San of Burma,* p. 101.

from Calcutta where he was flown out wounded from the battle-field at Meiktila. He went straight to report to Aung San at the conference, and Aung San introduced him to the assembly. The young man, straight and slim, dark as ebony, stood on the dais up high, beside his commander-in-chief, took the applause of the people modestly and spoke a few words. To the people the young soldier was a sharp reminder that the war and the resistance were not so far behind, and that there was no guarantee they did not wait round the corner in the future.

5

There were many confrontations between the Governor and the AFPFL. The one over the People's Volunteer Organization (PVO) was the most bitter and prolonged.

The PVO was started on December 1, 1945, primarily to or-ganize as a political force those PBF men who were not absorb-ed into the Burma Army. Hundreds and thousands of those veterans were wandering about all over the country, looking for jobs or something worthwhile to do. They needed help to resettle. They needed an organization as a home where they could feel useful and wanted. Bogyoke Aung San himself took on the leader-ship of the PVO; Bo Aung, Bo La Yaung, Bo Tun Lin, Bo Thein Dan, Bo Aung Min and Bo Taik Soe were among those on the Executive Committee. The PVO quickly attracted the veterans as well as young new recruits; it soon became much more than an ex-servicemen's association. In a matter of months, with member-ship of over 100,000 in units in every town and village, the PVO became, in effect, the unarmed private army of the AFPFL. As the rift between the AFPFL and the Governor became wider, the role of the PVO became more militant, reflecting the mood of the League and the people.

Men of the PVO drilled in the playing fields, and trained with dummy rifles. They wore uniform, and were organized on the military pattern. The veterans flocked to the PVO because it was home. Young recruits flocked to it because it satisfied their urges, gave them an opportunity to participate in the political struggle, and they liked playing soldiers. The AFPFL leaders, especially Aung San, saw the dangers of the PVO and decided that it must

Colonel Ne Win, Commander-in-chief of the Burma National
Army, 1943.

Some of the thirty comrades on the march of the Burma Independence Army, seen with Bo Mogyoe (seated in Burmese dress) and the Rev. U Nagai, in yellow robes. On Bo Mogyoe's right is Bo Aung San, and on his left is Bo Ne Win. (*Courtesy: Defence Services Historical Research Institute*).

Some of the thirty comrades in training at Hainan; Bo Aung San, on the left, and Bo Ne Win, on the right, in a group engaged in map exercises.

(*Courtesy*: *Director of Information*)

Reunion of comrades at Pyinmana, Colonel Ne Win in command of Operation Flush, and Bogyoke Aung San who had recently assumed office as Deputy Chairman of the Governor's Executive Council.

(*Courtesy*: *Defence Services Historical Research Institute*)

General Ne Win being welcomed by delegates to the Peasants Seminar at Popa, 1963.

General Ne Win and Revolutionary Councillors chatting with delegates to the Peasants' Seminar in Rangoon, 1965.

General Ne Win addressing the Peasants' Day mass rally in Rangoon on March 2, 1965.

(*Courtesy*: *Director of Information*)

General and Madame Ne Win welcome outstanding students for the year 1966 to a reception in their honour at the State House.

(*Courtesy*: *Director of Information*)

General and Madame Ne Win, in a rare moment of relaxation at the Taj Mahal, on a State visit to India, February 1965.

(*Courtesy*: *Indian Information Services*)

be dissolved once independence was attained. In the meantime, however, the PVO was essential, unavoidable, useful.

The Governor issued orders prohibiting drilling and training in uniform. When the PVO ignored the orders, several arrests were made. By May, 1946, the PVO controversy was leading to angry exchanges of words between the Governor and the League. The PVO, Sir Reginald accused, was either organizing resistance or was being organized as a private army by "a political party". Firm steps, it was warned, would be taken to provide peaceful conditions in which the cultivators could grow their paddy in season and to ensure that fair elections could be held "as soon as possible." Aung San retorted that the PVO were there in the country to protect the peasants, to enter the fields and lend helping hands during the ploughing season. There were "volunteer corps" before the war too, he pointed out, and "a certain political organization adopted openly, with the connivance of the Government of the day, methods of beating down its opposition with bamboo sticks and lathis." Regarding general elections the AFPFL wanted them without delay and would co-operate in conducting them fairly. "I challenge the British authority," Aung San said, "to set up a mutually agreed international commission to investigate into the question of who and which organization could constitute a threat to fair and free elections in this country."[15]

Words led to incidents. At Tantabin, as elsewhere, PVO leaders were thrown into jail. On May 18, a demonstration staged in that town by peasants and PVO were fired upon by the police, and several people were killed. Aung San went to Tantabin to deliver the funeral oration which thousands came to hear.

The situation in the country worsened rapidly.

Earlier in the year the Government had brought the politicians back from their foreign sojourns and let them loose. U Saw was returned from Uganda. He came back flashing a great big smile which cut his square face into two halves. "I am arranging things," he told newsmen at a press conference, with the air of a prime minister in control. But the whole situation was strange to him. He could not gather round him a decent following.

Dr Ba Maw was released by the American Occupation Forces from the Sugamo jail in Japan. The Royal Air Force flew him

[15] Statement in *The New Burma in the New World.*

12

back to Rangoon, and he stepped down on Burmese soil wearing a jungle-green bush-shirt and sporting a clipped moustache in the style of Adolf Hitler. He announced that he was above party politics, though willing to respond if the nation called him to duty. He waited, but the nation did not call.

Thakin Tun Oke returned from his war-time exile in Singapore. The Governor made him an Executive Councillor, and he made strong anti-AFPFL speeches in the Legislative Council.

Thakin Ba Sein came back from Java. He was a little too late to get a seat in the Executive Council. He honestly declared, however, that if he was offered a seat he would take it. Sir Reginald often repeated that the door was open to the AFPFL to come into office, on terms that he had previously offered. The AFPFL did not enter through the open door. Thakin Ba Sein, on his part, repeated often that if the Governor invited him to assume office he would accept. Sir Reginald, however, did not invite him. The situation was fast getting out of hand, and there was no point in making the Councils mere gathering grounds of anti-AFPFL elements who had no real following among the people.

Thakin Mya, Thakin Nu and others who had evacuated to Moulmein with the Adipadi in April, 1945, returned to Rangoon towards the end of the year. The former became a leader of the Socialist party when at last the party was started. The first endeavours were to keep the AFPFL as one united party, not merely an alliance of parties, and discourage the setting up of separate parties. The Myochit, the Sinyetha, and such pre-war political parties were welcome to come in as parties, but the leftist forces, it was hoped, would unite and give the lead in the march to freedom. When the Communist party was set up, against the wishes of some of the younger leaders of the AFPFL, attempts were made to preserve leftist unity by making that party the one united leftist force. The party, however, would not accept many of the Socialists who offered to join. Those who were acceptable, like Ba Swe, must start as members or candidate members; there was no room in the Central Committee for them. Kyaw Nyein was totally rejected. "He should retire from politics now," was the verdict of Thakin Than Tun and Thakin Ba Hein. Thus it was that, several months after the Communists had started organizing their party the Socialists decided to organize their's. Thakin Mya was elected chairman, Ba Swe the secretary of the party. On the executive committee were Thakins Tin and Kyaw Dun, U Kyaw Nyein, U Ko Ko Gyi, Ba Swe Lay, Bo Aung Gyi (who came in later from the 4 Burifs, after resigning his commission in the Burma Army) and others.

Despite the split in the leftist forces, the people were united behind Bogyoke Aung San. The PVO, organized on the military pattern, bound by something akin to military discipline, took orders from Aung San, their commandant. There was hardly any political opposition to speak of. U Saw, Dr Ba Maw, Thakin Ba Sein, Thakin Tun Oke,—or even Sir Paw Tun—could not possibly oppose the cause of freedom; all they could do was try to seize the initiative from the AFPFL and the national leadership from Aung San. In all their attempts they failed.

In a fit of desperation, Thakin Tun Oke spoke out in the Legislative Council that Aung San had once ordered the execution of some men while on the march with the BIA. This started a controversy and the Government considered whether a criminal prosecution against Aung San was called for. Thakin Tun Oke himself had written a book, *My Adventure,* in which he proudly recounted how he had ordered the decapitation of some bodies of British soldiers. Thakin Than Tun, as secretary general of the AFPFL, had anticipated Tun Oke's attack, and sent to friendly members of the House of Commons in London translations of excerpts from the book. Questions were therefore asked in the House if the Governor would be instructed to dismiss Tun Oke for what he had done during the war.[16]

The talk of prosecuting Bogyoke Aung San did not help to improve the already tense political situation. The AFPFL and the people prepared for the showdown. Sir Reginald, taking stock of his own forces, found them inadequate. Mountbatten, who had moved his SEAC headquarters to Singapore, was emphatic that it would be difficult to send British or Dominion troops to put down a rebellion in Burma. Lord Wavell also let it be known that Indian troops could not be used as public opinion in India would be deeply offended by such use. The officers and men who had been absorbed into the Burma Army from the PBF were sure to

[16] See *Hansard*, Commons, 1945-46. Vol. 420, 740-41.

rise if Aung San was arrested. Gen. Harold R. Briggs, General Officer Commanding, strongly advised Sir John Wise, who presided over an emergency meeting to consider the matter, against the arrest. Aung San's arrest would remove his restraining influence from the tense scene and rebellion would start and spread wide. Time had come, Gen. Briggs suggested, for the Labour Government in Britain to review its Burma policy and make a plan for the transfer of power to the Burmans.

The Labour Government, led by Prime Minister Clement R. Attlee, apparently had the same ideas as Gen. Briggs. News from Rangoon had been too conflicting, too confusing; the situation in Burma was getting too explosive. A review of policy was perhaps called for. A new policy would need a new Governor to carry it through. Sir Reginald needed a rest; he had also reported ill with dysentery. He was therefore recalled to London for consultations. He embarked at Rangoon on June 14, 1946, and disembarked at Liverpool on July 13. While he was still out at sea, the Labour Government's thinking on Burma had gone further. The necessity of a new policy, and a new Governor, was resolved. On the recommendation of Mountbatten, Major-General Hubert E. Rance, who had been Chief of Civil Affairs Administration (Burma), was chosen to go to Rangoon as Governor and work out a settlement with Aung San.[17]

Gen. Briggs was right. The PBF officers and men who continued to serve in the Burma Army would have risen if Bogyoke Aung San had been arrested. Already there were too many conflicts of loyalty in their minds: the Socialists wanted their support, and the Communists too, and there were loyalties to persons. But above all these conflicts the overarching loyalty was to the national cause of freedom. In that cause they would have had no hesitation to rise; they would have felt no qualms of conscience.

The 4 Burifs managed to a large extent to eschew party politics, but its dominant loyalty was to the national cause. It was not easy to keep that way, in the general situation of the country, in the circumstances surrounding the battalion, and with its internal composition. Bo Ne Win, however, led the men well in difficult

[17] Maurice Collis, *Last and First in Burma,* Faber and Faber, London, 1956, p. 281.

assignments. "Operation Flush" was one of them. The task was to restore law and order in the oilfields area, so that the rehabilita-- tion of the oil industry might proceed. Armed banditry was rife in the area. Political organization, especially by the Communists, was also active. The workers of the oilfields were a ready political force. There was also the PVO, militant, trained, with their hid- den arms. Operation Flush was therefore a sensitive and danger- ous assignment. Dacoity had to be put down, for the people must be protected. It was a poor desert area in which the people lived a life of bare subsistence. Bandits who preyed on them deserved no mercy. The political forces and the PVO, however, stood on a different plane: towards them a friendly neutrality must be maintained. Occasionally, they overstepped their bounds, or broke out in clashes among themselves. Then, Bo Ne Win would call in their leaders and try to get them to see reason and be patient.

Once the Communists instigated a "hunger march" starting from Seikpyu. It was an unwise, untimely move. The general poli-- tical situation was fluid. An outbreak of violence now might only complicate the situation. The hunger marchers might run into the police or the British "Black Cat" troops and get badly mauled. An incident here might well set off explosions all over the coun- try. Bo Ne Win met the leaders of the march at Sinbyugyun and advised them to call off the march. "You don't have a genuine cause," he told them, "for this is just a party affair. Save your- selves for the national struggle. We too will fight, if need be, in that struggle." The leaders would not listen; their blood was up, their numbers gave them courage, their slogans were catching. If they must go on, Bo Ne Win decided, the best thing would be to go along with them, to protect them as well as to prevent them from doing mischief. The hunger marchers thus went on their way, escorted by sections from the 4 Burifs. Nothing untoward happen- ed. The marchers, having let off steam, dispersed at their destina- tion.

The 4 Burifs was the first battalion to be completely "Burmaniz- ed". On assignments such as Operation Flush, in which tact and diplomacy were called for in dealing with the people, it would obviously not do to have British officers sharing commands. Thus, when it moved out from Prome, the 4 Burifs said good-bye to its British officers. Many of them had been good men, robust soldiers

who learned to respect Bo Ne Win. They understood the feelings
of the Burmese comrades; on their part, the one dear wish was
to go home.

Operation Flush, an independent mission for a completely
Burmanized battalion of Burmese troops, was therefore a challenge
to the men and their officers and more so to their commander.
Bo Ne Win worked hard with the men in the field, on the burning sands, under the hot sun. His aide would make him a sun
shelter under which he might sit and watch; but he was a worker,
not a watcher, and refusing the shelter, he would go out with the
troops. On inspection trips to outposts, he insisted on going the
way the men had to go. Going up a high hill to look at a bunker,
he climbed the way the men climbed, waving aside an easier route
over a smoothened path. "I must see for myself," he would say,
"what the men have to take." Out in the field, he would eat with
them, enjoying the same plain fare.

From Magwe, Lanywa and the oilfields, 4 Burifs moved on to
Pyinmana, another political hot-bed. There the Burma Defence
Army was reorganized in 1942. BDA units had been scattered in
the villages around Pyinmana which thus became a strong base
during the resistance. The Communists had got there ahead, after
the resistance, and by the time the 4 Burifs arrived, the area was
already their stronghold. The PVO were massed in strength too,
and rivalry between them and the Communists made for many
disturbances. The split in the Burma Communist Party also made
the interplay of political forces in the area more fierce.

Thakin Soe had consistently attacked everyone else: Aung San,
the Army, the older politicians like U Ba Pe and U Saw. He used
pithy language in his attacks, "rapist" and "traitor" being some
of the milder epithets which he employed. The party was, for a
time, led by a triumvirate of Soe, Than Tun and Thein Pe. Later,
cliques began to form behind each leader, and accusations took the
place of constructive criticism in the inner councils. Thakin Soe
accused Thein Pe and Than Tun of "Browderism"—compromis-
ing with the British, instead of carrying on the armed struggle. In
February, 1946, at a heated session of the Central Committee the
split became final. Thakin Soe and seven broke away, including
Daw Saw Mya who had served with the women's corps of the
BNA, and Thakin Tin Mya who had been close to Soe during the

underground years of the war and the resistance. Those who remained promptly branded Soe as a Trotskyite. Soe's party became known as the Communist Party (Burma)—the CPB, or the Red Flags. The party of Than Tun and Thein Pe was the Burma Communist Party—the BCP—or the White Flags.

Pyinmana was a cauldron in which political passions boiled. The Communists organized for a general rising, to steal the initiative from the AFPFL. The White Flags clashed with the Red Flags; the PVO occasionally collided with both. As the situation in the country became more tense, the AFPFL forces also became restive. There were hidden arms everywhere. If there was a national rising, they would be used in one cause; if not they would go off against each other. The Black Cats of the British forces, in sweeping the area, had committed excesses, driving men underground. Into such a situation the 4 Burifs went to keep the peace.

Bo Ne Win once again used his diplomacy and statesmanship to put the situation under control. He met the leaders of the PVO and the other parties and urged them to be patient. Those who had gone underground were contacted and coaxed to come out. Bo Tauk Htain and Bo Taryar, of the "thirty comrades", were leaders in the area and they respected Bo Ne Win. So did the politicians and the young leaders of the PVO. In their eyes he was neutral in the ideological conflicts, untarnished, and a patriot. Even those who spoke out against Aung San spoke well of Ne Win. Partly, it was a political tactic, to try and divide the Army or force a rift between the Army and Aung San. Partly it was from sincere respect for Bo Ne Win. A communist rising broke out at Lewe later in the year, but it was soon contained. The leaders of the rising attacked Aung San and the AFPFL, in their pamphlets and their declarations, but called Bo Ne Win a genuine leader, a hero.

Calling names was a major political activity. Whether the names were good or bad depended on the moods and the changing circumstances. A leader might be called a hero now, and branded a traitor soon afterwards. He might be a revolutionary today, and called a reactionary tomorrow. And "fascist" was another well-used epithet. If one's actions pleased, then he was a progressive, a patriot. The moment one began to displease, one began to show one's true character as "fascist ogre". These, Bo Ne Win knew.

The praises showered on him therefore found him unmoved, his
deep loyalties unshaken.

6

Sir Hubert E. Rance lost no time, on his arrival, in getting in
touch with Bogyoke Aung San. "I am not a soldier who has come
brandishing a mailed fist," the new Governor declared, "I want to
help find peaceful solutions to problems."

The AFPFL had started to step up the struggle. The first step
was the strike. The government servants, the postal workers, the
railwaymen, all went on strike demanding the early formation of a
popular Provisional Government. U Tun of the postal workers'
union, U Tun Aung Gyaw and U Ko Lay of the ministerial services union, and such other strike leaders made it clear that the
strikes were an inseparable part of the larger national struggle for
freedom. The police joined in on September 5, 1946. U Wan
Maung, U Aye and U Soe Shain, inspectors of police, took the
lead. "We shall not wear the crown any more," they declared at a
public meeting amidst cheers, "we shall be the people's police from
today or no police at all." Then they took off their cap badges and
changed them for new ones which had the peacock in its pride.
The police, always identified as the tool of the colonial power,
thus became one with the people.

In such circumstances Sir Hubert reached understandings with
Bogyoke Aung San. The old Executive Council was dissolved, and
the AFPFL was given the lead in forming a new Council. Aung
San became deputy chairman—the Governor was, in strict law,
chairman, but in practice he rarely took part in the Council's
deliberations—and Thakin Mya, Thakin Thein Pe, U Ba Pe,
Mahn Ba Khine, U Aung Zan Wai, Sir Maung Gyee and U Tin
Tut took their seats as AFPFL nominees. Thakin Ba Sein was
also appointed Councillor for Transport and Communications. It
was a Burman Council, with no British Civilians in it, and it
assumed office on September 27, 1946. Saw Ba U Gyi, U Mya
(Pyawbwe) and U Saw entered the Council in November. Prospects of a peaceful transfer of power improved with the entry
into office of the AFPFL. Tensions eased quickly. The strikers
returned to work. Office, Aung San declared, was not an end in

itself, but a means to work more effectively towards freedom. "We shall win independence within one year," he promised the people, "or we shall quit office."

The Burma Communist Party did not feel happy about the turn of events. Its leaders who had said during the war, and immediately after, that co-operation with the British was the only line of action, now began to say that real independence could not be gained without an armed rebellion. Thakin Thein Pe, representing the Party, sat on the Executive Council; but criticism of the AFPFL and Aung San personally became more violent in the public speeches of the Party leaders, and in its journal, *Pyithu-Arnar* (The People's Age). Aung San was branded a traitor, an imperialist stooge. The Executive Council, it was pointed out, was not a National Government, nor even a Provisional Government; its status was at the most that of the Council of Ministers under the Government of Burma Act of 1935.

The attacks persistently made by the Communist Party led the executive committee of the AFPFL to consider its expulsion from the League. Kyaw Nyein moved the resolution; Thein Pe, whose instructions were to say that the Party must keep its freedom of criticism and its separate entity, and under no circumstances to tender an apology, could only make a feeble reply. The motion was massively carried. The Supreme Council of the League endorsed the resolution on October 10, 1946. Thakin Nu, the vice-president of the AFPFL, broke into a triumphant cry, when the resolution was carried: "May communism flourish! May the Burma Communist Party perish!" Thein Pe had a quick retort. Turning a stern look on Aung San he said slowly, dramatically, "Vile King, I leave you to your fate!" even as Kyansittha, the hero, had said in history to his king whom he tried to rescue from the enemy but who, suspecting him, raised the alarm.[18]

Thakin Thein Pe resigned from the Governor's Executive Council on October 22. Differences of views between him and the Central Committee of the Party resulted in his being given six months' leave to study and think. The Party continued to pursue the path of attacking the League and Aung San in strong language. "Whither Aung San?" asked H. N. Goshal *alias* Yebaw Ba Tin,

[18] An account of this meeting appears in Thein Pe Myint's biography of *Kyaw Nyein*, (in Burmese), Rangoon, 1961, p. 86.

whose influence on the Party's thinking increased. Goshal, of Indian extractions, had studied economics and law at the Rangoon University, and was one of the founders of the Communist study group in 1939. Often jailed by the British, he trekked out to India from Mandalay after bombs had blown down the walls of the jail there. He worked with Thein Pe and the Communist Party in India. When war ended, he trekked back through Arakan to Rangoon. The Goshal thesis, developed and refined with the help of the CPI in later months, was that the AFPFL Government was anti-people, pro-imperialist; the AFPFL must be opposed, and the people must be prepared for an armed struggle.

The splits in the Communist Party affected the unity of the PVO. In October, 1946, a section broke away to form the "Red Army" of the Party. Bo Thein Dan became commandant of the Red Army and Bo Aung Min its chief of staff.

The splits among the leftist forces saddened Aung San. He saw that independence was coming soon. He also saw that after it was won, the leftist forces would fall upon each other, instead of working together to build the socialist State that they dreamed of. "I shall lead until independence is achieved," he confided to his close comrades, "then I shall leave to do some writing, and to look after my family, especially the education of the children. If there is no leftist unity, there will be no point in carrying on." To his older brother U Aung Than he said, "I shall quit office after independence, sit back and watch the scramble for power. It will be raw power politics then, and I am not made for it. It may be amusing to watch the scramble."[19]

7

In December, 1946, the Labour Government in London invited a delegation from Burma to come over and talk about the future. On December 20, Prime Minister Clement R. Attlee stated in the House of Commons that Burma would be helped to attain self-government by the quickest and most convenient path. "We do not desire to retain within the Commonwealth any unwilling peoples," Mr. Attlee said, "it is for the Burmese people to decide their own future."

[19] U Aung Than, *Sixteen Years* (Memoirs), Rangoon, 1963, p. 35.

The AFPFL's mandate to Aung San, who led the delegation, was to demand complete independence—as distinguished from dominion status. "I hope for the best," Bogyoke declared before departure, "but am prepared for the worst." On January 1, 1947, he flew to New Delhi, stopping off for a few days for talks with Pandit Nehru and the Indian leaders. He met the press on January 5. "Are you contemplating a violent or non-violent struggle, or both (if the talks proved unsatisfactory)?" a reporter asked. "We have no inhibitions of any kind," replied Aung San.

The delegation gathered in London. Thakin Mya, U Ba Pe and U Tin Tut were the other members of the AFPFL, with U Kyaw Nyein and Bo Setkya as advisers. U Ba Pe, whose wife was ill in Rangoon, followed up later and joined in the talks when they reached a crucial stage. Thakin Ba Sein and U Saw were also delegates, selected by the Governor; Thakin Chit and U Ba Yin went as their advisers. U Shwe Baw and U Tin Ohn, Secretaries to the Government, and some staff also accompanied the delegation.

The talks began on January 13. "I am a soldier, not a diplomat," Bogyoke Aung San said at the inaugural session which was held at Number 10 Downing Street. The people of Burma, he said, were united in their demand for "full and unfettered freedom." Their aspirations were to attain that freedom within one year. "When we speak of Burma," Aung San explained to Prime Minister Clement Attlee and the British delegation, "we envisage a Burma united and free. There are no insurmountable obstacles in the way of achieving that unity. If all the racial groups in the country are offered full freedom, and if they but meet together and work together without outside interference, they will unite."

There were details to discuss and legal technicalities to take care of, but the talks went off to a fine and friendly start. Aung San, a few weeks short of 32, made a good impression in the sophisticated diplomatic and governmental circles in which he moved. Attlee saw him as "a strong character", and "a statesman of considerable capacity and wisdom, as was shown by his proposals for dealing with the minority communities on generous lines."[20]

Some conservative elements among some of the racial groups

[20] *Aung San of Burma,* p. 107.

were not, however, so keen on building the Union of Burma together. Some British officers of the Frontier Areas Administration
also worked hard on those elements, persuading them that they
would have a better future in continued association with Britain.
A few Sawbwas (chieftains) of the Shan States, thus swayed, sent
a cable to the Labour Government in London, declaring that the
delegation led by Bogyoke Aung San did not have their support.
The AFPFL moved quickly to counter. Its young Shan leaders,
U Tin Aye, U Tun Myint and U Pe Khin covened mass meetings
in the hills at which resolutions were passed pledging full support to the Bogyoke. These resolutions were cabled to London.[21]

The AFPFL organized mass meetings in Rangoon and in towns
all over the country to lend moral support to the delegation which
was engaged in negotiations for the peaceful transfer of power,
and also to alert and prepare the people for prolonged struggle if
the negotiations should fail. A state of readiness prevailed throughout the country; the readiness to rise up in arms, if need arose,
was not concealed. The PBF officers and men in the Burma Rifles
battalions were ready too. The 4 Burifs at Pyinmana under Bo
Ne Win also waited for the signal.

Fortunately, there was no need to rise in arms, no need to
repeat the BIA story all over again. The London talks proceeded
well. There were a few snags, moments of deadlock. But the talks
had started out on broad agreements in principle; the details
could therefore be filled in. On Monday, January 27, 1947, the
Agreement—popularly known in Burma as the "Aung San-
Attlee" Agreement—was signed. Thakin Ba Sein and U Saw dissociated themselves from it, but Mr. Attlee rightly surmised that
their dissent was of no importance.

"The road to freedom is open now," Bogyoke Aung San reported to the people on February 4, after his return to Rangoon.
"We came to agreements in London for the election of a Constituent Assembly, an assembly of nationals only, which will draft
the constitution of independent Burma. The British Government
has also agreed to invest our Government with the powers of a
national government. As for the people of the frontier areas, they
must decide their own future. If they wish to come in with us,
we will welcome them on equal terms."

[21] Gen. Ne Win's *Statements of Policy on the National Races,* p. 56.

8

The next few months were furiously busy for Aung San. He never rested. He travelled all over the country, inviting the people of the highlands to join in to build the Union of Burma, campaigning for the AFPFL for the general elections that were fixed for April.

In February, delegates from the Chin, Kachin and Shan people gathered at Panglong to discuss their future in relation to the Union. Observers came to the conference from the Karen communities and the Karenni States. "The dream of a unified and free Burma has always haunted me," Aung San told the delegates, "we who are gathered here are engaged in the pursuit of that dream." Race, he said, was an artificial concept. "What is race, after all? What are its tests? We have in Burma many indigenous peoples; the Karens, the Kachins, the Shans, the Chins, the Burmese and others. In other countries too there are many indigenous peoples, many 'races'. China, Japan, and the Soviet Union provide such examples. In America, though the peoples may speak a common language, they spring from many stocks; there are the British, the Italians, and other peoples, but they have become assimilated, and they identify themselves as 'American'."

"Let us unite," Bogyoke Aung San called out. "If we want the nation to prosper, we must pool our resources, manpower. wealth, skills, and work together. If we are divided, the Karens, the Shans, the Kachins, the Chins, the Burmese, the Mons and the Arakanese, each pulling in a different direction, the Union will be torn, and we will all come to grief."[22]

On February 12, the delegates gathered at Panglong agreed to work together, accepting that freedom would come more speedily to the people of the frontier areas through co-operation. The "Panglong Agreement" signed on that day is regarded as an important milestone on the nation's march to freedom. Union Day, February 12 of every year, commemorates the Agreement, and is a national holiday.[23]

After Panglong began the hard campaigning for the general

[22] *Aung San of Burma*, p. 123.
[23] The Panglong Agreement is reproduced as an appendix in *Burma's Constitution*, by Maung Maung.

elections. The electoral machinery of the Government of Burma
Act, 1935, had to be used and there were communal seats in the
total of 255, leaving 210 seats for Burma proper (including 24
for Karens) open to the general contests. The AFPFL contested
every open seat. "Give us your trust," Aung San asked of the
electors up and down the country, "vote for our candidates. The
Assembly may yet turn into a Revolutionary Council. We therefore need men who are tested and true." The people responded
massively and gave the AFPFL a landslide victory on April 9.

The Red Flags led by Thakin Soe boycotted the elections. To
ask for votes, they said, would amount to submission to the authority of the Governor, and therefore a betrayal of the cause.
Dr Ba Maw's *Mahabama* (Greater Burma) party—an outgrowth
of the Sinyetha party—also boycotted the elections. So did U
Saw's Myochit party. The Burma Communist Party (White
Flags), however, put a few chosen candidates into the field, and
won seven seats.

On May 23, the AFPFL convened a national conference of its
delegates to draft the constitution. The basic principles were discussed and adopted. A committee of 111 members—10 from the
AFPFL executive committee, 25 Supreme Councillors, 45 mem-
bers-elect of the Constituent Assembly, and 31 AFPFL district
delegates—was assigned the task of preparing the first draft of
the constitution. Aung San was tireless. He attended to the chores
of the Government. He sat through committee meetings and full
sessions of the conference. He reported to the people. He kept
up a fast pace, as if he had to race with time.

In June the Constituent Assembly met. Young men from the
country, in their khaki uniforms, Socialist members similarly clad
and distinguished by their red neck-ties, members wearing European suits, members wearing pinni jackets, lady members in their
bright colours. The Assembly showed freshness and strength, and
it was very different from the legislative councils of old in which
flowing silk and smooth talk predominated.

Thakin Nu was elected Speaker, and the Assembly proceeded
to business without delay. Committees were formed to prepare
drafts on the different chapters of the constitution. Aung San sat
on the main committees, and his presence inspired confidence and
harmony. Agreements in principle were reached without much

bargaining when he was present. A chuckle from him, a joke, a promise, would get over obstacles. In a few weeks the draft of the constitution was in good shape.

The Communist members of the Constituent Assembly took part in the debates on the drafts of the constitution. The smooth progress, however, made their party desperate. In March, 1947, the party organized a peasants' rally in Pyu. Some 100,000 people attended. The massive turn-out gave Thakin Than Tun, who addressed the rally, and his comrades, an illusion of strength. More and more the party turned to paths of violence.

U Saw was becoming desperate too. He saw his chances of returning to power slipping away. The sight of Bogyoke Aung San—"a mere boy" he had called him—as national leader winning Burma's freedom irked him. There did not seem to be any way of constitutionally ousting Aung San from his place. U Saw too began to think in terms of violence and assassination. He started to gather round him a few young men. He indoctrinated them, trained and prepared them for the foul deed, first extracting from them the vow of absolute obedience to his will.

Rumours circulated in Rangoon that Bogyoke Aung San was in danger. Two hundred Bren guns, it was said in whispers, had been stolen from the British army arsenals, and that they had got into the hands of U Saw. That was more Bren guns than the Burma Rifles battalions collectively had. Colleagues wanted Aung San to be more careful. They tried to double his body guards and tighten security arrangements for him. But he put his trust in the people among whom he moved about even more freely. He had worn his khaki uniform during the election campaign. On more formal occasions, he wore the plain military suit about which he often quipped: "Look, this is all I got for myself in London, a suit of uniform!" Now he liked to wear Burmese clothes, in which he looked more relaxed. He smiled often, he was even gay.

On July 13, he addressed a mass meeting, gathered in Bandoola Square, from the porch of the Rangoon Corporation building. He gave the people "a few painful truths" as he called them, in his blunt and forceful manner and language. "Years of toil lie ahead of you," he said. "Maybe 20 years, at the least, will pass before you see the fruits of your toil. You must work with perseverance, with unity and discipline, always conscious of your duties as citizens of a free country. Rights carry responsibilities; you cannot enjoy the rights without discharging the responsibilities."

"You must work hard," he kept repeating, "be united and disciplined. Otherwise, the fruits of freedom will not be yours to enjoy, whether you have a Communist government or a Socialist government. You must mend your ways and build a New Burma together. These words I leave with you today."[24]

Those were his words of farewell to the people. On July 19, while he sat in Council at the Secretariat, the gunmen sent by U Saw broke into the chamber and sprayed it with bullets from their automatic weapons. Bogyoke Aung San rose from his chair making a gesture to the gunmen, as if to stay their hand or order them to go away. But they were not there to hold their hand; their vow of absolute obedience had been made to U Saw; their orders were to kill one and all.

Thakin Mya, Deedok U Ba Choe, Mahn Ba Khine, Mr. A. Razak, U Ba Win, and the Sawbwa of Mongpawn, all Executive Councillors, fell with Bogyoke Aung San. U Ohn Maung, a Secretary, and Bo Htwe, a bodyguard, were also killed in the shootings. U Ba Gyan and U Aung Zan Wai, Executive Councillors, escaped somehow from that chamber of death. Thakin Nu, Speaker of the Assembly, who was also on the list of intended victims, did not attend office that morning, and was thus saved.[25]

9

Bo Ne Win drove down from Pyinmana on hearing about the assassinations. An urgent message from associates in the Supreme Council of the AFPFL had also invited him to come to Rangoon for consultations. With him in the old-fashioned convertible sedan were Bo Maung Maung and Bo Ye Htut.

In Toungoo the party had to pass a check-point. British troops were already on the alert against threatened disturbances. Approaching Mingaladon, the party was stopped on the road, just past Kyaikkalo pagoda, when it began to descend to where the old military academy used to be during the war. Men of the 7 Gurkha Rifles manned the check-point, and their commander, Maj. Ford, was most apologetic. The situation was tense, he ex-

---

24 *Aung San of Burma*, p. 142.
25 Maung Maung, *A Trial in Burma: the Assassination of Aung San.*

plained, and his orders were to keep a check on armed military personnel entering the city. Bo Ne Win, his officers, and their men were therefore requested to leave their arms; they would then be taken to the camp of 3 Burifs where they could stay at the officers' mess and visit the city. Bo Ne Win broke into his choicest curses at the welcome. Bo Maung Maung and Bo Ye Htut joined in hearty chorus. Maj. Ford understood their feelings, but orders were orders. In the end, after an argument with General Stopford, the party arrived at the 3 Burifs mess, and made off for Rangoon.

The city was in mourning. The people were stunned. Rumours roamed the streets. Fortunately, Sir Hubert Rance, the Governor, had acted quickly to invite Thakin Nu to form a Government of AFPFL nominees. Rance had gone on the radio on the evening of July 19, to announce the tragic news, and to tell the country that though Bogyoke Aung San had fallen his work would continue, and the AFPFL would still be the Government.

Several meetings took place at the headquarters of the PVO in Lowis Road. Thakin Nu, Bo Let Ya (the new Defence Minister), Bo Aung, Bo Sein Hman and Bo Tun Lin of the PVO, Bo Ne Win, Bo Ye Htut and Bo Maung Maung were among those who discussed the situation and prospects for the future. It was agreed that the wise course would be to hold the country together, keep the people calm and march on to the goal that was within sight. The assassins must have support from outside, it was thought. In fact, rumours had it that foreign troops were coming in by air to seize Rangoon. Subversive elements in the country might also try to whip up the people's feelings and create disturbances, to throw obstacles on the road to independence. All these dangers must be guarded against, and a state of readiness must be maintained by the AFPFL and the patriotic components of the Burma Army.

Regarding political leadership, support for Thakin Nu was promised by all who were present at the meeting. Thus the man who wanted to be the "George Bernard Shaw of Burma" found himself political heir to Aung San at the moment of destiny. Aung San had brought Thakin Nu into the AFPFL when the latter was resting after the war. A member-elect of the Constituent Assembly for Mergui went down at sea with the *S. S. Anderson* while on

his way to the inaugural session. Thakin Nu was elected without
a contest to the vacant seat, and became the Speaker of the Assembly. U Saw's gunmen missed him, while Aung San and the
senior members of his Council were felled. Thus Thakin Nu remained, in that political scene of desolation, the one man of
stature round whom the forces for freedom could rally.

"We shall keep the Army united and ready," Bo Ne Win promised, "you hold the political front." This pledge he kept. He
visited the 3 Burifs and the 5 Burifs, met the officers and men
and told them to keep calm and prepared. "I grieve as much as
you for the fall of Bogyoke Aung San," he told them, "but nothing can be gained at this stage by hasty action. The best way to
salute his memory will be to carry on with his work, to strive towards the goals he set us. Death, after all, is no stranger to a soldier. Keep calm, be united, be ready." The Army listened to Bo
Ne Win's words. In all the units there were men who had served
under him in the BIA or the BDA. The BNA men, of course,
knew him and respected him as their commander-in-chief, and
since then the men had always acknowledged two Bogyoke's—
Aung San and Ne Win. That title does not only acknowledge rank,
but shows affection, trust and respect. In the resistance, and during the reorganization of the Burma Army, Bo Ne Win had spent
most of his time with troops in the field. Even when he took up
duties as commander of the 4 Burifs, the men in the other units
looked upon him as their leader, their Bogyoke. Now Bogyoke
Aung San had fallen on the march—as a good soldier should—
and only Bogyoke Ne Win remained.

Independence came within the time that Aung San had set.
Thakin Nu took another trip to London, with his advisers in October, 1947, to sign a final agreement—the "Nu-Attlee Agreement"
—for the transfer of power to Burma. The details were worked
out in protocols and supplementary agreements, but it was decided that Burma would become a sovereign independent republic outside the Commonwealth.

A few changes had to be made, on the advice of astrologers,
regarding the date of independence. First it was January 6, 1948,
then the 3rd, and finally the 4th at 4.20 in the morning. Everyone had to get up early on that auspicious day, therefore, and it
was a morning to remember. At the Government House, the Union

Jack was lowered, and the Flag of the Union of Burma was hoisted, while Sir Hubert E. Rance, and Sao Shwe Thaike—who had been elected the Provisional President of the new State—stood silently with the guests and the guards of honour in salute.

The early start of Independence Day made it possible for the Governor and his family to say their good-byes and embark early on the *S. S. Birmingham* which waited, with steam up, on the Rangoon river. A motorcade, preceded by ten police pilots on motor cycles, followed by guards and friends, drove to the wharf. Sir Hubert inspected an honour guard mounted by a troop of Gurkha Rifles, shook hands with Sao Shwe Thaike, Thakin Nu and Cabinet Ministers, officials and friends. The formalities and farewells over, Sir Hubert and Lady Rance embarked at 8.20 a.m.; then the ship sailed away.

At 10.15 a.m. U Mya (Pyawbwe) was sworn in as Speaker of the Provisional Parliament—into which the Constituent Assembly had turned, pending general elections of the two Chambers provided for by the constitution. Sao Shwe Thaike arrived at 10.30 a.m. to deliver his message to the people. "Let us rejoice," he said, "that independence has come not as a result of armed conflict but as the fruit of friendly negotiations with that great nation whose political bonds we replace by mutual consent today with the stronger bonds of friendship and goodwill. Today is for us not only a day of freedom but also a day of re-union. For a long time, the principal races of Burma, the Mon-Arakanese-Burmese, the Karens, the Shans, the Kachins and the Chins, have tended to look upon themselves as separate national units. Of late, a nobler vision, the vision of a Union of Burma has moved our hearts, and we stand united today as one nation determined to work in unity and concord for the advancement of Burma's interests and for the speedy attainment of her due position as one of the great nations of the world. It is unity which brought our struggle for independence to this early fruition and may unity continue to be the watchword for every member of the Sovereign Independent Republic to be henceforth known as the Union of Burma."

7

Trials and Tribulations

1

THE SOCIALIST State was the proclaimed goal of New Burma. The constitution embodied socialist principles. "Let me say at once," Thakin Nu had said, in moving the adoption of the draft constitution in the Constituent Assembly on September 24, 1947, "that the foundations laid for New Burma are those of a leftist country. And a leftist country is one in which the people, working together to the best of their power and ability, strive to convert the natural resources and produce of the land, both above ground and below ground, into consumer commodities to which everybody will be entitled each according to his need. In a leftist country there will be no such thing as a handful of people holding the monopoly over the inexhaustible wealth of the land while the poor and the starving grow more and more numerous. Then again, in such a country the aim of production is not profit for the few but comfort and the happiness of a full life for the many. Lastly, in a leftist country, there will be no distinction between the employer class and the employed class, or to put it simply there will be no such thing as the master-class and the governed-class."[1]

Those were the aims with which the nation-builders set out. Optimistically, a Two-Year Plan of economic development was drafted, and promises were made by the AFPFL leaders that in the abundance that would soon be reaped every family would, enjoying fair shares, own a house, a car, a radio, and earn a minimum monthly income of Rs. 800. The promises, however, were premature. The vision of a peaceful, harmonious and affluent society turned out to be a dream. Threats were soon posed to the safety and the integrity of the Union itself.

[1] Speech is reproduced in *Burma's Constitution,* by Maung Maung, p. 254.

The Red Flags had been up in arms for sometime when independence came. The Burma Communist Party—the White Flags—had participated in the making of the constitution and the celebration of independence: Thakin Than Tun was one of those who had risen from bed early on January 4 to attend the celebrations. After the assassinations, the party made some overtures for reunion with the AFPFL. In October, 1947, Thakin Nu and Thakin Than Tun had made a joint tour of districts which were badly affected by "terrorism" and there were talks of the party being readmitted into the League. After independence, however, the party once again resorted to strong language in attacking the AFPFL as a tool of the British imperialists, and the independence as a fraud. The Goshal thesis, brought back from India, it was said, ran into 27 type-written pages and outlined the "revolutionary possibilities for 1948". A national rising to set up a People's Government, was the line of action which the Communist Party accordingly adopted and pursued. The All-Burma Trade Union Congress (BTUC), a wing of the party, started to provoke labour strikes and unrest in Rangoon. In February, 1948, Thakin Than Tun and a delegation went to Calcutta seemingly to attend a conference of S.E. Asian Democratic Youth. In fact the delegates took part in the deliberations of the All India Communist Congress, and had close discussions with the members of the CPI. The time and the circumstances were right, it was resolved, to rise up in arms and take over.[2]

In March, the BCP held a peasants' conference in Pyinmana which was attended by more than 75,000 people. Thakin Than Tun was impressed and heartened. His words became even bolder and stronger when he returned to Rangoon.[3]

The Socialist party was submerged in the AFPFL. Party leaders took pride that their's was the largest single party in the League, which was true. But then the Communists were outside, in opposition. There were no other parties worth the name. There were some relics of parties, some relics of politicians, some racial and religious groups, some "independents" in the AFPFL. It was not difficult to be the largest single party in that set-up. The So-

[2] U Nu's statement on the Communist insurrection in *Premier Reports to the People*, Rangoon, Dir. of Information, 1957.

[3] *Burma and the Insurrections*, Rangoon, Dir. of Information, 1949.

cialist leaders, invested with office, busy with general duties, neglected the organization of the party. It quickly lost touch with the people. The AFPFL itself fast became a collection of individuals, a federation of political groups, a marriage of convenience.

The PVO had a bigger organizational network. It was more militant, for that was its training and its mission. The assassination of Bogyoke Aung San deprived them of a leader whom they could all trust. Bo Aung, Bo Sein Hman, and Bo Po Kun, the senior leaders, joined the Cabinet. Bo Tun Lin became a member of the Public Service Commission. Thus the mass of the PVO, and their young leaders in the towns and the villages, were without direction and ideological guidance. Many of their former comrades were in the Communist parties. Many of the younger PVO therefore felt more ideologically akin to the Communists who, however, looked upon them as the "blind young patriots". At one time the PVO had been useful and used; now they were useless, unwanted. That was how they felt, and the feeling hurt them.

Some elements in the various racial groups were restive. Those elements were by no means large in numbers; but they wielded influence within their communities, and they nursed hopes of foreign sympathy or assistance in their causes. The Shans who had their Shan State were fairly pleased. Their chieftains, the Sawbwas, had their reserved seats in the Chamber of Nationalities and kept their rights to collect revenue at gambling festivals, and their customary pomp and privileges. The socialist professions of the Burmese leaders, however, made the chiefs and the land-owners in the State nervous. The land nationalization law, which was passed soon after independence, did not reassure them. The law could not go into operation due to outbreak of insurrections. In 1953 a substantially redrafted law was passed, but the redistribution of the land was slow, in some areas inequitable.

The Chins got their schools, their roads, their Chin Affairs Council and their seats in the two chambers of Parliament. They were content. Land nationalization did not worry them for they had no land, only rocky mountains. Their main profession was soldiering, and for that the situation in the country provided ample scope. The Kachins up north were in similar circumstances. They had won their State, with the Myitkyina and the Bhamo districts added to their mountain ranges to make the State feasible and viable. Their leader, Sama Duwa Sinwa Nawng, a warrior chief, gave his full support to the Union Government and called on his people to do likewise.

The Karen problem did not admit of easy solution. The Karen communities are scattered all over southern Burma—in the Delta, along the Salween and the Sittang, in the valleys, on the highlands. To include in a Karen State all areas in which there were even sprinklings of Karens would have meant the turning over of most of lower Burma to the Karens. This would have been unfair to the Burmese, the Mon, the Kayah and other people who make their homes in the area. Saw Ba U Gyi and the more militant exponents of the Karen case, would not, however, be satisfied with less. There was also a distrust for the Burmese, and a belief among some sections of the Karen communities that the wiser course would be to carve out a separate State and stay within the British Commonwealth. Whether or not that was practical did not bother them.[4]

Brigadier B. E. Fergusson, who commanded the 16 Infantry Brigade during the Burma campaign, has written:

"Sometime in 1946 a letter appeared in *The Times,* signed by one Aubrey Buxton, asking that all those who had the interests of the Karens at heart should get in touch with him. He belonged, as I had guessed, to that great East Anglican clan of Quaker descent which is inextricably intermingled with Quaker Hoares, Barclays and the like, with a boundless tradition of public service behind them; he had served during the war with Force 136, which had sprinkled parachutists as though from a pepper-pot all over Southeast Asia to raise and arm the locals against the Japanese. Buxton told me that a delegation of Karens was on its way home to plead with the Government that they should be allowed to opt out of the plan, and to stay within the Commonwealth.

The Karen delegation, when it arrived, consisted of six or seven very likeable men, none of whom I knew. Its leader was Sydney Loo Nee, and one of its most forceful members Saw Ba U Gyi. I attended several parties given for them, including one at the Overseas League with Lord Mountbatten presiding.

[4] *The Karen Insurrection,* Rangoon, Dir. of Information, 1949.

But the high-light was a luncheon somewhere when the principal host was the Prime Minister, the then Mr. Attlee. The time came when Mr. Attlee made a speech. It was a good speech. None of us, he said, would ever forget the friendship, which had existed so long between the Karens and the British, nor what they had done for us during the war. Loo Nee rose to his feet to reply; what he said was this:

'Mr. Attlee has said some very nice things about the Karens. Everybody has been very kind to us since we came to London. There have been cocktail parties, dinner parties, receptions, and much generous hospitality. But we cannot get the answer to the question we came to London to ask. We have only one question. Some peoples want to leave the British Empire. We Karens don't. So here is our question, and it's all we want to know. May we please stay in the British Empire?'

Mr. Attlee looked at his watch, and said that he had an urgent meeting for which he was already late. He left the luncheon table."[5]

That brief account shows up the sensitive and difficult Karen problem in which so much sentiment, so deep distrust, so hard realities and so fond fancy were involved. The wounds of the Delta incident were not completely healed when independence came. The fall of Aung San and several older—and therefore perhaps more conservative—members of the Government disturbed the feelings of some of the Karen leaders. Thakin Nu, sweet and smiling, gave them some peace of mind, but not complete reassurance. The nationalization of land, even though only on paper at first, made the land-owning Karens unhappy. The constitution had made provision for the creation of a Karen State out of the Karenni State, the Salween district and such adjacent areas as were occupied by the Karens "if the majority of the people of these three areas and of the Karens living in Burma outside these areas so desire." Meanwhile, a 'Kaw-thu-lay Special Region' was set up around the Salween district and adjacent Karen areas, with its own Karen Affairs Council and some control over local affairs. The constitutional solution did not please the more ambitious

[5] Bernard Fergusson, *Return to Burma*, Collins, London, 1962, p. 102.

Karen leaders. On the other hand it offended the Karenni people who were quick to point out that they were different, ethnically, culturally, and historically, from the Karens, and had had their own independent identity ever since June 21, 1875, when the British in Lower Burma and the Kingdom of Upper Burma had signed a treaty to establish the Karenni region as a buffer state "separate and independent" over which neither side shall claim or exercise sovereignty or governing authority. The Karenni people therefore moved that the historic name of "Kayah" be restored to their State, and the constitution be amended to take it out of the list of territories earmarked for the Karen State.[6]

Those were some of the problems with which the Union of Burma set forth on its career as an independent state. The rising expectations of the people for a better life, the clashes and rivalries among the political leaders, ideological differences, the scramble for power at various levels, help of sorts from outside or the hopes for it, these made peaceful progress in unity hardly possible. Premier Thakin Nu, however, clung to his romantic vision and kept on promising that "gold and silver will rain from the sky, milk and honey will flow."

Eighty-three days after independence was declared, the Burma Communist party began its revolt on March 28, 1948, and the Union plunged into a bitter civil war that was to drag on for several years.

2

The timing of their rising by the Communists was tactically correct. The Union Government had not yet settled into power. The forces of law and order were in disarray. Dissatisfaction was widespread. Disorder was rife. "Workers in the B.O.C. (Duneedaw), Foucar and B.B.T.C.L. are now on strike," Thakin Nu reported to the people on the radio, the night of the Communist revolt, "and those in the latter two were forced to do so by threat of firearms by the Communists and the Red Army. The workers had on several occasions made appeals to the AFPFL to rescue them from the hands of the Communists."[7]

[6] Constituent Assembly (Parliament) *Proceedings*, vol. X, No. 7, pp. 150-75.

[7] *Towards Peace and Democracy*, p. 51.

Eleventh hour negotiations were made, Thakin Nu explained, to try to preserve the peace. The PVO had put forward four points for consideration: the purge of the AFPFL; timely prevention of civil war; the unification of the Socialists, the Communists (of both factions), and the PVO; a truce on all sides during which those measures might be taken. The AFPFL, the Government, and the Socialist party agreed, and Thakin Than Tun and the Communist leaders were invited to meetings. "An appointment was fixed with the Communists at 10 a.m. on the 26th of March," Thakin Nu said in his broadcast report, "but as that did not come off another one was fixed at 2 p.m. on the same day with the same result, while another timed for 8 p.m. did not materialize. And so Government, as requested by the PVO, postponed the meeting till 4 p.m. on the 27th of March. At the same time Government gave out that it will allow no other postponement. Information was received that, in the interim, the Communists had been transferring their smuggled firearms to different places and further that the Communists had made plans to go underground. A reply was received at about 5 p.m. (on March 27) from Thakin Than Tun, the Communist leader, to postpone the meeting to 5 p.m. on 28 March. As it was impossible for us to continue waiting further, we took action early on the morning of the 28th. We found, as we had anticipated, that the Communist leaders, Thakin Than Tun and Goshal had already gone underground, and only some of their followers were apprehended."[8]

The insurrection spread quickly. The Communists gained some initial advantages and quick successes. Small police outposts were overrun, their arms seized. Government treasuries in small towns were plundered. In the first few months, however, while they were yet alone, the Communists could not win spectacular victories; they could raid and plunder places but not hold them for very long. Their successes were brief. They did, on the other hand, shake political stability by dividing the parties and testing loyalties severely. The PVO were bothered and bewildered. The Socialists, in office and therefore identified as the evil genius behind the AFPFL, were unpopular. U Kyaw Nyein, the Home Minister, was perhaps the most unpopular Socialist among them all. His was the task to round up suspects after the assassination of Aung

[8] *Ibid* p. 53.

San and hold subversive characters under preventive detention.

U Saw and his men were given a fair trial by a special tribunal, headed by Justice Kyaw Myint of the High Court. Mr. F. H. Curtis-Bennett, K. C., flew out from London to lead the defence. The tribunal passed its judgment on December 30, 1947, awarding the capital sentence to each accused. Appeals were taken, unsuccessfully, to the High Court and the Supreme Court. The President, exercising the prerogative of mercy, reduced the sentences of three, but U Saw and the rest were hanged in May, 1948, about the time the first showers of the monsoon fell.[9]

In the Burma Army there were conflicting loyalties. Among the ex-PBF personnel there were Socialists and Communists, and those with loyalties to personalities. There were four Burma Rifles battalions on the eve of independence, and several racial units. Integration, rather than separation, of the races would have been the wise and correct policy, but the British thought that the racial battalions, especially the Karen Rifles were more "reliable". The one and only artillery, armed with 25-pounder guns, was manned by Karens. So were a Signals battalion, and a Transport battalion. In the hope that Karen public opinion would be better pleased, a Karen, Smith-Dun was made a Lt.-General and General Officer Commanding of the Burma Army after independence. The command of the Air Force was given to another Karen, Saw Shi Sho. Bo Ne Win and the senior Burmese commanders pointed out in the early stages that the Karen people should be given their fair political rights, and full support for the economic development of their areas. Giving them superiority and special places in the Army would not help their people, but only tempt them with the thought that they could dictate their terms by force. The protests went unheeded. A few months after independence, with insurrections all round, it was too late to mend.[10]

Bo Ne Win bid farewell to the 4 Burifs in December, 1947, to assume command of the North Burma Sub-District with the rank of Brigadier. His headquarters was in Maymyo, in the hills. His troops were dispersed all over upper Burma. They held together well under his leadership, and fought well in the field. The Communists could not penetrate further north than Pyinmana, and

---

[9] Maung Maung, *A Trial in Burma.*
[10] Gen. Ne Win's *Statements of Policy on the National Races,* pp. 67-8.

there too they kept well away from the road, the railway and the town. In August, 1948, when the situation in the country became desperate, Bo Ne Win was promoted Major-General, and made Vice-Chief of General Staff at the War Office in Rangoon. By that time more than half the PVO had gone underground. Several units of the Army were on the point of mutiny.

The PVO had pressed for peace parleys among the leftist forces, and the AFPFL had responded with a "15-point programme" to build leftist unity. Thakin Nu announced the programme on May 25, 1948, with main aim to build a socialist state by the united efforts of the leftist forces. A Marxist League, to be composed of the Communists, the Socialists, the PVO and "others who lean towards Marxism", was to be organized. When the League was achieved, the component parties would be dissolved. The Fifteen Points were not favourably received in England and America where charges were made that Burma had "gone red". The Government was so harassed and so unsure of itself, it sent a mission to London to offer explanations. Later the Marxist League idea was quietly abandoned, and the Fifteen Points became Fourteen.[11]

The Communists were uninterested in Thakin Nu's programme when they had their own. The PVO showed some interest at first, but insisted on face to face discussions, with the Communists participating. The AFPFL wanted the Communists to lay down their arms first, before taking their seats at the conference table. In this state of deadlock, the PVO broke up into two factions, the White Band PVO, led by Bo Po Kun and Bo Htain Win and Bo Tun Lin, and the Yellow Band PVO, led by Bo Aung and Bo Sein Hman. The White faction went underground on June 26. The Communists, who were getting feeble, thus received a much-needed respite.

Groups from the Burma Rifles battalions had been breaking away since the Communist insurrection began. Now whole battalions became restive. They must strike now for leftist unity, they thought, or be struck down by the reactionary forces. It would be easy to combine and take over, provided a leader of stature would consent to lead. That leader was obviously Bogyoke

---

[11] *Towards Peace and Democracy,* p. 106; the point that was deleted concerned the study and propagation of Marxism in Burma.

Ne Win. "Let's do a 'cook', Bogyoke," some of his young officers urged him, partly in fun, "for it will be so easy." When he came to the War Office, young officers urged him seriously to lead a coup, for they saw the country in dire peril. Politicians wooed him too. U Thein Pe, the Communist, who had his own plans to save the country, and his own thesis to advance, tried hard to win the Bogyoke over. Secret meetings were held in the first week of August at army camps in Mingaladon at which Thein Pe was the persuasive exponent of the Thein Pe thesis. The patriotic elements of the Burma Army would converge on Rangoon. The Air Force—with its few Spitfires—would land on the Turf Club grounds, which would become the command post of the revolution. Then, all the leftist forces would unite, form a National Government, from which reactionary elements would be excluded, and in due time general elections would be conducted. The grand plan sounded all right. Some of the young commanders were resolved, anyway, to rise. Gen. Ne Win, however, decided to hold the Army together as long as possible and stay loyal to the Government and the constitution. "When U Thein Pe failed to win me over," Gen. Ne Win recalled in later years in a parliamentary debate, "he and his friends tried to kidnap me; I had to keep away from them." That was true, U Thein Pe, M.P., admitted, "but then those were my foolish years."[12]

Planners of the Army rising had fixed August 10 as the D-Day. Changed circumstances called for a postponement till August 12. A message sent to Major Sein Tin, with the 1st Burma Rifles at Thayet, went over the wires and through the post office, instead of by army wireless, and the news leaked. Till the last moment the men were made to believe that Gen. Ne Win was going to lead them. When at last they knew he was not, many of them had second thoughts and decided to stay behind. Lt.-Col. Ye Htut, commanding the 3rd Burma Rifles at Mingaladon, gave the men a free choice, saying that it was a matter of conscience, and he would take only volunteers with him. The last moments were confused. Some men joined him, and the party climbed into trucks and drove out towards Prome.

Major Sein Tin moved with his battalion from Thayet towards

[12] Chamber of Deputies, vol. VIII, No. 10, (March 2, 1959), p. 817.

Rangoon on August 10, as originally planned. One of his tasks
was to open up the jails along the way and set the political prisoners free. The ultimate destination was the Turf Club, Rangoon, the site marked for the gathering of the clan. No serious
obstacles were encountered on the move south, nor were there
any welcoming parties. There was silence, and Major Sein Tin
soon sensed that something had gone wrong. Tharrawaddy was
reached. There a unit of the Territorial Force under Bo Kyaw
Sein was easily disarmed. There were no bad feelings; Bo Kyaw
Sein and his men were paid their salaries from funds collected
from the treasuries, and sent away unharmed. Two Spitfires flew
over and strafed the mutineers. No damage was done to either
side. The mutineers scattered in the fields and took cover intel-
ligently. They did not shoot back, for Spitfires were expensive and
hard to come by, and the aircraft would be their's after Rangoon
was taken. The attack from the air, however, served as a signal
to Major Sein Tin that the plans had gone wrong somewhere, for
if they had not, the Spitfires would have been at the Turf Club,
waiting and ready to fly for the rising, instead of against it. Major
Sein Tin decided to fall back with his troops to Prome, where
communications and terrain were good. Lt.-Col. Ye Htut and his
force joined up at Prome which became a stronghold of the insurrection.

Gen. Ne Win reorganized the decimated battalions and started
to forge them into a sword of steel to wield in the defence of the
Union. His own 4 Burifs did not mutiny. Elements of the 6 Burifs
had gone underground early. The 3 Burifs lost some men to Bo
Ye Htut, but the rest calmed down when Gen. Ne Win spoke to
them and asked them to stay loyal to the Union. All told, there
were perhaps 2,000 reliable soldiers left, with assorted arms and
a scanty supply of ammunition. The Karen units had been usable
against the Communist insurgents, but with the Karen problem
assuming serious proportions, the loyalty of the Karen soldier
was being put under heavy strain.

"The Government could not look on with folded arms,"
Thakin Nu reported to Parliament on the events of the latter part
of 1948, "while Communists and White PVO's were in revolt on
the one hand, and on the other the Karen Union Military Police
were creating havoc by looting arms, breaking open Government

treasuries and deserting from the ranks."[13] To defend the districts, 52 units of the Burma Territorial Force were planned to be raised in a few months. The BTF would then take over garrison duty, relieving the Army for action in the field. The urgent expansion of the BTF, however, further roused Karen suspicions, and the climate of mutual distrust only worsened. Foreign adventurers then turned up on the scene. Mr. Woodraw Wyatt, M.P. (Labour), taking part in a debate on Burma in the House of Commons, described a plot in these words: "There was the celebrated case of a Mr. Campbell, a *Daily Mail* correspondent, and a Colonel Tulloch, of Force 136, who went in for an extraordinary kind of schoolboy adventure in encouraging the Karens to believe that, if they started a revolt, they would get help from the City of London and that arms would be supplied from the same source. Of course, they had no business to say so, and British business men in Burma were bitterly against Campbell-Tulloch when the story was exposed. There is no question of British help for the Karens, even though they were made to think so."[14] Not the Karens only, but the Burmese too thought so. A loan of sterling requested from the British Government was held up in long debates. Requests for permission to buy needed arms were denied.

On November 24, 1948, Sama Duwa Sinwa Nawng reported to Thakin Nu that the situation had become desperate. "Delay will mean disaster," he said. "The Karens are now going too far." The Karen National Defence Organization (KNDO), he reported, was seeking the aid of the Kachins to seize power. "I was immediately reminded of the contents of one of the letters seized from Campbell," Thakin Nu recalled. "The letter said that Karens had started the revolt but the Frontier Areas peoples were still sitting on the fence. . . . I then sent for Bogyoke Ne Win and Bo Aung Gyi and instructed them to expedite the formation of the Territorial Force with 31st January, 1949, as the deadline. I then toured the Frontier Areas and explained to the people the real need of unity for the stability of the Union."[15]

---

[13] *Towards Peace and Democracy*, p. 167.
[14] *Hansard*, Commons, vol. 475, No. 43, col. 241.
[15] *Towards Peace and Democracy*, p. 212.

3

The insurrection of the KNDO did not break out on one day; it smouldered and burned for several months before it burst into flames. There were raids here, open defiance there, by KNDO units from July, 1948. The treasury was looted in Maubin; government firearms were seized in Insein. Thakin Nu tried hard to keep the peace. "There is no Karen problem, there are bad Karens and good Karens as there are good Burmese and bad Burmese," he kept saying. "Some of my critics called me 'Karen Nu' for being soft towards the Karens."[16]

On Saturday, October 9, Thakin Nu went to lunch with Saw Ba U Gyi and other leaders of the Karen National Union. Saw Ba U Gyi spoke up for peace and harmony. "I am not boasting when I say that I have been to many places in Burma," he said. "and my experiences of foreign lands comprise those which lie to the East, the West and the South. My experiences in those lands remind me of the Burmese saying, 'One cannot rely even on his own knees.' Can we put our faith in others when one cannot rely even on one's knees? We the indigenous peoples are our knees and the others are such countries as England, America, China and Russia. What I want to remind you is not to rely on those in whom you cannot put your faith. I do not rely on them, and let me remind and advise you to do the same."

"I admit that the Karens were responsible for the looting of arms at Insein," Saw Ba U Gyi said, "but there are good as well as bad Karens. The KNU is not responsible for that affair . . . but we request all those Karens to return those arms within two months from now. If I fail in my appeal, I will then presume that I have no influence as the president of the KNU and I shall resign the post."[17]

The situation, however, gradually worsened. On January 25, 1949, the KNDO insurrection got into full swing. Attacks were launched on Tantabin, Pyu and Toungoo, by the KNDO with the aid of Karen army mutineers. The towns were taken and the columns swept down towards Rangoon. On January 28 a KNDO attack on Bassein was repulsed. Insein, a few miles out of Ran-

---

16 *From Peace to Stability*, Rangoon, Dir. of Information, 1951, p. 70.
17 *Burma and the Insurrections*, p. 48.

goon, fell to the KNDO and Karen army mutineers on February 2. The 2nd Karen Rifles at Prome mutinied on February 5 and drove down to Rangoon in 20 buses. On February 21 Karen insurgents took Meiktila; when two government aircraft landed unaware of the situation, the insurgents seized the planes, flew on to Maymyo and captured the town. They issued arms to those Karen units in Maymyo whose arms had been taken away since the fall of Insein. On March 12 Karen insurgents and Communists, combining in an alliance of convenience, occupied Mandalay.

Those were the gloomy months when the situation changed from day to day. Rangoon lay in a state of siege. Foreign observers called the Union Government the "Rangoon Government", a nickname that stung. On February 1, when the KNDO insurrection was clearly out in the open, Karen officers and men were relieved from duty and put on leave. Many of their senior officers remained loyal to the Union Government, but it was obvious that they could no longer continue in active service in the situation. Bogyoke Ne Win, as Lt.-General, assumed duties as Chief of General Staff and Supreme Commander of the Armed Forces including the Police and the Union Military Police. His return as commander-in-chief gave heart to the soldiers in the Army who had been afield since the BIA and BDA days. "Bogyoke now leads us," they cried out jubilantly in the barracks when the news was heard, "we shall fight, and shall never go under!"

The people too rejoiced that Bogyoke Ne Win was in supreme command. There were many who wanted him to take up the political leadership as well. Thakin Nu toured troubled areas, running great personal risks, and he was also able to earn the confidence of the leaders of the highland people—which counted for much when the Government had few friends and many foes. But the AFPFL was no united party; it was an assortment of individuals, old and young, conservative and progressive, impelled by many motives. The Socialists in the AFPFL were under constant fire from the press and the people. If Bogyoke Ne Win assumed the political leadership as well, some thought, unity of the leftist forces could be forged, and peace would be quickly restored.

The older politicians, who were not in office nor in love with socialism, also looked to Bogyoke Ne Win as the one man who could give strong military and political leadership, bring peace

14

and build unity. "I suggest that Gen. Ne Win be given complete charge," said U Ba Pe in an interview published in *The Sun* of February 26. "Let parliament be suspended, military administration established under Bogyoke, until fair and free elections could be conducted."

Gen. Ne Win, however, had no political ambitions. The urgent task was to rally the Army and fight to hold the Union together. There were a few regular troops which were reliable, and these he moved constantly and committed to battle. Some were moved by a few available aircraft for engagement in one place, then withdrawn and flown into another area for yet another battle. It was like a game of chess, with the whole country for chessboard; it was a fast, furious and perilous game. When he was in Rangoon, he worked at the War Office or in a red-brick armoury of the police barracks on Prome Road, often in his vest, sweating in the heat. Requests for reinforcements or more supplies would come in from every direction, by wireless, by courier. Bad news poured in too. Now this town had fallen, now that. Now this unit had gone over to the insurgents, now that. But with back to the wall, the Army fought back, and Bogyoke Ne Win gave it the heart and the will to fight. There was never enough of men to send, nor ever enough of arms and ammunition. Territorial Force units were raised, quickly trained, and put into the field under young veterans of the BDA and the resistance. Recruits had to learn the art of war in battle, and they could not have found any school harder—or better. The Army, with its few thousand, did not dig in to defend; it went out to fight. Even while Rangoon was threatened, the Army fought in the north to recover Mandalay, Maymyo and Meiktila. The column of Karen insurgents which swept down towards Rangoon from Toungoo was scattered off Payagyi near Pegu. The 2nd Karen Rifles which came down from Prome was broken up in a pitched battle at Wetkaw bridge near Tharrawaddy. The Karen insurgents in Insein therefore waited in vain for reinforcements to strike the final blow at Rangoon.

For weeks the battle raged around Insein, often breaking out to Gyogon and Thamaing, six miles from the heart of Rangoon. Newspaper reporters made Thamaing their base. There the commanders would come from their conferences to launch the waves of attack with assortments of men and arms. Student volunteers from the University and the high schools, the levies, the regular forces, an old armoured car, these constituted the main force which the Government had to hurl against the entrenched insurgents. A few artillery pieces were available, though short of ammunition. These were mounted on the University campus, in Kamayut and elsewhere, and they flung hastily manufactured shells into Insein at intervals, making a lot of noise, inflicting some damage. The Air Force flew bombing and strafing missions; young pilots made up in daring what they lacked in ammunition. Naval boats, armed with Oerlikons, approached the battle areas through the creeks, and played their brave parts in the fighting.

The people of Rangoon sent food parcels for the fighting men —or rather, boys. Thamaing was busy like a market, with busloads of people and food parcels arriving every few hours. Every wave of attack would be applauded. Then, in a few hours the men would return, a mission done. Their dead would be laid down in a shed or under the trees, and the commander would tell the press about the battle. Reporters would take notes at furious speed, while shots from snipers sounded not too far away and flies settled on the blank faces of the dead. Those were sad days which also stirred the people into action. Rangoon was defiant. Life went on in the city. Schools were uninterrupted. Business was as usual; the cinemas, offering their four shows each day, were crowded.

General Ne Win often remembers the deeds of daring which his young men performed in those perilous years. "Once, a troop of men in front of Insein would not move on order to attack," he recalled. "They had grown weary and battly-shy. Tun Tin, their leader, jumped up from the trench and walked up and down with a little swagger telling the men that death would not come until one's time was up. Bullets whizzed round him like bees, but he remained untouched. The men then rose and marched forward to attack with Tun Tin leading them." Another man who seemed to have a charmed life was Bo Sein Hman. "Shells fell and burst round him," Gen. Ne Win said, "but he was unhurt. His nerves suffered, though. Now and then blood would clot up in his veins, and he would be petrified." Bo Sein Hman led troops against the mutineers of the 1 Burifs in the Tharrawaddy area. One day, he flew with a scouting mission over the town which was held by insurgents. A stray shot hit him, but he kept the fatal wound a secret so that the mission might be completed. Bo Sein Hman died the next day, April 8, 1949. His number was up.[18]

Bo Min Thein, leading 76 men, threw off from Bassein a force of insurgents several hundred strong. Officers and men of the 4 Burifs, moved in the nick of time by Gen. Ne Win, kept the Delta area free against the hordes. Bo San Yu went on special missions to Pyapon and other embattled areas to gather the men and mount operations.

Bo Chit Myaing, with two depleted companies of men (about 200) from the 3 Burifs, Bo Kyaw and Bo Sein Mya among his officers, stood at Wetkaw in the path of a column of Karen mutineers led by Lt.-Col. Mya Maung and made up of the full 2nd Karen Rifles and their families (some 2,000 in all), which rode down confidently from Prome on the road to Rangoon in 186 trucks. The defenders had a Boffor gun, borrowed from the Navy, and a few shells. The first shot put out of action the armoured car that led the advancing column, with a broadside hit. A few more shots, and the column scattered.

Bo Tin U fought in many areas, with a vow to stay single until insurgency was finally put down. "Get married, and this is an order," Gen. Ne Win told him after he was battle-worn for years. Thus fought many brave and dedicated men, some to the death. Gen. Ne Win fondly remembers them all.

The mutineers from the Burma Rifles battalions rallied to the call of Gen. Ne Win when Rangoon lay imperilled. The Karen insurrection posed a threat of foreign intervention, and this, Gen. Ne Win said in his message to the mutineers, must not be allowed to happen. Bo Ye Htut and Bo Sein Tin, in the Tharrawaddy-Prome sector, used their forces to thwart the plans of the Karen insurgents. For several nights, they had trucks driven back and forth, from the main trunk road to the river, giving the Karen insurgents who were marching to Rangoon the impression that Government forces were falling upon them in mass. Thus bewildered and alarmed, the insurgents broke up and scattered at the first serious encounter. The PVO insurgents in Tantabin area also

18 A brief biography of Bo Sein Hman is in *Encyclopaedia Burmanica,* vol. 4 at page 69.

observed a truce with the Government forces and fell upon the Karen insurgents. The army mutineers and the PVO were up in arms against the Government, but they were united in their resolve to keep off foreign intervention. Also, their leaders retained their respect and affection for Bogyoke Ne Win, and they listened when he spoke.

Insein was a vital test for the Government, but there were other towns which must be redeemed, other danger zones which must be watched. Gen. Ne Win therefore travelled extensively to inspect the scattered troops, to give them a feeling of unity and purpose, to plan the campaigns with them in the field. Once he drove up from Rangoon along the Mandalay road, through the Communist-infested Pyinmana area, then turned into the Shan State. He had a young Mon soldier with him, a few staff, and friends U Tin Maung and U Tha Gaung of A-1 Films. He would drop in on units on the way, chat with officers and men, then drive on. When he needed petrol, he would stop at a filling station in some small town, paying for it out of his pocket. Similarly he would feed the party at shops along the way, rather than have the units or the district officers make the arrangements. He did not bother to take accounts of expenses, for he never submitted bills for travelling allowances. All was in the line of duty. As the party got into the hills, the young Mon soldier felt compelled to tell U Tin Maung that funds had run out. "Uncle, can't you tell the Old Man to eat and fill the car at our units," he asked. "He just keeps paying out of his pocket, and never claims expenses. Now the money is gone." U Tin Maung had, fortunately, a roll of money which he had won at the races in Rangoon, and this supply came in useful in the situation. When the money gave out, he left the party to make a dash for Rangoon to be in time for the next race meeting of the Turf Club.

The party put up for the night at an army camp near Meiktila. In the middle of the night, however, Gen. Ne Win felt an urge to move on. He woke up U Tha Gaung, and got the party ready. "Let's move off," he said, "it is rather stuffy in here." He drove for an hour or two, then parked the car by the road to rest for the night. There was no traffic on the road at night in those days; all was silent and dark. In the morning, moving on, U Tha Gaung discovered that they had spent the night off Pyinmana in an area where the Communist insurgents prowled. The discovery made U Tha Gaung shudder. Gen. Ne Win, however, drove calmly on.

4

The Socialists came under increasingly heavy fire as the insurrection mounted. They were accused of being the evil genius behind U Nu, and the obstacle that stood in the way of peace and unity. The Karen insurgents had no love for them. The Communists hated them. The PVO blamed them for the breakdown of negotiations for leftist unity. Their leaders were attacked in the press; scandals were built of their public performance or their private behaviour. One scandal drove a Socialist Minister to leave office and lie low. Another roused a rally to anger and drove members to demonstrate and break up a few newspaper offices. In those circumstances, the Socialist leaders decided to resign as Ministers or Parliamentary Secretaries to prove their earnest desire for harmony and peace, and to open the way for participation of the leftist insurgent forces in the Government.

U Nu was out on tour in Sagaing—where the situation was grave, with Mandalay in the hands of insurgents—when the Socialists decided to resign *en bloc*. When he returned to Rangoon at the end of March, 1949, the resignations were on his table. "When I got back," U Nu said, recalling the event, "their decision had already been made, and I had to accept the resignations. But I did not accept their suggestion to invite insurgent leaders to join the Government. How could I have accepted these insurgents? If they came into the Government it would be through no good motive. I rejected the suggestion of my colleagues and in the place of those who resigned I appointed General Ne Win and U E Maung, and we went on fighting the insurgents with whatever small resources we had."[19]

Thus, on April 1, Gen. Ne Win became Deputy Prime Minister, with charge of the Home and the Defence ministries, in addition to his duties as supreme commander of the armed forces. His pledge to the people was that he would work for the restoration of peace, law and order, so that the first general elections might be held in fair and free conditions. The elections were due within

[19] Speech to University students. *Burma Weekly Bulletin,* Oct. 9, 1958.

18 months from the coming into force of the constitution. When Gen. Ne Win took office, the time limit was nearly up, and extension had later to be made by presidential decree. However, in the desperate situation which prevailed, the big question was whether the Union would survive at all.

It was a small, non-party Government which U Nu got together to meet the crisis. U E Maung, Justice of the Supreme Court, took care of the ministries of Foreign Affairs, Justice, and a few other subjects. U Tin, who had been associated with the nationalist movement since the days when he had managed the *New Light of Burma,* was Finance Minister. The rest of the Cabinet members were from the States and the Chin Special Division. The task was huge, resources were small, friends were few. But the Government carried on, and the people rallied behind it. For lack of friends abroad arms and ammunition could not be easily obtained. There was not only a shortage of sellers or suppliers, but of foreign exchange to buy with, or credit to depend upon. At home, salaries of government staff had to be cut by 25 per cent as a matter of dire necessity. A strike called by the Ministerial Services Union took some staff away from work for a few weeks, and that brought temporary relief to the Government whose obligation to pay the strikers was at least postponed.

Gen. Ne Win went to London in July and had talks with Mr. Ernest Bevin, the Foreign Minister, Mr. A. V. Alexander, the Defence Minister, Mr. Shinwell, the War Minister, Mr. Henderson, the Air Minister, and Field-Marshal Sir William Slim, the Chief of the Imperial General Staff. He and his party, which included ambassadors U Hla Maung and U Ohn and Wing-Commander S. Khin of the Burma Air Force, visited military installations and Burmese cadets in training. "We do not want highly mechanized equipment," Gen. Ne Win explained to reporters, "we cannot afford it. We have to reorientate our army on the lines of guerrilla warfare." The real situation in Burma, he also pointed out, was much misunderstood abroad, especially in Britain. It was a mistake, he said, to assume that all Karens were up against the Union Government; only about 5 per cent of them were with the insurgents. The backbone of the insurrection had been broken; insurgents were scattered in hill and jungle. The domestic situation in Burma was beginning to look up, with good harvests of paddy in prospect, and the flow to Rangoon of rice for export smooth and open. Gen. Ne Win denied that his mission was to purchase arms and military equipment, but the visit did help to expedite the approval of the Commonwealth loan that the Union Government had asked for. Procurement of training facilities for Burmese cadets became easier. U Hla Maung, with tactically timed diplomatic exuberance at a dinner party dropped the hint that if arms were not available from Western friends, inquiries must be directed to "you know who". This carefully delivered hint— which could always, if necessary, be blamed on too much wine— seemed to help dissolve some of the inhibitions and reservations held in London and elsewhere. A shipment of ammunition for Oerlikon guns came through soon after the dinner party.[20]

U Nu visited India and Pakistan, leaving Gen. Ne Win in charge at home as acting Prime Minister. Aid was sought on two separate fronts. U Nu wanted arms and ammunition for the fight against the insurgents. He also wanted the loan of sacred relics of the Buddha, and saplings of the sacred Bo tree to plant in Burma. India made available rifles and ammunition sufficient to keep the Burma Army in action for some months in the critical period. The relics were loaned too, so that U Nu could have them sent round the country to rejuvenate the Buddhist faith and boost up the people's morale. "Send us a few hundred saplings of the sacred Bo tree," cabled the Union Government to Burma's Legation in Colombo. In course of time, the saplings arrived by air in Rangoon, to be respectfully received by U Nu and his associates, and planted with ceremony all over the country. In those times, the saplings and the relics also formed a part of the mixed arsenal which the Union Government drew from in the bitter fight for survival.

Insein was recovered on May 22, 1949. In April it had looked as if a friendly settlement between the KNDO insurgents and the Government was about to be consummated. Saw Ba U Gyi and Mahn James Tun Aung came out under a flag of truce to have conversations with the Government leaders. Wearing a beret and a luxuriant growth of beard, Saw Ba U Gyi waved and smiled

---

[20] A report on the interview appears in *The Hindu,* July 17, 1949, based on a despatch from Reuters. See also profile of U Hla Maung, by Maung Maung, in *The Guardian* magazine, July, 1955.

to reporters as he came over. "All looks well," he replied to questions on the prospects of an agreement. The talks ended in an agreement which was signed on April 5 by the two Karen leaders on the one part and U Nu, Bogyoke Ne Win, Justice E Maung, and Sir Ba U, the Chief Justice of the Union, on the other. Amnesty, it was noted in the agreement, had already been granted. Karen army personnel who gave up fighting the Government would report to the Army, and an Army Reorganization Committee composed of Sir Ba U as chairman, and Lt.-Generals Smith Dun and Ne Win would consider their grievances, if any. There would be no discrimination, it was promised, between Karen personnel and military personnel of other races, nor between Karen civilian officers and others; all would receive fair and equal treatment. Karen civilians would also be permitted to hold such firearms as might be necessary for the security of their villages.

The agreement was received by the people with great joy. Saw Ba U Gyi and Mahn James Tun Aung were given their safe conduct back to Insein. In a few days, it was hoped, the agreement would be carried out, and the KNDO insurrection would be over. The joy, however, was shortlived. On April 8, a note signed by Saw Hunter Tha Hmwe and Saw Aung Sein was passed to the Government from the KNDO in Insein, rejecting the agreement, and making "counter-proposals" for cessation of hostilities as a prelude to parleys in which "responsible leaders, both military and political, from all other battle zones" could meet and discuss terms. Those, it was proposed, "should include other allied minority leaders such as the Chin, Kachin, Shan and Mons." The counter-proposals were clearly unacceptable to the Union Government. The fighting started again on the front. The cannons began to boom again.

The KNDO insurrection went on for some time. In terms of recommendations made by the Regional Autonomy Enquiry Commission headed by Sir Ba U—Saw Ba U Gyi had also taken part as a member of the Commission before he led the KNDO in their revolt—the Union Parliament amended the constitution in October, 1951, to establish a separate Karen State.[21] This too failed

---

[21] *Report of the Regional Autonomy Enquiry Commission, Rangoon,* Govt. Press, 1952; debate on the constitutional amendment, Constituent Assembly (Parliament), *Proceedings,* vol. XIV, No. 28.

to appease the KNDO. Thus the fight continued, in Insein, and beyond, for many weary, costly months.

Saw Ba U Gyi fell in the Hlaingbwe area, near the Thai border, in August 1950. The 3rd Burma Regiment, commanded by Lt.-Col. Aye Maung, with Major Than Win and Major Sein Lwin as deputies, came upon Saw Ba U Gyi's party in the swamps at dawn. The troops called out to the party to surrender. The party resisted; the troops opened fire. Saw Ba U Gyi fell. Another casualty was Capt. Vivian, a member of the party, who had broken out of Insein jail where he had been undergoing a sentence of imprisonment for stealing Bren guns to supply U Saw in 1947. Soldiers carried Saw Ba U Gyi's body on their shoulders through the swamps to Moulmein. There the Karen elders, the district officers and the officers of the 3rd Burma Regiment discussed how the last rites of the fallen leader should be conducted with full honour. A sea burial was decided, and after the religious service, the black coffin was taken out, attended by honour guards, to the ocean, four hours by motor-boat from Moulmein. Then, Saw Ba U Gyi's body was given over to the deep and peaceful waters.

Looking back across the years, Saw Hunter Tha Hmwe—who rejected the agreement of 1949 but concluded one with Gen. Ne Win on March 12, 1964—recalled with sadness the changes of heart that the KNDO leaders had along the long hard road of the insurrection. During the first period, 1949-52, he said in a message of thanksgiving broadcast to the people, the KNDO were rightists and they had sought the support of the Western Bloc. That was how Saw Ba U Gyi and Saw Sankey lost their lives while trying to enlist the aid of the West. They next placed their hopes in the Kuomintang troops which had trespassed on Burma's soil. Those hopes too were disappointed; the presence of the KMT only aggravated the complications. In the period 1953-60 they switched to the leftists of the Eastern Bloc. This change was attractive at first, but as time went on, the ideology was found to be detrimental to the interests of the people. Even he, Saw Hunter Tha Hmwe, who did not possess an acre of land or ten kyats of money, was called a wavering national bourgeoisie and attempts were made to retire him from leadership. Dissensions grew, and accusations were levelled at one another of deviation from the ideology. In the third period, 1961-64, guided by the Old Testament, the Karen Revolution found the path to peace and creative socialist construction. On that path the meeting with Gen. Ne Win and the Revolutionary Council of the Union of Burma took place.[22]

5

But we jump many years to hear Saw Hunter Tha Hmwe muse on the Karen revolutionary struggle. Those years were packed with events. They were years of conflict and confusion; yet the Union held together. There were trials and tribulations, yet the Union came through. There were political leaders who, weighed in the balance of history, were found wanting; but the working people, whose toils kept the Union going, bore more than their shares of the burden, made more than their shares of contribution, with more than the usual courage and fortitude. Since the Japanese invasion of the country in 1942, the people had not had peace. Yet they had unfailingly responded to all calls for sacrifices in the nation's cause. When the insurrections broke out, it was on them that the highest risks and the heaviest burdens fell. Their natural resilience, their sense of humour, their Buddhist tolerance, helped them to take their changing fortunes without bitterness.

The times and the circumstances posed a big challenge to the political leaders in power, and put them to hard, cruel tests. There were the insurrections to put down, the social revolution to push through. There were the rising expectations of the people for a better life after independence, their bitter disappointments and frustrations. Yet, the people needed to be given a sense of oneness, a sense of purpose and direction, the will to keep striving for the goals. There were so many odds against the Union, failure to attain the goals could be understood; yet, success was essential if the Union must keep faith with the purpose of its birth. The Union was not born merely to exist. Its pledge to the citizens was to open to them a braver, better life of socialist justice and

[22] Broadcast on March 22, 1964, reported in *The Guardian* daily, Mar. 23.

abundance. That pledge called for constant and continuing endeavour.

It is perhaps in the nature of politics that power becomes not a means to fulfil pledges and achieve goals, but an end in itself. When power becomes an end, not merely the means, then corruption and compromise, cliques, understandings, demarcations of spheres of influence, narrow and petty minds, slogans and pretty platitudes, grand plans which lack the will or intention to perform, these take over the political wheels. In such situations people talk of political machines and political bosses. Such machines, and such bosses began to appear in increasing numbers in Burma from 1951-52 when, as the insurrections gradually receded, general elections for Parliament were held in the cleared constituencies on a staggered arrangement. Even as, in the days of the GCBA, the lure of political office carrying power and privilege turned politics into a scramble, so now the first parliamentary elections started the stampede. As time went on, sharing the spoils and keeping the political managers and manipulators happy became the compelling goals, while the vision of the socialist society faded. That was the democracy as some elements in the leadership of the AFPFL understood it in fixing the phases of the national struggle; independence first; democracy second; finally socialism.

Gen. Ne Win kept himself strictly aloof from the darker side of party politics. Reorganizing the army took up much of his time. Whenever he could snatch time off from the daily chores of Deputy Prime Minister, he would dash off on tour, accompanied by a small staff. Office and political power did not spoil him; the ritual and the routine irked him. He did not enjoy, as some of his colleagues seemed to do, the long Cabinet meetings which yielded more resolutions than results. Now and then he would blow up when his aide reminded him of a Cabinet meeting he must attend. He would drive the aide away with a few pungent words, and swear he would never go near the Cabinet room again. When the hour of the meeting approached, however, he would relent, sweeten the sulking aide, and go off with him to the meeting. He liked to carry his own briefcase, and hail friends whom he passed in the Secretariat corridors. There was no pomp about him; and that was no pose, it was just his nature.

In his rare leisure, he liked to slip into a cinema hall, with a few staff for company. Partly from thrift, and partly because he felt uncomfortable in the posh exclusiveness of the dress circle, he would buy cheap stall seats for himself and the party. People saw him at the cinema, or in gay company at the clubs at night. They did not see him work night and day at the War Office or his command post which shifted about in the city. They saw him come to the parties or attempt the *fox-trot* on the dance-floor; they did not notice when he slipped out to get back to work punctually, on his own strict schedule. Perhaps it was a part of his strategy to be seen at play, to assure the people that all was well, and to give the enemy exaggerated ideas of the army's strength and readiness. Also, all the going about was in the continuing process of educating himself. He has a large appetite for learning; all pieces of information, all bits of knowledge are sorted out and neatly stored away in his well-stocked mind for future use.

Fighting the insurgents was not the only role of the army. Gen. Ne Win's vision went much further than just winning a few victories in the field or catching some insurgents in the hill and jungle. The jungle war would continue for long painful years, he foresaw. The army must not get lost in the jungle. It must build and modernize to become the national army with might and morale to defend the Union against foreign aggressors. The army must also retain the vital spark of idealism with which it had started. If the spark was lost, no amount of material could preserve its original character as the people's fighting army. This, Gen. Ne Win knew, and in the building of the army he constantly kept the emphasis on the quality and spirit of the men. In all the three services there were mixtures of the races, and of officers and men who had served in the British forces and those who had started their march with the BIA. These different elements had to be knit into a united and integrated army. Gen. Ne Win permitted no discrimination; his only test was the quality of service a soldier gave. His justice was fair and strict. No one enjoyed immunity from punishment for their misdeeds. Those who were close to him, being constantly under his quick and watchful eyes, got caught at once if they misbehaved, and then punishment was sure and swift. Those who served straight and true earned his lasting friendship. But no easy promotions, rather the reverse.

When at last he remembered that an aide was due for promotion he would send the aide to the troops where he could rise on his own merits.

The unity of the armed forces, acquired over the fighting years under the leadership of Gen. Ne Win, is such that the term "Burma Army" or the *Tatmadaw*, embraces all the three services. Soldier, sailor, airman, a comrade is simply a member of the *Tatmadaw*, and he is proud to be so identified. The building of the Army started even while it was out in the field in 1949, the peak year of the insurrection. Young officers would be taken out from the battlefield and shipped off for courses of training in England. On their return they would, likewise, disembark and go straight off to the field, with barely enough time to unpack and say hello to their families. A perfectionist and a great believer in training, Gen. Ne Win saw to it that the officers and men were always in form and up-to-date. Study missions were sent to Asian and European countries. Friendly links were established with Yugoslavia and Israel, and training facilities and arms and military equipment were obtained from the two countries. In later years, senior officers attended staff colleges in Australia and the United States. In this way the Army went out far and wide to gather knowledge and skills, while the home front provided a rich practising ground.

Gen. Ne Win decided in the later part of 1950 that his mission of restoring law and order was to a large extent accomplished. He therefore resigned from the Cabinet on September 9 to return to the Army which needed his whole attention. He had gone in, expecting to stay only for a few months. The task took him longer. Yet, typically, in those turbulent times when no one gave much thought to the constitution, he read it thoroughly and discovered a provision which fixed a time limit of six months for a non-member of Parliament to hold Cabinet office. U E Maung, Justice of the Supreme Court, was in the same position as Gen. Ne Win, and he stayed in the Cabinet from April to November, 1949, without bothering about the constitutional bar. Gen. Ne Win, however, "felt a qualm of conscience" and sought the advice of the Attorney-General before the six months were up. U Chan Htoon, the Attorney-General, gave his opinion that the bar would start to operate only after the first general elections were held and the Union Government was formed; Gen. Ne Win's staying in the

Provisional Government beyond the six months would not be unconstitutional.[23]

6

Adversity had held the AFPFL together. When the perils receded and power became a pleasurable and profitable thing, the AFPFL started to disintegrate—not on the surface, but deep down at its core. Had the differences been of policy, they could have been openly debated and settled, and that would have strengthened—not weakened—the organization. But they were not of policy or principle, for all were avowed leftists, dedicated to the building of a socialist society. They rose from personal rivalries and the ambition to monopolize—not merely share—power, and then for its own sake and for personal aggrandizement. The concept of power as a trust and a duty was soon lost sight of. "Our fellows can take adversity," Gen. Ne Win would often moralize, looking at the corruption spreading all over the political and social scene. "but prosperity spoils them."

The general elections of 1951-52 gave the AFPFL easy victory. It was only when an Elections Commission, headed by Sir Ba U and Justice E Maung, declared an area clear of insurrection that the elections were conducted in the area. Sir Ba U was hoping to be elected President of the Union, U E Maung could expect to succeed Sir Ba U, his uncle, as Chief Justice. In those circumstances, it was said, the Commission was more than friendly to the AFPFL for whose word it would wait before declaring a constituency safe and ready for elections. The Burma Army also served not only to keep the peace but to help the AFPFL win. There were many ways of helping. Villagers who were suspected of being anti-AFPFL were kept away from the polling booths by sudden military operations conducted right across their path. Or the booths would be raided, after the polling hour, by unidentified armed men. The Army had no qualms of conscience about helping, for the AFPFL was the united front which had led the nation to freedom, and it was in the first few years of independence the

[23] Gen. Ne Win's speech in the Chamber of Deputies, Feb. 13, 1959, reproduced in *Is Trust Vindicated?*

hope for national unity and prosperity. Even with the massive irregular support, however, some AFPFL Ministers and leaders succeeded in losing, and had to be pushed into Parliament through bye-elections.

The AFPFL held a brief conference in December, 1947, after Aung San had fallen. After that there were no national conferences. The headquarters became operational only during elections. At other times, it was empty and idle. Activity mainly revolved round the Government—winning and retaining office, demarcation of spheres of influence, the forming of cliques, the sharing of spoils. In the districts, the AFPFL leaders became the party bosses, wielding influence over the Government officers, making their occasional demands from the Union Government. Soon, understandings and comfortable working arrangements were established all round. That was democracy for the ruling gentry for which the people had to give their sweat and blood.

The predominant majority which the AFPFL enjoyed in Parliament for a decade after independence bred complacency in its ranks, including the parliamentary group. Premier U Nu himself showed little respect for Parliament, or the AFPFL members of it. At the opening of each session AFPFL M.Ps would be brought together and lectured to by U Nu, or one of his lieutenants—U Ba Swe, U Kyaw Nyein, or Thakin Tin. The members would be given a cursory preview of the legislative programme ahead, and told to keep in line, and avoid making too many speeches. There would be no discussion; the members of the parliamentary group were lectured to, not listened to, and many of the younger, more progressive members felt frustrated. Party discipline they understood and were willing to accept, but not this shabby treatment, especially when there was so much lip-service given to "parliamentary democracy".

U Nu had an expansive, extrovertive personality. He liked to dream aloud, and roam unrestricted on wide and lofty planes. The Chamber of Deputies, in which he would see the same members who owed their existence to the AFPFL of which he was the unchallenged leader, did not interest U Nu much. In the four years of the first full-fledged Parliament which was elected in 1951-52, U Nu did not make a single important policy statement. He preferred to meet the press at regular monthly or fortnightly conferences, and talk freely on minor matters or major policy. "There I failed in my duty to the Chamber," U Nu confessed in February, 1957, by which time AFPFL unity was already seriously undermined, "and there is really no excuse for my failure. In future I undertake to make policy statements in the Chamber, and also take part in debates."[24]

Gen. Ne Win, on his part, took his parliamentary duties seriously in the period 1949-50 when he was Deputy Prime Minister. There was only one chamber of the Provisional Parliament, then, but the sessions were held regularly, and the budget was voted. Attendance was small; 44 seats were rendered vacant because PVO and Communist members had gone underground. But Gen. Ne Win regarded Parliament as a gesture of faith, a living symbol of the Constitution. He believed in no half-measures. He hated hypocrisy. The Constitution accepted parliamentary democracy; the Army respected the Constitution and was pledged to protect it. He himself had joined the Cabinet in the discharge of his duty as a soldier to uphold the Constitution. Whether Parliament was big or small, whether its members were dull or brilliant, whether it was playing its role fully or only formally, he must respect it, report to it, and answer questions put by it. He attended sessions as regularly as he could, taking time off from directing military operations which were spread and scattered all over the country. When questions were asked, he gave honest answers framed after diligent research. When he promised that a matter would be looked into, he did follow up and report back. He made policy statements on defence requirements of the country, addressing the people through Parliament. He stressed that the Army and the people must march together and the people should appreciate that it was not enough to pay for the maintenance of the Army and leave the soldiers to do the "dirty work". That attitude would be right if the Army was a mercenary army, and the country could afford to keep a large one. Burma, however, could not afford to maintain a big standing army; the Burma Army was not a mercenary force; the people and the Army must therefore work together.

The Korean war caused a serious split in the Socialist party and the AFPFL. The Union Government supported the Security

[24] Chamber of Deputies, *Proceedings*, vol. III, No. 3, Feb. 28, 1957.

15

Council of the United Nations in its first stand on the Korean conflict, but dissociated itself from the later General Assembly resolution to brand the People's Republic of China as an aggressor. Nor did the Union Government impose any ban on the export of "warlike material" to North Korea and the People's Republic of China, pointing out that the total exports to China constituted only 1.1 per cent of Burma's annual export volume, and did not consist of warlike material in any case.[25] The Korean issue, however, roused the leftist wing of the Socialist party to bitter attack against the Government. Thakin Chit Maung (Tharrawaddy), Thakin Lwin, and several members broke away to form the Burma Workers and Peasants Party (BWPP), which was promptly dubbed as the "Red Socialist" party. The BWPP attracted some outstanding men. U Ba Nyein, son of a village postmaster who won his way into the coveted Burma Civil Service Class (I) by sheer merits, and an able economist, left the service to join. U Thein Pe Myint, U Aung Than (an elder brother of Bogyoke Aung San), and several intellectuals and leftist politicians came in. The BWPP was not strong enough in Parliament to muster enough votes to table no-confidence motions, but it resorted to several effective tactics, such as the sit-down strike and the walk-out, to make its presence felt. Its members were vocal, and well-armed with facts and figures. Their participation enlivened parliamentary debates.

Justice E Maung, half-judge, half-politician, since his brief sojourn in the Cabinet, could not resist political ambition. A bitter quarrel with U Nu further rendered his tenure on the Supreme Court uncomfortable, and U E Maung retired to start his "Justice Party". The BWPP and the Justice Party joined in a marriage of convenience in the National United Front (NUF) to fight the elections of 1956. By that time popular feeling against the AFPFL was so strong that the NUF won 45 seats in the Chamber of Deputies, and by allying with a few dissident individuals and groups it could marshal enough votes to table no-confidence motions against the Government. The AFPFL still enjoyed a massive majority in the Chamber of 250 seats, but the NUF and its allies had received 1,139,206 votes, as against the 1,743,816 won by the AFPFL, or 44.8 per cent of the popular vote as against

25 Maung Maung, *Burma in the Family of Nations,* p. 147.

AFPFL's 47.9 per cent.[26] This, for those who had eyes to see, was the writing on the wall for the AFPFL.

U Nu saw. He kept urging for a purge of the AFPFL, and a thorough reorganization. When the Cabinet was formed after the 1956 elections, he took leave from office for a year to devote himself full-time to his work as president of the AFPFL. U Ba Swe was made Prime Minister, with three Deputy Premiers to assist him—Sao Hkun Khio, who was both Minister for the Shan State and Foreign Minister; U Kyaw Nyein whose special interest was economic affairs and industry; Thakin Tin, president for many years of the All Burma Peasants Organization, an organ of the AFPFL, and whose subject, therefore was agriculture. U Nu, who had often declared his intention to retire from politics, had publicly named three political heirs—U Ba Swe, U Kyaw Nyein and Thakin Tin—saying generously that any one of them would be eminently qualified to succeed him. Three expectant heirs could not make for unity in leadership. Rather, such a situation encouraged factionalism, whipped up personal rivalries and bred dark suspicions. U Nu's absence from office did not help much either. He soon began to feel lonely, and to yearn for a return to office. He had often spoken of the need to separate the leadership of party from the leadership of the Government. "One man cannot carry two pots on his head," he said in his picturesque language. A few lonely months out of office convinced him that if he must hold only one office he would choose that of Prime Minister.

Another man who clearly saw the writing on the wall for the AFPFL was Gen. Ne Win. After leaving the Cabinet, he concentrated, with the support of a strong team of young deputies, to build the Army. He kept himself and the Army away from party politics, but urged U Ba Swe, the Defence Minister, and other Socialist leaders to start organizing the Socialist party on a strong and proper basis. The party had stayed out of office for a period, but its leaders returned to the Cabinet, one by one, and soon they were busy with governmental affairs and power politics, and party organization was neglected. "This will never do," Gen. Ne Win and his younger associates warned the Socialist leaders, "you must put down your grass-roots now, and start building the

[26] Chapter on Burma in *Constitutionalism in Asia*, ed. R. N. Spann, Asia Publishing House, 1963.

socialist economy without delay." But the party leaders were beginning to enjoy playing Ministers, and the constant warnings by the army officers became annoying. "We know what we are doing," they retorted, "politics is no easy thing. We shall mind our business, you mind yours." When time came for the elections in 1956, they were sweet again in asking the Army for some unofficial help. "Why can't you take care of your own business?" the young colonels asked, sarcastic, but not without sympathy. Gen. Ne Win threw out a few choice curses, then told his deputies to do what they could—within reasonable limits—to help the political comrades in distress. The AFPFL was undivided then, and though its character as a national front was fast fading, it could still be said—stretching a point—that helping the AFPFL to retain the leadership was a patriotic duty.

The Burma Army grew strong not too soon. The intrusion into Burma's borders of Kuomintang troops under General Li Mi, assumed serious proportions towards the end of 1952. The troops had been dispersed in Shan villages since the rout of Chiang Kaishek from mainland China, but they had not given much trouble. They engaged in opium-smuggling, gun-running and some cultivation in the valleys at the foot of the hills. Li Mi, however, started to make loud noises about his crusade to reclaim the mainland. The KMT became more active, and aggressive, on Burma's north-eastern borders. Air-drops of supplies from planes flying in from foreign bases became more frequent and blatant. The KMT aggression became an international issue which Burma could no longer ignore. The Government faced the issue on two fronts. First a complaint was lodged with the United Nations which, with speed and rare unanimity, recognized that Burma was the victim of an aggression by "foreign troops" and urged member states to refrain from supporting those troops. Secondly, military operations were mounted, on a divisional scale, against the KMT strongholds along the borders. It was the first engagement by the Burma Army with well-equipped foreign troops which were in mass— the KMT troops were estimated to be 12,000 strong. The Army proved itself in the hard test.

The Union Government was receiving American aid when the KMT issue erupted. Before going to the United Nations, therefore, the Government ended the aid programme, in order to end the anomaly, as U Nu put it, "of receiving aid from the United States Government on the one hand, and on the other fighting against an army which was controlled and supplied by the Formosan authorities whose continued existence was dependent on large scale American aid. At no time was there any suggestion that the United States Government itself had lent its support to the Kuomintang adventure."[27]

The United States Government might not have been officially involved, but there was strong suspicion in Burma that the Central Intelligence Agency was. William J. Sebald, the American ambassador in Rangoon, it was revealed in *The Invisible Government,* a book about the CIA, tried hard to obtain assurances from Washington that the CIA was not supporting the Chinese Nationalist troops.

"If U.S. relations were not to turn completely sour, he insisted, the Nationalists would have to be removed. Each time the State Department responded that the U.S. was not involved and Burma should logically complain to Taipeh.

Dutifully, Sebald passed along these assurances to the Burmese Foreign Office. But he never succeeded in convincing the Burmese of American innocence. The most determined of the skeptics was Gen. Ne Win, who as Chief of Staff of the Army, was leading the battle against the guerrillas. Fresh from a meeting with his field commanders, Ne Win confronted Sebald at a diplomatic gathering and angrily demanded action on the Nationalist troops. When Sebald started to launch into his standard disclaimer of U.S. involvement the General cut him short.

'Mr. Ambassador,' he asserted firmly, 'I have it cold. If I were you, I'd just keep quiet.'

As Sebald was to learn, and as high U.S. officials now frankly admit, Ne Win was indeed correct. The CIA was intimately involved in the Nationalist troops, but Sebald's superiors— men just below John Foster Dulles—were officially ignorant of the fact."[28]

[27] Speech in the Chamber of Deputies, Sept. 27, 1947; *Premier Reports to the People,* Rangoon, Dir. of Information, 1958.

[28] David Wise & Thomas B. Ross, *The Invisible Government,* Random House, New York, 1964, pp. 130-31.

A Four Power Commission—composed of military representatives from Burma, Thailand, Formosa, and America—helped to
evacuate a few thousand of the KMT from Burmese soil. The
evacuees, however, were old men or young boys, clearly not the
combatants. The arms they turned in were old and useless. Several thousand of the KMT remained, scattered, troublesome, flar-
ing up in fits of aggressive activity. The Burma Army mounted
several major operations against the marauders, and has remained
on vigilant guard on the borders. The KMT presence has continued to be an irritant in Burma's relations with the United States.

The Burma Army grew up fighting in the field. The numbers
increased in proper proportion to the needs and the means of the
country. The quality improved. Training facilities were set up
within the country, while missions and students kept going abroad
far and wide to bring home the latest skills and techniques. The
Officers' Training School continued to turn out young officers for
the immediate needs of the Army. For long term needs, a Defence
Services Academy was started at "Ba Htu Myo"—a site near
Aungban in the Shan State where Bo Ba Htu died during the
resistance. Young cadets who go to the Academy are put through
four years of training and schooling in the regular arts and science
studies and, on graduation, they are given their Bachelor's degree
in arts or science, and a regular commission in the armed forces.
The Staff College takes senior officers, Majors and above, gives
them good intellectual exercises, and provides them with opportunity to analyze and draw lessons from the campaigns in which
they have taken part. Pilot courses were occasionally conducted
for the colonels at which they were repeatedly urged to read widely and deeply. A foreign languages institute was started at the
Defence Services Institute for Army officers, and Gen. Ne Win
was a regular student in some of the first courses. Thus the Burma
Army went forth not merely to fight, but to learn.

A unity of command in the armed forces had grown out of the
long and hard campaigning. The practice happened mainly because of Gen. Ne Win. He was the one leader whom all the services accepted unquestioning. When the time came to reorganize,
the practice was officially accepted in constituting the offices of
Chief of Staff and a Vice-Chief for each of the three services—
Army, Navy and Air Force. The system reduced inter-service

jealousies and competition to manageable size. Carried down the line, the system of unified command made combined operations in the field much simpler. A unified code of law for all the services—the Defence Services Act and Rules—was accomplished after some concentrated study and research by Gen. Ne Win, senior officers of the Adjutant-General's department, and representatives of the three services. The code—which also established a Courts-martial Appellate Court, presided over by a High Court judge, as the highest appellate tribunal for courts-martial cases—has proved to be progressive and practical.

In the years when civil government was often confined to the town, the Tatmadaw moved and lived among the people in the villages. Several districts were placed under military administration, and young commanders of battalions or brigades found themselves called upon to render services far beyond the normal call of the soldier's duty. They learned to lead teams composed of soldiers and civilian administrators. They were charged with keeping the peace, as well as promoting the economic development of the areas in which they served. The troops built roads in the remote frontier districts, started schools for the children, serving as part-time teachers, helped to improve cultivation, and provided medical care to the villagers. "The yebaws (comrades) belong to the country, not the country to the yebaws," Bogyoke Aung San had repeatedly said. After he was gone, this reminder was kept up by Bogyoke Ne Win as the constant ideal by which the soldiers must be guided. "Ours is not a mercenary army," he has often said, "we come from the people, and must serve them. If the people are genuinely happy to see us, we are doing our duty well. If they hate to see us, then we must be failing in our duty, and we must examine ourselves to discover where and how, and mend our ways."

The Burma Army gradually became the best organized force in which young men served with discipline and dedication. Paradoxically, this force also became the most democratic of all organizations. The field commanders knew their troops intimately. Officers and men served together as brothers. The annual conferences of the commanding officers, held at various military camps—Maymyo, Meiktila, Mandalay, Mingaladon or Ratnabon—were occasions for free and frank discussions on wide-ranging subjects, such as strategy and tactics, military doctrine, logistical and other problems. Gen. Ne Win, the Vice-Chiefs, the departmental heads of the War Office, field commanders, battalion commanders, and commanders of special units, would talk and listen for several days, and map out plans for the year ahead and the long future. At such conferences, the philosophy of the Burma Army was often discussed. The political scene was a shifting one. The political leaders in the Government talked of a negotiated settlement with the insurgents one moment, then of a fight to the death the next. They talked glibly of building a socialist economy for the people's benefit, but the Army saw, more vividly than they—for they spent their time in Rangoon and the big cities—that the villagers were as poor as they were before independence, if not poorer. This lack of firm goals, this wide divergence between the words of the Union Government and its deeds, made the Army feel that it had to have an ideology of its own—a guiding star.

That star the Burma Army found in the Constitution. This charter envisaged a socialist State in which the citizens would be freed from want, hunger and exploitation. This charter enshrined socialist justice. Stay true to its basic principles, stand by them and fight for them, that became in brief, the ideology of the Army after much thinking and discussion at the conferences. After the ideology was adopted, the basic principles of the Constitution were taught to soldiers and officers, at their camps and in their schools, everywhere in fact where the soldiers gathered to discuss or learn. When the Burma Army started to take an active interest in the Constitution—its principles in theory and practice—the AFPFL, unfortunately, was still busy with small fights between the leaders and their cliques, petty controversy as to who should be general secretary of the League and who the president, or which minister should rank higher in the order of precedence. Few of the political leaders had time to re-read the Constitution—in the framing of which they had formally taken part—and make an honest appraisal to discover whether the ideals were being turned into living realities.

The annual conferences of the commanding officers gave an opportunity to Gen. Ne Win to meet the young officers many of whom had been in his BIA division when it marched up the

Irrawaddy to the far north. There would always be new faces too—young men who joined after the war, to rise to command responsibility in the many campaigns. He would know all the officers, Captains and up, by their names, and remember about their performances or their private lives in the long past. From the commanders who came to the conference he would ask about the junior officers or men in their troops whom he had known. "Is that fellow still drinking a lot?" he might ask, or "How is that So-and-So getting on with his two wives?" The men glowed when the questions were repeated to them, for they liked to be remembered by the Old Man.

8

The Caretaker Government

1

THE DECLINE of the AFPFL, which started somewhere in 1952 soon after the first general elections, was steady in the following years. After the elections of 1956, it became swift. The personal rivalries and factional conflicts which had been seething deep at the heart of the League began to break out on the surface.

The Socialists blamed U Nu whom they saw as master of the "divide and rule" tactics. U Nu talked grandly of democracy, they complained, but was an autocrat at heart. He had a speech for every occasion, but was no listener. At Cabinet meetings he was impatient of discussion. When a member developed a line of argument in which he was uninterested, he would sail off into daydreams, without even bothering to hide it; then, at the end, he would hand out his own decision, absolute and final..

In August, 1953, U Tun Pe, an "independent" member of the AFPFL and Minister for Culture, resigned from the Cabinet. A veteran journalist who had, as a reporter, covered the trial of Saya San, U Tun Pe gave a press conference to explain the reasons why he felt compelled to resign. "The Prime Minister," U Tun Pe said, "contrary to his illusion as a democrat, is imperceptibly moving towards absolute monarchism as the *Bawashin Mintragyi,* the Arbiter of Human Destiny." U Tun Pe gave examples. U Nu had, he said, committed huge sums of the State's money towards the expenses of the Sixth Great Buddhist Synod, without consulting the AFPFL Executive, or getting the approval of Parliament. "I accept in principle the holding of the Synod," U Tun Pe said, "as all Buddhists do. If the idea is merely a pretext to confer the title of Convenor of the Sixth Great Buddhist Synod on U Nu and to please his vanity, then I must object." In another important matter, namely finance, U Tun Pe complained that there

234

was never any full or free discussion. "Members of the AFPFL have never been given a chance to review the whole financial picture. Some are content with the 'kitchen economy' saying to themselves, 'We are satisfied because we have got what we want from the Finance Minister.'" Danger lay ahead, U Tun Pe warned. "If a small bureaucracy is allowed to handle the whole structure of democracy, it would really be as destructive as termites to the pivot of the Union."[1]

Many Socialist leaders agreed with U Tun Pe, and said so in whispers. But they did not resign. Gen. Ne Win, Brigadier Tin Pe, Colonels Aung Gyi, Maung Maung, Aung Shwe, Thein Maung and others, urged them to reorganize the Socialist Party, send out trained cadres to work among and rally the people, and forge ahead in earnest to build the socialist society of affluence. U Ba Swe, the Defence Minister, listened with interest. U Kyaw Nyein, who was more of the intellectual type, thought mainly in terms of putting down the Communist insurrection; if the Communists were down, he argued, the Socialists would come up automatically; anti-Communism thus became his ideology.

Gen. Ne Win and his associates urged that the Party should adopt an ideology that would be best suited to Burma's needs and conditions, then organize around a core of disciplined and dedicated cadres. "You must cultivate quality rather than quantity," they advised, "and observe strict discipline in running your affairs. In the collection and use of funds, for example, you need to be correct. You must not depend on the big traders who make big money by selling import licences to the foreign capitalists. If you do, you will continue to be under their obligation. Your socialism will begin and end in slogans." This kind of talk touched the Socialist leaders at sensitive spots, and they did not entirely enjoy the sessions with the army leaders. Whenever they could, they would find excuses to stay away from the meetings.

One last meeting was held at the residence of U Ba Swe. A rather heated discussion took place. Now or never, Gen. Ne Win warned. The Army must build itself into a People's Army, and with the fight against the insurgents and the Kuomintang marauders on its hands, it would be fully engaged. The Party too, Gen. Ne Win suggested should start organizing on proper lines with

[1] U Tun Pe, *Why I Resign from the Cabinet?*, Rangoon, 1953.

will and faith, without delay. "We have come to a parting of ways," Gen. Ne Win said. "You must go your's on the political front; we must go our way on the military. We only hope you will get off to a good and proper start." An element of the dramatic was introduced into the parting. An urgent 'phone call came to inform the meeting that students had started to riot at the Aung San Stadium towards the tail-end of a football match. The boys, annoyed with something, had started to throw things about and break fences. The situation was critical. Gen. Ne Win left the meeting to visit the scene. A few words from him calmed the students and brought the situation under control. As far as the Socialist Party was concerned, that meeting, which was broken up by the riot at the Stadium, was the point of final parting with the Army. That was in November, 1955, when Socialist leaders were in the Cabinet in sizeable numbers, and were therefore, despite their grumblings about U Nu, well content.

But not so the peasants who had to toil in the fields amidst dangers and difficulties. Their labours yielded the abundant harvests of paddy, which fed the people and also earned the precious foreign exchange through export of rice to the hungry world. U Nu announced the *Pyidawtha* plan to make the Happy Land, with the people working in willing partnership with the Government. Pyidawtha went off to the sound of music. In some districts it worked well. People helped to build roads, dig reservoirs and wells, build dykes to keep off the annual floods. In other districts, however, Government funds granted to projects were misused by the local AFPFL bosses or M.Ps. Soon the Pyidawtha became a white elephant, a political joke.

Pyidawtha was also the name by which an 8-Year Plan of economic development was popularly known. The first plan was the optimistic 2-Year Plan, announced in April, 1948, after two months of furious drafting. That plan turned out to be little more than "the AFPFL's economic testament." No serious effort was made to implement it. The 8-Year Plan came next. An American firm of engineers—the Knappen Tippetts Abbet Inc., or the KTA —was engaged in 1951 to draw up a comprehensive engineering and economic survey of the country, and to submit a report and recommendations to the Union Government. The KTA employed Robert R. Nathan Associates Inc., as its economic consultants.

The KTA studies were made the basis of the 8-Year Plan which was therefore also known as the KTA Plan. The American experts advised the Union Government to take "an ambitious and aggressive approach" in dealing with problems of development. "Spend more," they urged, "put money to work." That was the kind of advice the AFPFL leaders were willing to take. The world price of rice was good; export volumes were also considerable, despite the insurrections. Some Burmese economists foresaw a downturn in the price, and warned that the merry spending would lead to grief. The foreign experts, however, carried more weight; some of them had wormed their way so well into U Nu's confidence and affection that they obtained an appointment with him more easily than the top planners and economists in the Union Government.

The slump in the rice market came soon. Burma's foreign exchange reserves sharply fell from 1,269 million kyats at the end of June 1953, to 628 million at the end of February, 1955. Drastic measures had to be taken to arrest the drain. Heavy cuts were imposed on government spending. Imports were severely slashed. The 8-Year Plan itself was, for all practical purposes, abandoned. A 3-Year Implementation Programme was adopted for technical projects, and this was converted in 1956 into a 4-Year Plan. This plan ran into violent political upheavals and did not fare better than its predecessors. The failure in planning and development was due to many factors. The "ambitious approach" was perhaps one; the plans were often designed for prestige rather than tangible results. The resources were limited, the capacity for sustained endeavour was even more so. The factional warfare within the ruling party was harmful. Spheres of influence developed in the Government, under rival Ministers, and artificial controversies were excited, such as in the unnecessary fixing of priority between industry and agriculture. The foreign experts—who were imported in large numbers in the Pyidawtha years—were not wisely and effectively used. Some who flattered, or won favour somehow, were relied on too heavily. Those who were good in their fields, but not in winning favours, were often ignored. "The lesson about the use of foreign staff," wrote U Thet Tun, director of the Central Statistics and Economics Department, "is that personnel from academic institutions or disinterested governments would have been more useful than commercial firms who acquire vested interests and tend to work to perpetuate their contracts."[2]

There were thus economic plans, each looking better than its predecessor. But there was no serious execution. The promised land for the peasants and the workers remained only a dream. A house for every family, a car, a radio. and a monthly income of 800 kyats. these remained a promise unfulfilled. The battlecry of the AFPFL, as it went into the elections of 1956, was not a better life for the working people, but forty years of power for itself. With this noble battlecry the AFPFL plunged forward blindly to its own doom.

2

U Nu sought the role of bringer of world peace. He went out to Peking, Moscow, Washington, Jerusalem, Cairo, Belgrade, and everywhere, to try and change hearts and promote a world brotherhood of man.

In December 1954, U Nu spoke in Peking to an audience of Chinese leaders including Premier Chou En-lai. "The Americans are very generous and brave," he said. "The Chinese people are also very generous and brave. We do not want these two esteemed countries confronting each other with bitterness and hostility. As a friend of both we want these two countries to be on the friendliest of terms. . . . I will exert my utmost to bring about an understanding between the two countries." In Washington in May. 1955, U Nu explained: "Like all peoples, the Chinese have some good traits and some bad traits. Similarly the Americans have some good traits and some bad traits. Let the Americans pick out the good Chinese traits and not concentrate on their bad traits; similarly, let the Chinese pick out the good American traits and not dwell only on the bad American traits."[3] Then. slowly perhaps, but surely, love would bloom between the two countries.

At home, however, as events later revealed, love between old comrades in the AFPFL began to wilt and wither fast in the two years that followed. Instead of picking out the good traits in each

2 U Thet Tun, *Organization of Planning Machinery: Lessons from Burmese Experience*, JBRS, June. 1963.
3 *Premier Reports to the People.*

other, they picked out the bad and exaggerated them. Mutual fears and suspicions grew. *The Guardian* broke the story in May, 1958 —by which time the AFPFL had split into two halves—of a correspondence between U Kyaw Nyein and U Nu which took place in July, 1956. "U Kyaw Nyein, the most sensitively intellectual of the Socialists," reported the paper in its issue of May 6, "wrote several pages of a frank and accusing letter to U Nu on July 3, 1956, accusing mainly that U Nu was trying to eliminate the Socialists in the League by feeding them with Cabinet appointments while cutting them off from the masses, the ultimate source of power. He cited instances in support of his allegations. U Nu replied at length and eloquently, answering point by point, on July 6, and also, on the same day, submitted the correspondence to the AFPFL Executive inviting a thorough investigation and disciplinary action against himself if he should be found guilty."

Many charges and counter-charges were made in the two letters, some big, some small. "We faced perils together in the nationalist movement," U Kyaw Nyein wrote. "But those who were not with you in those perilous times, the big businessmen and the licensees, the black-marketeers and the exploiters, they began to worm their way into your company. They had the knack. Having acquired riches they could afford to make donations at your favourite charities." U Nu replied that he had observed a strict code of personal conduct, and with people who came to him as friends "relations must be pure and unselfish on both sides. I am a politician, and to my house came thieves and opium-eaters, drunkards and all. I could not turn them away. The main thing was not to become one of them."

"You began to like flattery and form so much," U Kyaw Nyein wrote, "you began to chide us if we did not rise when you entered the room. You began to show dictatorial habits. You would brook no comment on matters at Cabinet or other meetings. Your views must stand and all must bow to them." U Nu denied that he had developed into a dictator. "I have a temper," he explained, "and it has flared up too often too high. . . . These years as prime minister were enough to drive one mad. It has ruined my health. How could I set Socialist against Socialist and grab supreme power? Would the Socialists allow me; are they that stupid?"[4]

[4] *The Guardian* daily, May 6, 7, 8 and 9, 1958.

The letters expressed some of the fears and suspicions that were eating away the heart of the AFPFL. But if there was disunity within, the loss of contacts with the people and the forfeiture of their confidence were even more damaging for the League as well as the country. Since the brief and casual conference of December, 1947, the AFPFL had never convened a national meeting of delegates. In the decade that followed, U Nu kept promising that the League would be purged of undesirable elements and strengthened with the injection of new and wholesome blood. He made several attempts, but stopped whenever squeals of protests came from the entrenched party bosses. The Socialists complained—and U Kyaw Nyein made the complaint forcefully in his letter —that U Nu, under cover of cleansing campaigns tried to push the Socialists out of the League. U Ba Swe and U Kyaw Nyein, in their turns, promised occasionally to revive the Socialist Party, raise young and dedicated cadres, bring in fresh ideas, cut out straight and true paths to the socialist goals. But the Socialist leaders, caught in the chores of Government, busy with factional warring within the AFPFL, were too busy.

Thus national goals were lost. The people lost their faith in the Government; they became apathetic, resigned to their lot. Those civil servants of the old school, who were accustomed to look upon their's as a special privileged class, permanent and powerful, saw the AFPFL falling, and muttered among themselves that the League—which had, in its heyday, bullied them and threatened to break them—deserved to die. The younger civil servants, who wanted to serve, were frustrated. There was no collective responsibility in the Cabinet, only factional conspiracy. No clear directions were given to the civil servants; one order given by one Minister one day, might be cancelled by another Minister later on. There was, thus, stalemate everywhere.

The AFPFL, U Nu said often in his vivid language, "was like a putrid carcass of a dead dog which smelled to the heavens. I have said also that if the AFPFL leaders did not stop indulging in dirty practices, they would have a shamefully great fall."[5]

The fall was not long to come.

In a last effort to preserve AFPFL unity, a national conference

[5] Address to the All-Burma Conference of the 'Clean' AFPFL. *Burma Weekly Bulletin*, Sept. 11, 1958.

was convened in January, 1958. The delegates came, but for a few days before the opening of the conference, the top leaders of the League, and of the Socialist Party, grappled hard with the problem of patching up differences—at least on the surface and for the few days of the conference—and of finding a common platform. There were weepings, wailings, accusations, confessions, and many passionate outpourings, in the inner councils, the newspapers reported with great delight—their sales were soaring in those times—and it was not certain until the last moment that the conference would take place at all. But it did take place. The conference went off to a fine start with a growl from the tiger. "I used to be called Tiger Ba Swe not for nothing," U Ba Swe said sternly at the opening. "It was because I had the courage of conviction, and acted ruthlessly and without fear. Of late, due to circumstances, I had been inactive and my comrades had started calling me Nwargyi (the Cow) Ba Swe. But, to preserve AFPFL unity, I shall be the Tiger again. I shall stir, and ruthlessly pounce on anyone who undermined AFPFL unity, be he my closest friend." With that warning, *The Guardian* reported on January 30 on the inaugural session of the previous day, "the Tiger swept his fierce eyes over the vast assembly, then shook himself, and went back to his seat and sat down."

U Nu made a long speech at the conference. He declared that the AFPFL was a party, not a united front of parties. He also engaged in a discussion of ideology, and announced that democratic socialism, not Marxism, was the ideology of the AFPFL. The conference listened, applauded, shouted slogans, elected an Executive Committee and the Supreme Council and dispersed. In his note of farewell to the delegates, U Nu rejoiced at the unity which the conference had shown. He praised U Ba Swe, U Kyaw Nyein and Thakin Tin, saying that they were like the legendary heroes of Burmese history, each wielding the strength of a thousand men.

The unity, however, did not last too long. Two months after the conference, the AFPFL broke up from top to bottom, all the way. The split was final and irrevocable. He had done a lot of thinking, U Nu explained in a broadcast to the people on May 6, "on my role in the AFPFL, and I asked myself: Can you continue to control the organization any longer? If, knowing that you

16

cannot, you try to carry on, first by coaxing one side and then the other, will you not only fail to achieve unity but also lose your reputation and in the words of the saying, 'Not only fail to get the iguana but lose the *dah* (wood-chopper) as well'?" He then, he said, decided that the parting of the ways had come. On April 23 he called Thakin Tin in and announced his decision. Thus sprang up at once, as if by the wave of a magic wand, two factions of the AFPFL: the Nu-Tin and the Swe-Nyein, named after their leaders; or the 'Clean' AFPFL as U Nu called his faction, emphasizing that it was the corruption in the old AFPFL that he was out to combat, and the 'Stable' AFPFL as U Ba Swe and U Kyaw Nyein called their's, to make the point that they wanted eternal unity and the split was not their fault.

U Nu suggested that U Ba Swe and U Kyaw Nyein should stay on in the Cabinet until the August session of Parliament, at which the factions could submit themselves to a vote of confidence. The winner would then form the Government. As for the AFPFL, U Nu said he would be willing to persuade his associates to let the Swe-Nyein "inherit" the name, while the physical assets would be fairly divided between the two factions. "How would," *The Guardian* asked in an editorial of May 3, "the portrait of Bogyoke Aung San, such a sure vote-getter at election time, be fairly divided between the two factions? Perhaps they will cut it into two halves vertically and have half an Aung San each."

3

Gen. Ne Win kept the Army calm in the political crisis, and repeated that the armed forces and himself would show partiality to no faction but acknowledge undivided loyalty to country and constitution. That philosophy was not new, having been discussed and adopted at the annual conferences of commanders, and practised by all ranks. "There may be some of our comrades," Gen. Ne Win often said, "who find their personal attachments to some political leaders too strong. If they find their personal feelings in conflict with duty, then they should resign from the Tatmadaw. We ourselves shall serve the people and uphold the constitution. We would work under any constitutionally established Government. We would also, on our part, request the leaders of the Government to respect the constitution, and call on us to render only those services which are in keeping with it."[6]

The war between the AFPFL factions, however, grew fierce. Each faction, while blessing the strict neutrality of the Army, hoped that Gen. Ne Win would be a little more friendly to itself. Rumours were started that Gen. Ne Win would accept office as Deputy Prime Minister in charge of defence and security, and a terse statement came from the office of the Chief of Staff that the rumours were completely false. The Swe-Nyein faction, on the other hand, kept repeating, in their bid for support, that its leaders had fought in the resistance alongside the army leaders. Where was U Nu then, U Ba Swe asked. "I have never liked violence," U Nu retorted "but I helped in the resistance. Several of the secret meetings under the Japanese occupation were held at my house."

The mud-slinging between the factions became furious. "Power maniac" the Swe-Nyein group called U Nu. "If I was such a power maniac, why did they keep me as their leader for more than ten years?" U Nu asked. They called him a sex maniac next, and U Nu replied solemnly in a public speech that he had given up sex and practised celibacy since 1948. Thus did the intimate details of the private lives of the leaders come out into the open in the bitter war of words. A full-blooded Spanish wife of a foreign diplomat in Rangoon met U Nu at a party after he had declared that he had been practising celibacy. "Ah, Mr. Prime Minister," she teased him, "I would never allow my husband to do that!" U Nu becomingly blushed.

The two factions went all-out to win votes in the approaching parliamentary contest. Because of the worsening situation, it was decided that the contest should be held soon, rather than in the regular budget session which was due in August. A special session was therefore fixed for June, and the Chamber of Deputies was summoned. Members who had been treated with slight respect by the leaders of both the factions suddenly found themselves wooed vigorously. Promises of office and advancement were

---

[6] This was repeated after the voting in Parliament, e.g. address to a conference of commanding officers at Mingaladon, reported in *The Guardian* daily June 24, 1958.

made in return for their votes on the critical day. When they travelled to Rangoon, the M.Ps. were met on the way by representatives of the factions, wooed hard, and escorted to safe hiding places—with all comforts provided—and saved up for the voting. A few kidnappings of unwary M.Ps. were alleged. Keeping them nursed, nourished and safe became a major activity for each faction. Counting those who were safely in and calculating the prospects became another.

Not the people alone, but the *nats* (guardian spirits) were also wooed. "A young leader of the Swe-Nyein faction is said to be a great favourite of the nats," *The Guardian* reported on May 3. "As soon as the split showed, he rushed to the medium and made his offerings. The nats were said to have assured him that all the nats are on the side of his faction, and that when the other side makes its offerings, not the nats but only the devils come to the feast. The young leader, having now got the assurance that the nats are with him, is sending happy telegrams to AFPFL leaders in the districts, urging them to join his faction and the nats."

There was hardly any government from April to June, 1958. The Cabinet could not sit because one half of it was in bitter strife against the other. High councils for planning, security, and such vital subjects, could not work. The Secretariat waited; the civil servants passed their time reading newspapers, making bets on the coming race.

The Army remained cool, and kept the peace. Several people urged Gen. Ne Win to step in and take over. "We need a strong Government, capable of administering the country with clear cut policy and firm action for the effective realization of law and order and national reconstruction," spoke out Dr Ba Maw. "Political leaders have so far been only after exhibitionism, and they have indulged too much in play-acting. There have been too many speeches, too little action. We need a strong Government; I shall support such a Government."[7] So would the people. If Gen. Ne Win had assumed political power then, the people would have supported the move with enthusiasm. But the General was correct and proper, and faithful to his pledge to uphold the constitution.

He had not been interested in taking power in 1949, when

[7] *The Guardian* daily, May 3, 1958.

Rangoon was embattled, and power was his and the Army's for the taking. A few years later, when King Farouk was dethroned in Egypt by the military junta, close friends from outside the Army urged him again to consider assuming national leadership in the interests of national unity. He emphatically—even angrily —declined. Now in 1958 the call was more earnest, more urgent. But he did not respond. He had done his best to caution and counsel the leaders of the AFPFL on the need to preserve the unity of the League and the integrity of the Union. When they had gone and split up, there was little he could do, but keep the peace in the country, while keeping the Army out of the political fight.

The voting took place on June 9. The debate lasted one whole day. U Ba Swe introduced the no-confidence motion against the Government led by U Nu. There was much to say, yet little that the Swe-Nyein leaders could properly say, for they had been in the Government themselves until June 4, and it was yet too early to find fault with the new 5-day old Government. But they spoke of the past, accusing U Nu of betraying the country by dividing the AFPFL. The debate was dignified; the speeches were courteous, and bright with wit and humour. But the whole situation was strange and artificial. "The situation is the reverse of the general democratic practice," commented Dr Ba Maw. "Parliament is asked to vote on personalities, not on party nor on issues. If I were U Nu, I would have chalked out a definite policy about AFPFL unity, and given every one of my colleagues a warning that they must follow that policy. If they fail, or I fail to preserve unity, I would have dissolved parliament at once, and gone to the people. The people must choose. That is the only constitutional and democratic way."[8]

Instead of going to the people, the AFPFL had done strange things. "First U Nu, with his famed generosity, offered to keep his rivals in his Cabinet till the Chamber of Deputies could meet and decide which faction should form the Government," wrote the correspondent of *New Statesman*, London, in its issue of June 28. "Thus for 40 days till June 4, there was the strange spectacle of a nearly equally divided Cabinet, each half of which was actively and openly working for the downfall of the other. The no-

8 *The Guardian* daily, May 18, 1958.

confidence motion was debated on June 9, and lost by a narrow margin of 8 votes. U Nu was kept in power by 50 AFPFL members, 45 members of the NUF (which used to be a small and solitary opposition before), a bloc of 6 Arakanese members (of whom 3 became Ministers, and 2 Parliamentary Secretaries), and an oddment of minority votes. Swe-Nyein won a solid 100 AFPFL votes, and 19 other minority votes. The strange result is that the AFPFL Government is finely balanced on a thin edge with a massive AFPFL Opposition."

It was an expensive victory for U Nu. He had to hand out Cabinet appointments and privileges to get the votes. He promised to support the creation of new States in the Union if the minority peoples wanted them; this was in complete reversal to the firm, long-maintained policy of the AFPFL that the Union must be strengthened and separatism discouraged. U Nu owed his survival in office to the NUF which he himself had looked upon as a "Red Opposition", and this proved highly embarrassing. He invited into his Cabinet U E Maung, the ex-Justice of the Supreme Court, a leader of the Justice Party in the NUF. The Cabinet now represented an assortment of conflicting interests. It was a convenience, not a government.

The bitterness of factional strife did not end with the parliamentary decision. It only became more intense. The Swe-Nyein demanded the Nu-Tin faction to vacate the headquarters of the League and hand over the funds. Then the two factions got busy calling "Supreme Council" meetings to expel the rivals from the "AFPFL" for treachery.

U Win Maung, the President, gave a press conference on June 30, 1958, and made the disclosure that he had been reading the constitution. What he found there did not make him happy. He had no real powers as President, he complained. He had learned only three things in his term up to that date: putting on the flowing *pasoe* in 2 minutes; riding; golfing.

In Sagaing people brought out a coffin inscribed "Traitor U Pe Tin" (an NUF Deputy from the constituency who had voted for Swe-Nyein instead of for U Nu as directed by the party) and conducted a mock funeral in front of his house, a fortnight after the voting in Parliament. "U Pe Tin regarded the act as a bad omen and, in order to counteract it, he dressed himself as the

Thagyamin (King of Nats) and walked from his house to the monument in the football ground, chanting *mantras* all the way. When he arrived at the destination, he hopped several times, after counting One, Two, Three, as if the Thagyamin were flying. He also asked the news correspondents to take his pictures while so doing."[9]

The situation was amusing, yet it was tragic. It was not merely the AFPFL that was breaking up, it was an era that was ending. The principal opponents had shaken hands in the Chamber of Deputies after the results of the voting were announced. That was very well. But soon their followers throughout the country were shaking their fists at one another. In Rangoon, the Union Labour Organization (ULO) hastily raised by the 'Clean' AFPFL attained large numbers very swiftly, and soon it was in open and violent collision with the Trade Union Congress, Burma (TUCB), which had long been the labour wing of the undivided AFPFL. Rival women's organizations sprang up, one wearing blue *htamein,* one wearing red. Membership was one kyat per head, for which the new member received one *htamein,* and the party ticket. Some enterprising ladies joined both, and for two kyats received two *htameins*—which was a good bargain—and they could always wear the appropriate htamein for party rallies—for attending which also they were paid a fee.

The 'Clean' AFPFL survived in office in that strange situation for 3 months and 17 days. In that period, things drifted swiftly towards violence and bloodshed.

4

The situation that developed after the AFPFL split was, Gen. Ne Win reported to the Chamber of Deputies on October 31, 1958, after he had been voted into office as Prime Minister of a Caretaker Government, "approaching close to that sad spectacle of 1948-49."

"The effects of the political split," Gen. Ne Win said, "spread throughout the country like a rampaging forest fire. People who used to work together before now viewed each other with deep

[9] Report in *The Mirror.* Burmese daily, reproduced in the *New Burma Weekly,* July 5, 1958.

suspicion. Former close comrades and colleagues became deadly enemies. Political splits in some areas became so serious as to lead to violence and killings. The split led to a large increase in the activities of those elements who flout and violate the constitution of the Union of Burma, in their attempt to exploit the situation. Insurgents suffered intolerable damage, politically and militarily, during the last 10 years, at the hands of the Government, and were in such sad shape that in late 1957 and early 1958 many began to admit that the rebellion was a mistake and to 'enter the light' in increasing numbers. The Burma Communist Party had made overtures for peace. After the split, the BCP changed its tone and made new demands and put new pressures on the Government. Other insurgents too halted their steps when they were just about to emerge."

"The situation became more and more confused. There was so much confusion that units of the Union Military Police, assigned to certain district areas began converging on Rangoon in large numbers, some in uniforms and some in civilian dress; and when the Inspector General of Police was asked the reason why such large numbers of UMP were being called to Rangoon, he replied quite honestly, that he did not know anything about the matter at all."

"The situation," Gen. Ne Win said, "was that much confused. The governmental machinery also deteriorated to its present weak condition. The rebels were increasing their activities, and the political pillar was collapsing. It was imperative that the Union should not drown in shallow waters as it nearly did in 1948-49. So it fell on the armed forces to perform their bounden duty to take all security measures to forestall and prevent a recurrence."

There had, however, been no army *coup*. The situation became explosive towards the end of September, and it was U Nu who shrewdly decided that the only alternative to civil war would be a caretaker government led by Gen. Ne Win. The movement of the Union Military Police—which force was under the command of the Home Minister, then a 'Clean' AFPFL man—indicated that dark things were going on. Rumours of a *coup* by the UMP, in combination with insurgents who had lately 'entered the light', were rife. Assassinations were threatened, or feared. Elements of the Clean AFPFL started to level charges publicly against the Army, and this, pieced up with the mysterious movements of the UMP, presented a sinister picture.

Some delegates to a conference of the 'Clean' AFPFL, meeting from August 31 at the residence of U Nu spoke out loud against the Army. "It was only when I read the newspapers, including those of the previous days, on the morning of September 3," U Nu explained in a broadcast, "that I came across certain statements and allegations concerning the Burma Army which had been made by some district delegates. I was very surprised when I read those allegations. As a matter of fact, the delegates who made the allegations made them only because they were not aware of the real facts of the case." He went on to explain how the Burma Army had always acted strictly according to orders and consistently in the service of the country. "The entire country owes a great debt of gratitude to the Burma Army," U Nu said. "Who can deny that it was the Burma Army that saved the country from utter disaster when the whole of the Union was only two fingers' breadth away from the edge of the abyss, owing to the insurgents? Who can deny that Chiang Kai-shek's soldiers were driven out of our territories, in spite of formidable obstacles and difficulties, only because of the Army's courage, perseverance and spirit of sacrifice?"[10]

The situation, however, was too far gone to be saved by sweet words. Violence, bloodshed, civil war, foreign intervention, and the disintegration of the Union, were in prospect. "Such was my alarm and concern at these prospects," U Nu reported to Parliament on October 28, 1958, in moving that Gen. Ne Win be elected Prime Minister, "that I immediately gave my most anxious consideration towards finding a solution to these problems and thereby averting these grave dangers to the Union. The result of my deliberations was that I decided to urge Gen. Ne Win to assume the Prime Ministership, with a view to holding free and fair elections within 6 months. . . . Like the great patriot that he is, Gen. Ne Win accepted, though with some diffidence since he has never been anxious to exercise political power."

Once more, thus, Gen. Ne Win assumed political power and responsibility. "I have accepted this responsibility," he reported to Parliament in his first speech as Prime Minister on October 31,

[10] Broadcast on Sept. 4, 1958; *Burma Weekly Bulletin,* Sept. 18, 1958.

"in large measure to prevent any assault on the Constitution, which all of us revere and respect. I have taken this responsibility solely in my capacity as an individual, a citizen, and as a soldier." The General promised that "all those people who respect the Constitution will receive all the rights and privileges that they are entitled to. But, those who break the laws will be strictly dealt with. He also undertook to "do my best to hold fair and free elections within 6 months, if the insurgency and crimes are brought to an end within the period. The success of this undertaking depends not wholly on my Government but also on the leadership to be given by the Members of Parliament and by the political organizations. I wish to state here, most emphatically, that my Government will not work in the interest of any particular political party when the elections are held. All measures will also be taken to ensure that Government officials also do not work in the interest of any political party in the elections". In regard to foreign policy, Gen. Ne Win announced that there would be no changes. "My Government intends," he declared, "to continue in the practice of strict neutrality free from any entanglements."

"Mr. Speaker, Sir," Gen. Ne Win said, winding up his policy statement in Parliament, "I wish to state, in conclusion, that all that I have stated is really an elaboration of what I have frequently said, that the attainment of internal peace is dependent on an integrated policy of military and political action, and not through military means alone. This is the guiding policy of my Government."[11]

The change was welcomed by the people. The Caretaker Government, in their eyes, was not merely an unavoidable necessity and an expediency. Gen. Ne Win, they accepted, was a legitimate trustee of political power, and the Burma Army which he led was a patriotic, not a mere mercenary, army.

"Gen. Ne Win enjoys the prestige of a pioneer in his country's independence movement," wrote the *New Republic*, a liberal American weekly magazine. "The Army and Ne Win's late mentor, Aung San—the George Washington of Burma—are symbols of Burmese nationalism. Ne Win was one of the original Thakin nationalist group in the Thirties and became a military man only

[11] Speech reproduced in *Is Trust Vindicated?*

in 1940 when Aung San organized the anti-colonial precursor of independent Burma's Army with Japanese help. Thus Ne Win's government possesses unquestionable legitimacy—not only in the technical sense that the military is acting at the specific behest of the civilian leadership (for a designated temporary period), but in the deeper sense that the Army leadership is itself popularly rooted."[12]

5

It was on September 26, 1958, that U Nu had extended an urgent invitation to Gen. Ne Win to form and lead a Caretaker Government with special responsibility to restore conditions for holding fair and free general elections within 6 months from the assumption of office. It took one month to assemble the Chamber of Deputies in special session, so that it was only on October 28 that U Nu could move the election of Gen. Ne Win as Prime Minister.

The great sigh of relief that swept through the country on announcement of the proposed change was proof enough of its popularity. The Swe-Nyein faction also emphatically approved, for now they would have a chance of going before the people on equal terms with the Nu-Tin. The NUF, which held the whip-hand under the Nu-Tin regime, was bitterly disappointed. It raised loud cries that there had been a coup, and its leaders refused to be comforted even when Gen. Ne Win called them in to explain that there had been no such thing. The nomination of Gen. Ne Win as Prime Minister, however, was made by leaders of the Nu-Tin and the Swe-Nyein, Dr E Maung and several prominent Deputies, and the election was carried unanimously.

In the one month that he had before entering office, Gen. Ne Win worked hard on the operational plan for the six months that he expected to stay in political office. He met prospective candidates for appointment to his Cabinet. The choice was his, but he wanted to keep politicians out so that the Government might have both the character and complexion of impartiality. That necessarily reduced the number of eligibles, and since he also wanted to exclude army officers—to emphasize that there would be no

[12] *A view of Two Generals* in the *New Republic*, Nov. 10, 1958.

military regime but only a constitutional government led by him
—the choice was further narrowed to senior civil servants, judges, and university dons. In regard to State Ministers, Gen. Ne
Win offered to leave the choice to the respective State Councils,
and refrain from exercising his prerogative of ultimate choice except in extreme circumstances.

The composition of the Caretaker Government was announc-
ed ahead on October 14. The Cabinet was to be small: nine
members, including the Prime Minister, to take charge of Union
subjects. U Thein Maung, retired Chief Justice of the Union, a
GCBA veteran who had held the highest judicial offices; U Khin
Maung Pyu, the Chief Secretary to the Government; U Chan Tun
Aung, Chief Justice of the High Court; U Ka, Lecturer in Mathe-
matics, University of Rangoon; U Kyaw Nyein, Chairman of the
Union Bank; U San Nyun, a retired Election Commissioner; U
Chit Thoung, the Government Chemical Examiner, U Ba Kyar,
a retired District Judge. The Ministers for the Shan, Kachin and
Kayah States, and the Minister for Chin Affairs made the number up to 13, which was tiny compared to the Cabinet of 30
Ministers (assisted by 32 Parliamentary Secretaries) before the
AFPFL split. But then the Caretaker Government was a func-
tional, not a political government. It did not have to nurse and
woo votes in Parliament; it did not have to feed and humour
political groups and bosses outside. It was meant for working, and
go to work the Caretaker Government did immediately after it
was sworn in on October 29.

Gen. Ne Win made it clear from the start that in the discharge
of his duties as leader of the Government, he would be calling
upon the armed forces to strive harder to put down insurgency
and lawlessness, and to help out in bringing down the costs of
living, fighting "economic insurgency" and improving communications. The rewards for the extra labours would be the satisfaction of jobs well done, duty to the country discharged. No
soldier must swagger because the Chief of Staff was Prime Minister. In several directives and addresses made to conferences of
commanding officers Gen. Ne Win drove home that message.

The men responded with enthusiasm. Soldiers and sailors
brought fish from the Delta and sold them in the streets of Rangoon to give the citizens more choice of food at cheaper prices.

They brought in firewood and went round in trucks to sell. Meat was made available on the market; poultry became cheaper. The soldiers also helped to clean up the streets, joining hands with citizens and civil servants, and to clear up slums and re-settle the squatters. They repaired or built roads. Those services were rendered in the time that the soldiers could spare from their duties of suppressing insurgency and lawlessness.

The easing of political tensions itself was a big contribution to creative work. The people began to feel happier, safer, and more hopeful. A "welcome lowering of the political temperature," was thus seen by *The Times* of London, two short months after Gen. Ne Win had taken office. "The main casualty," the paper noted in its editorial on December 30, "of a decade of disorder in Burma has been the disappearance of justice at the lower levels of society. Every job was seized by one political faction or another for its henchmen and the peasants were ground between their ambitions and power." Now, under the Caretaker Government, that justice, for so long in flight, returned.

"Gone are the huge heaps of garbage that littered the streets," reported *Time* news-magazine of February 6, 1959, "the packs of wild pye-dogs that fed on them. Buildings are getting their first coats of paint since 1941. Night trains are running from Rangoon to Mandalay for the first time in years, attesting to greater security in the countryside. . . . Hordes of corrupt, bribe-taking political hacks have been replaced by army officers."

Actually, however, the number of army officers seconded to civilian departments was not large. In the field, Security Councils were revived or revitalized. Those Councils were nothing new. For many years, in many districts, the Councils had served well as joint army-civilian teams which kept the peace and ran the administration. These Councils were coordinated and directed, during the Caretaker Government, by the Central Security Council, chaired by U Khin Maung Pyu, the Home Minister. Colonel (later Brigadier) Maung Maung, director of military training, served as deputy chairman, and thus as the coordinator in security matters. Colonel Ba Than, director of psychological warfare and Lt.-Col. Kyi Han of the Defence Ministry were among the few senior officers who worked with the CSC.

The gathering in of illicit arms in Rangoon, Insein—a nest of

crime—the towns and the villages kept the security forces busy
for several months. The harvest was rich. Then, there were the
pocket armies to disband. The constitution had clearly provided
in its article 97 that the raising and maintenance of "any military
or semi-military organization of any kind" could only be done by
the Union Government with the consent of Parliament. This requirement was respected even in the first years of independence
when the emergency called for the creation of auxiliary units such
as the Burma Territorial Force. Later, however, as the power
struggle within the AFPFL became resolute, small armed organizations were raised by various departments such as the Electri-
city Supply Board and the State Timber Board on the excuse of
necessity to protect their plants and personnel in the countryside.
The organizations did not show on the departmental budgets, nor
was parliamentary sanction sought to keep them. These units were
disbanded, and suitable personnel were taken into the regular
armed forces or the Union Military Police.

The UMP itself was in need of reorganization, a definite aim
and purpose and inspired leadership. The British had raised a few
UMP units, on the pattern of the Burma Frontier Force, for police
work and frontier security. Army officers had commanded UMP
and BFF units in those days. After independence, the Burma
Army took over frontier duty, and the BFF—which acquired
bad odour because some of its British officers were identified with
separatist movements in the highlands—was not revived. The UMP
continued playing its part—often under officers seconded from
the Army—at the height of the insurrections. Later, however,
its discipline became lax. Its officer corps also became, to an
extent, the dumping ground of politicians who could not be usefully employed elsewhere. Whole units of the UMP were sometimes used for purely political purposes, and even in University
campus politics which the AFPFL tried in a clumsy way to control.

To the UMP went Colonel Min Thein, and several young officers, to reorganize, train, and inspire. The ultimate aim, it was
announced, was to absorb the UMP into the regular Burma Army,
for there must be unity of command over the Union's armed forces—which was what the constitution called for. The UMP personnel welcomed the proposal. They had been a hybrid force—

neither police, nor army, used by unscrupulous politicians as a convenience, forgotten in other times and left alone to lick its shame. Now the UMP had good leadership, a proud role alongside the Burma Army with which it would soon become one.

The Army also lent its senior officers to give leadership to some of the strategic services. Thus, Col. Kyaw Soe went to the Inland Waters Transport Board, Col. Saw Myint to the new Frontier Areas Administration, Col. Khin Nyo to the Burma Railways, Air Commodore T. Clift to the Union of Burma Airways, Col. Ba Ni to the Telecommunications Directorate, Col. Hla Aung to the Survey Department, Lt.-Col. Chit Khaing and Commander Maung Maung Gyi to the Directorate of Labour, Col. Chit Myaing to the Directorate of National Registration. The officers gave spirit and sense of purpose and direction to the departments. Improved services, increased earnings, progress on or completion of projects long shelved, were among the results. There had been too much politics, too much talk, too little real work. Now with party politics exiled from the executive sphere, the staff felt free to work. Politicians who were in charge of State boards and corporations were retired off; officials who were grossly inefficient and notoriously corrupt were replaced. There were few other changes in personnel; the Army lent help at the leadership level, and that was enough.

Gen. Ne Win had promised that his Government would also try to bring down the high costs of living and send the law after the blackmarketeers and the racketeers. In that drive Brigadier Tin Pe and Colonel (later Brigadier) Aung Gyi served as coordinators. They supervised a team of senior officers who were seconded to several key departments and corporations. Col. Kyi Win went to the Agricultural Resources Development Corporation, and also kept an eye on the Income Tax Department. Col. Kyi Maung looked after the State Timber Board. Col. Mya Win took charge of the Union Purchase Board. Col. Khin Nyo, with the Railways, also ran the Trade Development Corporation. Lt.-Col. Mya Thaung was assigned the task of expanding the overseas markets of the State Agricultural Marketing Board, and of expediting the export of rice. Port facilities and shipping became important for the export and import trade, and Lt.-Col. Saw Mya Thein was seconded to the Port Commissioners, and the Customs,

while Naval Commander Baroni was sent to the Union of Burma
Shipping Board. The Burma Pharmaceutical Industry was totter-
ing along; Captain (Navy) B. O. Barber and a few officers were
sent in to pull it up. The Industrial Development Corporation, a
huge, sprawling organization with several industries and projects
under its charge, needed streamlining. U Maung Maung, Secretary to the Ministry of Defence, was made director-general of the
IDC, with Wing-Commander Parry Aye Cho as his deputy. Thus,
one thing led on to another, and in a few months Army officers
or Defence Ministry officials found themselves taking on additional duties in economic and industrial enterprises. The private
sector raised loud protests that the Army was going far beyond
its mandate, and that business enterprises started by the Defence
Services Institute were encroaching. Yet, there was no denying
that national earnings vastly improved during the Caretaker Government, and the cost of living indices showed sharp and consistent downward trends.

Gen. Ne Win gave Rangoon a new Mayor. Col. Tun Sein, a
brigade commander who had led in operations against the Kuomintang marauders, was brought from the field to clean up Rangoon.
It required an operation at least as massive as those which were
mounted against the KMT, to accomplish the task. Mayor Tun
Sein used all his leadership abilities in the job and worked won-
ders. The slums and the squatters presented a big challenge. Previous governments had sometimes tried to re-settle the squatters,
but a demonstration or two in protest would put an end to the
feeble efforts. The slum-dwellers and the squatters had votes—
thousands of them—and even if they did not know what was good
for them, the politicians needed their votes, and were willing to
humour them.

Col. Tun Sein, however, had clear orders from Gen. Ne Win
to clean up, and he started a combined operation without delay.
"Army engineers surveyed three satellite cities on the rice fields
northeast and east of Rangoon," reported a correspondent of the
Chicago Daily News, "and built 150 miles of streets and roads.
Tap water was piped in to each block and some street lights were
erected. Each squatter family was registered and assigned a lot
in the new towns. They hold the lot on a 30-year lease. They were
given a deadline for evacuating Rangoon. The army provided

trucks to carry squatter belongings. Also, the army is shipping in building materials for sale at cost in the new cities, including trainloads of bamboo, lumber and roofing. And with the possession of a plot of land, many squatters who formerly lived miserably are now building solid two-storey homes. So far, 170,000 squatters have moved out and another 80,000 are scheduled to be transferred by next autumn."[13]

Some squatters grumbled. Some politicians, with eyes on the elections that were to come, made capital of the situation. U Nu himself was unable to resist the temptation to extract votes out of the grumblings. In a passionate speech which he delivered on May Day of 1959 at the Martyrs' Mound, he said that the squatters were in tears because they had been forcibly removed.

6

Gen. Ne Win has the reputation of being the "most press-shy national leader."[14] He met the Rangoon press just once when he was leader of the Caretaker Government and answered some of the questions which had been submitted in writing beforehand. That was the last formal meeting with the press. "My duty is to report and answer to Parliament," he said. He did attend parliamentary sessions as regularly as possible, answering members' questions himself. In debates on important bills—such as the one which empowered the Government to introduce national service— he would participate. That was, for him, a consistent practice going back to the dangerous days of 1949 when Parliament met within sound of cannon-fire from Insein.

A visiting team of West German journalists obtained a rare interview with Gen. Ne Win on October 17, 1958. The journalists asked him some questions, which he took with good humour. "Do you think you will be able to hold elections within 6 months?" they asked. "I shall try," he replied, "with confidence." "What will

[13] Albert Ravenholt, *Burma Army Gives Rangoon a New Face,* in *Chicago Daily News,* June 15, 1959.

[14] This was the description used by the Israeli press which covered his 8-day visit to their country in June, 1959, without getting from him much more than a brief recorded statement; see *The Guardian* daily, June 18, 1959.

17

you do if you find that you can't accomplish the task within that brief time?" they pressed. "I shall resign", Gen. Ne Win answered without hesitation, "and convene Parliament for the election of a new Prime Minister."[15]

That was exactly what he did as soon as he found that he could not guarantee the conditions for holding fair and free elections in April. "I would say," Gen. Ne Win stated in Parliament on February 13, 1959, after submitting his resignation to the President earlier in the morning, "that an election if held within this period, would be merely a token. The deep antagonisms and constant bickerings between the various political organizations in the country continue unabated today. The strong urge towards bloodshed and violence has not lessened to any perceptible degree. During the election it is a certainty that voters will be exposed to intimidation by those in possession of arms." The drive against insurgency and lawlessness was beginning to bring results; the people were rising in support. Yet, three months had been too short, and to let off just when the drive was gathering momentum would be unwise.

Choose a new Prime Minister, Gen. Ne Win urged, and he would, as Chief of Staff, continue to serve in the cause of restoring law and order. If, however, Parliament could not find a suitable substitute, and wished him to remain as leader of the Caretaker Government, he must first have article 116 of the constitution suitably amended. That article provided that a member of the Government "who for any period of six consecutive months is not a member of Parliament shall at the expiration of that period cease to be a member of the Government." He had been mindful of this provision, Gen. Ne Win recalled in his report to Parliament, even when in 1949-50, he had to overstay the period when he served in the Cabinet. He had then sought the opinion of the Attorney-General who gave an assurance that it was all right, because there was only a Provisional Government until the first general elections could be held.

The situation, however, had changed. Article 116 was fully operative. It would stand in the way of his continuing as Prime Minister beyond April, and as he had found that he could not satisfactorily discharge his duty in that period, Parliament must

15 *The Guardian* daily, Oct. 18, 1958.

either elect a new Prime Minister or amend article 116 suitably to allow him to continue. "The law should not be stretched in its interpretation according to one's wishes," Gen. Ne Win said. "If an amendment of this constitutional provision is deemed necessary in the interests of the country, then a suitable amendment should be made, temporarily, to suit the circumstances obtaining, and only for the necessary period."[16]

There were eminent jurists who offered unsolicited advice to Gen. Ne Win that he could resign on the last day of the six months, enter office again the next day and continue for another six. This could go on without end, and article 116 would not be offended. That kind of dealing was not, however, to Gen. Ne Win's taste. A law must be complied with both in the letter and the spirit. If the law was found unsuitable, it must be amended to meet the situation; but there must be no clever, cunning legal hair-splitting.

President U Win Maung posed a question for the Supreme Court, the answer to which, he thought, might dispose of the problem and eliminate the need for a constitutional amendment. The President apparently acted on his own, and not at the instance of the Government. Perhaps he wanted to help. The Supreme Court too would perhaps have been favourably inclined to render an opinion, rich with legal learning and references to precedents in other countries, which would give the colour of legality to Gen. Ne Win's continuing in office within the provisions of article 116. The presidential request for an advisory opinion was taken up with dispatch by the Supreme Court. The case, however, was closed on Gen. Ne Win's resignation and his clear statement that his conscience would not be set at rest by mere interpretations, however learned, but an amendment, which the people could read and understand, should be made if Parliament wanted him to stay.[17]

Parliament suspended the operation of article 116, by constitutional amendment, and voted that Gen. Ne Win should continue. U Nu wanted to negotiate a compromise. Let the elections be held in April, he suggested to Gen. Ne Win, and let senior

[16] Speech reproduced in *Is Trust Vindicated?*
[17] The question posed was whether Parliament could re-elect a non-member premier who had resigned, and if so when would the six months begin to run; *Supreme Court Reference* 1 of 1959.

army officers named by the General continue to serve in the Cabinet until their tasks were accomplished; if more than six months was needed, then one set of officers could resign from the Cabinet at the end of that period, and another set go in. The compromise, however, was unacceptable to Gen. Ne Win.

The NUF protested strongly against the constitutional amendment. Its leaders in Parliament said that the heart was being torn out of the constitution. Twenty-nine NUF M.Ps voted against the amendment, but it was carried massively.

Gen. Ne Win made minor changes in the composition of his Cabinet. He brought in Brigadier Tin Pe as Minister for Mines, Labour, Public Works and National Housing. U Thi Han, the director of Defence Supplies, was appointed Minister for Trade Development and Industries. The two new Ministers were the only exceptions which Gen. Ne Win made to his policy of keeping army officers and Defence Ministry officials out of the Cabinet. The exceptions had to be made because the choice was so severely limited. For the Ministry of Health, Gen. Ne Win chose U Tun Tin, a barrister and a retired Secretary. U Tun Tin was called in by the General and asked if he would be willing to join the Government. He answered, "Yes", and that was that.

The Caretaker Government, paradoxically perhaps because it was led by a soldier, tried hard to give new life to the constitution and their true roles to such institutions as Parliament, the Executive and the Judiciary. Thus, the *New Statesman* of London, in its issue of January 24, 1959, called Gen. Ne Win the "constitutional soldier" and noticed that "one happy feature of the Caretaker Government is its respect for the constitution and parliament. U Nu, leading his factional government for 3 months after the AFPFL split, felt compelled to pass the budget by presidential ordinance. Ne Win promptly convened parliament to pass the budget in the regular way and has so far refrained from making any law by ordinance."

No special power was, in fact, used by decree or ordinance during the whole period of the Caretaker Government. When laws needed to be made, the drafts were first placed before joint meetings of parliamentary leaders of the two AFPFL groups and thoroughly discussed until consensus was reached. Then, the bills were moved in Parliament, with ample notice, and ample time for debate. Those draft laws which could not obtain warm support from the parliamentary leaders were dropped. Many were dropped by Gen. Ne Win, when they came before the Cabinet, because he considered them to fall outside his mandate. Several draft commercial agreements with foreign firms, and several proposals for the taking of foreign aid or loans, were similarly vetoed. "We have no right to commit the future governments," he would rule, "and as for loans, it is easy to take them, but the future generations which will have to repay with interests will curse our memory."

Members were given more time in Parliament to ask questions and introduce bills and motions on Wednesday, the day reserved for private members. Laws were drafted by the Caretaker Government to increase the salary of members, the salary and allowances of Ministers, and to create the office of the Leader of the Opposition with status, salary and privileges of a Minister. The bills gained enthusiastic support from the parliamentary leaders, and quick passage in Parliament. The laws were to become operative when a new government assumed office after the elections.

To the Executive, Gen. Ne Win's constant message was: "Be loyal in your public service to the country and the people, not to any party. Be brave, and do what you think is right, guided by your conscience. Be honest. Do not get involved in the party political warfare; do not exploit that warfare for your own undue advancement or profit. Build a good tradition of efficient and honest service to the country. Have no anxiety about honest mistakes. But don't feel too confident that disloyalty or dishonesty will always remain undiscovered or go unpunished." Executive officials generally responded with enthusiasm in the first months of the Caretaker Government. There were some who marked time, and watched how the winds would blow. The rest, however, put their hearts into their work, and everywhere—in the Secretariat, the districts, the towns and the villages—government became more efficient, punctual and prompt. Later, after the elections were announced, the morale of the civil servants declined again. Party governments were coming back, and the civil servants knew that the best policy to pursue under such governments was "Safety First".

Gen. Ne Win also had a law passed to raise the status of the

Auditor-General. The constitution gave that official some per-
manency of tenure in that after he was appointed by the President with the consent of Parliament, he could only be removed
on successful impeachment "in the like manner and on the like
grounds as a Judge of the High Court." In regard to salary and
allowances, however, the Auditor-General was on the same standing as the most senior civil servant. That, Gen. Ne Win decided,
was not right. The Auditor-General must control all disbursements
and audit all accounts of moneys administered by the Union Government; he needed a status of authority and terms of service
which encouraged him to do his duty with impartiality and independence. A law was therefore piloted smoothly through
Parliament by the Caretaker Government to give the Auditor-
General the same salary as a Judge.

The Judiciary was not in too good a shape when the Caretaker Government entered office. The constitution established the
Judiciary as an important pillar of the State. The Supreme Court
had the power of judicial review, its writ jurisdiction to exercise
in the protection of fundamental rights, its supervisory jurisdiction over courts and "quasi-judicial" bodies throughout the Union,
and its special function of rendering advisory opinions on questions of law of public importance referred to it by the President.
The judges of the Supreme Court and High Court stood high on
the order of precedence, and were the first to receive high honours
and titles. When the President of the Union was to be elected
after the first general elections, it was Sir Ba U, the Chief Justice
of the Union, whom the AFPFL chose. It was no doubt a fitting
honour for a distinguished man; but such honours, or the hope of
receiving them, became temptations to some judges. The quality
of the Supreme Court began to visibly decline once the ambition
for the presidency started to seize the senior justices.

There were other ambitions—for titles, for promotion as Chief
Justice, for elevation from the High Court to the Supreme Court,
for appointments to special commissions. These ambitions which
gripped some of the judges and led them on unbecoming paths,
lowered the high tribunals in the esteem of the people. Most of
the judges did their work conscientiously and with dignity. But a
few senior judges behaving badly could do irreparable damage to
the prestige of the entire Judiciary.

Gen. Ne Win invited U Chan Tun Aung, Chief Justice of the High Court, to join his Cabinet, but then the Caretaker Government was non-party, and it was called into being, for a limited period, by exceptional circumstances. In regard to the Judiciary, however, Gen. Ne Win took a correct and proper attitude. "We shall not interfere in the work of the Judiciary," he instructed U Ba Sein, the Attorney-General, "and we shall respect its decisions. But don't consult individual judges of the Supreme Court or the High Court on particular cases. That is wrong in principle. You must, as our chief law officer, give us your best advice, and we shall be guided by it. If the law as it stands does not sanction what we must do, don't stretch it, or get round it. We shall stay squarely within the law, and if necessary, openly amend it. Similarly, if cases go to court, we must do our best to present our case, then abide by the court's decision."

In these ways the "constitutional soldier" set about to strengthen the law and the constitution. In the hands of the Caretaker Government the constitution did not lose its heart; it gained a new lease of life.

7

Gen. Ne Win undertook and accomplished two other major tasks in his time as leader of the Caretaker Government: the introduction of popular government in the Shan and the Kayah States; and the execution of an agreement with the People's Republic of China on the long disputed demarcation of the border between the two countries. These were tasks which previous governments had undertaken without reaching clear and final decision. They were not included in the tasks set to Gen. Ne Win when he was invested with the premiership. He took them on because he saw that his Government, united and enjoying massive support in Parliament and in the country, had unique advantage to negotiate.

The chieftains (Sawbwas and Saophalongs) of the Shan State and the Kayah State retained their feudal rights and privileges after the Union of Burma—dedicated to democratic and socialist principles—came into being. Representation for the two States in the Chamber of Nationalities was not by election. The chiefs went to the Chamber by right. The Shan State had 25 seats and the Kayah State had 3, so that there was a solid feudal bloc of 28 in a Chamber of 125 seats. In drafting the constitution, it was agreed that this arrangement would be tried for 3 years, and later reviewed and changed after a referendum.[18] There was, however, no review. When the NUF became a vocal Opposition in the popular Chamber, it moved, at every opportunity, a constitutional amendment to abolish the reserved seats. The AFPFL found itself in the uncomfortable position of having to vote down the amendment though it had pledged itself to carry out its principle.

The chiefs had also promised that they would give up their hereditary rights and their reserved seats in Parliament. A few matters of detail stood in the way of a final agreement between the chiefs and the Union Government. When Gen. Ne Win became Premier, he gave respectful treatment to the State Councils, and showed fairness in making budgetary allocations to the States. In response the chiefs were willing to work over the details together and conclude the agreement. By March, 1959, the agreement was approved in principle. The amounts of compensation to be paid to each of the chiefs had been worked out, and other terms had been settled in a spirit of give-and-take. The Shan and the Kayah State Councils approved the draft agreements in March, and Parliament proceeded to unanimously repeal those constitutional provisions which reserved seats in the Chamber of Nationalities for the chiefs. Thenceforth, the chiefs stood on equal terms with other citizens of their States and the Union; they gave up their prerogatives and became "popular" in return. On April 21 the chiefs signed their "acts of renunciation" in a ceremony at Taunggyi. "Popular government came to the Shan State yesterday," reported *The Nation* in its issue of April 22, "when the chiefs or Sawbwas signed an act of renunciation or a modern Magna Carta giving up their hereditary rights."

Gen. Ne Win went to Taunggyi later to join in the celebrations. After expressing his admiration for "the wholehearted and sincere way in which the chiefs had set about divesting themselves of their rights and prerogatives," Gen. Ne Win, in his speech of April 29, had a few words to say on the future of the Shan State.

[18] Minutes of the Constitution Drafting Committees, Sub-committee on the Shan State, Aug. 14, 1947.

"Now that they have divested themselves of all their hereditary powers and privileges and have also participated fully in setting up a popular Government, the Saophalongs and Sawbwas should, in close cooperation with the people, work diligently for the welfare of the peoples of the Union as well as the Shan State. I would like to urge them to devote their brains and their financial resources to the promotion of the social, economic and industrial development of the Shan State. To the people of the Shan State also, I would like to say this. The fact that the Saophalongs and Saophas have given up their powers does not mean that you may behave disrespectfully towards them."

"I shall conclude," Gen. Ne Win said, "with an exhortation to you all to foster and safeguard the Panglong spirit, to cultivate Union-consciousness, to fight those who would attempt the disintegration of the Union, to abandon narrow parochial attitudes as regards race, and to endeavour towards the common welfare of the whole Union."[19]

The incomplete demarcation of the boundary between China and Burma had given rise to occasional controversy ever since the British annexed upper Burma. After Burma attained independence the Union Government had had occasion to exchange notes or register protests with the Kuomintang Government. The collapse of the KMT, and the rise of the People's Republic, postponed but did not extinguish the problem. In December, 1954, Premiers U Nu and Chou En-lai met, and declared in a joint communique that the border question should be settled "in a friendly spirit at an appropriate time through normal diplomatic channels."

In 1956, however, the question leapt into the headlines of the Burmese press, with reports that there had been large scale crossings of Burma's northern borders by Chinese troops. A hue and cry was raised by the press and the people, and negotiations to settle the border question were resumed with some urgency. U Nu, in his period of leave from the premiership, went to Peking to talk. Correspondence between Premiers U Ba Swe and Chou En-lai followed, and visits and correspondence were exchanged at various levels. In the words of U Nu, reporting to Parliament on April 28, 1960, the negotiations proceeded on the following

[19] Speech reproduced in *Is Trust Vindicated?*

course: "Matters then remained static until the advent of the Bogyoke Ne Win Government. Bogyoke Ne Win had always been
interested in the Sino-Burmese boundary question, and I had kept
him informed from time to time of important developments. During the first few months of his premiership, heavy preoccupations
with more immediate matters made it impossible for Bogyoke Ne
Win to take up the question. As a statesman and a realist, he recognized that it was very much to Burma's interest to have this
question settled as early as possible, and he turned his attention
to it as soon as his other imperative duties permitted. After giving
the matter the most careful study, he came to the conclusion that
we should try to reach a settlement on the following lines. Gen.
Ne Win consulted the leaders of both the Clean and Stable
AFPFL, and obtained their consent to his making an attempt to
settle the question on those lines. He then consulted the Shan
leaders and, thanks to his high qualities of leadership and persuasion, succeeded in obtaining their consent."

"Gen. Ne Win's proposal was communicated to the Chinese
Government on June 4, 1959. The Chinese Government's reply
was dated September 24, 1959. Without going into details, they
suggested that the latest proposals of both sides should form the
basis for further negotiations, these negotiations to take place
between delegations appointed by the two Governments. The
Union Government's response was contained in Bogyoke Ne Win's
letter of November 4, 1959, to Premier Chou En-lai. Bogyoke
Ne Win emphasized that it was only his position as a non-partisan
Prime Minister which enabled him to secure the agreement of the
major political parties and of the State Governments concerned.
As such the compromise proposal embodied the maximum offer
it was possible for us to make and, in his view, represented an eminently fair and equitable basis for an agreement. Instead therefore of turning the question over to delegations of the two countries for further negotiations, Bogyoke Ne Win expressed his
belief that the Chinese Government would find it possible
to take a further step with a view to eliminating the small
difference that still remained between the two sides. Bogyoke
Ne Win concluded by saying that if this belief was shared by the
Chinese side, he would be prepared to go to Peking at the earliest
possible date to discuss and formalize an agreement in principle

on the Sino-Burmese boundary question."

"Premier Chou En-lai's reply, welcoming Gen. Ne Win's suggestion that he should visit Peking, and extending a formal invitation to him to come at any convenient time during January, 1960, was received on December, 22nd 1959. After an exchange of further correspondence in an attempt to clear up the positions of both sides, Gen. Ne Win led a high-powered team which included the Foreign Minister, the Attorney-General and the Vice-Chief of Army Staff, to Peking on January 23, 1960. The results of that mission are embodied in the Sino-Burmese Boundary Agreement which was concluded on January 28, 1960."

"I believe that the Burmese interests have been well served by the conclusion of this agreement. For the first time in history we shall soon have a well-defined mutually agreed boundary between Burma and China. Thus a boundary, which has defied solution for three quarters of a century has now been settled. The constant uncertainty which attended the absence of a mutually agreed boundary between China and Burma has been removed by this Agreement. It has thereby eliminated a major source of misunderstanding between our two countries and peoples, and I believe that it is not inaccurate to say that both Burma and China have gained by the agreement."

In moving that the Agreement be ratified by Parliament, U Nu paid tribute to the political leaders and government officials who had taken part in the long negotiations. "But the main credit on our side for this settlement belongs to one man. That one man is Bogyoke Ne Win. As the Head of a Caretaker Government whose primary responsibility was the restoration of law and order and the holding of general elections, it would have been easy, had he been so minded, for Bogyoke Ne Win to side-step this extremely difficult issue, and to leave it to the successor Government to work out a solution. That he did not choose this path and, putting the larger interests of the country first, decided instead to make a frontal attack on this problem, is the measure of Bogyoke Ne Win's greatness. This bold and courageous decision, the able and democratic manner in which he obtained the support of the main political parties and State Governments, and the high degree of diplomacy which he brought to bear on the problem in the final stage of the negotiations with China, are a testimony to his statesmanship and patriotism. On this issue alone, the entire country owes him a debt which it can never hope to repay. In more ways than one, the Union has been extremely fortunate to have had Bogyoke Ne Win at the helm of affairs at this juncture in its history."[20]

8

One important contributory factor to the success of the negotiations on the border questions was Gen. Ne Win's keen sense of timing. He had already announced that general elections would be held early in 1960. After the elections a party government would come into office, and however strong it might be, it would still have to face an opposition in Parliament. If the Chinese Government wanted to conclude the negotiations with a strong Burmese Government commanding national support and respect, it had to be in the few weeks before Gen. Ne Win relinquished the premiership.

Gen. Ne Win also saw that the time was ripe for agreement. Thorough research on the course of the negotiations also convinced him that China had been favourably disposed all along; though the correspondence had gone on over a long period, it was often the Burmese responses which had been delayed. If he himself went to Peking, Gen. Ne Win thought, with a clear and concise proposal containing the maximum offer that could be made and the minimum that would be expected in return, a final agreement would not be elusive.

Thus it was that Gen. Ne Win went to Peking towards the end of January, 1960, a few weeks before the elections were due. The first session, held in friendly privacy between the two Premiers alone, led to a full and unreserved meeting of minds on the main points of substance. Both the leaders knew all the facts. No notes or memoranda were needed or referred to. Gen. Ne Win had scribbled a few points in a small pocket diary. Those were useful for checking, but the spirit of agreement which prevailed and

[20] Speech in the Chamber of Deputies, April 28, 1960, reproduced in booklet published by the Dir. of Information. Details of the terms of agreement are left out; for those see *Burma's Constitution,* by Maung Maung, and *The Making of Burma,* by Dorothy Woodman.

the full knowledge possessed by the two Premiers of the entire history of the border question were decisive. The "experts" of both sides met later in several sessions, and talked long over words and forms. But the substance of agreement, arrived at between the two leaders in their first meeting remained unaltered.

The border agreement marked a fitting end to the Caretaker Government. Time had come, Gen. Ne Win decided, a few months before he went to Peking, to hold general elections and make way for a party government. The politicians were clamouring; the months out of power were making them restless, hungry, desperate. The Army, harnessed to the thankless task of cleaning up, was weary and in need of consolidation. The discipline and the hard work, hallmarks of the Government, were not fully appreciated by some people who had been long accustomed to drifting.

Time had come to go, Gen. Ne Win decided. The Army and he had done what could be done. Conditions were favourable for holding fair and free elections. The constitution had been revitalized. New high standards of administration had been set. New values in the doing of justice had been established. Besides, the Army must not get too deeply drawn into the political warfare. Some elements in the Army were showing partisan leanings, which was bad for the integrity and unity of the Army. Power had intoxicated or corrupted some soldiers, which was bad for them and the Army too. The thankless tasks which the Army had had to take on had in the end done damage to its popularity, prestige, and public image. The Army must be saved, for it was an organization of young men, trained, disciplined, idealistic, dedicated to high purpose. If the Army was gone, there could be little left to hold the country together.

On his way to Israel in June, 1959, Gen. Ne Win was interviewed by some reporters at the Calcutta airport. Asked when he would be holding elections in Burma, he promptly replied: "Around April, next year." This was big news, good news, for the politicians in Burma. When the Chamber of Deputies met in August, 1959, an NUF member asked the Government for a confirmation of what Gen. Ne Win had said in Calcutta. The Judicial Minister replied that the general elections would be held in January, or February, 1960.[21]

[21] Chamber of Deputies, *Proceedings,* vol. IX, No. 2, Aug. 14, 1959.

Constitutionally, it would have been proper to dissolve Parliament in June, 1960, when its normal life would run out, and conduct the elections within 60 days of the dissolution. The Caretaker Government could thus hold office till August, or later, for the new Chamber of Deputies must assemble and elect a new Prime Minister to whom power could be handed over. But Gen. Ne Win had Parliament dissolved on December 19, 1959, and fixed February 6, 1960 as the date for the elections for the Chamber of Deputies, and February 29 for the Chamber of Nationalities elections.

The political parties gave a whoop of joy at the announcements. They began energetically to organize their campaigns, brushing up old slogans, coining new ones, drafting manifestoes, framing powerful charges against their rivals, thinking up the promises to make to the voters.

On December 21, the last conference of the Security Councils was held in Rangoon by the Caretaker Government. "When we formed our Government," Gen. Ne Win said at the opening session, "we undertook to conduct elections which were as fair and free as possible. That was a promise which we solemnly gave, and not just to please the people and win their applause. Now we shall keep that promise. All government servants, including personnel of the armed forces, should be absolutely non-partisan during the forthcoming general elections. There should be no oppression or victimization of the party you do not like. Let the people make their choice in freedom. The country will get the government it deserves."

9

Interlude

1

THE ELECTION campaign was hard and bitter. Mudslinging, name-calling, washing one's dirty linen in public, these the party leaders did unashamed, and unaware—or uncaring—that in the end politics and politicians would be debased in the public eye. The campaign cost money—heaps of money—and businessmen who had made their fortunes in the decade of AFPFL power were called upon by both factions to contribute. Unable to pick the winner, the businessmen, except those who were firmly committed to one faction, made their contributions to both, hoping that when one was returned to power they would be able to recover their lost fortunes.

The Socialist leaders had always said that U Nu was no organizer, a mere orator, a spell-binder. He could never, they had said, win an election without them. In the campaign, and indeed in the months preceding it, U Nu proved that they were all wrong. He could not only win without them, but against them also. He outclassed and outfought them, strategically, tactically. Quietly, sweetly, more often uttering Buddhist sermons than making political speeches, U Nu set the pace and called the tune. His rivals followed, dancing to his tunes.

At a conference of the Clean AFPFL, held in September, 1959, U Nu pledged himself to the establishment of Buddhism as the state religion. This went over very well with the monks, who wield considerable influence on the daily lives of the people, especially the villagers. The army psychological warfare directorate, in its anti-communist drive, had launched a campaign with the cry that the "Dhamma is in Danger". Pamphlets in their millions were distributed throughout the country by the army, to prove that the Communists had burned pagodas, looted temples,

271

called Buddhism opium of the worst kind, and attacked the
Buddha as the people's enemy number one who preached nothing
but propaganda which chained the people to their misery. The
director of religious affairs appealed to the Buddhist monks to
meet the serious threat posed to Buddhism by the Communists.
The monks responded massively.[1] The campaign became a gift
to U Nu with his sermons and his promise that he would strive
to make Buddhism the state religion.

The Stable AFPFL accused that U Nu was exploiting religion
in the election campaign. U Nu retorted that he was not, that
while the Clean AFPFL was committed to making Buddhism the
state religion that was a party programme, not an election issue.
U Nu also pointed out that the undivided AFPFL, in convening
the sixth Great Buddhist Synod, had agreed about the state religion. He also stood on his record of honouring the basic constitutional principle of non-discrimination on religious grounds. He
had, he recalled, even banned the teaching of Buddhism in state
schools in 1954, against strong opposition from the monks, because he was convinced that the teaching of Buddhism only
would be unfair and discriminatory.

U Kyaw Nyein made a slip of the tongue and said that a
politician did not need to observe the five precepts. This was
played up by the Clean AFPFL, and U Kyaw Nyein had to
explain that he did not say what he said in seriousness, but in
any case U Nu himself was not above breaking the vow of truth-
fulness in the five precepts. That might or might not be true, but
the voters did not care. In their eyes, U Nu was the devout man,
the pure, while the Swe-Nyein were the breakers of the precepts.
To the cadres whom the Clean AFPFL trained and sent out to
the villages, U Nu preached: Be good men; observe the five
precepts; wherever you go, pay your respects to the monks, the
elders. Those cadres proved more effective than the professional
organizers who promised the leaders of the Stable AFPFL that
all was well in the districts, and stayed in Rangoon, hanging round
their chiefs.

U Nu lived in a modest cottage, rode about the town in a jeep.
He invited newsmen to his house, and showed them round, telling

---

[1] *Dhammantaraya—Dhamma in Danger,* in *Burma Weekly Bulletin,*
Apr. 30, 1959.

them that even that small cottage was not his own. He publicly gave away some of his clothes and belongings. In contrast the two leaders of the Swe-Nyein lived in style, rode about in their Mercedes.

"Whenever Bo Khin Maung Gale opens his mouth the Stable lose half the votes to the Clean," said U Nu about a vocal and voluble opponent. "But let him abuse me to his heart's content, I bear him no ill-will."[2] Bo Khin Maung Gale was not, however, the star loser of votes. There were other Stable leaders too who made famous—and costly—slips of the tongue. Some of them had, during the first months of the Caretaker Government, made out that there had been a *coup* and the Stable had arranged it, and the soldiers were "our boys". The Stable found, too late, that their being identified with the Army by the people was not making them too popular. They tried to change their tactics, but without much result. "We shall send the soldiers back to the barracks if we form the next Government," promised U Kyaw Nyein, "we shall not keep army officers in civilian jobs. But what will U Nu do if he wins?"[3] The army, however, had already made it clear that it was returning to the barracks after the elections. U Kyaw Nyein's challenge, flung at that late hour, only had a false ring.

A few days earlier U Ba Swe was said to have remarked that the Stable would win, whether they won the elections or lost. That was another famous vote-loser. U Nu, quickly pouncing on it at a rally, asked the audience if they too had heard about the remark. "Yes", the people shouted back. "Then", U Nu declared, "the implications are clear: if the Stable can win by fair means they will do so; if not, they intend to win by foul means."[4]

"Give us your vote," U Nu asked the people, "the precious vote which you must draw forth from the deep recesses of your heart. The issues at stake are large, but they boil down to this. Do you want democracy, or would you prefer fascism?"

The Clean AFPFL chose yellow—indicating religion and purity —as its colour. Its polling boxes carried the picture of U Nu, sweetly smiling. The colour and the picture were sure winners.

2 *The Nation*, Jan. 25, 1960.
3 *The Nation*, Feb. 3, 1960.
4 *The Nation*, Dec. 28, 1959.

"Anyone carrying the Clean ticket will win," predicted a Clean candidate in Rangoon in a gush of confidence.

The omens were indeed bad for the Stable AFPFL. Municipal elections, long overdue, were held in the cities ahead of the parliamentary elections. U Ba Swe went to Moulmein to campaign for the Stable candidates. "We must win the municipal elections in Moulmein, otherwise the Clean AFPFL will jeer: 'Old Ba Swe's back is broken,' and we cannot tolerate that."[5] The results were 25 seats out of a total of 25 for the Clean, with 29,649 votes out of a total of 41,252 cast.[6] Similar results were shown in Mandalay, and every city in which municipal elections were held.

The Stable AFPFL issued an election manifesto, full of promises. Agricultural loans would be doubled, taxes would be cut, controls would be abolished. Education would be free to the middle school level; free education in the high schools and the universities would be introduced by stages. More pay was promised for teachers, more security for the civil servants. Efforts would be made to fulfil the principal needs of the country in the fields of national solidarity, peace and prosperity, stability of the Union, growth of democratic ideals, and rehabilitation of the national economy.[7]

U Nu, on his part, kept repeating that the issue was clear and simple: Democracy or Fascism. But what did those words mean, asked Dr Ba Maw who observed the scene with pessimism. "The people don't seem to mind the mess they are in," he said, "they only object to anyone trying to save them from the mess and trying to change the way they have been used to living. They have been taught a new word for it, which is Fascism."

"Doing what they like without caring a damn what happens to them or to others or to the country as a whole, they have been told, is Democracy. Ruling the country and wasting its substance and allowing crime and corruption to grow rampantly is called Democracy; every attempt to make Democracy to mean not only rights but also obligations is called by some Fascism."

"An intelligent understanding of Democracy," Dr Ba Maw said, "and its obligations would have made people, who are re-

5 *The Nation*, Dec. 4, 1959.
6 *The Nation*, Dec. 20, 1959.
7 *The Nation*, Dec. 23, 1959.

sponsible for the past ten years of ruin and crime, ashamed even to face the electorate, let alone asking to be returned to power. They think it is enough to say that they are sorry for the past. Any criminal would be prepared to say he is sorry for his crime, if he could get free that way; even more, if he could get back the same chance to do all he had done before. Democracy very definitely does not work that way."

"Also, since the voters are not facing the real problems bedevilling the country, those problems will go on after the elections, and even get worse. If the old gang get into power again in spite of their past record, it will mean for them that no record, however black, matters to the people and they could go on with the same old foolery as before; in fact they would go on with greater audacity, seeing that such things don't count at all with the majority of voters."[8]

2

Gen. Ne Win took every step to get the message across to all officers and men that they must remain strictly neutral in the elections. Directives were issued. Commanding officers were ordered to drive the message home by all possible means. But personal feelings were hard to ignore. Many of the young leaders of the Swe-Nyein were old comrades, and the temptation to treat them more equally than the others was almost irresistible for some of the young army officers. Besides, U Nu was going round campaigning against the "fascists", and the soldiers, bent under several additional loads of duty, felt that they were the undisclosed targets, and they were hurt.

Thus, there were cases of army officers helping the Swe-Nyein. Despite the help, or because of it, the Swe-Nyein went down in municipal elections in some districts. The Swe-Nyein who were happy to get the help, grumbled when they lost, and claimed that it was the army which was getting unpopular while they had to go before the people as "substitutes for the real accused." This ingratitude also hurt the soldiers. As for the Clean AFPFL, the proved cases of army help to their rivals became a potent propaganda weapon for the election campaign. U Nu and the Clean

[8] *The Nation,* Jan. 24, 1960.

AFPFL appeared before the people as the martyrs, oppressed and persecuted, yet forgiving. This image had a huge emotional appeal.

Gen. Ne Win travelled on November 9, 1959, to Meiktila, Mandalay, and other army camps to meet the commanding officers and make his message clear. "We must stay strictly neutral," he explained, "because that is our pledge and also because that is the only wise policy for the Tatmadaw to pursue in these times of political conflict. You have your personal feelings; so have I. Most of the leaders of the two major factions were our comrades. When the AFPFL was undivided, we accepted it as the political leader and the legitimate custodian of national power. When the AFPFL split, the country was torn by political strife. Our loyalty to the country and the people is, however, undivided. We stepped in to save the situation and hold it until fair and free elections could be held."

"I did not lightly promise to hold fair and free elections. As you know I ponder deeply and weigh my words with care before I speak. My word is a bond. We have, as the Tatmadaw, always served the people loyally, keeping our promises, doing as we say, saying only as we do. Some of you may think that even though I declare that the Tatmadaw shall serve as the neutral umpire in the elections, I will pretend not to notice any quiet help that you may give to one side or the other. That is not so. Let me emphasise that I mean every word of what I have said."

"Let the people choose freely. Let those who wish to contest the elections, as the Clean AFPFL, the Stable, the NUF or as independents, do so without hindrance. To vote freely, to contest freely, are the rights of citizens. Let the winner form a government and have a good try at doing a good job."

"You will want to ask me: what if the new government makes a mess of things again? Well, we can only wait and see before finding a clear answer to that question. Two things can happen. Or, rather, three. The new government may do a good job; its leaders may mend their ways. If that happens, we shall be content, and we shall devote ourselves to our duties as soldiers. The other possibility is that they will fall back into their old ways, and things may become as bad as they were before. Yet another possibility is that things may get even worse. If things get bad or worse, what shall we do? You may ask me: shall we look on with folded arms while the country plunges towards disaster?"

"I must answer that question with a question. If we should feel that we must rise to the call of higher duty to save the country, can we achieve any success if we do not have the affection and respect of the people? The answer, clearly, is 'No'. We must march arm in arm with the people, be with the people and for the people always. All the victories the Tatmadaw has won in its career are due to this unity with the people. If we have to engage in greater battles in the future, we must retain and reinforce this unity."

"You cannot earn the respect and affection of the people by helping this side in the elections, or oppressing that side. You must do your duty impartially, win the confidence of the people. We must uphold the discipline of the Tatmadaw. There have been some laxities in some quarters of the Tatmadaw lately. There are some who are intoxicated by power. Those must be corrected. If you see your comrade weakening, help him and pull him up. If he refuses to be helped, but commits grave errors, he must be disciplined. There is no immunity for any wrong-doer. We cannot have the people say that the soldiers are above the law, or that there are double standards of justice, one for the soldiers, one for the civilians. When the country was on the verge of chaos we could step in and rescue it because the Tatmadaw was there, united, disciplined, dedicated, enjoying the respect and affection of the people. Now if the Tatmadaw lost its unity, discipline and dedication, or the respect and affection of the people, which organization would be there to save the country if the need arose again?"

"So, let us strengthen our own ranks, uphold our discipline, improve our battle-worthiness, and keep our ideals undimmed. Also, we must never lose the affection and respect of the people. Then we shall always be fit and ready to respond to any call of duty. But let us hope that the new government will do well, that its leaders will mend their ways and take the country on the right path in the right directions. If that happens we shall remain, happy and content, in our barracks, doing our soldier's duties."

Gen. Ne Win's address, informal, impressive because of its sincerity, was taped, and copies of the tape were sent to all military units and stations for repeated playbacks. Well before the elections, therefore, the soldiers came to fully appreciate their role and where their duty lay. They served to keep the peace and clear the political arena for the most free and fair parliamentary elections the country had ever witnessed.

The result was that U Nu rode on the crest of a huge emotional wave that swept through the entire country and carried him to massive victory.

3

The battle of the giants was fought in Rangoon. U E Maung of the Clean took on no less a person than U Ba Swe of the Stable. It was whispered about in town that perhaps the Clean was feeding U E Maung, a former NUF leader, to the Tiger. U E Maung refuted the rumours and said that he had asked his party for the privilege of fighting the Tiger. Thakin Tin of the Clean entered the lists against U. Kyaw Nyein. U Nu, considered a sure winner, did not have much opposition to meet; the Stable entered against him, perhaps mockingly, one Yebaw Ba Thein who was unknown, but who proved in the end to be quite a fighter.

All the Stable candidates went down in crushing defeat. The results, announced from the City Hall, were hailed by huge crowds of people who waited through the night. What happened in Rangoon was repeated almost everywhere. The elections were held simultaneously for each Chamber, throughout the country; only for ten constituencies were they postponed for a few months. The state of the parties in May, 1960 was: 159 Clean, 42 Stable; the rest being divided between 'independents', small parties and racial groups. The NUF, which put 135 candidates into the field, polled a total of 297,062 votes among them, but did not win a single seat. Thus, with the NUF wiped out, the Clean AFPFL enjoyed the predominant majority which the undivided AFPFL had once enjoyed, and the Stable AFPFL became the small and lonely opposition that the NUF was in those days.

The Caretaker Government had compiled the electoral rolls correctly and thoroughly. There were 9,915,216 voters on the rolls, as against 8,570,308 in 1956. There was a better turn-out of voters: 59 per cent as against 42 per cent in the earlier elections. Of those who voted, 52 per cent gave their votes to the Clean, 31 per cent to the Stable, and 5 per cent to the NUF. In 1956, 42 per cent of the voters voted for the undivided AFPFL, and 31 per cent for the NUF, returning 144 AFPFL members as against 46 NUF.[9]

The Stable promptly accused that the Clean had not won a clean victory. The victors had violated the constitution, the Stable cried, by using Buddhism as a stepping stone. They had also, it was alleged, poured millions of kyats into the campaign, buying votes and favours freely. The insurgents helped the Clean, it was also said, and U Nu's smiling picture on the ballot boxes was a deception because voters in the districts thought he was their candidate and they put their ballots in the boxes carrying his picture.[10]

But the Stable too were not known to have spared money in the election campaign. Regarding Buddhism, the Stable had come out with a statement, at the peak of the campaign, that a Stable government would introduce compulsory teaching of the religion for Buddhist pupils in schools, open new state primary schools at monasteries and a separate teachers' training college and a university for the monks. The Stable also undertook to consider establishing Buddhism as the state religion, after the elections and in consultation with the monks and the people.[11] Thus, if U Nu exploited religion in the elections, the Stable could not plead innocence either.

As for the picture on the ballot boxes, the electoral law only prohibited the use of Aung San's picture. The undivided AFPFL had always brought out the Bogyoke's picture at election times, and used it on the ballot boxes. Neither U Ba Swe nor U Kyaw Nyein had complained then that the use of the picture was unfair. And, if the Clean used U Nu's picture on its boxes, the Stable could have used U Ba Swe's on its own boxes if it chose.

A deeper, more objective, analysis of the elections was offered by Dr Ba Maw who had not himself contested. He had seen the election campaign move forward "roughly in five stages." The first consisted of "a general absence of political consciousness in a real sense among the people. None of the facts or issues now

[9] *The Guardian,* May 6, 1960.
[10] *The Nation,* Feb. 14, 1960.
[11] *The Guardian,* Dec. 14, 1959.

seething in the country seemed to bother the masses. The fact that, as the London *Times* has commented, although their country is one of the richest, the Burmese are with the people of Laos, the poorest in Asia and that their span of life is shorter than that of the others left the people unmoved and indifferent."

In the second stage the widening of the AFPFL split dramatized the activities of the two factions in a way that the people could understand. "Mass politics turned more and more into just a choice between those two factions and their colours—yellow for the Clean and red for the Stable. All other issues began to disappear at this stage; if the people did not like the reds it was the yellows, or the other way round. Burma seemed to have no other problem or issue to think about; the waste, the corruption, filth and chaos of the ten AFPFL years did not matter."

"Then followed the third stage with an appeal to the religious side of the people, religion as the average Buddhist in Burma understands it. It turned the election further away from the actual issues. Soon it became almost a religious crusade working below the surface and arousing the most deep-rooted passions. The monks came in massively to support the man who promised to make Buddhism the state religion. As the London *Times* has said, the masses showed that religion mattered more than higher economics."

"The fourth stage proved to be the culminating point in the factional struggle. The Clean faction concentrated on a whispering campaign against the Stable which spread like a fire across the country. It accused the Stable faction of almost all the dirty things done by the pre-split AFPFL in the past and of being in league with the army in doing the dirty "fascist" things happening at the moment. It was a very simple hate campaign based upon the shrewd calculation that if in a contest between the two parties one is sufficiently hated the other will draw the votes. Very curiously, the Stable people as a whole did not seem to mind the accusations associating them with the army acts; in fact they often went out of their way to encourage them. Their arrogance even seemed to justify the worst of these accusations. This in the end proved to be their undoing."

"On account of their long historical and religious conditioning the Burmese are inclined to regard all government as evil and tyrannical. They are therefore willing to believe in most stories told them about the wickedness of those ruling them. But this also produces an opposite result. When the Burmese masses are persuaded by his open religious life and acts that a person in power is devout and a promoter of their faith, he makes a big appeal to them. U Nu has succeeded in exercising such an appeal, especially among the women and the less literate part of the population, and it was partly this that made the phenomenal victory of the Clean party possible."

"The Burmese have believed for a thousand years or more," Dr Ba Maw wrote, "that a government exists only to promote their religion especially by building pagodas and other rich and costly edifices, to collect taxes which it may use as it likes, and to punish the law-breaker and for nothing else; everything else is quickly suspected to be tyranny. They just want to be left alone by the government. Progress means change and all sorts of rules and regulations they cannot understand, and so it is an interference with their lives, or fascism as it is called in Burma nowadays. The people have heard a lot about their democratic rights, but hardly ever of their democratic obligations. All these facts added to the further fact that owing to their political immaturity they find it hard to distinguish big matters from small ones, led many people to remember disproportionately the small personal wrongs and hardships they had at times to suffer and to forget the big long-term gains achieved in consequence of these hardships. This psychological conflict between the army authorities who believed that the end justified the means and its temporary hardships, and those people who believed that no end would justify any hardship put on them helped the Clean party's whispering campaign tremendously."

"At this critical stage, both the army and the Stable party showed a strange lack of leadership. They took no notice, or very little, of the whispering campaign going on; they did nothing to explain in the countryside why they had to do the hateful things they did and the need to do them in defence not only of democracy in the true sense but of the people for whom democracy must exist. Much of the things they did could perhaps have been explained that way, although certainly not all of them; there were certainly needless wrongs and excesses for which the army should have taken open and organized action against the wrong-doers in a way that all could see. But it often failed to to do so."

"As for the Stable party, it seems that they did not know their own minds at this critical stage. Instead, they tried to follow where the Clean led, readily agreeing with that party's view of demo-cracy and fascism which was clearly designed to put both the army and the Stable in the wrong at every turn. The socialists in the Stable leadership were afraid to admit that their socialist task was to change the social conditions and to start doing it at once. If they had taken a longer and bolder view and fought the battle on their own ground instead of their enemy's, and so proved that they had a better understanding of our problems, their defeat would have been much less and more historically worth while. It might even be that they would not have been defeated. In any case, it would have raised our politics to a higher level; and the future would have been their's as the more progressive and vital party, and therefore more in harmony with the times. But the Stable leaders, in their arrogance, were blind to all this."

"Perhaps their costliest error was that they never explained to the masses the real issues involved in the elections. They were content to fight on the issue raised by the Clean party. That was how religion and fascism became the only issues. Religion was U Nu's strong suit, and fascism was something that could plausibly be charged against an army that had to clear up within a few months the mess of ten years left behind by the past AFPFL Gov-ernment. The army even backed a widespread religious movement, "The Dhamma in Danger", which weakened the Communists, but at the same time strengthened the yellow party immensely by putting the country in a strong religious mood. Thus the Stable party had lost the battle before it was fought."

"At the last stage, the saying that nothing succeeds like success again proved to be right. First of all there were those people always numerous in an immature country, who acted on the herd instinct and did what they saw others doing. They became yellow because a lot of others were yellow; they disliked the reds and the army for the same reason; and they liked to be on the winning side which would form the government and so could help them in future. Next, there were the usual opportunists and camp follow-ers. Guessing the party that would win, they have backed it in full force. And, of course, the insurgents everywhere campaigned for a yellow victory, believing that they could come to terms more easily with that party."

"This is the basic picture," Dr Ba Maw wrote, "of the general elections in Burma which have just ended."[12]

4

U Nu took office on April 4, 1960, forming a small Cabinet without appointing any deputy prime minister. In his first speech in the Chamber of Deputies on April 5, he paid handsome tribute to "Gen. Ne Win and the government that he led for their great contribution in preserving the ideal of democracy in our country and making it possible for it to grow and flower on our soil." He would, U Nu promised, strive "to carry out our principal mandate of establishing democracy and developing it as a way of life for our people during the Government's tenure of office. Four years of course is too short a period for the achievement of such a gigantic task, but we are not going to repeat our past mistake of thinking that we shall continue in power for forty years or base our action on the basis of that wishful thinking."

The *Pyidaungsu* (Union) Party, into which the Clean AFPFL had been reorganized after the elections, would "practise the principles of party conduct and organization in a democracy" and "we will not use our majority to oppress the minority in any way." As for the parliamentary opposition, U Nu pledged, it shall receive a fair deal and full opportunity to play its part in the affairs of the country. Political parties which did not gain seats in Parliament, would also be consulted, whenever possible, and given their opportunity to participate in the political life of the country. There would be the rule of law, security of service to insure the independence and efficiency of the civil servants.

Economic plans would be drafted, U Nu said, in accordance with "the democratic principles of discussion, consultation and compromise." He admitted that "the decisions and actions we took in the economic sphere during the ten years that we were in power before the AFPFL split were characterized by the same undemocratic trend that I have described in the political sphere.

[12] *The Nation,* Feb. 11, 1960.

Most of our decisions were arrived at on the initiative of one, two or three leaders without adequate discussion and consultation with other members of the party, and far less with persons and interests outside the party." That would, U Nu promised, be reversed. Also, "during the ten years before the split, we had permitted government's economic policies to be used to some extent for the entrenchment of the party in power, and particularly for the benefit of party adherents and the followers and sycophants of individual leaders. I do not mean to imply that this was the motivating factor in all government actions in the economic sphere; the AFPFL did much which benefited the masses in general, and business, industrialists, workers and individuals who did not belong to the AFPFL. But we were not careful enough to ensure that party adherents and followers of individual leaders would not receive any benefits, or preferential treatment, merely on the strength of their party membership or of their being followers of particular leaders." That, U Nu promised, would not happen again. The controls in the fields of trade and industry would be turned over to nationals as much as possible, and there would be "a gradual withdrawal of the State from economic activity until its scope becomes narrow enough for our available man-power resources to handle it with efficiency, or alternatively to strengthen our civil service to the required extent."

U Nu also promised to create separate Arakanese and Mon states "after ascertaining in a democratic manner whether the people themselves in these areas desire statehood, and in a manner which will ensure peace, harmony, understanding, happiness and welfare for all who inhabit these areas." In fulfilment of another promise, Buddhism would be made the state religion "as speedily as possible", while protecting "fully the rights and privileges of the other religions and religious groups in Burma."

Many committees and commissions were appointed to carry out the many promises. A permanent advisory committee with the former President, Dr Ba U, as chairman was appointed "to advise the Union Government on implementing the Prime Minister's promises to the country, and to give opinions on questions which may be referred to it from time to time by the Prime Minister or any member of the Cabinet." The AFPFL (which could now drop its prefix 'Stable' because U Nu had started his Pyidaungsu Party, shedding the name 'Clean AFPFL') promptly retorted that the advisory committee was unconstitutional. The committee of the "five wise men", as the newspapers called it, took many questions, pondered deeply, and—according to the newspaper cartoonists—gave the expected answers. "This is so, is it not?" was a question referred to the committee, as depicted in a cartoon. "Yes, that is so," was the reply. "This is not so, is it not?" was another question. The wise men shook their heads vigorously and replied, looking solemn and wise, "No, that is not so."

There were the lay commission and the commission of monks to study and report on how Buddhism should be made the state religion. U Nu made it clear that the commissions were not to deal with the question whether Buddhism should be made the state religion, for that was decided; they were only to study and report on how. A committee was appointed to study and report on how the public services should be organized, and what sort of law should be passed to guarantee the security of the public servants. A "parliamentary democracy promotion committee" was appointed to "ensure the widespread flourishing of the tenets of parliamentary democracy in the country." On all these committees the opposition parties—the AFPFL, the NUF, the Arakanese National United Organization (ANUO) and others—were given representation.

There were committees for the creation of the Arakan and the Mon states. Committees to draw up another Four Year Economic Plan. The Bandoola Square was to be turned into a "Hyde Park" where soap-box orators were to enjoy freedom to speak on any subject. A committee was appointed to organize the *Hittine* Corner (Open-air Public Forum).

First things must come first, U Nu declared on his return to power, and the first thing was to lay firm foundations for democracy. Pyidawtha, the Happy Land, could wait. The grand plans for the welfare state must also yield place to the first task of establishing democracy. Burma was like a patient, U Nu said, for whom the doctors had just about given up hope. The administrative machinery was like a broken-down jeep, without tyres or even the essential parts of the engine: "I can't drive this affair at 160 miles an hour!"

Democracy, however, was for the articulate few, the few who

knew how to make demands, manipulate and pull strings. For the
millions of the peasants and the workers things went on as they
did before the AFPFL split. They had drawn the precious votes
from the deep recesses of their hearts in the elections; now they
were forgotten. They were the voiceless millions in the democracy about which so much was spoken in Rangoon.

The democracy which the Pyidaungsu party held so precious
only raised expectations, increased appetites and provoked demands from the vocal, articulate people who were skilled in the
mechanics of parliamentary government. Even in the Pyidaungsu
party itself conflicts of interests and ambitions soon resulted in
open splits. U Nu had kept his Cabinet small; the ambitious in
the party pressed for entry. He had made parliamentary secretaries out of some new-comers—retired civil servants, lawyers and
professional men. The new-comers considered themselves to be
minister material, and looked upon the "uneducated" veterans
with contempt. The veterans, on their part, looked upon the new-
comers as upstarts, bandwaggon-climbers. A few months after the
Pyidaungsu party had entered office rival factions began to form
in the party, irreconcilable, actively organizing and fighting for
the party leadership. U Nu had let it be known that he was not
interested in being the party leader—he would concentrate on the
premiership—and that the contest for the party leadership was
open. This set the factions on a furious campaign into which they
poured all their considerable resources. The Pyidaungsu party
which commanded such an overwhelming majority in parliament,
and had set forth with such good prospects, lost its unity even before the end of its first year.

5

On one thing the political parties were united. They did not want
the army to return to political power again. They would work together, do anything, to keep the army out. That was a negative—
no army—policy. What the Pyidaungsu government needed to do
was adopt positive programmes of development and forge steadily
ahead. Then, they might show the people that they could do just
as good a job as the army, using gentler means.

Some senior civil servants who had during the Caretaker Government spoken only ill words about "those politicians" now had only derisive things to say to their political chiefs about "the trousered rulers", meaning the soldiers. Those civil servants started joyously to undo many of the good things that the Caretaker Government had done. Many projects in which good progress was being made were stopped, seemingly merely to emphasize who the new masters were.

Gen. Ne Win had told his officers, on the eve of their relinquishing civilian duties, that they must not feel hurt if some of the things they had done were changed or undone. "I did not hesitate to change if I felt the need, when I was Prime Minister," he said, "similarly, the new government may drop some of our plans or change some of them. You should not feel unhappy if it does so."[13]

One of the first projects to be dropped was the resettlement of the squatters. Col. Tun Sein was ordered by the new government to stop, hand over and go. The municipal corporation had, *The Nation* noted on April 7, three days after U Nu's return, "already removed hundreds of hutments and encroachments which were unhygienic and were fire hazards and hide-outs for criminals After dismantling the huts the corporation did not just leave their tenants to find their own accommodation. They were resettled in the new towns of Okkalapa and Thaketa which were built within a short time with the cooperation of the civilian departments and the armed forces. Over 10,000 huts still remain to be removed from the city, yet the corporation will not be able to touch them because of the Ministry's order."

U Nu, personally, took great pains to try and keep Gen. Ne Win in good humour. Gen. Ne Win went to America and to England in June, 1960, for a medical check-up, and some rest and recuperation. U Nu went at midnight to the airport to see the General off. Flight schedules through Rangoon were such that the return flight also touched down in the early hours of the morning. But U Nu was there at the airport to welcome Gen. Ne Win back. The General returned the courtesy. When U Nu went to India Gen. Ne Win sent him off; when the premier returned, the chief of staff greeted him at the airport. These personal courtesies were fine. But the important thing was to get on with

13 *The Nation*, April 22, 1960.

the nation-building, mobilizing the creative forces of which the army was a major one. In that direction, however, policy was either wavering or negative.

In Washington and New York, journalists and political scientists who met the General in informal sessions found him relaxed and cheerful. He was, they found, no ambitious general plotting for a return to power. They suggested to him that perhaps Burma should try the presidential system of government, as the parliamentary system had proved to be a failure. Gen. Ne Win would not entirely agree. Both systems had their good points and their bad, he said. The parliamentary cabinet was always answerable to the people, while the president, once elected by direct popular vote, was the supreme executive for his term, unchallengeable by no-confidence motion. Parliament, on the other hand, could easily fail to reflect the people's will; even if the right men had been elected, they often became slaves to the party machines. Deep study and thinking was necessary, Gen. Ne Win said, to create a system which could work well in a country in the context of its circumstances and the education, the cultures, the beliefs and the economic conditions of its people.

In London some journalists asked Gen. Ne Win if he was holding himself in readiness for an expected call to return to power. "Oh no," he replied laughingly, "I am doing no such thing. I am happy as I am."

But things were becoming unhappy in Burma.

U Nu ate many dinners with leaders of the opposition parties, made many speeches, appointed many committees. He still seemed to think that he could run the country by moral re-armament: change your heart, embrace your enemy, then live in love and happiness forever. Eating dinners with the opposition leaders consumed so much of U Nu's time that members of his own party found they were shut out from him. They were disgruntled and frustrated. The opposition parties however began to feel that U Nu was leaning on them, and could not do without them. Leaders of the AFPFL expected an invitation from U Nu to join a coalition government. "We can't refuse, can we?" the expectant leaders were said to have asked each other often, "he needs us so badly, and we owe it to the country to serve." To the younger leaders of the AFPFL, the expectant seniors said: "There may not be seats for you in the cabinet, but you must not despair. It is a patriotic duty for us to go in and help."

U Nu must have been amused—or irked—by all this talk of a coalition government, for he spoke out in Parliament that he was not asking for help, and that he could manage the government very well. All his overtures to the opposition were in the cause of building democracy. Because he was being generous, he must not be taken to be weak and helpless, he warned.

But the warning came a little too late. The political and social fragmentation was too far gone by that time.

6

On August 26, 1961, U Nu finally pushed through parliament a constitutional amendment declaring that "Buddhism being the religion professed by the great majority of the citizens of the Union shall be the state religion." Previously Buddhism was recognized as having a "special position as the faith professed by the great majority of the citizens" while Islam, Christianity, Hinduism and Animism were also recognized as "some of the religions existing in the Union at the date of the coming into operation of this constitution."

The change was therefore slight, especially because U Nu proceeded to move another constitutional amendment to guarantee the right to practise and teach all religions in schools and to impose on the government a duty to protect the religions from all dangers, including insult and false representation. The guarantee of non-discrimination was already in the constitution. Offences in regard to religion were in the penal code. The constitutional amendments therefore left the law just about where it stood before.

The State Religion Protection Act declared the days of Buddhist sabbath as public holidays, and provided for facilities in state schools and universities for the teaching of Buddhism, the opening of primary schools at suitable monasteries, the allocation of broadcasting time to religious sermons and discourses. These also had been done before, without anyone complaining, or protesting that they were against the law or the constitution.

The establishment of the state religion, thus, only whipped up

19

emotions and angered or alienated the non-Buddhists, without effecting any substantial changes. The Kachins, the Karens, the Chins, and other racial communities protested. When the enquiry commission of laymen went to Myitkyina, the capital of the Kachin state, it ran into angry demonstrations; it had to withdraw under police and army protection. Tension gradually mounted, and when parliament assembled to vote on the constitutional amendments heavy security measures had to be taken in the city and around the chambers. The passage of the first amendment was hailed by the Buddhist monks and the laity with joy, and they called U Nu the great protector of the faith, of the same standing as the early kings. When the second amendment was passed— giving guarantees to other religions—they called him a traitor, of the same standing as the betrayers of the Buddha.

Mixing religion with government often led to hypocrisy and bigotry. Government officials took to becoming monks for brief sojourns, some sincerely, some showingly. Religious meetings were frequent and fashionable. Those who meditated furiously in strategic places which U Nu passed on his regular visits to the pagoda were often the regulars on the cocktail circuits. It was difficult to distinguish between devoutness and religiosity. Turning sabbath days into public holidays led to confusion, for the sabbath, rotating by the moon, often falls on different days of the week. Sabbath days were dry days for the official class and the "elite", and blackmarkets in liquor began to boom on those holy days.

Some Buddhist monks rioted when the protection given to the other religions was passed into law. They seized a Muslim mosque in the city, and the riot squads had to be called out. Thus Buddhism—which preaches peace, love and tolerance—was made to provoke anger, enmity and strife. Buddhism, a jewel of purity, was cast into the mud of passion.

The deterioration that set in was fast. The states—their chiefs who had already relinquished hereditary powers, and their leaders —began to clamour for more rights, more equality, for privileges which they claimed in the name of "pure federalism". At first the demands were mild, couched in suggestions for constitutional amendments. Later there was organized pressure, stepped up in inverse ratio to the decline of the Union Government. Threats of secession were made. The constitution, curiously enough, provided for the secession of the Shan state and the Kayah state, after a trial period of ten years—if the people of the state concerned expressed their clear desire to secede. The threat of secession had been used before by the states as a useful bargaining factor in their relations with the Union Government. Now the threat was seriously posed in angry words of command.

All groups were asking for more; none offered to give back to the state, or give in to compromise. The civil servants wanted constitutional guarantees, no less; U Nu promised they would get what they wanted. The businessmen were up, protesting against the government's proposed 'nationalization' of the import trade.

The so-called spokesmen of the Arakanese and the Mon people wanted speedy establishment of their separate states; they could not, among themselves, settle the question of who should be ministers or head of the state, but that did not matter; U Nu gave them his promises, and had the constitutional amendments prepared. Nothing short of amending the constitution would satisfy the groups with their insistent, often angry, demands. Mere statutes would not suffice. The leaders of the states also wanted the constitution to be thoroughly re-written to provide for pure federalism. The leaders met in conference in Rangoon towards the end of February, 1962, and said: "Now, or Never."

At this point, Gen. Ne Win decided that things had gone far enough. It was time to step in and save the situation. The people had been hoping for his return. Friends had urged him. A few young colonels had put it to him even before the Pyidaungsu party had been in office for a year that a return to power was a duty. But Gen. Ne Win had waited, resolved to give the government a full chance, wanting to be sure that there was no other alternative. When a few young colonels became too involved he retired them off, or relieved them of commands.

Tensions mounted in the country. Splits and divisions grew. But Gen. Ne Win waited. He went to Pagan a few times to rest and think amidst the magnificent ruins of the city where once Buddhism had flourished. "Is it better to leave this splendour—which must one day fall to dust—as a monument to one's memory, or to free men from the misery of want and hunger and give them full opportunity for material and spiritual fulfilment?"

This question Gen. Ne Win asked his aide as he looked out on the city of the pagodas, thousands of which were already no more than mounds of dust. It was a question to which he did not need an answer.

Only the historians may, as they dig hard for the facts, discover exactly when Gen. Ne Win decided that he must once again assume the leadership. It was a momentous decision, heavy with responsibility, and he probably did not consider it fair to have more than a very few of his young deputies share in its making. It was a deeply considered decision, not reached on impulse, nor prompted by irritation. Yet, no long or laborious plot preceded its translation into action. None was necessary, however, for the people longed for a change and an end to all the democratic disorders.

Gen. Ne Win attended the performance of a visiting Chinese ballet troupe on the night of March 1. The show went on till fairly late. When it ended, Gen. Ne Win went onto the stage and shook hands with the performers. There was a lot of clapping of hands and the beaming of smiles. It had been a good show; all went home happy. Around midnight troops began to move into Rangoon to take up strategic positions. U Nu, some of his ministers, and the leaders of the clamorous racial groups were taken into custody; many were sent back home in the morning. When the people of the city woke up, the change had already been made.

At 8.50 a.m. on March 2, Gen. Ne Win spoke on the radio to announce the change:

"I have to inform you, citizens of the Union, that the armed forces have taken over the responsibility and the task of keeping the country's safety, owing to the greatly deteriorating conditions in the Union.

I appeal to you to carry on with your daily tasks as usual, without fear or anxiety.

I also call upon the government servants to continue to attend to their duties without any interruption.

I urge the Education authorities and the students who are in the midst of their examinations to carry on with their work.

We shall do our best to promote the happiness and well-being of all the people of the Union."

By noon the people of the cities and the towns knew that Gen. Ne Win had returned to the national leadership. They rejoiced. They also went about their business and their work calmly. The high school students took their examinations while history passed a turning point outside in the streets. A few enterprising newspapers put out special editions which were quickly sold out.

U Nu had said that there were 16,000 problems of state which would require national committees and at least 20 years to solve. Now the problems were bequeathed to Gen. Ne Win. U Nu had asked the people to build 60,000 sand pagodas to bring good luck to the tackling of the problems. Some wise elders had shaken their heads and whispered that U Nu's insistence on sand pagodas indicated the running out of the sands of his time. Now the shifting sands had slipped away, leaving a vast desolation in which the building with solid rock and stone must start anew.

10

A Sense of Purpose

1

AND so the soldier is back. Called to higher duty again, this time he attacks the very roots of the social evils, poverty and hunger, exploitation and injustice.

Gen. Ne Win set about quickly to construct an administration, prescribe the procedures and get the country moving on. The Revolutionary Government was formed on March 2. Its Council of Ministers is the approximate equivalent of the Cabinet under the old system. The Revolutionary Council, formed on the same day, is the policy-making organ of State.

Parliament was dissolved. The Advisory Committee and the Election Commission were abolished. The State Councils, so torn with strife, were replaced by State Affairs Councils which are smaller but better fitted for sustained and serious work.

Gen. Ne Win, as chairman of the Revolutionary Council and head of the Revolutionary Government, is the repository of the sovereign powers of the State. This, however, is the formal arrangement of necessity. In practice Gen. Ne Win started at once to share the powers with the Council and the Government, and to open up channels of direct communication with the people. In the past there was a parliament which the prime minister sometimes ignored for years on end. The Revolutionary Council, on the other hand, meets frequently, and engages in full discussion of high policy. The Cabinet could also be a mere form in the parliamentary days. The prime minister, or some pre-eminent minister, would take the lead, lay down the law, and the rest of the ministers would nod their heads. Members of the Revolutionary Government, however, have to do a lot of homework on their subjects before they present their cases at the regular meetings. There would be thorough discussion, with Gen. Ne Win coming in with a few questions which cut through to the root of the matter, or drawing from his prodigious memory which covers a variety of subjects. If memory proves a little tardy, he would beat a tattoo on his forehead with his fingers, and in a little while the needed information would come out from the well-stocked storehouse within.

Power held for its own sake is both a corruption and a corruptive influence. Of this Gen. Ne Win is fully aware. He keeps on repeating that power is a trust, and an instrument for building a better life for the people. The best safeguard against the abuse of power is to have the people participate as fully as possible in as many spheres of activity as possible. In the economic field, as well as in the political, therefore, the guiding principle is: "From the people to the people."

On the land, in the factory, in the ward of the town, in the village, the people will manage their affairs, producing more so that the fair shares will be richer, holding courts to decide or settle their disputes, making the rules by which their society will be bound for their common good, seeing to it that they live those rules. The gradual emergence of that society will see the gradual passage of power from its trustees to the people to whom it belongs. This is the vision.

Leaders of the three principal political parties—the Pyidaungsu, the AFPFL and the NUF—who were invited to lunch with Gen. Ne Win on March 4, 1962, found him anxious to forge national unity and march forward with the people to the socialist goals. "Let us work together," he urged. "The goals that we have set are nothing you cannot accept. You are welcome if you wish to join us in the march. If you do not, please do not hinder us. You have had a full opportunity to do things your way for over a decade. Now give us a chance to do it our way." Over lunch there were reminiscences about those days of the struggle for freedom in which the comrades had worked together. There were smiles, expressions of goodwill and support, promises of a deeper study of the situation and a full statement from the party executive. But the parties clung to the hope that the Revolutionary Government would serve only as another caretaker for a brief period, then conduct parliamentary elections and return power to the victor. "We accept Gen. Ne Win as the national leader," the

AFPFL announced, "and we give him full support in the present task. We believe, however, in parliamentary democracy, and hope that Gen. Ne Win will hold elections at a suitable time in the future."

But the Revolutionary Council was deeply disillusioned with parliamentary democracy. In "The Burmese Way to Socialism", a terse and powerful statement of policy issued by the Revolutionary Council on April 30, 1962, it was pointed out that "parliamentary democracy has been tried and tested in furtherance of the aims of socialist development. But Burma's 'parliamentary democracy' has not only failed to serve our socialist development but also, due to its very defects, weaknesses and loopholes, its abuses and the absence of a mature public opinion, lost sight of and deviated from the socialist aims, until at last indications of its heading imperceptibly towards just the reverse have become apparent." The new course must therefore be to "develop, in conformity with existing conditions and environment and the ever changing circumstances only such a form of democracy as will promote and safeguard the socialist development."

The Burmese Way to Socialism was charted out with great care. There were several long sessions of the Revolutionary Council before the fine points of policy were resolved. Several more were needed to polish the drafts. Words were carefully weighed. Gen. Ne Win would work on the drafts late into the night, or early in the morning, awakened by the alarm set on his wrist-watch. A perfectionist, and a purist in the use of language, he would have several discussions with the scholars before he passed a word or an expression. The final draft of the statement of policy was presented to a conference of commanding officers by Gen. Ne Win, and consensus was obtained on each paragraph and clause. The Burmese Way to Socialism is thus an act of faith, a definition of the goals, and a chart of the path to the goals.

"In setting forth their programmes as well as in their execution," it is declared, "the Revolutionary Council will study and appraise the concrete realities and also the natural conditions peculiar to Burma objectively. On the basis of the actual findings derived from such study and appraisal it will develop its own ways and means to progress." In the march forward deviations to the left or to the right will be avoided with vigilance and the basic interests of the nation will be constantly kept at heart. The Revolutionary Council will also "critically observe, study and avail itself of the opportunities provided by progressive ideas, theories and experiences at home, or abroad without discrimination between one country of origin and another." With firm faith in the people and "their creative force" the Revolutionary Council "believes that the people will with an active awareness of their duties and responsibilities, play their part in full in this national revolutionary progressive movement and programme."

The next logical step, after the declaration of policy, is to form a party to carry it out. "The Revolutionary Council, forged by peculiar and powerful historical forces is revolutionary *in essence,* but wears the outward garb of a military council," reads the Council's announcement of July 4, 1962. "This the Revolutionary Council deems undesirable . . . the natural leader of a revolution should be a revolutionary political party."

"On three different occasions," it is pointed out, "the Revolutionary Council has explained and discussed its convictions and programme with the leaders of political parties, inviting them to strive together in unity. All the parties unanimously announced their agreement and support for the socialist programme—the Burmese Way to Socialism—but disagreements emerged on the question of forming a party." In the circumstances the Revolutionary Council has decided to proceed with the building of the Burma Socialist Programme Party (BSPP) as a cadre party, with emphasis on quality of the cadres rather than their quantity. "In this process, the political parties are welcome to offer their sincere and constructive criticisms, but the Revolutionary Council urges them to refrain from indulging in destructive measures."

2

The dream of a free and resurgent Burma, united and strong, forging ahead steadily to socialist goals has haunted the leaders before. Soon after independence plans were laid for the organization of a united front, or one single party, of all leftist forces. The insurrections shattered the plans. Or it could be that the failure to seriously execute the plans in time unleashed the insurrections.

Bogyoke Aung San had thought deeply about it even before freedom was won. When he was in Japan with the "thirty comrades" he wrote a "Blueprint for Free Burma" which, re-read today, rings in many places with the tone and temper of The Burmese Way to Socialism. Aung San did not use the word "socialism", for he was in Japan, among military leaders who had no great fondness for the word. But his meaning was clear.

"Our aim," he wrote, "is finally to establish an independent republic adapted to our own conditions and needs. . . . In this connection it might be pertinent to answer the question whether or not monarchy would be suitable for the new Burma that is to be resurrected. Monarchy, as we had in the past history of Burma, is out of the question now. The history of Burma has clearly shown the weakness of this form of state particularly in a country like ours. . . . In the conception of the Burmese people, everything goes well if the head leads correctly but everything goes wrong if the head misleads or is unable to lead. There were many cases in our history in which chaos and confusion arose out of the debacle of the top leadership."

Would a constitutional monarchy be more suitable for Burma then? Aung San answered: No. "It is against the Burmese temperament which always demands a strong capable leadership and does not want merely a figurehead. Moreover under constitutional monarchy the facade only is monarchy but in essence it is what is generally called parliamentary government which fosters the spirit of individualism and thus gives chance to individualistic disruptors and obstructionists to disturb or delay the course of administration."

"What we want is a strong state administration. . . . There shall be only one nation, one state, one party, one leader. There shall be no parliamentary opposition, no nonsense of individualism. Everyone must submit to the state which is supreme over the individual. This form of state we call Republic for want of any other name, but it may become, when actually in existence and operation, quite a new state form, peculiar to our own country."

What would become of such a state if no able leader could be found for it? "Our answer to that question," Aung San wrote, "is that the party will create the necessary strong leadership, for the party will not be created on a loose basis but will be an iron-bound order of all the best elements of the state for which, therefore, it would not be difficult to find any future leadership. Again, another question may be raised as to what will happen if the party itself breaks down because of the factional struggles that may grow within. Our answer is that factional struggles in such a party are rare or seldom become serious, and at any rate we consider that one party rule is so far the best form to give and maintain a strong stable administration, although we cannot say that it will remain the ideal form forever."

"For the creation of the above form of state, the essential pre-requisite is the building of one united nation. In concrete terms it means we must bridge all gulfs now existing through British machinations between the major Burmese race and the hill peoples, the Arakanese, the Shans, and unite all these peoples into one nation with equal treatment, unlike the present treatment which divides our people into 'backward' and 'administered' sections. All the natural barriers that make mutual associations and contacts difficult shall be overcome, for instance by construction of effective modern communications, such as railways and roads."

"In the emerging independent new Burma, our policy is to create a happy, strong and modern nation, and to ensure such conditions as will contribute to this policy. We shall have to raise the standards of living of the people, which at present are not high in a country like ours, raise the amount of income per capita, increase our population as fast as possible, educate the people, develop their health, physique and discipline. We shall have to simplify and rationalize the present top-heavy administration, so bound up with red-tape. We shall have to reform the legal system, check immigration, make for harmony between labour and capital, introduce universal compulsory primary education and make education more practical and technical. On the economic side, we shall cancel all domestic debts of the poorer classes, check usury, decide a definite land policy to ensure land for the landless, regulate tenancy, abolish landlordism (especially absentee landlordism), modernize agriculture. A definite policy must also be determined for the industrialization of our country, the extraction of raw materials, the search for new raw materials, the immediate introduction of small scale industries. New progressive commercial and fiscal policies must also be adopted."

There must also be, Bogyoke Aung San envisaged, the "control of exports, regulation of imports, marketing and price control, an enlightened system of taxation which shifts the burden from the poorer community to the propertied on a progressive scale, stabilization of new currency, establishment of new coinage, etc."[1]

Thus a one party political system is neither new to Burmese thinking, nor alien to the Burmese temperament. Whether the system prospers depends on the quality of the leadership and its continuity. It is generally accepted that Gen. Ne Win provides the needed leadership in these crucial times. The Revolutionary Council and the Burma Socialist Programme Party, actively raising and testing the cadres, take care to ensure its continuity. "I do not believe in the indispensable man," Gen. Ne Win has often said. "There is no miracle worker. But a willing man with a stout and true heart can accomplish a lot. Placed in bad conditions, he can make them good. Placed in good conditions, he can make them better. With a few hundred of such men we can push the revolution through."

3

Gen. Ne Win is a believer in deeds, not words. When something is done he wants to show it by results achieved, rather than announce it beforehand with promises. "You should perhaps have put it at about 6 per cent," he told the Minister of Labour who had announced at the workers' seminar preceding May Day, 1965, that the aimed economic growth rate for the following year was 8 per cent. "Then, the people would have been pleasantly surprised if the announced rate was exceeded. If we fell a little short of 8 per cent, and hit, say, 6 per cent, then you would still have achieved what you promised." Understatement. Talk less and do more. Promise less and deliver more. These are the habits of life which Gen. Ne Win has brought to the national leadership.

But even the doers have to speak sometimes, and Gen. Ne Win

[1] This note was circulated and discussed among the members of the Minami Kikan. Recovered from the private papers of Mr. Higuchi, it was presented to the Defence Services Historical Research Institute. The note was reproduced in *The Guardian* magazine, Mar. 1957.

has spoken on a variety of subjects. He has spoken at seminars of musicians, of artistes and performers, of writers, of public servants, of educationists, of scholars and lexicographers. He has spoken at seminars of peasants at Ohndaw, Duya, Popa, Kabaung and Rangoon. He has spoken at seminars of the workers in Rangoon and in Chauk. He has spoken at the gatherings of the national races—the big get-togethers of the Union family—in Rangoon, Loikaw and Mandalay. Whether it is to a huge rally, or in a small circle of delegates that he speaks, he likes to engage in an informal chat, with only a few scribbled notes for guide. He would draw the words from the depths of his feeling, and throw in a few anecdotes stored up from his long experience with the nation's affairs. He listens well, reads a lot, enjoys private conversations with people. These also give him the points to speak on which closely concern the people before him, or beyond in the entire country.

A devoted family man, and a respecter of the sanctity of the family and the good traditions of society, he speaks of the current decline in morals: "The basic cause for this decline can be found in economic hardship and a deterioration in the traditional social and cultural values of all races in the country—the Burmese, Shans, Karens, Kachins, Chins, Kayahs and others. For example, in pre-war days all our people were in the habit of helping one another in time of need. Even during the war when conditions compelled a good many to flee their homes, their more fortunate fellow-countrymen would provide them on the roads with parcels of food. However, since the attainment of independence these very people have apparently lost their former virtues of kind-heartedness, and spirit of mutual help, year by year. In a similar way, there has been a deterioration in the relationship between parents and children, teachers and pupils, husbands and wives. Mutual assistance and co-operation between individuals is now virtually non-existent, while the number of selfish people is increasing. All these are the results of the decline in our traditional observance of the obligations governing the relationship between parents and children, teachers and pupils, husbands and wives. If nothing is done to preserve this traditional observance, it is likely to disappear in the near future."[2]

[2] Independence Day broadcast, Jan. 4, 1963, *Forward*, vol. I, No. 12.

The traditions and the classics should be preserved, but not merely as curiosities or relics for the museums or the dusty archives. They must be turned into living forces which can inspire and help in the nation's progress in these modern times. This is a constant theme with Gen. Ne Win. Thus he said at a seminar of theatrical artistes: "I am advocating the preservation of our cultural heritage because the current trend is that people in towns, including myself, do not even know how to speak Burmese correctly. Those who do can only be found in the countryside; and among the urban people, only those who belong to the theatrical world speak correct Burmese. We wish to revive and preserve our Burmese literature including classical songs in their original form, and in implementing this project, the responsibilities of dramatists and stage artistes are by no means small. And on their part, dramatists should portray, in keeping with the needs of the new era, more of scenes calculated to foster patriotism, promote physical and moral courage, as well as a capacity to evaluate intellectual and physical labour. For dramatizing such inspiring themes, we can pick out suitable episodes from the usual sources —the *Jatakas* (Buddhist birth stories) and our history. We can easily do that as these sources are rich with ageless stories. Dramatization of inspiring stories is the most important aspect in our schemes to educate our people and bring them abreast with modern times."[3] At his instance marionette artistes, some of them in their 'seventies and 'eighties, were invited from Mandalay, early in 1966, to perform at the State House and in public shows in Rangoon. Thus an art that faced extinction was revived. At the end of a series of performances at the State House, Gen. Ne Win, in the best Burmese tradition, bowed low on his knees to pay his respects and present gifts to the old artistes.

The poverty of the people in a country which has abundant natural resources is the haunting picture of Burma today. To free the toiling peasants and workers from hunger and humiliation and give them a happier, fuller and more hopeful life should be the inspiration of all citizens. Thus, in speaking to the graduating students of the Rangoon University in 1959, in his capacity as their Chancellor, he said: "Those of you who are leaving the world of students today should not be satisfied with doing the routine

[3] *Forward*, vol. I, No. 21.

work in the routine ways, but must strive to innovate by introducing new ideas and new ways of promoting economic development. Only then will you be doing your duty to our country and our people."[4] In the same vein, in his opening speech at the Seminar of the Burma Socialist Programme Party on November 14, 1966: "We must dare to innovate and run calculated risks; if we are tame and timid the fruits of national independence will never be for our people to enjoy."

More adequate and decent provisions of food, clothing and shelter for the toiling millions—that, in brief, is the basic policy of the Revolutionary Council. The rest follow naturally. "Before the war," Gen. Ne Win often says to explain his aim and purpose in a nutshell, "a man could buy three longyis (man's garment) a year. In the years after independence, he could buy two at the most. I would like to see that he can buy at least four."

Material well-being alone, however, is not sufficient. Mental happiness is also important. The two are doubtless interdependent to some extent, but it is a fact that there are people who are wealthy, yet unhappy. "It may be worthwhile," Gen. Ne Win said in opening the first national research congress on March 21, 1966, "to initiate research on how to give peace and happiness to man. This should be a fruitful field of research which invites our attention, and that of people in all countries."

"In my younger days," said Gen. Ne Win, inaugurating the first cooperative village of Amara in Pegu district on May 8, 1963, "there were no sharp distinctions in the economic levels of villagers. In Prome district where I come from, however poor a villager might be, he usually owned a cart and a pair of bullocks and some five or six acres of land. Besides, he could rent an equivalent area. At transplanting or harvesting time, all the womenfolk in the village lent a hand. What joyous occasions those were, each helping the other. Hired hands came into existence only later, following the unequal distribution of wealth in the villages. All they have is their physical strength, and none of them owns a cart or a yoke of oxen. Although I had heard about hired hands vaguely, I came to know fully about them only at the Duya peasants' seminar. Now we are giving priority to improve their lot."

But there will not be any feather-bedding of the farmers. To

[4] Speech reproduced in *Is Trust Vindicated?*

the pioneer families of Amara, his advice was: be frugal. "I am asking you to be frugal because I have heard that a shop which was opened here yesterday sold about K.4000 worth of goods in one evening. By all means buy food and clothing, but avoid extravagance. We want to see all citizens of the Union free from debt and living in reasonable comfort. Use your capital wisely and save for your own future. You will not benefit if, because our loan is insufficient, you try to raise money from others against your crop or paddy. Work hard and put up with austerity for a couple of years."[5]

If the lot of the peasant is poor, that of the urban worker is no better. Thus, at the May Day rally, 1963, Gen. Ne Win said: "In order to know what the life of the workers and the farmers was like in the past, we have only to study those of their representatives on this dais. Their ages range from 50 to 60. Working all their lives, they have had to tax to the utmost their physical or mental powers, but have their lives been smooth, have they ever been free of anxiety about their livelihood? Up till now they have not been free from worry as regards livelihood, food and clothing. Our endeavours are directed towards ending this state of affairs: we want to promote the well-being not only of the farmers, and workers present at the rally, but also of all the working people in the Union."

And "working people" is an inclusive, not an exclusive, term. It includes the peasants and the workers—both manual and mental. There will be no artificial preferences for, or prejudices against, any type of worker. Peasant, factory worker, office worker, professional or intelligentsia, he is one of the family of the working people if he gives his best and takes only his fair share. "Many of the mental workers have changed their attitudes," Gen. Ne Win pointed out in addressing the Workers' Seminar on April 30, 1966, "and are giving loyal and devoted service. They gave outstanding service, for example, in the nationalization of the banks. We have still to show proper appreciation for that."

To the farmers present at the May Day rally of 1963 Gen. Ne Win appealed: "Do not squander the agricultural loans which we have issued, as it were, by scraping the barrel. Please use them wisely, and repay promptly. Although these are government loans,

[5] *Forward,* vol. I, No. 20.

they belong to all the citizens, and when you repay them we will be able to use them for other projects. We need to implement expensive projects for the workers, but as we have spent generously for farmers, we have not been able just yet to allocate funds for the good of the workers. Workers and farmers are interdependent, so I request the farmers to be punctual when repayment is due."[6]

Rights and duties go together. Peasants and workers must earn their new rights by working harder and producing more. Peasants who draw agricultural loans but do not grow and advance excuses for failure to repay, workers who demand increased wages for less work, such people must not be encouraged. "We must not let such people have their own way," Gen. Ne Win warned in opening the Party Seminar, 1966, "even though they call themselves peasants or workers. It is not the capitalists alone who may exploit. The so-called peasants and workers who resort to easy living by sharp practices are exploiters too. We must change those attitudes, partly by education."

Hard work, discipline, service to country and community in the awareness that by such serving one's interests are also served, self-reliance, humility, the dignity of labour, these are some of the values which Gen. Ne Win wishes to see restored and revitalized. There is no short-cut to the socialist society of affluence, he emphasizes. The road is long and hard. Quiet, sustained, unflagging endeavour is called for from those who march. He himself is no quitter. Once he is at a job he must keep at it till it is done. To do the job well and complete it is what matters. Applause or blame, while he is at it, or after it is done, matters little.

The importance of earning, and keeping, the affection and support of the people in all the endeavours is what Gen. Ne Win has constantly reminded all comrades of the Tatmadaw. "We all come from working class families—farmers, workers, teachers, doctors, public servants, and so on. Our army has risen out of the struggle for national freedom; our duty is to the people. We must never look upon ourselves as a separate or privileged class. So long as we keep faith with our mission, we shall succeed. If and when we commit a breach of that faith, we shall go down in defeat."

[6] *Forward*, vol. I, No. 19.

20

Power is a trust, not a special privilege. Thus, Gen. Ne Win warned, "all persons who are entrusted with power, from members of the Revolutionary Council and the Revolutionary Government to leaders of local bodies which will be elected by the people, must be strong enough to withstand the corruptive influence of power. We must strive to achieve that strength. We have seen in the case of the Saya San Revolution how that movement, which began with honourable motives, deviated later from its original course because of power corruption. We ourselves in the Revolutionary Council and the Revolutionary Government, are daily reviewing our actions to see that we do not deviate from our set course. If at any time you see us deviating, bring us down from our position. The peasants and the workers have the strength to do that."[7]

And power belongs to the people. "We shall restore power to the people," Gen. Ne Win declared at the Peasants' Seminar in Rangoon on March 1, 1966, "and towards that end we shall build political institutions in which the peasants, the workers and the working people fully participate."

4

"My ears were bored by my grandmother when I was a few days old," remembered Gen. Ne Win once. "Until I became a novice in the monastery I wore a top-knot. For at least three generations our family has been pure Burmese. My forebears made offerings to Talaing nats. I, as the eldest son, am supposed to carry on with that custom. I stopped it, but nothing untoward happened. You can't find the graves of our ancestors in the village graveyard now. When our grandmother died—and I was very fond of her—I wanted to have a proper tomb erected over her grave. My father, with his Buddhist philosophy, advised that we should not mourn too long over a body that must turn to dumb dust; the law of impermanence touches us all. So, we buried her and raised no tombstone. In this way, in course of time all traces of our ancestors disappeared under layers of earth."[8]

[7] Peasants' Day address, Mar. 2, 1965, *Forward,* vol. III, No. 15.
[8] Speech at the Workers' Seminar on Apr. 30, 1965. When his father, U Po Kha died in Jan. 1965, after years of illness in his care, Gen. Ne

That was in good-humoured reply to some rumours that were circulated that Gen. Ne Win was not of pure Burmese blood, and that he was not a Buddhist. He practises Buddhism but does not exploit it for political ends. He has no use for religiosity, for hypocrites, bigots, false prophets, and exploiters of the religion. Buddhism teaches that a true Buddhist must live it. Lavish gestures and loud proclamations do not get a person anywhere. And one cannot obtain vicarious merits from the good deeds of other people; one must do the good deeds oneself. This is a belief that Gen. Ne Win has held from his youth.

Gen. Ne Win's oft-stated policy towards religion is clear and simple. The Burmese Way to Socialism states briefly that "the Revolutionary Council recognises the right of everyone freely to profess and practise his religion." A more elaborate statement of policy on religion was issued in April, 1964, when the Revolutionary Council saw that some opposition elements were building up a religious issue and trying to gain the support of some monks. The statement reiterated that freedom of faith and worship would be respected, while a distinct line of demarcation must be drawn between secular affairs and the religious. The Revolutionary Council would not solicit the support of the monks in running the affairs of state or in political activities, and would also expect the monks to stay aloof. The purification of Buddhism, and the weeding out of false elements from the order is desirable and if the Sangha would do the cleansing themselves—as they should—the Government would be willing to make any necessary support available.[9]

"Attempts must be made," it is stated in The Burmese Way to Socialism, "to do away with bogus acts of charity and social work for vainglorious show, bogus piety and hypocritical religiosity, etc., as well as to foster and applaud *bona fide* belief and practice of personal morals as taught by ethics and traditions of every religion and culture." This has been distorted to imply that the Revolutionary Council is out to extinguish the order of the Buddhist monks which subsists on public alms. But Gen. Ne Win explains:

Win had simple Buddhist rites performed, without any publicity, and the body was cremated, the ashes scattered.

[9] Proclaimed on Apr. 18, 1964, published in the *Burma Gazette*, vol. 17, No. 18, dated May 2, 1964.

"It has become fashionable among our people in holding charitable functions, to place more emphasis on showy prestige than
on earning religious merit or fulfilling the actual needs of the re-
cipients. The result is that those who hold such showy functions
invariably spend more than they can afford, and have to lead a
miserable life thereafter, burdened with huge debts. It is time,
therefore, for our people to adjust their charitable acts more on
sincerity than on vainglorious show so that they will be able to
donate, regularly and not sporadically, towards the four main requirements of the Sangha."[10]

The need to purify Buddhism and weed out false elements from
the Buddhist Order has long been widely felt. The eminent Sangha have felt the need acutely. At the All-Denomination Therava-
din Sangha Convention held in Hmawbi near Rangoon in March,
1965, the venerable Zawtikaryon Sayadaw put it thus: "During
the time of Emperor Asoka, 60,000 *ditthis* (unprincipled persons)
donned the yellow robe for easy living and as a result the prestige of the true Sangha suffered. Today too, we have many im-
posters among us; and the laymen, unable to distinguish the good
monks from the bad, have come to hold a low opinion of the
Order."[11]

The problem is old. Previous governments had tried to have
the monks registered and issued with identity cards, but when
protests were raised by some monks, the attempts were abandoned. There were some young monks who wanted heroic roles
in the political life of the nation, remembering U Ottama, U
Wisara and other monks who had made their marks during the
nationalist struggle. There were some who found the discipline
of the Order too strict for their liking. True monks, like good
soldiers, must live under two sets of laws. Soldiers must obey
the military code as well as the civil laws. So must the monks
acknowledge the civil laws which bind them as citizens, and the
Vinaya which binds them as members of the holy Order.

The Burma Socialist Programme Party has also stated its position towards religion. Distinguishing some of its "specific characteristics" from those of Social Democratic parties on the one hand
and Communist parties on the other, the BSPP has explained:

[10] Independence Day broadcast, Jan. 4, 1963, *Forward*, vol. I, No. 12.
[11] *All-Denomination Sangha Conference, Forward,* vol. III, No. 16.

"A Social Democratic party permits its members freedom of faith and worship. However, it would draw no clear borderline between religion and politics, often deliberately mixing the two. Abuse of religion in promoting the cause of the party is not uncommon. A Communist party has neither religious faith nor worship. The rules of the party forbid its members such faith or worship. The BSPP gives full freedom of conscience and religion to those who believe and worship and to non-believers and free-thinkers alike; all of them unite in working for the improvement of their mundane life. . . ."[12]

These occasional statements have helped to clear the air and dissolve the strangeness which once existed between the Sangha and the Revolutionary Council. The eminent Sangha are discovering with pleasure what U Wiseitta of Mingun, the Tipataka Sayadaw of great learning who played a leading part in the Sixth Great Buddhist Synod, found out several years ago. "Bogyoke Ne Win is no Communist," says Sayadaw U Wiseitta: "and he is a good Buddhist. Once, during the Synod, we drove in a procession from the Great Cave, where the recitals were being done, to the Shwedagon Pagoda. Bogyoke Ne Win's car happened to come up from behind. He could have passed us. He was probably in a greater hurry than we. But I saw him in our rear-view mirror, calm, modest and humble, instructing his driver to trail along. Thus his car formed the tail-end of our procession right up to the Pagoda. Is that how an irreligious General behaves?" The Sayadaw who resides in a lonely monastery in the hills of Mingun, is known to have given away all the lavish donations which his disciples have laid at his feet. He lives an austere life and on a spare diet of vegetable and fruit. He weighs his words with care. His words about Bogyoke Ne Win were not lightly spoken.

5

The restoration of peace and the building of national unity have taken priority in the programme of the Revolutionary Council.

A general amnesty was proclaimed on April 1, 1963. Previous offences were wiped out; for those who had troubled conscience,

[12] *The Specific Characteristics of the Burma Socialist Programme Party*, declared on Sept. 4, 1964, and published also in booklet form.

a clean chapter of life was to begin. "Go home," Gen. Ne Win said to the inmates of the Rangoon central jail whom he visited, "and don't come back here again. Serve your families and your communities; make your contributions to the nation-building."

"The amnesty is aimed at helping to restore peace and unity," Gen. Ne Win explained on April 2 at a conference of the Security and Administrative Committees. "It is a move to dispel fear of punishment from those who might have transgressed the law at some time or other, and to encourage them to come forth and work with the Government with a clear conscience for national unity and welfare. Moral deterioration in the country had affected not only civil servants, merchants and politicians, but also the armed forces personnel. Those who offend the law in the future will, however, be strictly dealt with."[13]

On June 11, the Revolutionary Council followed up with an invitation to the insurgents to come out to "parley for peace" without any preconditions. National strength and unity must be found within the country's borders, it was pointed out, and all progressive forces should find ways and means of putting an end to the bleeding, wasteful civil war, and of working together to build a happy socialist state. The invitation was a bold and generous gesture. Governments had granted partial amnesties before, and offered to legalize the insurgent groups if they laid down their arms first and renounced the path of violence. But no Government had gone so far as to invite the insurgents to the conference table without any preconditions.

The response was good and prompt. One of the first to turn up was Thakin Soe, the leader of the Red Flags. A few young girls, barely out of their 'teens, wearing khaki shirts, over their short htamein and canvas shoes, his wife-cum-secretary Yemay Daw San, and Comrade Kyaw Win made up the delegation which Thakin Soe led to the conference table in Rangoon. He had been in the jungles continuously for some sixteen years, and Soe was clearly out of touch and out of his depths. It was a new world which he saw, a world with which his old slogans did not quite fit. He was given opportunities to meet old friends, and the press as well. At the press conference, he placed a picture of Stalin on the table before he started, and denounced Khrushchev whom his

13 *Forward,* vol. I, No. 17.

party had tried *in absentia* in the jungle and sentenced to death. He talked grandly about a national convention which must be called, under international supervision, to decide the future of the Union. All parties, groups and races must be represented, and the armed forces must be represented by sergeants and below. After a few days of futile talks the negotiations were terminated and Soe and his team were given their safe conduct back to their lairs. Soe protested that he had not yet finished talking, and would like to have more time, or come again.

A top-ranking delegation from the National Democratic United Front (NDUF) came after Thakin Soe had gone. The Communist Party of Burma (CPB) led by Thakin Than Tun, and the Karen National Unity Party (KNUP) led by Mahn Ba Zan were the principal parties in the NDUF. The delegation, under the leadership of Comrade Htay, the CPB secretary, Mahn Ba Zan, Bo Zeya, Comrade Aung Gyi and others, was better prepared for the talks. It studied the situation more carefully. It stayed longer, its members visiting their families, friends, the Shwedagon pagoda and Thakin Kodaw Hmaing. The talks lasted over a few months and were finally broken off on November 14, 1963, by the Revolutionary Council. "Despite the generous concessions granted by the Revolutionary Council in the interests of constructing peace in a practical way," a communique explained, "the CPB and the KNUF were found exploiting these very concessions to strengthen their organizations militarily, politically and financially, and from such an improved position they were making insidious attempts to win the Revolutionary Council's recognition of the parallel governments set up in their jungle domains. Furthermore they were constantly engaged in organizational activities, both aboveground and underground, designed to show off their strength with a view to blackmail the Revolutionary Council to accede to their demands."[14]

The Karen Revolutionary Council, led by Moosso Kawkasa (Saw Hunter Tha Hmwe), however, came to stay. Saw Hunter Tha Hmwe, the authentic Karen leader who had sent back a note from KNDO-held Insein in April, 1949, repudiating the agreement signed a few days previously by Saw Ba U Gyi in Rangoon, now concluded a final agreement with the Revolutionary Council

[14] *Peace Talks, Forward,* vol. II, No. 9.

on March 12, 1964. The agreement, its preamble states, is reached after "deep and thorough discussions on the basis of the Declaration of Policy and Faith of the Revolutionary Council of the Union of Burma regarding the Indigenous Races and the Principles propounded by the late Saw Ba U Gyi on internal peace" and with a sincere desire on both sides to restore internal peace.

"The Karen Revolutionary Council agrees with the Revolutionary Council of the Union of Burma that a constitution of the Union of Burma on the basis of the Burmese Way to Socialism and the pattern of socialist democracy, should, at the appropriate time in the future, be written and adopted by representatives of the indigenous races of the Union in convention, after full participation and thorough discussion." So reads article 1 of the agreement.[15]

6

The statement of policy on the national races was drafted by Gen. Ne Win with considerable care. Madame Ne Win and he went to Mandalay to participate in the celebration of the 17th Union Day (February 12, 1964), and he had spent the after-dinner hours of February 11 with some members of the Revolutionary Council, going over a draft. There were a few words in the draft which did not quite sound precise or right, and he kept mulling over them in bed. In the small hours of the morning, he stole out quietly—in order not to disturb his wife—and went downstairs to work over the draft again. When time came to go to the mammoth rally at the foot of the Mandalay hill, the final draft was only just about done. The statement has so far been the only one which Gen. Ne Win wrote and read out. His other speeches were extempore.

The Union, Gen. Ne Win points out, is the home of many indigenous races. To make the Union a happy and prosperous home, the races who form the members of the family must live and work together in unity, amity and harmony. They must accept that theirs is an indissoluble union, their destinies cast together through weal and woe. Only when this feeling of indissoluble unity prevails will the animosities and suspicions of the past fade into insignificance.

[15] *Accord with Kawthoolei, Forward,* vol. II, No. 16.

To preserve the unity amidst diversity all the national races must recognize that in matters of common interest—such as the protection of the integrity of the Union and the promotion of the economic and social welfare of the nation—all must share, irrespective of race or religious belief, in the toils and the receiving of commensurate rewards. Without such sharing, the Union cannot prosper. There are large gaps in the social and economic conditions of the individual races. The more fortunate must therefore help the less fortunate in order to reduce the gaps.

There are, on the other hand, the cultures, the arts, the languages, the literatures, and the customs of the races which should be preserved and promoted. They form the wealth of each individual race, and those which are not obsolete or do not hinder progress should be preserved.

"It is most important," Gen. Ne Win said, "that we should always remain members of one family, and partners in progress. In previous times there was bargaining—using all kinds of pressures—rather than sharing. Now we must march forward together, arm in arm, with mutual trust and confidence."

The details of the structure of the Union must be determined after full discussion at a future national convention of the peoples, Gen. Ne Win said. "But let us begin the tasks of social and economic development, sharing in the toils and the fair rewards."

7

In international relations the traditional policy of non-alignment is even more strictly and scrupulously pursued by the Revolutionary Council. Self-reliance and building of national strength and character to protect and preserve the integrity of the Union, these must of needs come first. Independent and strong, Burma would then be able to make her contribution, positively but without any slogan-shouting or flag-waving, towards a more happy and harmonious world.

Gen. Ne Win has visited countries East and West, to cultivate friendships, to study, but not to ask for aid. "It is not possible for a nation to remain isolated," he explained in addressing the opening session of the Party Seminar, 1965. "It must have relations with others. It must establish friendships and avoid generating ill-will. This is the principle. It is a good one and must be followed. But the practice is difficult. It is said that union is strength. This should be accepted. But it is difficult to attain complete unity in practice. That is why in our relations with other nations we will never attempt to reap advantage at the other's expense. Also, we will not let others reap advantage at our expense. We will fraternise with others on a basis of equality. Of course, our relations will be close with those countries which have programmes similar to ours. But even nations which have close relations with each other break out into quarrels arising out of misunderstandings. When lovers quarrel the ensuing hatred is more bitter. This is evident to our eyes. Therefore, we should be measured and moderate in our relations with others."

Again, at the close of the Seminar; "Both the Eastern and the Western blocs have good features as well as poor ones. We do not say that whatever the Western bloc does is correct or that whatever the Eastern bloc does is correct. We will study objectively the Western bloc as well as the Eastern bloc and take for ourselves the good features that we consider useful to us, and discard the bad. But we shall not speak ill."

Quiet diplomacy. Mutual help and respect on terms of equality. Positive contribution, without claiming grand roles. Faith in and support for the United Nations Organization. And above all self-reliance which is the essential source of strength and self-respect. These form the firm fabric of foreign policy.

"We in Burma believe," Gen. Ne Win summed up in replying to President Lyndon Johnson's toast at a dinner in Washington on September 8, 1966, "that every country has the right to fashion its own destiny. We have sought to build our relations with all other countries on the basis of mutual respect, of equality and of non-interference in each other's internal affairs. We shall persist in this policy and we entertain the hope that it will in course of time come to be generally accepted as a basis for a stable and peaceful international order."

8

On the qualities which make Gen. Ne Win the natural leader in these times, U Khin Zaw, scholar and poet, has written: "Bogyoke

Ne Win is Burmese to the core; honest to the core; patriotic to the core; Buddhist to the core.

"To expand each item in the reverse order: He is a Buddhist but would not mix religion with the business of governing. When U Nu, after he had been elected by a landslide vote, thanks to Bogyoke Ne Win's holding the election as fair as he could make it, offered to let him gain merit by putting his signature to the Act banning the slaughter of cattle, Bogyoke Ne Win declined. True, he was demitting office and this last official act would gain great merit for his future existences. But he would not waver from his principle of not mixing religion with government.

"Immediately after U Nu took over from the Caretaker Government of Bogyoke Ne Win I took the most intimate measure to remind U Nu that Bogyoke was his most dependable ally. I quoted Shakespeare to him, 'Please grapple him to your heart with hoops of steel.' U Nu nodded. My impression was that he meant he knew and it was hardly necessary. Later on, politics misled him.

"After March 2, 1962, quite a few countries thought that Bogyoke was going communist. I happened to have helped in the translation of the first statement of fundamental policies called the Burmese Way to Socialism and I knew that Burma would be a socialist country, may be more effectively, but would certainly not be a communist country. I said as much to those who sought my opinion. To their 'so many people who are around him are Communists; might he not be swayed by them into communism' my reply was that the man who could sway him or influence him was not born yet. His was an extremely uncanny mind. He knew where he was going and would go straight on doing his best the best thing for Burma, as far as he knew, in his characteristic forthright manner. I neither could nor would say more.

"He is patriotic. That was precisely why he, who could live his own life in comfort and security, chose laborious days and studious nights, and personal danger day and night. He never did care for power for its own sake. People like him needed not any hankering after power. Political power is for those who had no sense of personal power within themselves. He hated the bad-taste-in-the-mouth privileges that political power brought, all the insincere adulations and deprecatory approaches. And presents!

Soon after the takeover, someone made the mistake of sending to
him as present a magnificent golf set with his name inscribed. He
publicised this fact with strict injunctions that no one in his government was to accept such presents. His patriotism is unmixed
with any consideration of self. It shines clear and pure.

"He is honest. Therefore he insisted on this quality in those in
responsible positions. We have had under previous governments
enough anti-corruption drives without effect enough. Only now
direct action is taken against any suspected corruption. This action is no respecter of persons. It strikes swift and sure, far more
effective than any propaganda against corruption.

"His Burmeseness. This comes out in his attitudes and relations
with others and also in his broadcasts (his use of the word *'khin-
bya'* in all his speeches is like a Burmese signature tune). It is
this quality which endears him to the army, from the privates to
the brigadiers. He is big enough not to have long memories, not
to mind small matters, so long as it touches not love of Burma.
That is the point. He cares for those who love Burma. For Burmans who do not love Burma he has no use whatsoever."[16]

9

In the statement of the philosophy of the Burma Socialist Programme Party it is said:

"Things in this universe are transient and every period in
its life is all too brief.

Names are forgotten as fast as all things fade; history books
become obsolete even as they are written. Founders of religions and ideologies, men of world renown—statesmen, generals, scientists, authors, kings—all are prone to this universal
law of transience. They live and die as every other being on
this earth; when they die, they leave behind a faint echo of
their existence, but this echo does not resound forever. It is
very unlikely that this echo will be heard for another ten thousand years. It is almost certain that it will have died out completely in another one hundred thousand years; and what an
insignificant fraction of time even one hundred thousand years
are!

[16] *"The Union and Bogyoke", Working People's Daily*, Feb. 12, 1966.

Members of our Party must not therefore take the ideology and programmes of the Party to be final and complete beyond the need of alteration or amendment.

The programmes of our Party are mere relative truths. Nevertheless, for a man to work during his lifetime for the welfare of fellow citizens, for that of the majority and for that of man in brotherhood is indeed a beatitude.

The Burmese Way to Socialism is the Programme of Beatitudes for the society in the Union of Burma.

We shall constantly try our best to make the ideology and programme of the Party more and more entire. We shall constantly endeavour by critical reviews to cleanse them of errors. We shall constantly apply our minds to improve them.

Thus alone shall our Party leave to the future generations of the society in Burma worthy environments for their heritage."

Gen. Ne Win, who took a big part in expounding the philosophy and drafting the statement, will probably answer, if asked about the prospects of the revolution that he leads, that time alone will tell. He may also add that his comrades and he and the people are trying hopefully to build the good society within the limits set by the law of *sankhara* (perpetual change in conditioned being), and all that they can do is do their best.

Yet, despite the fact that things are transient and life is too brief, memory too short, these times in Burma, this soldier, those with him, and the people who rise to their call to march—all will certainly leave impressions on the nation's history, impressions which will endure for a long long time.

Bibliography

Burmese language material—the titles are in free English translation.

AUNG SAN, *Burma's Revolutionary Struggle for Freedom*, article in the *Bama-Khit* daily, Aug. 1, 1943.

Bogyoke Aung San, ed. Bo Thein Swe, collection of biographical essays, Rangoon, 1951.

U AUNG THAN, *Sixteen Years*, Rangoon, 1963, political memoirs—1945-61

————, *Aung San*, Rangoon, 1965.

Armed Forces Day, 2 vols. for 1959 and 1960, Institute of Military Science, Rangoon, collection of accounts of the Resistance.

DAW AH MAR, *Artistes the People Love*, Mandalay, 1964, profiles of famous composers, singers, theatrical performers.

U BA KHINE, *Burma's Political History*, Rangoon, 1937, reprint 1964.

BA SWE (Rangoon), *Into Battle*, Rangoon, 1960, (the fight against insurgents).

————, *This Wind, This Weather*, Rangoon, 1964, a fictionalized account of the BIA period.

————, *Creature of the Times*, Rangoon, 1964, post-independence life of intrigue and corruption.

BOHMU BA THAUNG, *A History of Burma's Revolutionary Struggles*, Rangoon, 1965.

CHIT KAUNG, *Twenty Years*, Rangoon, 1961, memoirs of a veteran who turned Communist insurgent.

Encyclopaedia Burmanica, 14 vols., Sarpaybeikman, Rangoon, containing information on the GCBA, Thirty Comrades, Who was Who, etc.

U HLA (Ludu), *The Newspapers are Speaking History*, Mandalay, 1963, the Kingdom of Mindon from contemporary newspaper reports.

————, *War-time Burma as Spoken by Newspapers*, 4 vols., Mandalay, 1968.

BO HTAIN LIN (with U Thein Pe Myint), *The Peace Talks, Inside Stories*, Rangoon, 1964.

BO HTUN HLA, *Bogyoke Aung San*, Samameitta, 1955, a short biography.

MAUNG MAUNG (Ngathaing-gyaung), *Burma's Revolution*, 2 vols., Rangoon, 1953 and 1954.

————, *Living History*, Samameitta, 1956, profiles of Gen. Ne Win, U Ba Swe, U Kyaw Nyein, U Thein Maung, and others.

MAUNG MAUNG KHIN, *Reminiscences*, serialized daily in *The New Light of Burma*, from 27th October 1966, to July, 1967.

"MYADAUNGNYO", *Thirty Comrades*, Rangoon, 1943.

GEN. NE WIN, *Speeches,* Rangoon, Dir. of Information, 1963.

————, *Statements of Policy on the National Races,* Rangoon, Burma Socialist Programme Party, 1964.

U SOE MAUNG, *The Sawbwa of Wuntho,* Samameitta, 1956.

BO TAIK SOE, *Colonel Ba Htu,* Rangoon, 1946.

BO TAYAR, *Return of the Thirty Comrades,* Rangoon.

THAKIN CHIT MAUNG, *Notes on Burma's Politics,* Rangoon, undated, about 1949.

U THANT, *Pyidawtha Journey,* Rangoon, 1961, two volumes of contemporary history.

U THEIN HAN ("Zawgyi"), *Thakin Kodaw Hmaing (U Lun: Man and Poet),* Rangoon, 1955, about the man and his times.

U THEIN MAUNG, *A History of Rangoon,* 1962.

THAKIN TIN MYA, *In the Socialist Life,* Rangoon, 5 volumes 1964-68, memoirs of a young Thakin who served in the resistance, and with Thakin Soe for long years in the underground.

————, *The Ten Zones of the Resistance,* Rangoon, 1968, the organization of the resistance in zones and the military operation in some detail.

U THEIN PE MYINT, *Traveller in War-time,* Rangoon, (reprint 1966), about his trek out to India to serve as an agent for the Burmese Resistance.

————, *Burmese Envoy and the Allies,* Rangoon.

————, *Like the Sun Rising in the East,* Rangoon, novel with the nationalist struggle as background, winner of the Sarpaybeikman Prize.

————, *The Student Boycotter,* Rangoon, 1938, about the strike of 1936.

————, *Kyaw Nyein,* Rangoon, 1961, biography of a contemporary.

————, *Political Experiences,* Rangoon, 1956.

————, *Searching for the Truth among the People,* Rangoon, 1964, studies of the daily lives of students, peasants, villagers, and of elections he had fought.

THAKIN TUN OKE, *My Adventures,* Rangoon, 1943, reprint 1964, on the thirty comrades and their return.

U TUN PE, *Why has Parliamentary Democracy Fallen?,* Rangoon, 1962.

THAKIN THEIN MAUNG, *The Revolution of 1300 B.E.,* Rangoon, 1939.

THAKIN SOE, *Burma's Revolution,* Rangoon, 1939.

THAKIN BA HEIN, *The Capitalist World,* Rangoon, 1939.

THAKIN BA SEIN, *The Struggle waged by the Thakins,* Rangoon, 1943.

Proceedings of the Constituent Assembly 1947-48.

Proceedings of the Provisional Parliament, 1948-52.

Proceedings of the Chamber of Deputies, 1952-62.

Forward, magazine.

Myawaddy, Shumawa, Ngwetaryi and *Thwethauk* magazines.

The Botataung, The Hanthawaddy, The Mirror, The New Light of Burma, The Rangoon, and the *Working People's Daily,* newspapers.

PUBLICATIONS OF THE BURMA SOCIALIST PROGRAMME PARTY:

  The Burmese Way to Socialism, The Constitution of the B.S.P.P., and *the Philosophy of the B.S.P.P.* in one booklet;

  Party Seminar, 1965 with the opening and closing speeches by Gen. Ne Win, published 1966;

  Party Affairs Bulletin, a monthly; *Party News,* a bi-monthly newspaper;

  Party Seminar 1966, Political Report of the General Secretary;

  Speeches of Gen. Ne Win, 1966; and other educational booklets.

PUBLICATIONS OF THE DIRECTOR OF NFORMATION:

  Proceedings of the *Peasants' Seminars* at *Ohndaw,* 1962; *Duya,* 1963; *Popa,* 1963; *Kabaung,* 1964, and *Rangoon,* 1965, 1966;

  Proceedings of the *Workers' Seminars* at *Rangoon,* 1963; *Chauk,* 1964 and *Rangoon,* 1965, 1966;

  The Development of the Union States 1962-65;

  The Peasants' Revolution (*Saya San Rebellion*) published on Peasants' Day, March 2, 1965;

  Annual Budgets for popular reading; and others.

ENGLISH-LANGUAGE MATERIAL

Note: Only Burmese sources are cited. Several comprehensive books on modern Burma by non-Burmese scholars exist. An outstanding example, covering very fully the British annexation and the Burmese resistance, the history of the disputed border with China and the final settlement of the problem, is Dorothy Woodman's *The Making of Burma*, Cresset Press, London, 1962. A contemporary historical and political analysis is Frank N. Trager's *Burma from Kingdom to Republic*, Praeger, 1966; the book has a wealth of valuable references.

AUNG SAN, *Burma's Challenge*, Rangoon, 1946.

————, *Blueprint for Free Burma*, *The Guardian* magazine, March, 1957.

BA HAN, DR, *The Planned State*, Rangoon, 1947, on economic planning activities of the Burmese Government in war-time.

BA MAW DR, *Burma at the Beginning of the Second World War*, *The Guardian* magazine, Dec., 1959.

————, *In Search of a Revolution*, The Guardian daily, July 19, 1964.

————, *The New Order Plan*, Burma, 1944.

————, *The Making of a Revolution*, The Nation, Jan. 4, 1960.

————, *The Military Takeover in Burma*, The Nation, Mar. 9, 1962.

————, *It Happened during Thingyan*, The Nation, Apr. 13, 1964.

————, *Breakthrough in Burma*, Yale University Press, 1968, his memoirs.

BA SWE, U, *The Burmese Revolution*, Rangoon, 1957.

BA THAN, Ex-Colonel, *The Roots of the Revolution*, Rangoon, 1962.

BA U, DR, *My Burma*, New York, 1958, memoirs of a former Chief Justice and a retired President.

Burma and the Insurrections, Rangoon, Dir. of Information, 1949.

Burma's Fight for Freedom, Rangoon, Dir. of Information, 1948.

HTIN AUNG, DR, *The Stricken Peacock,* Nijhoff, 1966.

HTIN FATT, U, *Aung San and His Ancestors,* The Guardian daily, July 19, 1964.

————, *The Story behind the AFPFL Split, New Burma Weekly,* May 31, 1958.

Is Trust Vindicated?, Rangoon, Dir. of Information, 1960, account of the Caretaker Government, contains some speeches by Gen. Ne Win and a list of army officers who were seconded to the civilian departments during the period.

KHIN MAUNG NYUNT, DR, "Supannaka Galuna Raja" in *The Guardian* magazine, Apr., 1968.

————, "Japan 'Khit' in Retrospect" in *The Guardian* magazine, May, 1968.

————, "A Tribute to My Great Neighbour (Mr Razak)" in *The Guardian* magazine, August, 1968.

KHIN ZAW, U, ("K") *Burma in My Life-Time, The Guardian* magazine, Feb., 1956 to Mar., 1957, and Apr., 1961, autobiographical sketches by a sensitive poet and scholar, with vivid snapshots of his times.

KHIN MYO CHIT, *The 13-Carat Diamond, The Guardian* magazine, Sept., 1955, a humorous story about life in wartime Burma.

————, Memoirs serialized in *The Working People's Daily,* 1963-64.

KYAW MIN, U, *The Burma We Love,* Calcutta, 1945.

Manifesto of the Dobama Asi-ayone, 1940, in *The Guardian* magazine, Jan., 1959.

M. B. K., *The Burmese Resistance, The Guardian* magazine, Mar., 1960.

————, *The Thirty Comrades, The Guardian* magazine, Jan., 1960.

————, *The Panglong Agreement, The Guardian* magazine, Feb., 1960.

————, *War Comes to Burma, The Guardian* magazine, May to Sept., 1964.

————, *I Escaped from the Communists, The Guardian* magazine, Dec., 1956 to June, 1957.

MAUNG MAUNG, *The Forgotten Army,* Rangoon, 1946, the resistance as seen by a young soldier.

————, *Burma's Teething Time,* Rangoon, 1949, talks and articles on the resistance and the gaining of independence.

————, *Grim War against the Kuomintang,* Rangoon, 1953, reports on the military offensives in the hills.

————, *Burma in the Family of Nations,* Amsterdam, 1956.

————, *Burma's Constitution,* Martinus Nijhoff, The Hague, 1959; the first part gives brief account of the nationalist movement and the constitutional history of Burma; the second deals in some detail with the working of the constitution.

————, *A Trial in Burma: the Assassination of Aung San,* Nijhoff, 1962.

————, *Aung San of Burma,* Nijhoff, 1962, self-portrait by Aung San, with his speeches and writings, and about him by his comrades and contemporaries.

————, *Law and Custom in Burma and the Burmese Family*, Nijhoff, 1963.

————, *Gen. Ne Win*, a profile, *The Guardian* magazine, October, 1954.

————, *Bo Khin Maung Gale, The Guardian*, July, 1954.

————, *U Kyaw Nyein, The Guardian*, Mar., 1955.

————, *U Ba Swe, The Guardian*, Mar., 1956.

————, *U Hla Maung, The Guardian*, July, 1955.

————, *Thakin Than Tun, The Guardian*, Oct., 1956.

MAUNG MAUNG PYE, *Burma in the Crucible*, Rangoon, 1951.

NE WIN, GEN., *Our Fight for Freedom*, broadcast of May, 1945, reproduced in *The Guardian* magazine, Apr., 1957.

NU, U, *Burma under the Japanese*, Macmillan, London, 1954.

————, *Towards Peace and Democracy*, Rangoon, Dir. of Information, 1949.

————, *From Peace to Stability*, Rangoon, Dir. of Information, 1951.

NYI, NYI, DR, *A Short History of the University of Rangoon*, Annual magazine of the Rangoon University, 1955-57.

————, *The University of Rangoon, a Factual Survey*, the *New Burma Weekly*, July 19, 26, August 2 and 16, 1958.

N. N. *Out of the Past, The Guardian* magazine, Feb. to July, 1962.

————, *My Karen Diary, 1945, The Guardian* magazine, June 1957, account of a goodwill mission among the Karens during the war.

New Burma in The New World, Rangoon, 1946, containing speeches of Gen. Aung San, press interviews, AFPFL statements and manifestoes.

Nine Months after the Ten Years, Rangoon, Dir. of Information, 1959, account of the first nine months of the Caretaker Government.

N. C. SEN, *A Peep into Burma's Politics*, (1917-42), Allahabad, 1945, contains a good account of the Boycott of 1920 in which the author was a leading participant.

SEIN WIN, *The Split Story*, Rangoon, 1959, on the AFPFL split.

THA HLA, DR, *The Rangoon University Strike*, 1936, New Burma Weekly, June 21, 28, July 5, 19, 26, and Aug. 2, 1958.

THEIN PE MYINT, U, *What Happened in Burma*, Allahabad, 1943.

THET TUN, U, *Young Burmans in Wartime Japan, The Guardian* magazine, August, 1954.

————, *A Review of Economic Planning in Burma, JBRS*, Jan. 1960.

————, *Organization of Planning Machinery: Lessons from Burmese Experience, JBRS*, June, 1963.

TUN PE, U, *Sun Over Burma*, Rangoon, 1949, a journalist's view of wartime Burma.

————, *Why I Resign from the Cabinet?*, Rangoon, 1953.

VUM KO HAU, *Panglong Memories, The Guardian* magazine, Feb. 1955.

————, *Burma's Charter of Liberty, The Guardian* magazine, Feb. 1954.

————, *The July Murders, The Guardian* magazine, July, 1954.

Who's Who in Burma, Rangoon, 1961.

Official Reports:

Burma Round Table Conference Proceedings, Rangoon, 1932.

Burma: A Statement of Policy by His Majesty's Government, London, 1945.

Enquiry Commission for Regional Autonomy, Report, Rangoon, 1952.

The First Interim Report of the Administration Reorganization Committee, Rangoon, 1949.

Report of the Rebellion in Burma, London, 1931, (HMSO, Cmd. 3900).

Report of the Riot Enquiry Committee, Rangoon, 1939.

————, Bribery and Corruption Enquiry Committee, Rangoon, 1940.

————, Secretariat Incident Enquiry Committee, Rangoon, 1939.

————, Tantabin Incident Enquiry Committee, Rangoon, 1947.

Proceedings of the Legislative Council, vols. I-XXXII, 1923-30.

Newspapers and Periodicals:

The Guardian, monthly magazine, and daily newspaper; *The Nation* (1948-1964); *The Working People's Daily; Forward,* a bi-monthly magazine.

New Burma Weekly (1958).

Publications of the Burma Socialist Programme Party:

The System of Correlation of Man and His Environment, Rangoon, 1963, containing the Philosophy of the Party, The Burmese Way to Socialism, and the constitution of the Party.

The Specific Characteristics of the Burma Socialist Programme Party, Rangoon, 1964.

Party Seminar, 1965, with the opening and closing speeches of Gen. Ne Win, published 1966.

Index

(Note: This index is largely one of Burmese names, and to the reader who is not familiar with such, a brief explanation may be useful. The family surname is not used, though it is being adopted by some Burmese families. Each Burmese name is therefore separate and independent. Many names are fairly common, a typical example being "Maung Maung". Prefixes or titles go with names, e.g. Maung Thant, or young Master Thant; Ko Thant, when he is a young man, and U Thant when he is an adult. U Thant would, however, refer to himself or sign his name as Maung Thant, out of modesty. The title may denote not age but social status. A young man who would, by age, qualify for the "Ko" title, may be addressed as "U" due to his education or office. Again, the prefix employed may show the relationship between two persons, rather than age or status. His mother would call U Thant, if she uses his name at all, "Maung Thant"; the wife would call him Ko Thant, if she does not use some other more affectionate mode of address.

Similarly with women who advance from "Ma" to "Daw". The title may denote age, social or marital status, or the degree of relationship between two persons. Thus, Ma Khin Khin becomes Daw Khin Khin in later life, or when she becomes wife, mother, doctor, teacher, etc.

"Thakin" is the title assumed by male members of the Thakin Party (the Dobama Asi-ayone), and "Thakinma" is the title used by the female members. "Bo" is officer, a serving member of the armed forces, or veteran of the independence struggle.

The index, for simpler identification, lists all the references under one name disregarding the different titles its owner may be using at different times. When the name is the same, but the owners are different, separate listings have been made.)

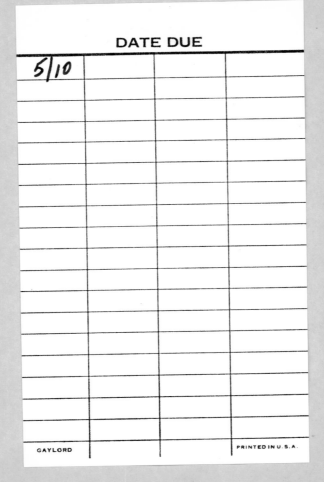

DATE DUE

5/10			